Scott,

May your love for Christ and His Church continue to increase.

In grace,
David

"Stevens offers a fresh and much-needed theological approach to multiethnic ministry . . . This book encourages the reader to think theologically through the key issues in reaching across all barriers within the church, not just the most visible ones. If you are seeking a strong biblical and theological understanding of multiethnic ministry, *God's New Humanity* is a must-read."

—**RODNEY WOO**
　Author of *The Color of Church*

"The greatest picture of the church is found on the pages of Revelation. There we see all of God's people gathered from around the world and down through the ages. There we can't help worshipping the One who paid the price to bring us together as one . . . If you're a Christian leader, this is must reading. Highly recommended!"

—**DAVID SANFORD**
　Executive editor of the acclaimed *Holy Bible: Mosaic*

God's New Humanity

God's New Humanity

A Biblical Theology of Multiethnicity for the Church

DAVID E. STEVENS

Foreword by
PAUL LOUIS METZGER

WIPF & STOCK · Eugene, Oregon

GOD'S NEW HUMANITY
A Biblical Theology of Multiethnicity for the Church

Copyright © 2012 David E. Stevens. All rights reserved. Except for brief quotations in critical publications or reviews, no part of this book may be reproduced in any manner without prior written permission from the publisher. Write: Permissions, Wipf and Stock Publishers, 199 W. 8th Ave., Suite 3, Eugene, OR 97401.

Wipf & Stock
An Imprint of Wipf and Stock Publishers
199 W. 8th Ave., Suite 3
Eugene, OR 97401

www.wipfandstock.com

ISBN 13: 978-1-61097-466-0

Manufactured in the U.S.A.

All Scripture quotations, unless otherwise indicated, are taken from the New International Version®. Copyright © 1973, 1978, 1984 by International Bible Society. Used by permission. All rights reserved.

All Scripture quotations marked NASB are taken from the New American Standard Bible®. Copyright © 1960, 1962, 1963, 1968, 1971, 1972, 1973, 1975, 1977, 1995 by The Lockman Foundation. Used by permission. All rights reserved.

All Scripture quotations marked NEB are taken from the New English Bible®. Copyright © Cambridge University Press and Oxford University Press 1961, 1970. Used by permission. All rights reserved.

All Scripture quotations marked NKJV are taken from the New King James Version®. Copyright © 1982 by Thomas Nelson, Inc. Used by permission. All rights reserved.

All Scripture quotations marked RSV are taken from the Revised Standard Version®. Copyright © 1946, 1952, and 1971 National Council of the Churches of Christ in the United States of America. Used by permission. All rights reserved.

All Scripture quotations marked Moffatt are taken from The Bible: James Moffatt Translation by James A. R. Moffat. Copyright © 1922, 1924, 1925, 1926, 1935, Harper Collins, San Francisco. Copyright © 1950, 1952, 1953, 1954, James A. R. Moffatt.

All Scripture quotations marked NLT are taken from the New Living Translation®. Copyright © 1996, 2004, 2007 by Tyndale House Foundation. Used by permission. All rights reserved.

I dedicate this book to our firstborn, Jonathan.
In life we loved you dearly, in death we do the same.
Your love for people of other cultures and languages continues to inspire us.
What joy you now know as you serve and worship
with those of God's multiethnic New Humanity in heaven.

Contents

Foreword by Paul Louis Metzger / ix
Acknowledgments / xiii
Abbreviations / xv

Introduction: A Crisis of Identity / 1

1. The Dividing Walls / 13
2. Humanity, the *Imago Dei* / 35
3. The *Imago Dei* Deconstructed / 57
4. Babel and the Sons of God / 75
5. The New Humanity / 95
6. Babel Reversed / 120
7. The New Humanity as *Ekklēsia* / 137
8. A Change of Clothes for the Church / 156
9. The Powers That Divide / 178
10. The End of the Story / 203
11. On Earth as It Is in Heaven / 220

Conclusion / 253

Bibliography / 259
Index of Subjects and Names / 269
Index of Ancient Documents / 279

Foreword

THIS BOOK ISN'T POLITICALLY correct. It's biblically correct. The church is God's New Humanity in union with Christ Jesus. This driving conviction has a profound bearing on how we see ourselves and how we approach diversity in the body of Christ. We need to come to terms with the radical call to unity envisioned by God's breaking down dividing walls between people through Christ's atoning work and our new life in the Spirit. Drawing from the whole counsel of God, my friend Dr. David Stevens has provided an invaluable resource to the church in responding to the New Testament mandate for ecclesial existence: *We are to experience and model our New Humanity identity in Christ rather than revert to our old ways bound up with various forms of societal separation. In God's New Humanity—the church—there are no ethnic, economic, and related divisions. So, be one as God is one.*

There are so many good books out there that discuss the multiethnic church. However, there is a glaring need for more biblical-theological exposition. This volume is a significant foundation stone for the building of authentic multiethnic churches through careful recourse to Scripture. David develops his argument through attention to the unfolding biblical drama, beginning with Genesis and ending in Revelation. He shows that God's heartbeat is to build a diverse community that reflects his multifaceted glory. God builds the new community of Pentecost on the ancient ruins of Babel. We need the biblical grounding offered here along with one another's long-suffering love if we are to keep from building new divisions on the ash heap of our own attempts at making a name for ourselves.

The pursuit of diverse unity in the local church and Christian community at large is a marathon race, not a fifty-yard sprint. We have such a long way to go. Ethnic, class, gender, and generational preferences, along with various other specialized groupings bound up with branding and niche comforts in our consumer-oriented culture, so easily keep us divided. God's Spirit breaks through the divide and builds Christ's church as a people made up of many cultures.

The church is to be the microcosm of Christ's kingdom unity in its witness to the world. However, we often look to such spheres as the state or the entertainment industry rather than the church to bring about diverse unity in our society. Unfortunately, Dr. Martin Luther King Jr's words in his sermon "Paul's Letter to American Christians" are still true today: "there is more integration in the entertaining world and other secular agencies than there is in the church." Now if the church is the concrete manifestation of Jesus' eschatological kingdom and not these secular enterprises, we must make sure that we as the church are bearing witness to our unity in Christ here and now. If Jesus and his eschatological kingdom are not divided, why is the church divided presently? We need to live now in light of what will be true of us as the church. While the government and other agencies tend to enforce integration, making sure we comply, we as the church will move forward into diverse unity only by appealing to God's kingdom vision for unity in and through Christ, compelled by God's winsome love.

David practices what he winsomely and thoughtfully preaches and teaches. You will find here biblical wisdom coupled with practical insights and honest, humble reflections involving personal struggles and difficulties as David seeks to foster and encourage ecclesial life that is grounded in our collective identity in Christ. As senior pastor of Central Bible Church in Portland, Oregon, he is actively engaged in leading and shepherding an increasingly multiethnic congregation. David is also a fellow leader of The John 17:23 Network. The John 17:23 Network exists to encourage, exhort, and equip the multiethnic Body of Christ in the greater Portland area to fulfill Jesus' prayer that we might all be one. I cannot wait to get this book into the hands of people in the Network! It will provide much needed biblical instruction for us as we combat our individualistic and consumer-driven tendencies to reinforce divisions. If the Network and the church at large are to flourish, we will need to see that God's vision for unity calls us beyond our individual desires and impulses that so often confine us to separate, homogeneous local churches. We are to make visible in our local assemblies our diverse unity in Christ, just as the early church often sought to model in its day.

We don't know what we're missing when we divide the church in ways that cater to our own niche affinities. There is so much richness and beauty to be experienced when the church celebrates—not tolerates—diverse oneness in Christ. Such unity also bears upon our mission in the world. As John 17:23 makes clear, the world will know that God has sent his Son when we live in the unity flowing from the love of the Triune God. This book makes clear what we are missing when we fail to experience and reflect who we are as the New Humanity through union with Christ. We settle for so little, but God is calling us to so much more. So, what are we waiting for? Realize in thought and action our New Humanity identity in Christ as you respond to God's word and love that makes us one in the full array of our intercultural splendor. You and your church will never be the same.

Paul Louis Metzger, PhD
Professor of Christian Theology & Theology of Culture
Multnomah Biblical Seminary/Multnomah University
Author of *Consuming Jesus: Beyond Race and Class Divisions in a Consumer Church*

Acknowledgments

I AM GRATEFUL FOR the many who helped make this book a reality. Every author is shaped by those who have gone before in the past or journey alongside in the present, speaking fresh insight into the writer's life. I am no exception.

I first want to thank the members of Central Bible Church whom God has given me the privilege of serving as pastor for the past eleven years. Thank you for granting me a sabbatical to finish this project. Most of all, your willingness to move in fresh directions and embrace the various ethnicities that God has brought to our church family is exemplary. As Paul expressed to the Philippians, "I give thanks to God each time I remember you" (Phil 1:3).

I am also deeply grateful to my colleagues in ministry—the pastoral staff and elder team of Central Bible Church. In both times of blessing and difficulty, you have remained faithful to the vision God has given us. May we continue to become a church *of* the nations and *for* the nations.

Several have mentored me theologically over the years, particularly in areas relating to the theme of this book. I think particularly of Dr. Dale Wheeler who, during my days at Dallas Theological Seminary, first influenced my thinking concerning the corporate implications of the apostle Paul's concept of the "new man." I am also indebted to Dr Emile Nicole and Dr. Samuel Bénétreau of the Faculté Libre de Théologie Évangélique near Paris, France. Your mentorship in my doctoral studies and theological reflections on several portions of Scripture related to this book were invaluable. I cannot thank enough my good friend and colleague in ministry, Dr. Paul Louis Metzger, who has written the foreword to this book. I have deeply appreciated your critical analysis and candid suggestions throughout the process of writing this book.

Through their patience and prayers, my own family members have participated in the writing of this book. My wife, Mary Alice, has added the balance that only a pastor's wife can offer, and my children have demonstrated great patience and understanding when my thoughts were elsewhere. I am also deeply indebted to my father who, as a pastor in a racially divided community, modeled before my young eyes a genuine heart for reconciliation.

Finally, a special thanks to Ellen Bascuti, my meticulous copy editor and member of Central Bible Church. Your experienced eye for details and heart for the message of this book contributed greatly in bringing it to completion. Also, thank you Jenni Brown for your excellent and creative work on the illustrative graphics within the text. A picture is worth a thousand words!

David E. Stevens
Portland, Oregon

Abbreviations

ANET	*Ancient Near Eastern Texts Relating to the Old Testament.* 3rd ed. Edited by James B. Pritchard. Princeton: Princeton University Press, 1969.
APOT	*The Apocrypha and Pseudepigrapha of the Old Testament.* Edited by R. H. Charles. 2 vols. Oxford, 1913.
BAG	Walter Bauer, W. F. Arndt, and F. W. Gingrich, *A Greek-English Lexicon of the New Testament and Other Early Christian Literature.* 4th ed. Chicago: University Press, 1952.
BDB	Francis Brown, S. R. Driver, and Charles A. Briggs. *A Hebrew and English Lexicon of the Old Testament.* Oxford: Clarendon, 1970.
BTL	*Biblico Theological Lexicon of New Testament Greek.* Translated by William Urwick. Edinburgh: T & T Clark, 1962.
CD	*Church Dogmatics.* Karl Barth. Edited by G. W. Bromily and T. F. Torrence. Translated by J. W. Edwards et al. Edinburgh: T. & T. Clark, 1958.
HALOT	Koehler, Ludwig and Walter Baumgartner, *The Hebrew and Aramaic Lexicon of the Old Testament.* 4 vols. Leiden: Brill, 1995.
KBL	Koehler, Ludwig and Walter Baumgartner. *Lexicon in Veteris Testamenti Libros.* Grand Rapids: Eerdmans, 1953.

LSJ	Henry George Liddell, Robert Scott, and Henry Stuart Jones. *A Greek-English Lexicon*. 9th ed. Oxford: Clarendon, 1996.
LXX	*Septuaginta*. Edited by Alfred Rahlfs. 2 Vols. Stuttgart: Privilegierte Württembergische Bibelanstalt, 1935.
MM	Moulton, J. H., and G. Milligan. *The Vocabulary of the Greek Testament*. London, 1930. Reprint, Peabody, Mass., 1997.
NCS	National Congregations Study, Wave 2–2006/07. Online: http://www. soc.duke.edu/natcong/wave 2.html.
NIDNTT	*New International Dictionary of New Testament Theology*. Edited by C. Brown. 3 vols. 1975.
TDNT	*Theological Dictionary of the New Testament*. 10 vols. Edited by Gerhard Kittel and Gerhard Friedrich. Translated by Geoffrey W. Bromiley. Grand Rapids: Eerdmans, 1964–76.
TWOT	*Theological Wordbook of the Old Testament*. Edited by R. Laird Harris, Gleason L. Archer, and Bruce K. Waltke. 2 vols. Chicago: Moody, 1980.

Introduction

A Crisis of Identity

> *The greatest good you can do for another is not just to share your riches, but to reveal to him his own.*
>
> Benjamin Disraeli

Today, the church is in crisis. I see it all around me. Like an adolescent struggling with identity problems or a male with his midlife eccentricities, the church is in a crisis of identity.

Actually, this crisis has been going on for years, even centuries. From the very moment that Jesus uttered those astounding, prophetic words to Peter—"Upon this rock I will build my church"—the church has been struggling to understand and live out her true identity.

How do I know? Ask yourself a simple question: What immediately comes to *your* mind when you hear the word "church"? In Europe, where I spent fifteen years of my adult life, the term inevitably conjures up images of immense cathedrals adorned with flying buttresses designed in gothic architecture. The distinct impression is of an institution frozen in time, hardened in concrete, and weighted down in the traditions of the past.

In the minds of others, the church is that sectarian group of self-righteous moralists who gather on a weekly basis up the street. They are, in fact, intent on "reclaiming America." Somehow their political views or blanket condemnation of contemporary society takes precedence over the faith, hope, and love of the gospel—or so it seems.

Still others think strictly in denominational terms: "I'm of the Baptist 'religion'" or "She's a Presbyterian." Maybe you view the church primarily through a historical lens, the important feature being your identification with an influential figure such as Martin Luther, John Calvin, or John Wesley. For such individuals, to cross over denominational lines requires nothing less than a spiritual conversion of sorts.

On the other side of the spectrum, some view the church today in purely individualistic terms. Possibly disillusioned by the seemingly insurmountable difficulties of life in community with others, some have retreated to the "church of God and me." As one respondent to a recent Gallup poll replied, "I am my own church."

It could be that none of these images of the church reflect your perspective. For you the word "church" evokes thoughts and feelings that are far more personal, maybe even painful. Though deep inside you believe in the church, the harsh experience of gossip spoken behind your back or lack of integrity in the leadership left you disillusioned and disengaged. Maybe you withdrew from one local church to escape the crucible, only to find the next experience decidedly worse. You may be thinking, *How could I ever go back to the very people who hurt me so deeply?*

THE UNSOLVED PROBLEM

Yes, today the church is in crisis. At the heart of that crisis is our own self-identity as the church. After all, when *you* hear the word "church" what comes to your mind? Your answer to that question will be shaped largely by what you believe the church to be in the first place.

According to theologian Emil Brunner, this is the "unsolved problem" of the church today.[1] Though Brunner wrote his *magnum opus* on the church in the 1950s, the problem remains unsolved more than fifty years later. In fact, the religious landscape today is more diverse, complex, and confusing than ever.

The confusion and complexity of this unsolved problem is particularly epitomized in the ethnic divides that presently segment the body of Christ.[2] Some significant works have been published in recent years

---

1. Brunner, *Misunderstanding*, 5. Writing about the same time, W. A. Visser'T Hooft states, "Any discussion of the Church and the race question can only be carried on in the light of the Church's understanding of its own nature." Visser'T Hooft, *Ecumenical Movement*, 8.

2. Except when citing other authors, I give preference throughout to the term "ethnicity" over "race." My rationale for this is explained in Chapter 2 under the subheading:

concerning the rapid growth of ethnic diversity in America. The most recent research reveals that, largely due to the change of immigration laws in 1965, the percentage of the white population in the United States is decreasing rapidly, from 85 percent in 1960 to only 64 percent in 2010. In that same time period, the black population has increased to 12.5 percent, the Asian population has grown to 5 percent, and the Hispanic population has spiraled upward to 16 percent of the population! Moreover, people of multiple racial groups, not taken into account in 1960, today comprise about 3 percent of the population.[3]

This growing mosaic of ethnicities holds out an unprecedented challenge and opportunity for the church. Scottish historian Andrew Walls has argued that "the great issues of twenty-first century Christianity" will concern factors of ethnicity. He goes on to state that *"more than in any other nation in the world, the body of Christ could be realized—or fractured—in the United States."*[4] The challenge is that, in stark contrast to our surrounding culture, the vast majority of local churches today are homogeneous in character. Less than 8 percent of Christian congregations in the United States today are ethnically diverse. Put in other terms, more than 90 percent of worshipers attend ethnically homogeneous congregations.[5]

Does such homogeneity reflect God's design for the church? What does the Bible say about diversity in unity among God's people? Why is it that Sunday morning remains the most segregated moment in American society? Finally, how do we address divisions within the church caused by ethnicity, socioeconomic class, and even generational preferences?

The surrounding culture is doing much better at something that should be one of the distinguishing marks of the church. Billboards often are written in Spanish or the predominate language of that neighborhood. Most consumer products will likely carry a picture of an African-American, Asian, or some other ethnicity. Diversity training is required in many schools and businesses. The high school my children attended, located up the street from our home in Portland, Oregon, boasts some three thousand students representing more than fifty languages. Yet somehow when it comes to the church we have forgotten, or

"Race, Ethnicity, and Culture."
    3. Emerson, "Changing Demographics," 62.
    4. As cited by Priest and Nieves, *This Side of Heaven*, 7 (emphasis mine).
    5. DeYoung et al., *United by Faith*, 2–4.

maybe have never really discovered, who we are and what God created us to be—a mighty force of reconciliation in a deeply broken world.

As will be demonstrated, the disheartening fact is that the church is not only marked by ethnic segregation, but also actually—although at times unknowingly—contributes to the construction of such dividing walls. Michael Emerson and Christian Smith convincingly argue:

> In fact, far from knocking down racial barriers, *religion generally serves to maintain these historical divides, and helps to develop new ones.* . . . The structure of religion in America is conducive to freeing groups from the direct control of other groups, but not to addressing the fundamental divisions that exist in our current racialized society. *In short, religion in the United States can serve as a moral force in freeing people, but not in bringing them together as equals across racial lines.*[6]

The paradox, of course, is that the church should be leading the way when it comes to the "racial lines" or ethnic divides in society. Among the hundreds of Christians interviewed for their study, Emerson and Smith found one refrain repeated: "If anyone should be doing something about the racialized society and if anyone has the answers to the race problems . . . it is Christians."[7]

SEEKING SOLUTIONS

What is the solution? How do we find our way in the maze of opinions and ingrained traditions about the church? How do we strip away the caricatures, the fluff, the stereotypes, and the misunderstandings and get back to the essentials of our collective identity as God's people? How do we resist the powerful forces that move us toward affinity groups, homogeneity, and consumerist choices all of which only strengthen the division in Christ's church between white and black, Asian and Hispanic, young and old, and rich and poor?

Is it possible to reimagine the church purely through the lens of Scripture? Though we have certainly muddied the waters over the years, the biblical writers are not to blame. On the contrary, they have left us with graphic, inspiring images of the church that offer clarity, color, and insight. Like an intricately woven fabric, these complementary images

---

6. Emerson and Smith, *Divided by Faith*, 8 (emphasis mine).
7. Ibid., 17.

taken together reflect the manifold beauty of the church as God intended it from its inception. To understand these images and to allow them to transform our life in community is to appreciate our "riches" as the people of God.

In these images of the church, God speaks to us in language that we can understand. Utilizing the creativity of the biblical writers, the Divine Author draws an analogy with the familiar, such as the family, a house, a bride, the human body, or a vine and its branches. The dynamic, organic beauty of each picture resonates with the deepest longings of the human heart. Why? Because this is what you and I were created for, a longing for belonging that only God can satisfy.

Of the some eighty images of the church either directly mentioned or alluded to in Scripture, it is Paul's image of the church as the "new man" (i.e. the New Humanity; Eph 2:15; 4:22–24; Col 3:9–11) that best synthesizes the overall biblical portrait of God's intentions for the church. The vocabulary of the New Testament immediately links the New Humanity with the first man, Adam, and God's original intentions for humankind. It also brings to mind the grand redemptive work of the second man, Christ, and the New Humanity conceived through Christ's work on the cross. No other biblical image of the church so profoundly weaves together the various themes of creation, fall, re-creation, and heavenly destiny than that of the church as the New Humanity.

We cannot effectively *be* the church if we fail to understand and experience the essential nature of the church. I say "understand and experience" because throughout this book the call to understand our identity is not merely intellectual in nature, but also experiential. I am speaking throughout of an intimate, life transforming understanding that results in a change of one's values and priorities. "Be who you are!" is the incessant call of the New Testament writers. If we don't know who we are, however, it is impossible to *be* . . . and to do. Furthermore, our understanding and appreciation of who we are *as* a community of believers will inevitably determine how we live *in* community with other believers who are different from us. I cannot emphasize this enough. I sincerely believe—and the Bible teaches—that all the failures and foibles characterizing the church today can, in one way or another, be traced back to this one issue—*a crisis of identity*. Where there is a crisis of identity, there is a dearth of authenticity, genuine community, and ethnic reconciliation.

On the other hand, the opportunity facing the church today is self-evident. It's the opportunity to *be* the church God intended all along, marked by diversity in unity in fulfillment of the Jesus' high priestly prayer (John 17). It is also the opportunity to be a "house of prayer for all nations" (Mark 11:17), reaching the mosaic of people who have come to our doorstep. Finally, it's the opportunity to live out our true identity as the New Humanity in whom reconciliation between Jew and Gentile, black and white, male and female, rich and poor, young and old, and every variety of background, culture, taste, and preference finds its realization in vivid, living color for the entire world to see.

In view of this, a movement is sweeping the church today, calling for multiethnic congregations as the biblical response to centuries of segregation and division. Noted Christian leaders are engaged in reflection on the issues as never before. The cry of an increasing number is: "The twenty-first century *must be the century of multiracial congregations.*"[8] Some who have previously held to commonly accepted principles of homogeneous church growth are calling into question their dearly held assumptions and are beginning to catch a more biblical vision of diversity in unity.

Various works have been written recently on this growing concern to confront issues of ethnic segregation within the church. The vast majority, however, are written largely from a historical, sociological, or pragmatic viewpoint. Far too little has been written providing a thorough biblical-theological framework for such reflection.[9] Mark DeYmaz, in his book *Building A Healthy Multi-Ethnic Church,* urgently reminds us: "It is essential that the growing fascination with the multi-ethnic church be informed by sound theological reflection. . . . The emerging movement must be based on biblical *prescription* rather than on current cultural *description* if it is to succeed in bringing the first-century church to the United States of the twenty-first century and beyond."[10] For this reason, nine of the eleven chapters of this book are exclusively devoted to the biblical-theological foundation and motivation for nurturing multiethnicity within local churches. It is my prayer that this book, *God's*

---

8. DeYoung et al., *United by Faith*, 2 (emphasis mine).

9. An excellent starting point has been provided in DeYmaz, *Multi-Ethnic Church*, 3–39; DeYoung et al. *United by Faith*, 21–37; Fong, *Racial Equality*; Hays, *People and Nation*; Woo, *Color of Church*, 2–72.

10. DeYmaz, *Multi-Ethnic Church*, 27.

New Humanity, will contribute to the ongoing theological reflection and lead to a fresh understanding, appreciation, and experience of our collective identity as the New Humanity in Christ. In turn, I believe this will enable us to better address the ethnic, generational, and socioeconomic divisions in both the contemporary church and society.

CHARTING THE COURSE

Yes, we need "biblical prescription" rather than "cultural description" if we are to chart our course in the ethnically pluralistic culture in which we live. That is my purpose in laying out the biblical teaching on God's New Humanity. My goal is *to define the scriptural truth of the church as the New Humanity and its relevance to the contemporary challenges and opportunities of nurturing multiethnicity in and among local churches.* In doing so, we will better understand and appreciate the diverse riches that are ours as the multiethnic body of Christ. While I focus primarily on issues of multiethnicity in the church, the principles drawn from our study will also apply to other issues that divide local churches today—socioeconomic class, culture, generational preferences, and the pervasive attraction of affinity groups, not to mention the secondary doctrinal issues at the heart of so much denominational sectarianism in the church. All of these are dividing walls that must be "deconstructed" if the church is to live out her identity as the New Humanity. They are strongholds in our thinking that must be demolished (2 Cor 10:3–4).

Chapter 1 highlights the current crisis facing the church; that is, the segregation of God's people along lines of ethnicity. Sociologists such as Michael Emerson and George Yancey have done the church a great service by outlining the present racial divides in the contemporary church.[11] These landmark works have greatly contributed not only to our understanding of the present dividing walls, but also to the underlying causes. We will see that attempts to meet the basic human needs of meaning and belonging in a market place fueled by consumerism, choice, and competition inevitably leads to internal similarity (homogeneity) in local churches. Such homogeneity only perpetrates the present ethnic divides in the church and in society.

---

11. See especially Emerson, *Divided by Faith*; DeYoung et al., *United by Faith*; Perry, *Building Unity*; Yancey, *One Body*.

While chapter 1 summarizes the present crisis, chapters 2 and following present a substantive biblical theology outlining God's solution to the fragmentation of humanity. God's solution is found in the New Humanity, God's new society, the church. In these chapters, I will make every attempt to let the scriptural text speak for itself. I'll begin in chapter 2 with God's original intentions described in Genesis 1:26–27 where humanity is created as the *imago Dei*. This chapter will explore the meaning of humanity as the image of God and its implications for a theology of oneness. Here we will discover that humankind does not *have* the image nor is it created *in* the image; rather humankind as a corporate solidarity *is* the image of God. I will develop the implications of humanity as the *imago Dei* under the three concepts of rule, resemblance, and relationship that together provide an interpretive framework for understanding the church's identity and vocation as the New Humanity.

We know, however, the rest of the story. The great divider of humanity, Satan, performed his insidious work sowing doubt, disobedience, and discord. Such sowing immediately brought a harvest of rebellion and alienation. Relational oneness with both God and fellow man was grievously compromised. Babel is man's answer to the problem. At Babel, humanity arrogantly ascends toward heaven, attempting to restore on its own terms relationship with God and fellow man. The initiative proves disastrous. The languages are confused and the people are dispersed. In chapter 3, I will trace the effects of sin that have deconstructed (but not obliterated) the *imago Dei*. Special attention will be given not only to the immediate context of Genesis 3, but also to the division of humankind at the Tower of Babel described in Genesis 11.

The tragic events on earth are a mere reflection of turmoil in the heavenlies. Not only is humanity fallen, but also the entire cosmos is tilted. Because of this, we cannot understand the alienation of ethnicities on earth apart from what the Bible says about the divisive influence of Satan and his demonic minions. Special attention will be given in chapter 4 to the division of humanity at Babel according to the number of the "sons of God" (Deut 32:8) and the resulting demonization of ethnicities and cultures (Dan 10) that only accentuates the racialization of humanity. This topic is rarely—if ever—addressed in writings on the church or on multiethnicity. It remains a neglected emphasis in biblical theology. The discussion of this chapter will set the stage for a more complete development in chapter 10 where we will consider the New

Testament "powers" and their divisive influence on the New Humanity as well as on society.

The creation of collective humanity as the *imago Dei* and the deconstruction of humanity through the devastating effects of sin set the stage for the creation of the New Humanity as detailed in Ephesians 2:11–22. This is the New Testament response to the most pressing Old Testament questions concerning the fracturing of humanity. Based on a thorough exegesis of this crucial passage, we will explore in chapter 5 the implications of Paul's teaching concerning the New Humanity as it relates to the dividing walls of ethnicity that presently segregate the body of Christ. Many interpret the concept of the "new man" as a new "nature" in the individual Christian. This chapter will demonstrate, however, that the concept is best understood corporately as the church. The "old man" stands in relation to Adam as its head and is characterized by division and alienation. The "new man" stands in relation to Christ as its head and is the sphere of unity and reconciliation. This chapter will explore how the church as the New Humanity fits into God's unfolding plan of the ages to bring reconciliation to a broken world.

Just as a human is conceived and then born, so also the New Humanity was conceived at the cross and born at Pentecost. At Pentecost, the Spirit of the triune non-homogeneous God united into one living organism people of multiple cultures, ethnicities, and nationalities. Chapter 6 will explore the significance of Pentecost in relation to the dividing walls that confront the church today. This chapter will also highlight the mosaic of ethnicities and socioeconomic classes that made up the early church as detailed by Luke in the book of Acts.

It could be argued that, while such diversity characterizes the church universal, there is no biblical precedent to indicate that such multiethnicity should also characterize the local church. Foundational to this discussion is an understanding of the term *ekklēsia*. I begin chapter 7, then, with a discussion of George Barna's recent book *Revolution* in which he minimizes the importance of the local church as a concrete manifestation of the universal church. This discussion is critical to the issues of multiethnicity and diversity in the local church. For if the New Testament only emphasized the universal church and not the local church, then in what specific ways would the multiethnic aspect of God's people be concretely reflected on a local scale? This chapter will clearly define the New Humanity as *both* the universal and local church.

Life together in God's "United Nations" is immediately confronted by the challenges of diversity. The reality of life in Christ, where there is "neither Jew or Greek, slave nor free" is fleshed out only as the New Humanity puts on a new set of "clothes," the garments of unity and reconciliation. This is what Paul describes as essential to the renewal of the New Humanity according to the image of his Creator (Eph 4:22–24; Col 3:9–11). Often these passages are interpreted from a purely individualistic mindset. In chapter 8 the focus will be on the corporate interpretation of the New Humanity already developed in chapter 5 and the implications of such renewal for the present dividing walls of ethnicity.

The New Humanity's renewal into the likeness of his Creator does not go unnoticed by the demonic forces that originally inspired the cataclysmic division of humanity. Paul reminds us that our battle—that is, the battle of the New Humanity—is not against "flesh and blood," but against the general headquarters of hell itself, including the very powers that Moses (Deut 32:8) and Daniel (Dan 10:10–21) describe as influencing ethnicities and nations. Chapter 9 will focus on gaining a better understanding of the spiritual powers that oppose the New Humanity and the unity for which he is destined (Eph 6:11–18). Here I will give particular emphasis to an understanding of our collective identity in Christ as we confront the divisive powers opposing the New Humanity.

Our identity and unity as the New Humanity is incomplete without an understanding of our destiny. While living in the "in-between," the "already/but not yet," we keep our eyes on the expectant hope of the ecstasy of community when those of every tribe, language, people, and nation will worship the great Three-in-One in perfect harmony. We must live the present with the end in view, as Christ himself endured the cross for the joy set before him (Heb 12:2). All of history begins with a man and woman (Gen 1:26–27); it will conclude with a man and his bride (Rev 19–21). This will be the focus of chapter 10.

Having explored the present crisis facing the church (chapter 1) as well as the biblical response (chapters 2–10), the purpose of the concluding chapter (chapter 11) is to explore several directives for deconstructing the walls that contribute to the ethnic divides in the contemporary church. Much has already been written on the multiethnic church and the opportunities and challenges that it presents. Not intending to duplicate the fine works already published, I will touch on certain areas I feel may have been overlooked or simply need further development.

We will further explore, for example, the importance of understanding our biblical identity as the people of God and the implications of this for the life of the local church. Nothing will better overcome the pernicious influences that shape our segregationist tendencies than a renewed understanding of our collective identity as God's New Humanity. I sincerely believe this is the starting point for lasting ethnic reconciliation and unity in the church of the twenty-first century. Our churches must become New Humanity churches.

My sincere hope and prayer is that through this reflection you will grow in your understanding and appreciation of the diverse riches that God has called his people to experience *together* in authentic community. May your vision be enlarged, may your heart be stirred, and may the church of Jesus Christ become all she was meant to be.

1

The Dividing Walls

Before I built a wall I'd ask to know
What was I walling in or walling out,
And to whom I was like to give offence.
Something there is that doesn't love a wall,
That wants it down.

Robert Frost

SITUATED IN SOUTHERN FRANCE stands a unique church building. It is located in the heart of the region most favorable to the Protestant Reformation. While many Protestant structures throughout the country were decimated during the awful days of the counter-reformation, some still remain in the region of the Rhone River valley. The uniqueness of this particular church building is that it is *both* Protestant and Catholic. However, the two congregations do not share the same sanctuary, for a massive dividing wall separates one from the other.

I'll never forget speaking in that church (the Protestant side) one evening during a regional prayer gathering. The memory remains indelibly etched in my mind. Our prayers echoed Jesus' prayer that his followers might be one "so that the world might believe" (John 17:23). How ironic that behind me stood the very wall that symbolized a seemingly irreconcilable division between Protestant and Catholic dating to the sixteenth century. As I inquired about the history of the wall, I learned that since the two congregations could never decide who was to have final ownership of the building, they split it right down the middle by building an impenetrable barrier.

We, too, have built our walls. They come in different sizes and shapes. Their color and building materials may vary, as well as the way in which they are constructed. Some are denominational, others are socioeconomic. Still others are generational or determined by gender. Our particular focus is on the walls built by ethnicity. Our walls, like that literal wall made of stone and mortar that still divides two congregations, are massive and seemingly indestructible.

Michael Emerson and Christian Smith describe the construction of racial and ethnic walls as a process of "racialization." This process results in a "society wherein race matters profoundly for differences in life experiences, life opportunities, and social relationships." Such a perspective results in allocating differing economic, political, social, and even psychological rewards to individuals and groups along racial lines that are socially constructed.[1] In some parts of the world, these "differing rewards" are ultimately defined in terms of life and death. Emerson and Smith go on to claim that we in America also live in a racialized society. What is worse, the church of Jesus Christ not only reflects such realities of racialization, but also contributes—though often unintentionally—to the process.

OUR CHANGING SOCIETY

Before discussing how the church today reflects such racialization and even contributes to the process, we need to remind ourselves of the rapid ethno-demographic changes within our American society today. Consider these facts:

- Racial and ethnic minorities accounted for roughly 85 percent of the nation's population growth of 27.3 million people over the past decade (2000–2010).[2]
- In the year 2010, the United States had well over 30 million *more* people considered racial and ethnic minorities than it did in 2000.[3]

---

1. Emerson and Smith, *Divided by Faith*, 7.
2. Yen, "Census Estimates," A10; Humes et al., "Overview of Race," 3. Of these, the Asian population experienced the fastest rate of growth, increasing by 43 percent.
3. Humes et al., "Overview of Race," 4–5.

- As of 2010, 36.7 million of the nation's population were foreign-born, up from 19.8 million in 1990 and 31.1 million in 2000.[4]
- Today, we have more Jews in the United States than in Israel; we have more blacks than in any country apart from Nigeria, Africa; and we are the third largest Spanish-speaking country in the world. One out of four people is a minority.[5]
- The number of Hispanics in the United States has grown dramatically from 7 million in 1960 to more than 50 million in 2010. The number of Hispanics in this country outnumbers the total populations of Panama, Costa Rica, Nicaragua, Honduras, Uruguay, Paraguay, and Bolivia combined. Only Mexico has more Hispanics than the United States. In fact, there are more Hispanics in the United States than Canadians in Canada.[6]

What is projected over the next fifty years?

- By the year 2050, minorities who are now roughly one-third of the US population will become the majority, comprising approximately 54 percent of the US population.[7]
- The Hispanic population will nearly triple, from 46.7 million to 132.8 million during the 2008–2050 period, growing from 15 percent to 29 percent of the American population.[8]
- The Asian population is projected to climb from 15.5 million to 40.6 million. Its share of the nation's population is expected to rise from 5.1 percent to 9.2 percent.[9]
- New immigrants along with their children and grandchildren (born in the United States) will account for 82 percent of the projected population increase from 2005 to 2050. By 2050, 19 percent of the population will be foreign-born, up from 12 percent in 2005.[10]

4. "Foreign-Born Population: 2000"; "Nation's Foreign-Born Population," para.1.
5. Cooper, "People Just Like Me," 156.
6. Priest and Nieves, *This Side of Heaven*, 7; Emerson, "Changing Demographics," 62; Humes et al., "Overview of Race," 3.
7. "Minorities expected to be majority in 2050;" para. 1; "People of Color," under "Population."
8. Nasser, "U.S. Hispanic population," para. 1.
9. Ibid.; cf. Humes et al., "Overview of Race," 4–5.
10. Nasser, "U.S. Hispanic population," para. 7.

- Also by 2050, African, Asian, and Latin American Christians will comprise 71 percent of the world's Christian population.[11]

In light of these momentous demographic changes, Philip Jenkins reminds us there will be some surprising developments for the church at large: "Soon the phrase 'a white Christian' may sound like a curious oxymoron, as mildly surprising as 'a Swedish Buddhist.' Such people can exist, but a slight eccentricity is implied."[12] Truly the American society has rapidly become a "stew pot" of multiple ethnicities and the cultures they represent. However, are we living up to our motto, *E Pluribus Unum*—out of many, one?

I HAVE A DREAM

Let's backup nearly fifty years. One of the greatest speeches of the twentieth century was delivered on August 28, 1963, on the steps at the Lincoln Memorial in Washington, D.C. Who can forget the impassioned words and eloquent delivery of Martin Luther King Jr.?

> I have a dream that one day this nation will rise up and live out the true meaning of its creed: "We hold these truths to be self-evident: that all men are created equal." I have a dream that one day on the red hills of Georgia the sons of former slaves and the sons of former slave owners will be able to sit down together at a table of brotherhood. . . . I have a dream that my four children will one day live in a nation where they will not be judged by the color of their skin but by the content of their character. I have a dream today.[13]

Five years later, on April 4, 1968, King was shot in Memphis, Tennessee. The following year my family moved to Memphis from Chattanooga, my birthplace. At that time, my home state was racked with racial strife. More than once police were called to my junior high and high school campus to calm demonstrations. On one occasion, as soon as the high school band broke out with the school's theme song "Dixie" (we were called the "Rebels!"), a large portion of the crowd in the stadium exploded in a riot. This was only four years after King's death.

What progress has been made in the last fifty years?

11. Rah, *The Next Evangelicalism*, 13.
12. Jenkins, *The Next Christendom*, 3.
13. King, "I Have a Dream," para. 17–21.

E PLURIBUS UNUM

One would expect that in a society so rapidly becoming pluralistic, there would be a significant decrease of racialization as defined above. Indeed, as we will see, few white evangelicals rank racism as a significant issue. The perspective of white evangelicals is somewhat typical of American society at large. A 2010 *Washington Post* poll of 1,083 adults nationwide (including 153 African Americans) shows that many Americans think race relations are improving. When asked if African Americans have achieved racial equality, 37 percent indicated that they have, 31 percent indicated that racial equality will soon be achieved, and only 27 percent felt that it would never be achieved, at least not in their lifetime. As for King's famous "I Have a Dream" speech, a full 51 percent felt that his dream has already been fulfilled, with 47 percent indicating that it hadn't yet been realized.[14]

In spite of these statistics, our world experiences little of the brotherhood of which King dreamed. While certain progress has been made in terms of racial reconciliation since the 1960s, we are probably not as far along this road as we would like to think. Melissa Harris-Lacewell states it well:

> Substantial evidence shows that the economic, social, and even political gains made by African Americans in the 1960s and 1970s have leveled off or reversed in the past decade in areas such as urban education, the number of black elected officials, and the racial wealth gap. . . . These sobering realities indicate that race still vastly over-determines the life chances of Americans. . . . To be born black in America is still a tremendous disadvantage compared with being born white in this country.[15]

A NEW BRAND OF RACISM

Our tendency may be to look at the tragedy of Rwanda or the hatred of the Ku Klux Klan or the enforced segregation of the Jim Crow laws and stereotypically categorize any form of racism or ethnic snobbery in such radical terms. What makes racial divisions so subtly powerful in American society today is that they are frequently fueled by deeply imbedded, covert, nearly invisible attitudes and values that are far more

---

14. "Race and Ethnicity," PollingReport.com.
15. Harris-Lacewell, "Racial progress," para. 22–23.

palatable and politically correct than the overt racism of bygone days. In other words, our prejudices *are* enforced against others, but in subtle and sometimes unconscious expressions that are more difficult to identify. Contemporary racism is *adapted* to the times in which it manifests itself. It manifested itself in one way in the slave culture of the 1800s, in another way during the period of Jim Crow segregation, and now in much more subtle but equally lethal forms in the post-Civil Rights era. Practices that produce racial division in the United States today are increasingly covert, embedded in normal operations of institutions, without direct racial terminology, and invisible to most whites.[16]

That's why Emerson and Smith conclude: "Because racialization is embedded within the normal, everyday operation of institutions, this framework understands that people need not *intend* their actions to contribute to racial division and inequality for their actions to do so."[17] This may well explain why in one recent national survey conducted of more than 2,500 Americans, only 4 percent of white evangelicals ranked racism as a significant issue. However, for those who are sensitized to the sociological subtleties of racism, the problem still exists and in some cases is growing. Even Billy Graham has publicly stated that "racial and ethnic hostility is the foremost social problem facing our world today." African American Protestants seem to agree, with nearly one-third citing racism as a pressing issue and nearly one-quarter citing it as the single most important issue for Christians to address.[18] As George Yancey concludes, "The dirty little secret in America is that we *are* a racially segregated society and we are comfortable with this segregation."[19]

THE MOST SEGREGATED HOUR OF CHRISTIAN AMERICA

As goes the culture, so goes the church. One would hope to discover that God's new society of believers better depicts the ideals of which King so eloquently spoke. Here, too, our hopes must be tempered by the harsh realities that characterize Christ's church both in America and abroad. The passionate vision of King extended far beyond societal reconciliation to the very core of the American church. He fully recognized that

---

16. Bonilla-Silva and Lewis, "New Racism," 2.
17. Emerson and Smith, *Divided by Faith*, 9 (emphasis mine).
18. Ibid., 4, 87.
19. Yancey, *One Body*, 113.

since the church is the conscience of society, any genuine repentance of racialization must begin there, with the house of God (1 Pet 4:17). In his famous sermon "Paul's Letter to American Churches," he reiterates that well-known expression, "the most segregated hour of Christian America":

> There is another thing that disturbs me to no end about the American church. You have a white church and you have a Negro church. You have allowed segregation to creep into the doors of the church. How can such a division exist in the true Body of Christ? You must face the tragic fact that when you stand at eleven o'clock on Sunday morning to sing "All Hail the Power of Jesus' Name" and "Dear Lord and Father of All Mankind," you stand in the most segregated hour of Christian America. They tell me that there is more integration in the entertaining world and other secular agencies than there is in the Christian church. How appalling that is.[20]

How well these words describe my own church in what is considered the Upper South during the 1960s. My father was a pastor in the racially segregated city of Chattanooga, Tennessee, during the 1950s and 1960s. Our all white church was located in a neighborhood that was about 30 percent black. The in-church fighting over whether or not to allow blacks into our Sunday services remains permanently impressed on my memory. Yet as a young boy I would heartily sing with our all white church family that well-known hymn, "Onward Christian Soldiers": "We are not divided, All one body we, One in hope and doctrine, One in charity." About the time we were singing that famous hymn, King also wrote these words, describing the typical lifestyle of African American Christians:

> If your family attended church, you would go to a Negro church. If you wanted to visit a church attended by white people, you would not be welcome. For although your white fellow citizens

---

20. King, *A Knock at Midnight*, 30–31. As to the origin of the expression, John McManners writes: "Critics noted that the Sunday Protestant worship hour was the most segregated time of the week. Indeed, the once righteous churches of the North, after proclaiming triumph over slavery and the evils of the South, came during the next century to adopt southern styles of regard for blacks and their churches, and there was little positive contact even within denominational circles" (McManners, *History*, 423).

would insist they were Christians, they practiced segregation as rigidly in the house of God as they did in the theatre.[21]

It is estimated that in the 1950s approximately 14 million blacks lived in the United States. Of these, about 8.3 million belonged to some Christian church. Yet of these 8 million blacks, approximately 7.5 million were in separate black denominations. While about 500,000 were members of predominantly white denominations, this did not mean that half a million black church members worshipped with their white brethren on Sunday morning. The vast majority belonged to and worshipped with black congregations. A parallel study published in 1948 indicated that only about 8,000 blacks belonged to white congregations. At that time, that amounted to one tenth of one percent of the black Protestant Christians.[22]

Such segregation is often a reflection of what is being taught (or not being taught!) in our nation's seminaries and Bible colleges. It often has been said that if there's a mist in the pulpit, there's a fog in the pew. That is certainly true when it concerns issues of racial segregation. One example is Bob Jones University, well-known for it's commitment to the authority of Scripture. However, in the 1950s and 1960s, BJU not only promoted racial segregation, but attempted to support its stance biblically. In a 1960 pamphlet entitled *Is Segregation Scriptural?*, Bob Jones III writes, "A Negro is best when he serves at the table. . . . When he does that, he's doing what he knows how to do best. . . . And the Negroes who have ascended to positions in government, in education, this sort of thing, I think you'll find, by and large, have a strong strain of white blood in them."[23]

Now more than fifty years later, what is the state of the church in America in terms of racial and ethnic segregation? Admittedly, some encouraging trends have arisen in recent years. Since the late 1980s, the evangelical community has produced a plethora of books, conferences, research, and mergers of once racially divided organizations. Even the *Wall Street Journal* in 1997 referred to evangelicals as "the most energetic element of society addressing racial divisions."[24] One of the top news

21. King, *Why We Can't Wait*, 48.
22. Visser 'T Hooft, *Ecumenical Movement*, 19–20.
23. Cited by Tony Evans, *Embrace Oneness*, 233.
24. Emerson and Smith, *Divided by Faith*, 63.

stories of 1995 was a formal apology by the Southern Baptists for their involvement in the sin of slavery. They asked for forgiveness and encouraged reconciliation.[25] Today, of the approximate 300,000 congregations in the United States, predominantly white and non-Hispanic congregations are somewhat less white and non-Hispanic than they were in 1998. Moreover, the number of people in congregations that are completely white and non-Hispanic decreased from 20 percent in 1998 to 14 percent in 2006–2007. All of this may represent a positive shift. Studies show that since 1998 the impact of immigration on American congregations has resulted in predominantly white congregations becoming somewhat more ethnically diverse rather than in simply increasing the number of congregations predominantly composed of Latinos, Asians, or immigrants of whatever nationality.[26]

While these observations are encouraging, such subtle shifts are minimal in light of the challenge of being the church in a racially alienated society. The most recent research demonstrates that:

- Churches today are more segregated than they were prior to the abolition of slavery.[27]
- Churches are ten times more segregated than the neighborhoods in which they are located and twenty times more segregated than nearby public schools.[28]
- If a racially mixed congregation is one in which no racial group comprises 80 percent or more of the congregation, then according to the latest research 92.5 percent of churches in the United States are racially segregated.[29]
- The most recent *National Congregations Study* indicates that merely 28.6 percent of churches have any type of joint worship services with a congregation of a different racial/ethnic makeup.[30]

25. Ibid., 64.

26. *NCS*, under "Explore the Data."

27. Woo, *Color of Church*, 23.

28. Severson, *Religion & Ethics Newsweekly*, para. 6; DeYmaz, *Homogeneous*, Introduction.

29. DeYoung et al., *United by Faith*, 2. Approximately 12 percent of Catholic churches, just less than 5 percent of evangelical churches, and about 2.5 percent of mainline churches can be described currently as multiethnic. See DeYmaz, *Homogeneous*, 30.

30. *NCS*, under "Explore the Data."

These figures are not surprising, given the fact that the seminaries that train the pastors of these local congregations exemplify ethnic homogeneity. In 2000, half of all the accredited seminaries in America lacked even one ethnic minority on the faculty, and half of the rest had but one.[31] Nor is it surprising that Emerson and Smith conclude that "after hundreds of years of efforts, far from being brought closer together, white and black evangelicals, and Americans in general, are widely separated, perceiving and experiencing the world in very different ways."[32] They also observe that when white evangelicals speak of integrating their congregations, they refer primarily to a sense of "openness" to all people. As a pastor, I have heard this attitude expressed time and time again. Obviously, no Bible believing Christian would ever say he or she was "closed" to those of another race or ethnicity. There are probably few if any evangelical churches—where whites are in the majority—that would knowingly turn away a non-white. It is quite another thing, however, to actually become part of a mixed or non-white congregation or to diversify the way a predominantly white congregation does things to become ethnically mixed.

The fact is the vast majority of white American evangelicals live in an ethnically homogeneous world. Beyond occasional acquaintances, few have interethnic contacts. Many live in worlds that are at least 90 percent white in their daily experience. Those interviewed by Emerson and Smith admitted they were "sheltered, unexposed to racial diversity, insulated, in their own small world."[33] Because of this, while some may passively favor congregational integration, it is difficult to conceive of it actually taking place on any large scale. The conclusion of these same authors is stunning: "when the racial composition of congregations is surveyed today, little seems to have changed since the civil rights movement, . . . most congregations remain racially segregated. Since the 1960s, a proportionately small number of congregations have struggled to be multiracial, and a few seem to have succeeded, but they are the exceptions to be sure."[34]

When we think of racial segregation, our minds most often go to the black-white divide in America. However, long before the black-white

---

31. Priest and Nieves, *This Side of Heaven*, 4.
32. Emerson and Smith, *Divided by Faith*, 88.
33. Ibid., 80–81.
34. Emerson and Woo, *People of the Dream*, 23.

divide existed in America, our country was already guilty of the most heinous forms of racism in its treatment of the indigenous peoples. In fact, the genocides of the last century pale in comparison to the number of indigenous peoples abused, murdered, and displaced. It is estimated that nearly 200 Native tribes in America have become extinct. Richard Twiss describes the continuing divide in the evangelical church:

> In all this time the non-Native evangelical community has yet to say to the Native American Christian community, "We need you." Why not? Because differing cultural worldviews determine how value is assigned, measured, or determined, whether for a person, group, or thing. The ethnocentric (based on the belief that one's own group is superior) and biased Euro-American worldview has greatly hindered the church community's ability to see Native believers as valuable and necessary members of the Body of Christ.[35]

What is true in the area of ethnic segregation is equally observed when it comes to other factors that fragment the church into atomistic affinity groups. While our primary focus is on the dividing walls of ethnicity in the body of Christ, the same observations and principles can be applied to socioeconomic and generational divides that separate believers and churches from one another. Since race and income tend to track one another in the United States, class divisions are a natural by-product of the racial divide. The vast majority of American congregations are situated in the same social class milieu that they were in over ten years ago.[36] While there has not been (at least statistically) much upward mobility, there certainly hasn't been the downward mobility that is called for in the gospel.

Beyond the issue of segregation by ethnicity and socioeconomic status is the phenomena of generational preferences that fragment the church. One of the most noticeable characteristics of the local churches in Portland, Oregon, where I presently live is the piecemeal effect of generational isolation. Massive numbers of twenty-somethings have left already established congregations to create an environment of worship more conducive to their cultural preferences. While initially such

---

35. Twiss, *One Church*, 59.

36. *NCS*, under "Explore the Data." Even here, only 10 percent of all religious service attenders affiliate with a congregation that is located in a census tract in which at least 30 percent of the residents are poor.

congregations attract large numbers of "birds with the same cultural feathers" and appear to be growing numerically, the long-term effect weakens the broader church in the city at its very foundations. We compromise the very unity for which Jesus prayed, and in doing so sacrifice the very apologetic that could result in so many more believing that Jesus has truly come in the flesh (John 17:21). In our desire to multiply the church, we have denied the very unity that should most characterize the church as well as the power of Christ that can make such unity a reality.

THE BUILDING MATERIALS

Every wall is built of something. The same holds true of the walls that divide the church today along lines of ethnicity. It will be difficult to identify the walls or to deconstruct the walls unless we understand how they are constructed in the first place. Any casual, simplistic answer that merely attributes the construction of the dividing walls to sin, prejudice, racism, or ethnic bigotry will not suffice. We must identify and describe the sociological currents that push us in the direction of segregating ourselves into affinity groups defined by color of skin, language, age, culture, and socioeconomic status.

In what ways do evangelicals actually reproduce and contribute to ethnic segregation? In other words, how are the dividing walls that fragment the church today constructed? Why is it that African Americans often attend African American churches, Koreans often attend Korean churches, Hispanics often attend Hispanic churches even though they all drive by largely white Euro-American churches to arrive at their own? Why such congregational homogeneity in spite of the ever increasing cultural heterogeneity?

The answer to those questions is not complicated. It is not valid to conclude that the present divisions in the church—whether ethnic, socioeconomic or generational—are due entirely or even primarily to prejudiced Christians within our churches. The dividing walls can be traced to sociological factors that are determinative for any group, whether Christian or not. The bottom line is that we are influenced more by sociological factors than we would like to admit. All the while claiming to be the *ekklēsia* of God, a new community, the body of Christ that cannot be divided (1 Cor 1:13), we nevertheless find ourselves acquiescing to the natural, sociological tides that determine the relational patterns of the population at large. Jim Wallis puts it bluntly: "The life of

North American churches has become utterly predictable on sociological grounds. Factors of race, class, sex and national identity shape and define the lives of Christians just like everybody else. No one expects anything different of Christians."[37] No one, that is, except Christ, the head of the church.

Before moving on to the biblical response to the present day crisis, I would like to briefly examine why the life of our churches has become predictable on sociological grounds. This will enable us to better appreciate why the biblical response to the present fragmentation of the church is so applicable. It also will allow us to identify our *natural* responses that are sociologically motivated so that we can better live out *biblical* responses that are supernaturally motivated.

A LONGING FOR BELONGING

The starting point is the basic human need for meaning and belonging. We each have an innate longing for belonging that, as we will see in chapter 2, is integral to who we are as the image of the triune God. Such longing for belonging is critical in our search for meaning. An understanding of who *I* am cannot be achieved apart from an understanding of who *we* are. My basic human need of meaning is fulfilled when I am loved and my basic human need of belonging is fulfilled when I am linked or connected to others.

Emerson and Smith describe two social dynamics that groups—even religious groups—provide in response to the basic human needs of meaning and belonging: boundaries and social solidarity.

Boundaries are symbolic and help a group distinguish itself from other groups. Essentially, we know who we are by defining who we are not. That is why, from a purely sociological perspective, permeable and fuzzy boundaries result in less of a sense of meaning and belonging, thus weakening the group.

The other dynamic is solidarity. Boundaries contribute to solidarity. When a group identifies who it is by defining who it is not, greater solidarity is the result. If a group lacks solidarity, it will eventually fail. Translated into biblical terms, "A house divided cannot stand." Generally, groups who are able to provide a sense of boundaries and social solidarity

---

37. Wallis, *Call to Conversion*, 19.

best respond to the innate human need of meaning and belonging and are thus more successful.[38]

This is where the difficulty begins. When an intense craving for meaning and belonging (innate to who we are as the image of God) is confronted by negative sociological patterns typical of a particular society, an inevitable dissonance develops. It is the dissonance between the biblical approach to finding meaning and belonging and the natural, human approach characteristic of one's cultural norms.

What are these cultural norms that make the life of the church so predictable? The first is a pervasive individualism so characteristic of American society. Such individualism has nurtured a society marked by personal choice, consumerism, and competition, resulting in an ever increasing homogeneity of groups well-defined by symbolic boundaries and social solidarity. It is precisely this predictable sociological process that constructs the dividing walls of ethnicity, socioeconomic class, and affinity groups within the church today. Figure 1.1 depicts these sociological dynamics.

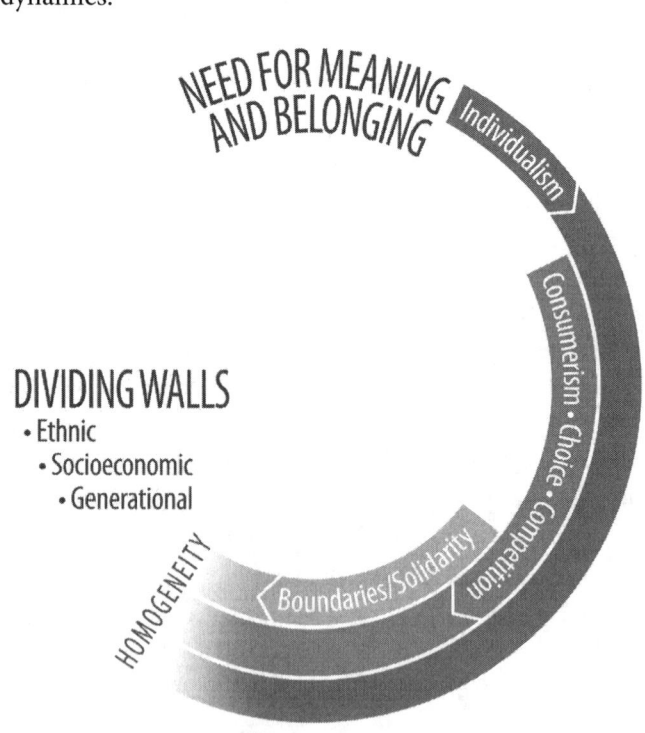

DIVIDING WALLS
- Ethnic
- Socioeconomic
- Generational

Figure 1.1

38. Emerson and Smith, *Divided by Faith*, 143.

WHEN LONGING FOR BELONGING MEETS RADICAL INDIVIDUALISM

One societal phenomenon typically characteristic of western culture is what Robert Bellah terms "radical individualism." "Individualism lies at the very core of American society," he writes. "We believe in the dignity, indeed the sacredness, of the individual. Anything that would violate our right to think for ourselves, judge for ourselves, make our own decisions, live our lives as we see fit, is not only morally wrong, it is sacrilegious."[39]

While in many countries around the world, religion is considered a family or societal affair, in America it is more often than not an individual affair. For fifteen years, my family served among the Protestant and evangelical churches of France. Though France is definitely influenced to some degree by the individualism of the western mindset, when it comes to religion one's familial, cultural, or even national identity often prevails. For the vast majority of nations and cultures around the world, religion is not so "privatized" as in the United States. While in America we think of reaching people with the gospel one-by-one, in certain cultures around the world, entire villages and tribes experience conversion at the same time.

Paradoxically, some of the seeds of our postmodern individualism were planted during the Protestant Reformation. As evangelicals, we are indebted to the reformers for their clarion call to the Scriptures as the sole authority for faith and practice. But with that came the pendulum effect of moving churches more and more toward a privatization of Christianity.

> In telling believers that only Scripture is the Christians ultimate authority, that God's revelation is given today only through the Word, and that the church is in error when it contradicts Scripture, and in emphasizing the priesthood of the individual believer (all biblically true), the seeds were sown for individuals to stand ultimately above the church, judging it and not considering themselves accountable to it, but rather the other way around.[40]

About the same time outside of the church, we find the powerful influence of the Enlightenment. Jean-Jacques Rousseau (1712–1778) was one

---

39. Bellah et al., *Habits of the Heart*, 142.
40. Bacote, "Fade to White," 53.

of the most influential thinkers of the Enlightenment, and his writings have greatly influenced the world view of Western society. His concept of *amour de soi* (self-love) stated that ultimate reality is discovered in individual choice driven by an innate desire for self-preservation. This is the original, pre-social condition he called the "state of nature." Consequently, *all social relationships are not ultimately real but only secondary to the primacy of the individual.* His famous line from *The Social Contract* has reverberated through the past 200 years: "Man is born free, and everywhere he is in chains." While often interpreted to refer to the chains of political oppression, Rousseau was speaking rather of the oppressive *personal* relationships of our lives like marriage, family, church, and the workplace. Other early modern political thinkers like Thomas Hobbes and John Locke followed this same line of thought, describing the original condition of humanity as purely disconnected, atomistic individuals. The resulting call was to throw off the "chains" of the present social order and create "the new man" in which one is liberated from all relationships except those that are the product of personal choice.[41] This rationalistic movement began to radically alter the cultural and religious landscape of America.

In colonial America, "religion was simply not left to the individual choice, nor was it often imagined that it could be."[42] Yet the emphasis on the individual found in both the Reformation and the Enlightenment began to change all of this, leading to a major shift in *Weltanschauung*, or worldview. As Sidney Mead describes it, such "internalization or privatization of religion is one of the most momentous changes that has ever taken place in Christendom."[43] This process of privatization was later intensified during the first and second Great Awakening in American history. The emphasis on the individual, so prevalent in the political philosophy of the day, was carried over into the life of the church. While the revivalists of the first Awakening had appropriately denounced the abuses of the established churches that had turned the clergy into a privileged class, the leaders of the second Awakening in many cases denounced church authority itself. The cry to cast off *civil* authority became equally an appeal to throw off *ecclesiastical* tyranny. Some leaders of the second Awakening transferred the rhetoric of independence

---

41. Pearcey, *Total Truth*, 137–42.
42. Emerson and Smith, *Divided by Faith*, 138.
43. Mead, *Brave New World*, 4.

uncritically from the sphere of politics to the sphere of the church. As a result, "the priesthood of all believers was taken to mean religion of the people, by the people, and for the people."[44] All the while bringing spiritual revival to otherwise dead churches, the Awakenings also promoted an ever increasing separatism among American Protestants, polarizing churches and leading to a plethora of denominations. "As liberal individualism was taking root in politics," Nancy Pearcey writes, "it was being uncritically applied to the churches, producing a highly individualistic and democratic ecclesiology. Modern values like autonomy and popular sovereignty became simply taken for granted in evangelical churches."[45]

Today, American evangelicals are even more individualistic. In a poll taken in the mid-1990s by sociologist Wade Clark Roof, more than 54 percent of evangelical Christians said that "to be alone and meditate" was more important than "to worship with others."[46] In his recent book *Revolution*, George Barna predicts that "future models of 'church' will be almost impossible to categorize or market."[47] Beyond the traditional parachurch movements and the bourgeoning emerging church, we find numerous Internet-based faith groups, marketplace fellowships, and coaching groups, to name a few. The Barna Group estimates that more than fifty million Americans practice their faith through a variety of alternative faith models. They further predict that by the year 2025 the local church will lose roughly half of its current "market share" and alternative forms of spiritual expression will pick up the slack. Much of this is fueled by a rampant individualism that has touched the very core of modern day evangelicalism. As Emerson and Smith point out: "Individualism is very American, but the type of individualism and the ferocity with which it is held distinguished white evangelicals from others. . . . Contemporary white American evangelicalism is perhaps the strongest carrier of this free-will individual tradition."[48]

Lack of clarity as to the essence of the church is at the heart of our crisis of identity as the people of God. No wonder so many believers today view themselves as individual Christians rather than as part of a living, organic community. Peruse the shelves of any Christian bookstore

44. Pearcey, *Total Truth*, 274–75.
45. Ibid., 277.
46. Pearcey, *Total Truth*, 293.
47. Barna, *Revolution*, 64.
48. Emerson and Smith, *Divided by Faith*, 76–77.

and you go away with the distinct feeling that the Christian life is about "Jesus and me." The quintessential question being asked is, "What will promote *my* faith experience?" "It is as though most Christians expect to fly solo to heaven," writes Michael Griffiths, "with only just a little bit of formation flying from time to time!"[49]

The same pervasive individualistic world view influences how we as Christians approach societal ills, whether it concerns racism or other problems. More often than not we think in individualistic terms. When asked how to have a transforming effect on the broader culture, a Baptist woman replied: "I just feel that if each individual lived the Christian life . . . it influences society. We just need to live the life that Christ wants us to live, the best we can, to influence society in general."[50] On the other end of the denominational spectrum a Presbyterian man suggested: "I think our country has a perceived race relations problem. I think that we have individuals still that have race relation problems. I don't think that the country has in its current form a race relation problem."[51] Evidently, an individualistic, atomistic view of the church also leads to an individualistic, simplistic approach when it comes to finding solutions to societal concerns.

MARKETPLACE CHRISTIANITY

Individualism is the *Weltanschauung* in which the seeds of choice, competition, and consumerism can sprout and flourish. And flourish they do! A marketplace is inevitably full of choices, consumers, and competition, and American Christianity provides all three in ample doses. There are suppliers (churches that are in competition with one another), consumers (Christians looking for the "perfect" church to meet their needs), and to a great degree the freedom to choose. If a consumer can choose where to go to church, and the survival of churches (the "suppliers") is dependent upon the consumer's choice, then churches are inevitably placed in competition with one another. Evangelicals have capitalized quite well on the social dynamics of American religion.

This phenomenon has historical roots. By the end of the eighteenth century, Thomas Jefferson's Virginia Bill for Establishing Religious

---

49. Griffiths, *Cinderella*, 23.
50. Smith, *American Evangelicalism*, 188, 190.
51. Emerson and Smith, "Color-Blinded," para. 17.

Freedom (1785) along with the passing of the First Amendment to the Constitution ("Congress shall make no law respecting an establishment of religion, or prohibiting the free exercise thereof") had led to a foundation being laid for our present day religious marketplace. At last, religion was disestablished from any governmental influence at the national and state level. While it can be argued that circumventing the religious oppression so characteristic of European societies is a positive step, such disestablishment also led to pluralism, increased competition, and a growing marketplace consumerism.

> When religion becomes disestablished, it opens the doors for creative religious entrepreneurs to market their alternative faiths to religious consumers. The general public, likewise, is freed—at least in the ideal—to choose among options. Disestablishment in the context of a new, pluralistic nation led to a religious marketplace. With only slight exaggeration, the United States can be characterized as the "mega-mall" of religious consumerism.[52]

One natural consequence of this "mega-mall" environment fueled by consumers, choice, and competition is an ever increasing ecclesiological pluralism. Churches choose to "specialize" by targeting certain age groups, ethnicities, or preferred styles of worship. Over and beyond the racial and ethnic divide, we have churches for the young and churches for the old, traditional churches, contemporary churches, and emergent churches. The determining factors are really insignificant. As Emerson and Smith observe, it could be something as ridiculous as ear size. "If ear size came to be an important social dividing line, we would begin to find big-eared congregations and little-eared congregations. Prejudice is not needed for this to occur. Rather, real cultural differences would develop by ear size and interactions with like-eared people would become easier, smoother, and ultimately more satisfying."[53] A consumer mentality and its counterpart of niche marketing play into this dynamic, resulting in the sharpening of boundaries. Whites want to be with whites, baby boomers tend to hang with baby boomers, the Generation X culture gravitates toward others who are like them. Gradually, distinct identity boundaries are developed that separate one local church from another. While each church may grow in size and/or strength, it may be more due to sociological principles of group identification rather than to a healthy,

52. Emerson and Smith, *Divided by Faith*, 139.
53. Ibid., 145.

collective biblical identity. Paul Louis Metzger puts it pointedly: "We live in an age of consumer culture, the grand supermarket or shopping mall of desire, and many progressive, culture-engaging churches have unwittingly taken the bait—hook, line, and sinker."[54]

IDENTITY AND HOMOGENEITY

The result of "taking the bait—hook, line, and sinker" is more often than not the establishment and maintenance of homogeneous churches. So much of recent church growth theory and practice has focused on the "homogeneous unit principle" popularized by Donald McGavran. His classic statement that people "like to become Christians without crossing racial, linguistic, or class barriers" has been the rallying cry for the establishment of homogeneous churches around the world.[55] C. Peter Wagner argues extensively in his book *Our Kind of People* that such an approach is not only natural from a sociological perspective, but also biblical and pragmatic. It "gets the job done" from the standpoint of numerical results. This is because no individual, according to Wagner, should be required to abandon his culture to become a Christian. The theory's primary concern is that we should never add culturally offensive prerequisites to the message of the gospel. For McGavran and Wagner, it is clear that multiethnic churches are in most cases counterproductive to evangelism. In fact, McGavran goes so far as to argue that race prejudice "can be understood and should be made an aid to Christianization."[56] This is the "consecrated pragmatism" of the Church Growth movement.

The Church Growth movement of the twentieth century was built on the premise that "people meet together for worship within the basic sociological groupings into which they are born."[57] This is what sociologists call the "status quo bias." The status quo bias says that we tend to stick with what we have, even if gains could be had by choosing an alternative. In other words, leave well enough alone. When applied to congregations in America, the conclusions are obvious. Preferences, perceived similarity, and the degree to which meaning and belonging are met are

54. Metzger, *Consuming Jesus*, 55.
55. McGavran, *Understanding Church Growth*, 223.
56. McGavran, *Bridges of God*, 10. For a balanced assessment of Donald McGavran's "homogeneous unit principle," see Mark DeYmaz, *Should Pastors Accept or Reject the Homogeneous Unit Principle?*
57. Wagner, *Our Kind of People*, 11.

the key factors that shape people's choices. These factors, however, are initially shaped by a person's history. Given the fact that US congregations since the Civil War have been largely racially homogeneous, the status quo bias indicates that they will probably remain so.[58] This also accounts for the reality that a social structure—a church, a community group, or the business place—can be racialized even though the choices of the individuals within the structure are not explicitly racial. People are simply complying with the "default setting" of the system. In Paul's terms, this is conforming to the patterns of this world.

Unfortunately, we have—oftentimes unconsciously—taken up the building materials of radical individualism, consumerism, and status quo bias to subtly but surely build our own dividing walls. Motivated by our longing for belonging, we have acquiesced to the natural status quo tendency by gathering with believers of a similar ethnic feather, resulting in largely homogeneous churches as defined by ethnicity. Indeed, we are more influenced by sociological factors than we would like to admit. We have become utterly predictable. After all, it's just easier that way. However, as René Padilla asks:

> What can this missiology say to a church in an American suburb in which the bourgeois is comfortable but remains enslaved to the materialism of a consumer society and blind to the needs of the poor? What can it say to a church in which a racist feels at home because of the unholy alliance of Christianity with racial segregation? . . . Of course it can say that "men like to become Christians without crossing racial, linguistic and class barriers," but what does that have to do with the gospel concerning Jesus Christ, who came to reconcile us "to God *in one body* through the cross?"[59]

In the following chapters, I will contend that the Scriptures call us to redefine our boundaries and sense of solidarity uniquely in light of our New Humanity identity. The biblical response to the present crisis of dividing walls that fragment the body of Christ is "understand and be who we are!" I will argue that we must intentionally shift our focus from *natural* groupings in the church to *supernatural* groupings in the church, finding our point of commonality—not in such determinants as color,

---

58. Emerson and Smith, *Divided by Faith*, 146 (emphasis mine).
59. Padilla, "Unity of the Church," 169.

culture, or class—but in our shared identity as members of God's New Humanity.

CONCLUSION

I, too, have a dream. It is not so much a dream for America, but a dream for the church. This dream is not original with me. It is found throughout the Bible, particularly in the New Testament teaching concerning the church as God's New Humanity.

In one sense, this dream has already become a reality. God's provision of the cross has brought reconciliation to an otherwise alienated world. With those final words, "It is finished," the second Adam more than replaced what the first Adam had erased. With those final words, vertical reconciliation with God and horizontal reconciliation at the heart of humanity were made possible. Those final words spoken by the Man for all nations indicated God's full provision for a true "table of brotherhood." Today, this table of brotherhood is compromised by the dividing walls of ethnicity and culture that fragment the church in America. While the surrounding culture is becoming more and more ethnically diverse, eleven o'clock on Sunday morning continues to be the most segregated hour of American society.

Having looked at the dividing walls of ethnicity, class, and generational affinity that piecemeal the church today, our desire in the following chapters is to take a fresh look at God's design for his church as detailed in the biblical record. Here, many pertinent and pressing questions can be asked to guide us in our exploration: What does the Bible say about such dividing walls? What, according to the Bible, is at the source of these divisions? More positively stated, what is God's original design for mankind and how is this ideal to be pursued? What is God's provision for deconstructing the dividing walls in the contemporary church? Finally, what is the responsibility of believers individually and collectively in this process?

2

Humanity, the *Imago Dei*

> *Today, more than at any time, the question, "What is man?" is at the center of theological and philosophical concern.*
>
> G. C. Berkouwer

THE PRESENT CRISIS FACING the church today cannot be viewed in isolation from the biblical record. It is not sufficient to simply take isolated proof texts, sometimes removed from their context, to argue a case for diversity in unity. We need rather a substantive, overarching biblical theology of oneness. However, this requires not only an analysis of the key biblical texts, but also a synthesis of the larger biblical context. We need to step back to see the larger narrative of Scripture. We need, as my friend Rodney Woo has put it, to see "the beginning, the end, and everything in between."[1]

The following chapters explore the biblical theology of diversity in unity. While there are multiple and colorful images employed by the Scriptures to describe the unity and diversity of God's people, one in particular stands out as a synthesis of both Old and New Testament theology—God's people as the New Humanity (Eph 2:15; 4:22–24; Col 3:9–11). While the specific Pauline terminology is limited to the New Testament, its roots are deeply imbedded in the Old. We begin, then, with an exploration of humankind as the *imago Dei* in the opening chapters of the Bible. We'll then proceed to the devastating effects of

---

1. Woo, *Color of Church*, 2–20.

humanity's fall into sin—the image of God deconstructed. This sets the stage for the promise of hope in a new society, the New Humanity, of which Christ, the second man and last Adam, is the head. Effectively, Christ more than replaced what Adam erased!

This is no dry, sterile theology. The practical and pressing implications for the church are spelled out by Paul in his exhortations to put on a new set of "clothes" fitting to our calling. We discover that, as we do so, we are individually and collectively being renewed into the image of our Creator. Here there is no segregation of ethnicity, socioeconomic class, or age. We are *already* one in Christ, even though we have *not yet* experienced to the fullest the "mature man" (Eph 4:13) for which our hearts long!

BACK TO THE BEGINNING

To understand our collective identity as the New Humanity, we must begin with the creation of the first man, Adam. Genesis, the book of beginnings, brings us face-to-face with God's original intentions for humanity. Genesis 1 beautifully describes in poetic form the historical realities of humanity's beginning. This dramatic account cannot be read without the distinct impression that humankind stands as the apex of the created order. "Let us make" stands in stark contrast with "Let the earth bring forth."[2] All that precedes the grand finale of God's creation of humankind, though receiving the divine affirmation as "good," is clearly distinguished from humanity who alone exists as the very image of God. The inspired wording is unmistakable:

> Then God said, "Let us make man in our image, in our likeness, and let them rule over the fish of the sea and the birds of the air, over the livestock, over all the earth, and over all the creatures that move along the ground." So God created man in his own image, in the image of God he created him; male and female he created them. (Gen 1:26–27)

Here lies the enigma. What is this "image"? Is it man himself, or does it belong to his Maker, an image *after which* man is created? What is the significance of the often contested "let *us*" of verse 26? To whom is God speaking? Furthermore, why would "man" (singular) be called "them"

---

2. Kidner, *Genesis*, 50.

(plural) in one verse and "him" (singular) in the next verse, leaving average readers questioning either the reliability of the text or their own English grammar? To complicate matters, man is further described as the "likeness" of God. What significance could this little addition have on the understanding of the image motif? Beyond all these interpretive questions lie the broader issues of the relevance of this passage to the dividing walls so evident in both society and the contemporary church. It is to these questions we now turn, for without clear answers, "the beginning, the end, and everything in between" won't make much sense.

THE *CRUX INTERPRETUM* OF SCRIPTURE

In many ways, the doctrine of the image of God functions as the *crux interpretum* both for one's understanding of the unfolding drama of redemption in Scripture and, more specifically, for one's anthropology. Concerning the latter, James Barr has pointedly noted that if the doctrine of the image were absent from the structure of Genesis 1, man would exist as nothing more than a dominant animal.[3] Of course, this is not the case.

The doctrine of the *imago Dei* in Genesis 1 stands as a reminder of our true humanity with all of its privileges and responsibilities. It tells us who we are and who we are to become. As F. R. Barry has noted, "God created man in his own image. All the rest of the Bible is a commentary on that phrase."[4]

Unfortunately, the importance of this doctrine has in no way excluded it from interpretive difficulties. Much of the problem lies in the fact that the Old Testament references to the doctrine of the image of God are "tantalizing in their brevity and scarcity."[5] Actually, there are only three:

> Let us make man in our image . . . so God created man in his own image. (Gen 1:26–27)

> When God created man, he made him in the likeness of God. He created them male and female and blessed them. And when they were created, he called them "man." (Gen 5:1)

---

3. Barr, "Image of God," 14.
4. Barry, *Recovery of Man*, 61.
5. Clines, "Image of God," 53. There are, of course, two significant New Testament passages that mention the doctrine: Jas 3:9 and 1 Cor 11:7.

> Whoever sheds the blood of man, by man shall his blood be shed;
> for in the image of God has God made man. (Gen 9:6)

INTERPRETATION THROUGH THE CENTURIES

As expected, the brevity and scarcity of references to the *imago Dei* have resulted in a tremendous amount of controversy throughout the centuries. Outside the canonical books of the Old Testament, there is little mention of the image of God until the intertestamental period. Then in the apocryphal books Sirach 17:1–3 and Wisdom of Solomon 2:23, we find two examples. The latter passage states: "But God created man for immortality, and made him the image of his own eternal self" (NEB). In the Targums, the rabbis seemed hesitant to make definitive statements regarding the image of God.[6] The Mishnah, on the other hand, understood the image in an allegorical sense (following Philo) as a reminder of the dignity and value of each human individual. More recent Jewish opinion is as diversified as Christian interpretation.

Most of the church fathers tended to emphasize the intangible part of man—that is, man's soul—as that which reflected the image of God. For Athanasius, it was the divine Logos as located in the intellect, while Augustine declares in neo-Platonist style: "For not in the body but in the mind was man made in the image of God. In his own similitude let us seek God, in his own image recognize the creator."[7] The majority of the Reformers followed suit, interpreting the image along the lines of moral integrity, purity, justice, and holiness. Illumined reason, true knowledge, and righteous will—all originally inherent in man—made up the surpassing excellence of human nature. Finally, the typical rationalist interpreted the image as the "divine spark"—the religious quality of man that includes self-consciousness, self-determination, and intellect. For G. W. F. Hegel, the very nature of man was divine. For A. E. Biedermann, it was the cultivation of a spiritual life in harmony with the spirituality of God himself.[8]

More recent Old Testament scholarship has taken a different twist from all the above interpretations, arguing strongly for a physical

---

6. The *Targum Onqelos* is an example of this, leaving the phrase "as (in) the image of God" completely untranslated.

7. As cited by Clines, "Image of God," 86.

8. Barth, *CD*, III.1.193.

interpretation of the image. According to this view, man was created "with the same physical form as the deity, of which he is a molded three-dimensional embodiment, delineated and exteriorized."[9] Such an understanding has been built off of lexical studies that, with strong reason, define "image" (*ṣelem*) as "an actual plastic work, a duplicate."[10]

Another view is that of Karl Barth, whose writings in the twentieth century marked a watershed in the study of the image doctrine. Barth notes that for centuries expositors have neglected the plain witness of the text itself as to the meaning of the image: "male and female he created them." For Barth, the image is an *analogia relationis* that finds its essence in the "I-Thou" relationship within the Godhead, between God and man, and between man and woman.[11]

It appears that in the history of interpretation scholarship has reached somewhat of an impasse over the problem of the image. Apart from Barth, all of the above views fail to take into account the Hebrew concept of man as a totality—as spirit *and* body—choosing instead to emphasize (or completely exclude) one or the other. To make matters worse, there are those such as James Barr who reason somewhat fatalistically that there is no way of determining the meaning of the image. Because of certain higher critical presuppositions regarding the Genesis passages, he concludes: "There is no reason to believe that this writer had in his mind any definite idea about the content or the location of the image of God."[12]

THE NATURE OF THE IMAGE OF GOD

Admittedly, such divergence of interpretation through the centuries could lead us to adopt Barr's pessimistic conclusion. Yet I believe the passage itself yields several clear indications that point us toward the meaning and function of the image. Furthermore, as we take our findings concerning the image and view them in relation to the New Testament

---

9. P. Humbert as cited by Clines, "Image of God," 56.

10. Rad, *Genesis*, 56. This understanding is further supported by translators of the LXX who most often rendered the Hebrew *ṣelem* as *eikōn* in Greek, having reference to statues. For a survey of *ṣelem* in relation to similar words in the same word group, see Barr, "Image of God," 21.

11. Barth, *CD*, III.1.192–97.

12. Barr, "Image of God," 13.

passages that speak of the creation and renewal of the New Humanity (Eph 2:15; 4:22–24; Col 3:9–11), the full nature of the image as well as implications for the issues at hand begin to take shape.

What then are these indications in the Genesis account that point us in the right direction? There are several of a more exegetical nature that need to be addressed. These include: the meanings of the terms "image" and "likeness" as used in the Old Testament, the interpretive question of man "as" or "in" the image of God, the thought behind the plural "Let *us* make man," and the significance of the concept of "man" in Genesis and in biblical theology.

I believe these issues, once addressed, yield three conclusions concerning the "image of God" motif as introduced in Genesis. These can be summarized by the terms *rule, resemblance,* and *relationship.* I also believe these three concepts set the stage for the larger biblical-theological framework contributed by the New Testament. On a more practical level, they also give us insight as to God's intentions for his people as they confront the dividing walls of ethnicity in the life of the church.

RULE: HUMANITY AS GOD'S VICE-REGENT

In any attempt to understand the meaning of man as the image of God, we must first establish the significance of the term "image" (*ṣelem*) as used in the Old Testament. The basic meaning is "something cut out, image, likeness, semblance" or a "statue, image, copy, drawing."[13] The emphasis of the word is on *physical shape* or *form*. This is seen, for example, where the word is used in reference to three-dimensional images such as idols or statues of heathen gods (Num 33:53; 2 Kgs 11:18; Amos 5:26) or of men or animals (1 Sam 6:5, 11; Ezek 16:11). Apart from the uses of the term in Genesis, there are *no* examples where *ṣelem* is used in a strictly metaphorical or spiritual sense, referring to intangible entities or qualities as "reason," "moral consciousness," "love," or "justice."[14] It seems most natural, then, to understand the term "image" in Genesis 1:26–27 (cf. 5:1; 9:6) in a very concrete sense referring to a fashioned image or a representative figure. This is further supported by the use of

---

13. BDB, 853; KBL, 2:804; *ANET*, 93.

14. There are two Old Testament passages where the meaning of *ṣelem* is questionable: Ps 39:6 and 73:20. Even in these passages, the term *ṣelem* is not void of the idea of shape or form. The major lexicons understand the term even in these passages as an extension of the nuance of physical shape.

the term in the relatively clear passage in Genesis 5:3. There, Seth is born according to the *image* of his father, Adam, lending strong support to the physical meaning of "image."[15] If in Genesis 1 "image" refers uniquely to God's spiritual qualities found in man, no other biblical example of the term remotely matches it.

Man as God's Image

This concrete, tangible understanding of "image" cannot be disassociated from a further question posed by Genesis 1:26. Is man created "in" or "as" the image of God? The phrase "Let us make man *in* our image" demonstrates how crucial a two-letter preposition can be, not only to our understanding of a single verse, but also, in this case, to an entire doctrine!

At first glance, God has an image *in which* man has been created. In this case, the Hebrew *bêt* ("in") is understood as the *norm, standard,* or *pattern* after which man is created.[16] However, does God have a tangible, concrete form? Admittedly, the Bible does speak of God by means of anthropomorphisms (Gen 6:6; 8:21), direct statements concerning his outward form (Exod 33:18–23; Deut 4:12; cf. Isa 40:18), and theophanies (Exod 3:1–12; Josh 5:15). He is described as hearing (Exod 22:27), seeing (Ps 10:14), walking (Gen 3:8), and even as whistling (Isa 7:18). Nevertheless, the Scriptures are explicitly clear that God is spirit *(rûaḥ;* Eccl 12:7; Isa 31:3).

It is in reaction to such a crass bodily understanding of God that many have adopted a metaphorical understanding of "image," understanding it to consist in such immaterial concepts as "self-consciousness" and "self-determination," "original righteousness," "reason," "personhood," "spirit," "soul," or "heart." The major objection to this interpretation, however, is that it finds no support in the tangible, concrete meaning of the term "image" (*ṣelem*), as we have already seen. A further problem is the emphasis on one part of personhood (the spiritual) to the exclusion of the other (the physical). Such a superficial dichotomy is never warranted by Scripture or by Semitic thought. Rather, the body

---

15. A comparison of Gen 1:26 with 5:3 also underscores the distinction between humankind created *as* (*bêt*) the image of God and Seth who was *according to* (*kaph*) the image of Adam. When *bêt* is used with *ṣelem* the reference is invariably to God and not to man.

16. Kautzsch, *Hebrew Grammar*, 379, §119.h.

is understood "as in all its parts the medium of a spiritual and personal life . . . and finds its reality in being God's image."[17] It would seem, then, that any interpretation of humanity being created "in" the image of God can easily lead to two extremes—either to an unbiblical view of God's essence or to an unbiblical view of personhood.

There is another way of understanding the meaning of the Hebrew *bêt*. It can be translated "as," carrying the idea of "in the capacity of."[18] A classic example is Exodus 6:3, "And I appeared to Abraham . . . *as* (*bêt*) God Almighty." (emphasis mine).[19] As applied to Genesis 1:26, the verse reads, "Then God said, 'Let us make man *as* our image, according to our likeness." This is the preferred interpretation of this verse. God created man *as* his image. Man does not *have* the image, nor was he created *in* the image, but he himself *is* the image.

The implications of man existing *as* the image of God are noteworthy. When it is understood that man himself *is* the image of God, it necessarily follows that the *entire* man exists as such. No allowance is made for a superficial Platonic dichotomy between body and spirit. This makes man as the image of God something quite tangible, visible, and concrete. "In so far as man is a body and a bodiless man is not man, the body is the image of God; for man is the image of God. *Man is the flesh-and-blood image of the invisible God."*[20]

The entire man as the image of God is visible and concrete, but also living and dynamic. While Genesis 1:26 merely informs us that humanity *is* the image of God, Genesis 2:7 tells us the specifics of *how* that image was made and in what it consists. Adam was formed from the dust of the ground and is in essence a physical creature. Then into his nostrils God breathed the breath ($n^e\bar{s}\bar{a}m\hat{a}$) of life and man became a living soul. As Walther Eichrodt has noted, "Man does not *have* a body and soul; he is both of them at once."[21] In stark contrast to man as the living image of the living God stood the inanimate images of the pagan gods or even hand-hewed statues arrogantly established by ambitious

---

17. Eichrodt, *Theology*, 2:149.

18. Kautzsch, *Hebrew Grammar*, 379 §119.i. For a complete and convincing discussion, see Clines, "Image of God," 76–77; Ross, *Creation and Blessing*, 112.

19. Other examples include Num 18:26; Deut 1:13; Ps 78:55.

20. Clines, "Image of God," 86 (emphasis mine).

21. Eichrodt, *Theology*, 2:124.

kings. It was to such lifeless images that man as God's living image stood as an ever-present polemic.

This leads us to a final implication of man *as* the image of God. Not only is man as an entirety the image of God, but humanity as God's image functions in a *representative* capacity. This is crucial for understanding the development of this concept throughout the rest of Scripture. It was not uncommon in the Ancient Near East for a king to set up an image of himself in a remote province for the one purpose of extending his authority and rule. In many cases, the image (statue) itself represented the king's occupation of the conquered land. In fact, such a close correlation existed between image and king that to revile the image was to dishonor the king. Similarly, man *as* image is God's authoritative representative on earth with the unique role of exercising dominion. Even as a pagan king would establish his statue on foreign soil to signify his presence and ownership, so the transcendent Creator of Genesis 1 has become tangibly immanent through his authoritatively established vice-regent, humanity. Therefore, the role of man as image is to *express* God more than to *depict* God. "For the image does not primarily mean similarity, but the representation of the one who is imaged in a place where he is not."[22]

That this is true is evident from the structure of Genesis 1:26, "Let us make man *as* our image . . . and let them rule," which is best translated "Let us make man *as* our image . . . *in order that* they might rule."[23] Man himself is the image of God; the commission to rule is the function of the image, that to which man is called and capable of because of who he is. This function of dominion is further described in verse 28 as "subduing" ("bring into bondage") and "ruling" ("to tread down, subdue"). This is God's *Magna Carta* for all human progress and dominion. Thus man as the image of God is the Creator's authoritative vice-regent on earth entrusted with the unique role of exercising dominion. In creation, God fashioned man out of the dust to reign. Eric Sauer states it well:

> These words plainly declare the vocation of the human race to rule. They also call him to progressive growth in culture. Far from being something in conflict with God, cultural achievements are an essential attribute of the nobility of man as he possessed it in

---

22. Clines, "Image of God," 87.

23. E. Kautzsch, *Grammar*, 320 §108.d. See also Hens-Piazza, "Theology of Ecology," 107–10.

Paradise. Inventions and discoveries, the sciences and the arts, refinement and ennobling, in short, the advance of the human mind, are throughout the will of God. They are the taking possession of the earth by the royal human race (Genesis 1:28), the performance of a commission, imposed by the Creator, by God's ennobled servants, a God-appointed ruler's service for the blessing of this earthly realm.[24]

Psalm 8: God's Majesty, Man's Dignity

No better commentary on Genesis 1:26 exists than Psalm 8. This psalm takes us from the majesty of the heavens above to the humility of young children below, from the creation of all things to the culmination of God's kingdom purposes. It talks about the strong, the weak, the spectacular, and the obscure. It begins and ends, however, with God himself and the exclamation of praise: "How majestic is your name in all the earth!"

Psalm 8 deals with two extremely important questions: Who is God, and who is man? In stark contrast to Charles Darwin, Thomas Huxley, and company, this psalm answers those two questions by pointing us to the majesty of God (vv. 1–3) and the dignity of man (vv. 4–8). The two are inseparable. Human dignity—*your* dignity as an individual and *our* dignity corporately—is derived from our recognition of God's majesty. It is this sense of dignity the psalmist describes in verses 3–5: "When I consider your heavens, the work of your fingers, the moon and the stars which you have set in place, what is man that you are mindful of him, the son of man that you care for him? You made him a little lower than the heavenly beings and crowned him with glory and honor."[25] The heavens, with all their planets and stars, are miniscule in contrast to God. After all, they are the "work of his *fingers*" (emphasis mine). However, in contrast to the heavens, man is miniscule. Yet God cares for humanity in our smallness, in our weakness: "What is man that you are mindful of him, the son of man that you care for him?" (Ps 8:4). The author is precise in the selection of his terms, preferring 'ĕnôsh ("man") that emphasizes humankind as feeble and impotent (Gen 4:26; Ps 103:15), all the while

---

24. Sauer, *King of the Earth*, 80–81.

25. Concerning the Hebrew term 'ĕlōhîm. the NIV translation "heavenly beings" rather than "God" (cf. NASB and RSV) is preferable. The context where this verse is cited in Heb 2:5 concerns a comparison with the angels.

viewing him as a social being. Amazing! God is more interested in frail *people* than in planets.

Because the God of all creation cares for you and me, he has given us a position of honor in his creation: "You made him a little lower than the heavenly beings" (Ps 8:5). Humankind is not a little higher than the animals, but a little lower than the angels. Mankind is the crowning apex of all creation. He has been entrusted with a position of inestimable honor. When man is viewed as the haphazard result of some freak evolutionary process, however, the God-given dignity of man is blindly dismissed. Where there is no dignity, there is no morality; where there is no morality, there is the oppressive rule of one ethnicity or nation over another.

Here, I believe, is where we get at the heart of what motivates the most extreme forms of racism that plague society. It is the inherent belief that some are endowed with more dignity than others. Such a perspective fueled the seventeenth-century view in America that considered black slaves as less than human, without souls, and incapable of learning. The truth of the dignity of *all* was distorted into the lie of the superiority of *some*. The tragic results are written in history books and reported daily in our news.

The psalmist reminds us that such a high, honorable position characterizing *all* humanity brings with it great privilege and responsibility.

> You made him ruler over the works of your hands;
> you put everything under his feet: all flocks and herds,
> and the beasts of the field, the birds of the air,
> and the fish of the sea, all that swim the paths of the seas.
> (Ps 8:6–8)

In the Ancient Near East, only the pagan king stood as the image of god (or the gods). According to the creation account, however, such a privilege knows no limitation. No preferential distinction exists between king and laborer, Israelite and non-Israelite, man and woman. Everywhere, humankind is essentially the same, sharing *equal* status as God's authoritative vice-regent over the earth. Any supposed distinction between one individual and another fades into insignificance in light of the fundamental standing of *every* human as the image of God. No mention is made of groups, species, races, classes, or peoples. "By the doctrine of the image of God, Genesis affirms the dignity and worth of man, and elevates *all* men—not just kings and nobles—to the highest status conceivable, short of complete divinization."[26] No allowance is made for part of humanity to be less than the image of God. The natural conclusion is that *every* individual and *every* ethnicity that makes up created humanity exists intrinsically and equally as the image of God.

Apart from this truth, we cannot understand the motivation for this sixth commandment. At the very heart of the sixth commandment ("You shall not murder"; Exod 20:13) is a deep reverence for human life. Humanity, created as the image of God, stands as the crown of all of God's creation. That's why God tells Noah as he exits from the ark and establishes directives for a new government of humankind: "From each man, too, I will demand an accounting for the life of his fellow man. Whoever sheds the blood of man, by man shall his blood be shed; *for in* ["as" = *bêt*] *the image of God has God made man*" (Gen 9:6; emphasis mine). God's warning is explicit: Any individual or group that would attempt to gain wrongful advantage over another *will be penalized*. Such truth strikes hard at any concept that views one group of people or any individual as inferior to another. Unfortunately, this primeval and biblical doctrine failed to penetrate the minds and hearts of so many Euro-American social scientists in the early history of the United States. By the end of the nineteenth century, the inequality of races and the necessary domination of the many by the few was a given.

The idea of humankind as God's official representative on earth is revolutionary in light of many of the ancient religions surrounding Israel that taught that man is helplessly and irreversibly caught up in fatalistic, rhythmic cycles of fertility. No such pessimistic fatalism can be seen in the psalmist's words! Rather, he underscores the role of *all* humanity as God's designated vice-regent over the earth. Furthermore, the words of both the psalmist (Ps 8) and God himself (Gen 1:26–27) hint at the anticipated conflict with evil "powers" that humanity encounters. To "rule" and "have dominion" seem to speak not only of the inanimate created order, but also of the evil forces that must be trampled underfoot. As Allen Ross explains, "The terms used suggest putting down opposition and were perhaps used in anticipation of the conflict with evil. As the Scriptures unfold . . . God's new creation must trample underfoot all evil forces."[27] We will see that these evil forces include the powers that seek to fragment humanity in general and the New Humanity in particular.

26. Clines, "Image of God," 64.
27. Ross, *Creation and Blessing*, 113.

Humanity, the Imago Dei

As we progress in our study, the relevance of man as the tangible, living image of God on earth will become increasingly clear. Though the first humanity failed in its ordained role of faithfully representing the Three-in-One on planet earth, the New Humanity has been both created and commissioned *as* God's image (Eph 2:15; 4:22–24; Col 3:9–11). As the New Humanity, we are God's tangible, visible, living representative on earth. We are destined to rule.

RESEMBLANCE: HUMANITY AS THE "LIKENESS-IMAGE"

Humanity as image effectively represents God, not only to the degree that he *rules* over creation, but also to the degree that he *resembles* his Creator. That is why in Genesis 1 man is further described as the "likeness" ($d^e m\hat{u}t$) of God. Though the term is more abstract in meaning than *ṣelem*, it nevertheless predominantly conveys the idea of visual, exterior appearance.[28] Just how does collective man, as the image of God, resemble God?

It is important to note that the descriptive "likeness" merely explains the term "image." As G. C. Berkouwer concludes: "Because of the variable usage of the two terms in Genesis, it is difficult to escape the conclusion that it is impossible to hold that *ṣelem* and $d^e m\hat{u}t$ refer to two different things."[29] Rather, the descriptive term likeness tells us what kind of image man is. Man is the "likeness-image" of God.

If this is so, in what ways does man as the image of God resemble God? If man indeed exists as a whole and cannot be dichotomized into various parts—thus allowing one to define humanity's likeness to God strictly in spiritual terms—how then is the image like its Creator? Is there a literal resemblance?

Most likely the answer is to be found in that the "breath ($n^e\check{s}\bar{a}m\hat{a}$) of life" was imparted to man's body of dust (Gen 2:7). As Ross explains:

> This word for breath is used in the Bible for God and for the life imparted to man—never for animals. Here the very breath of God is being given in a moment of inspiration. This breath brings more than animation to the man of earth (2:7); it brings spiritual understanding (Job 32:8) and functioning conscience (Prov 20:27). In short, we may conclude that moral capacity is granted to human beings by virtue of this inbreathing. It truly is a breath

---

28. BDB, 198.
29. Berkouwer, *The Image of God*, 69.

of life; that is, it produces life. It probably is this inbreathing that constitutes humankind as the image of God.[30]

Such inbreathing gave man the capacity for self-awareness and self-determination. It constituted man as open to divine address and rendered him capable of responsible conduct, in relation to his Creator and fellow man. Certainly this aspect of mankind as the image of God approaches the view of the majority of the Reformers who placed the emphasis on the moral integrity, holiness, and justice of humankind prior to the Fall. These are among the communicable attributes of God that man as the image of the Creator can experience. Having the breath of life sets humanity apart as unique among all living beings. Man (as are the animals) is a living soul (*nepeš*); but only man (never the animals) is termed the image of God infused with the breath (*nešāmâ*) of God. The key, therefore, to understanding man as the likeness-image of God is found in both the definition of man and the description of God in these verses (Gen 1:26–27). Both definition and description point to *relationship*.

RELATIONSHIP: HUMANITY AS REFLECTION OF THE THREE-IN-ONE

Genesis 1:26 reads, "Then God said, 'Let *us* make man as *our* image.'" Hidden away in the unexplained "us" and "our" of this verse is the veiled allusion to the most intimate of relationships between Father, Son, and Holy Spirit. The relational oneness of the great Three-in-One is the template expressing God's most cherished intentions for all of humanity—relational oneness. God intended man to experience the ecstasy of community.

Certainly the plural designation for God (*'ĕlōhîm*) poses no problem in this passage as it is used extensively throughout the Old Testament. However, what has been the subject of lengthy discussions is the plural "Let *us* make." The problem is further complicated when the phrase "*our* image" in verse 26 reads "*his* own image" in verse 27. A parallel problem is seen in the object of God's creative activity, which seems to move from "man" (v. 26) to "them" (v. 26) to "him" (v. 27).

---

30. Ross, *Creation and Blessing*, 122–23.

Over the years, several explanations have been proposed concerning the plural "*let us* make." It has been viewed as a remnant of myth;[31] others have understood it as God deliberating with his creation or with his heavenly court.[32] Still others see here a "plural of majesty," referring to the fullness of the divine powers possessed by the Creator.[33] However, the interpretation that has the most contextual support understands the plural "let us" as referring to plurality in the Godhead. In this case, the emphasis is placed upon God addressing the Spirit (*rûaḥ*). The Spirit has already been seen "hovering over the waters" (v. 2) and is depicted as having a creative role in other biblical passages (Job 26:7; 33:4; Ps 33:6; 104:29–30). "Although the Christian Trinity cannot be derived solely from the use of the plural, a plurality within the unity of the Godhead may be derived from the passage."[34]

No doubt this latter interpretation has definite implications for understanding man as the image of God. God is a social being and as such has enjoyed eternal fellowship within himself. God is one essence, yet exists as three persons. Even so, man as image exists—not singularly—but as two (man and woman) and then in relation to the many. Therefore, the plural "them" of verse 27 is in perfect harmony with the singular "him" in the same verse. The collective designation "man" (*'ādām*) properly corresponds to both. The age-old polarization between collectivism and individualism finds a solution in the Trinity. Nancy Pearcy states it well: "Over against collectivism, the Trinity implies the dignity and uniqueness of individual persons. Over against radical individualism, the Trinity implies that relationships are not created by sheer choice but are built into the very essence of human nature. *We are not atomistic individuals but are created for relationships.*"[35]

That this is true is emphasized by the intentional vocabulary of Genesis 1:26. The author could have depicted God as saying, "Let us make *man* (*'îsh*) as our image." This term, *'îsh*, views man *as an individual*. It is commonly translated "husband" (Gen 3:16; Ruth 1:3) and often

---

31. See Clines, "Image of God," 64; Rad, *Genesis*, 57.

32. The inherent problem with this view is that whatever is involved in the "us" must be active in the creative work. The involvement of either creation or God's heavenly court is contrary to Old Testament theology (Deut 32:39; Isa 44:24; 45:7).

33. Keil and Delitzsch, *Pentateuch*, 1:62; Cassuto, *Genesis*, 55.

34. Mathews, *Genesis 1–11:26*, 163.

35. Pearcey, *Total Truth*, 132 (emphasis mine).

describes the general distinction between male and female (Lev 15:16; Isa 4:1). On the other hand, the vocabulary of Genesis 1:26—(*'ādām*)—though occasionally referring to an individual man and only rarely to man as opposed to woman, most often describes humans or humankind in a generic sense, that is, collective humanity.[36]

Man was not created as an originally androgynous individual, but only with a view to relationship with woman. In the end of Genesis 1, God saw all that he had made and it was "very good" (v. 31). While man exists apart from woman, however, God's pronouncement is telling: "It is *not* good" (2:18). It is incorrect to regard the "male and female" of verse 27 as entirely definitive of the image, but it cannot be excluded from the image. The image is not complete until the creation of Eve. This is what Barth termed the *analogia relationis*—man as God's image implies the reciprocal relationship of human being with human being.

> Why, asks Barth, . . . have theologians resorted to speculations and neglected the importance of the difference between man and woman, which is basic for the Scriptural picture of man? The similarity, the analogy, between man and God is here, not an *analogia entis* (analogy of being), but an *analogia relationis* (analogy of relation). The relation between "I" and "thou," which is already present in God ("let *us* make man in *our* image"), finds its creaturely analogue in the relationship between man and woman. Just as there is an "I-thou" relationship in God . . . so also is there in man an "I-thou" relation, a "face-to-face" relation; and thus the pattern of human life is analogous to that of the divine life.[37]

Essentially, man is viewed as what I might call a "relational solidarity" in the creation account. Henry Wheeler Robinson termed this "corporate personality." This is a concept of "unity" in which any constituent or particular part may be addressed as the whole, or the whole may be addressed as the particular part.[38] After all, God could have chosen to create each new individual directly from the dust, but he chose to do oth-

---

36. Cf. Gen 6:7; 7:23; 9:6; Exod 9:25; Num 8:17; 1 Sam 16:7; 1 Chr 29:1; Job 20:4; Ps 8:4.

37. Berkouwer, *The Image of God*, 72; cf. Barth, *CD*, III.1.192–97.

38. Robinson, *Corporate Personality*, 3. Several examples of this in the Old Testament are the sin of Achan for which all Israel suffered (Josh 7), the execution of Saul's descendents to expiate Gibeonite blood shed by Saul (2 Sam 21), Leverite marriage (Deut 25:5ff), and the visitation of the father's iniquity upon the children (Exod 20:5).

erwise. Each human being is inextricably connected to all of humanity and carries both the privileges and responsibilities of that relationship of solidarity. Given such solidarity of the human race, it follows that no one individual or group of individuals manifest the fullness of the image of God. Rather, "The image of God is, as it were, parceled out among the peoples of the earth. By looking at different individuals and groups we get glimpses of different aspects of the full image of God."[39]

Not only does man as image speak of solidarity of relationship, but also of intimacy and transparency of relationship. Adam and Eve were both naked and they "felt no shame" (Gen 2:25). This is not merely a description of their literal, physical state, but also of something much more profound. It describes the physical *and* psychological intimacy and transparency that characterized their relationship. They were at ease in one another's presence without fear of exploitation. Even as they were physically naked, sharing their bodies with each other, so also they were psychologically and spiritually transparent, sharing their souls with each other. In this way, the relational intimacy of the non-homogeneous Creator was reflected in his creation of humanity as the image of himself. As already observed, we each have an innate longing for belonging that is integral to who we are as the image of the triune God. Such longing for belonging is critical in our search for meaning. An understanding of who *I* am cannot be achieved apart from an understanding of who *we* are. Additionally, we cannot understand who *we* are apart from understanding the relational character of Father, Son, and Holy Spirit. "The three members of the Trinity are 'person' precisely because they are persons-in-relationship; that is, their personal identities emerge out of their reciprocal relations . . . [hence] the Creator's intent that humans be the representation of the divine reality means that the goal of human existence is to be persons-in-relation."[40]

It seems, then, that a crucial factor in understanding the nature of the image of God is understanding the solidarity of the human race in relationship. Relational man is the image of his relational Creator. That is why Gabriel Marcel can say, "To exist is to co-exist." To the degree that the solidarity and transparency of relationship is severed or marred, to that degree humanity's representative role as the likeness-image of God is compromised.

39. Mouw, *When the Kings*, 47.
40. Grenz, *The Social God*, 332.

RACE, ETHNICITY, AND CULTURE

Humanity as the image of God exists as God's authoritatively mandated vice-regent on planet earth. Humanity *in its entirety* is entrusted with the dignified vocation of ruling over creation, resembling his Creator, and experiencing the relational community that characterizes the non-homogeneous Three-in-One—Father, Son, and Holy Spirit. This being true, it follows that there is only one race—the *human race*. Therefore, any concept of "race" as a biological construct that separates humanity according to perceived physical/biological differences must be dismissed as not only unbiblical but *anti*-biblical.[41]

The concept of "race" is one of the most damaging ideologies of the modern and postmodern world. The concept must be deconstructed. It is one of the "arguments" and "imaginations" in people's thinking that must be torn down (2 Cor 10:3–4). While as a biological construct the concept of "race" has no scientific or theological foundation, it nevertheless remains in people's minds as a *social* construct. Jenell Paris points out that "the idea of race developed in piecemeal fashion, emerging first in sixteenth-century Europe, North America, and South America as an informal ideology that legitimated slavery and oppression of Africans and indigenous people."[42] As Europeans began exploring the world in the fifteenth century, they developed ideologies that justified a new social order of domination. Prior to this time, they had simply explained human differences (in-groups and out-groups) in terms of ethnicity: language, custom, religion, and regional habitation. Now, however, the world began to be viewed differently. As the British began colonizing America, they encountered Native Americans with whom relations soon became violent due to land disputes. The name "Indian" was soon used as a categorization of these Native Americans, associating the generalized "Indian" physical characteristics with violence, savagery, and suspicion. A similar phenomenon took place with regards to African slave labor. "Negroes" transported from Africa to North America not only

---

41. The typical categories used until modern times to denote the five major racial groupings are: Caucasoid (European "White"), Mongoloid (Chinese/American Indians), Negroid (African "Blacks"), and Australoid (Australian Aborigines). Today, the US Census Bureau uses five "race" categories: White, Black or African American, American Indian or Alaska Native, Asian, and Native Hawaiian or Other Pacific Islander.

42. Paris, "Race," 20.

made ideal plantation workers, but they were controllable. Their language, color, and appearance made it difficult to escape and assimilate into normal life in other colonies. Within thirty years of the founding of Jamestown, colony legislation referred to color as a way of defining social status and privileges. Thus race began to emerge as a way to legitimatize colonization. Only later did racially minded scientists begin to formalize such cultural understandings, lending credibility and authority to the term "race." Essentially, the concept of "race" began as a folk category, was later codified in science, and consequently became part of the American worldview.[43]

Later, in the 1800s, the worldview of Darwinian evolution further promoted the concept of "race," identifying certain races as being more like their apelike ancestors than others. This is fully explained in Darwin's *Origin of Species*, which carries the explanatory phrase in its complete title: "*or the Preservation of Favoured Races in the Struggle for Life.*" Much more recently, even the leading evolutionary spokesperson, Stephen Jay Gould, has stated that "Biological arguments for racism may have been common before 1859, but they increased by orders of magnitude following the acceptance of evolutionary theory."[44] This, in fact, fueled the spirit of colonialism as Rudyard Kipling's well known poem suggests:

> Take up the White Man's Burden
> Send forth the best ye breed
> Go, bind your sons to exile
> To serve the captives' need:
> To wait in heavy harness,
> On fluttered fold and wild—
> Your new-caught, sullen peoples,
> Half devil and half-child.

Such statements blatantly contradict the affirmation of Scripture that God made from one man *every* nation of men (Acts 17:26). As long as we believe that humanity is divided into biological "races," we will continue to attribute a significance and finality to certain ethnic groups that is not warranted.[45] While the supposed biologically determined categories of "race" are, in fact, nonexistent, there are many other factors that provide

43. Ibid., 20–22.
44. Gould, *Ontogeny and Phylogeny*, 127.
45. Meneses, "Science and the Myth," 35.

boundary markers enabling a group of people to distinguish itself from others—markers such as phenotype, language, culture, and religion. Essentially, these are ethnic distinctions. In contrast to the concept of "race," ethnicity stresses the cultural rather than the physical aspects of group identity. An ethnic group distinguishes itself and is so recognized by others via factors of shared heritage (having real or supposed common ancestry and memories of a shared past) and shared identity (as indicated by any combination of cultural, linguistic, and religious markers). An ethnic group will share language, dress, food, customs, values, and sometimes even religion. However, all of these are variables; they change easily. Such similarities can also unite people considered to be of different races all the while dividing those considered to be of the same race.[46] Therefore, designations such as Chinese, Jew, Serb, Croat, Hutu, Tutsi, Latino, African American, or European American are all, in fact, *ethnic* categories. The determining factor is not genetic racial codes, but *ethnicity*.

Furthermore, ethnicities develop their unique cultures. What is culture? Most simply put, "culture is a way of behaving, thinking, and reacting."[47] It refers to all learned behavior acquired through the social networks in which we live. The social networks designate the tangible individuals who share life, whereas the culture speaks of the more intangible perspectives and behavioral patterns that are the by-product of the social network. Color, in fact, says little about culture. Rather, culture is "a social group's distinctive way of life, the beliefs and practices that members find 'normal' and correct."[48]

Given the above distinctions, racism is far more than simple prejudice. We are all prejudiced to one degree or another, but not everyone is racist. We all have personal opinions of other ethnicities, cultures, or backgrounds, and all too often these opinions are not based upon fact. Sometimes we hold on to those opinions even after the facts are known. Such is prejudice. Racism, however, is more than being prejudiced. As Joseph Barndt puts it, "Racism is prejudice plus power."[49] When we enforce our prejudices against another race, that is racism. Racism is an extreme expression of ethnocentrism. It is the result of viewing the dif-

46. Ibid., 34.
47. Nida, *Customs and Cultures*, 28–29.
48. Jindra, "Culture Matters," 64.
49. Barndt, *Dismantling Racism*, 28.

ferences in another ethnicity as biologically inherent and hierarchically organized.[50] Soong-Chan Rah describes this as America's "original and most deeply rooted sin":

> The problem of defining race is an example of a vicious circle. Racism created the categories of race (commonly-held, social perceptions of physical differences); and in turn, racial distinctions became codified legally, leading to further expressions of racism in individual, social, political and legal forms. The American creation of race as a social category ultimately had a negative social impact. If the category of race was created under the auspices of equality and affirmation of difference, the outcome may have been different. However, the creation of race as a social category had dysfunctional and sinful origins. This original sinfulness has crept into our society and culture and begins to determine how we value the 'norm' in American society (and subsequently the American church). Racism, therefore, ends up creating social values and norms that become the way our culture conducts business. Racism is America's original and most deeply rooted sin.[51]

CONCLUSION

Yes, God created humankind as his own image. All the rest of the Bible is a commentary on that phrase. If we want to discover what the Bible says about the dividing walls of ethnicity, we must go back to the beginning. We must see afresh God's original intentions for all humanity. Critical to understanding humanity as the image of God are the concepts of "rule," "resemblance," and "relationship."

Humanity is not created *in* the image of God, nor does humanity *have* the image of God. Humanity *is* the image of God. Furthermore, humanity *in its entirety* is the image of God, inclusive of all ethnicities and nationalities. This image is tangible, visible, and living. It is designed to be seen. Man as image makes the transcendent God tangibly imminent. Humankind stands as God's authoritative vice-regent over the earth, mandated with the stewardship of subduing the earth. This is *rule*.

Humanity's mandate to rule is realized as man fulfills his role as the likeness-image of God. As the image speaks of the authority of the

---

50. Hiebert, "Western Images," 98.
51. Rah, *The Next Evangelicalism*, 68.

king, so also the image speaks of the personality of the king. Man was created to reflect the Creator's personality, having been endowed with the capacity for self-awareness, divine address, and responsible conduct. Man was created to reflect the communicable attributes of God, such as "love," "righteousness," and "truthfulness." This is *resemblance*.

Man as the likeness-image of God best resembles his Creator as he lives in the solidarity of relationship. The community of the non-homogeneous Three-in-One is the template of the community God intends for all humanity. This is the *analogia relationis* infused into the very heart of man. The I-thou relationship inherent to our Creator is likewise integral to the essence of who we are as humans. This is *relationship*.

We cannot appreciate the answers the New Testament offers apart from understanding the questions the Old Testament poses. This is likewise true as it relates to the dividing walls that segment both society and the church today. As one reads the Genesis account of man as the image of God, numerous questions begin to surface: What happened to man as God's image as a result of sin? In what specific ways did humanity's fall into sin damage his roles of rule, resemblance, and relationship? More positively, what hope does the Bible offer concerning humanity's renewal to the image of his Creator? It is to these questions and answers that we now turn.

3

The *Imago Dei* Deconstructed

We have thus far been baffled in all our attempts to account for the differences between races of man.

Charles Darwin

DEATH. THE VERY WORD is disconcerting, like so many words in the English language that begin with "D": depression, disease, doubt, discord, division, and *deconstruction*.

Each Friday, my wife and I visit the cemetery where our oldest boy is buried. We water the *living* plants, we trim the *living* grass, and we pray to the *living* God, giving thanks for a life well lived. Nevertheless, each time we visit we are reminded of what feels like the finality of death. Oh, it's not that we doubt our son is alive and well in the presence of his Creator. Rather, the separation that death brings *feels* so definitive, so final. To die is to be shut out from life *as we know it*. Death is separation. Physical death is the separation of body and spirit. Spiritual death is the separation of one's spirit from God. Eternal death is separation from God throughout eternity. Death is the essence of the deconstruction of humanity as the image of God.

Separation lies at the very heart of sin's impact upon the three expressions of man as the *imago Dei*: *rule*, *resemblance*, and *relationship*. The tragic results of self-assertive sin profoundly marred humanity's privileged role as God's image, bringing alienation to man's relationship vis-à-vis God, fellow man, and all of creation.

First, sin struck at humanity's mandate to rule. Though mankind was created to have dominion as God's vice-regent over all the earth, a creature—the very embodiment of Satan—exerted dominion over man and thus disrupted creation order. Consequently, corporate humanity became estranged from the very creation over which he had been given dominion. "Thorns and thistles" and "painful toil" became part and parcel of man's struggle to fulfill his role as God's image over an alienated world. Evil was now crouching at humanity's door (Gen 4:7).

Second, sin struck at man's resemblance to his Creator. Humanity's essence and role as the "likeness-image" of God was severely compromised. Consequently, corporate humanity became disabled in its capacity for self-awareness, its openness to divine address, and its spiritual responsiveness. Humanity's experience and expression of the communicable attributes of the Creator such as "love," "righteousness," "holiness," and "justice" were now compromised. Though man ever remains the image of God, he nevertheless must now contend with both physical and spiritual disease, deformity, and ultimate death.

Finally, sin dealt a death blow to man's relational capacity. With the intrusion of sin came also consequent alienation, both between man and God and between man and fellow man. Relational alienation became the rule of the day. Explicit trust and transparency—illustrated by man's nakedness—vanished, leaving only insecurity and fear. Humanity was fractured at its core.

All of this is part of the deconstruction of man as the image of God. As Francis Schaeffer has described it, "These separations (and others related to them) are like titanic sonic booms in the sociological upheavals coming down to, and perhaps especially in, our day."[1] We cannot understand the present day dividing walls within humanity without exploring these "titanic booms" as outlined in Genesis 1–11. Nor can we appreciate what God has done in creating the New Humanity until we take a closer look at the progressive deconstruction of the Old Humanity as depicted in the Book of Beginnings.

THE *tôlᵉdôt* OF GENESIS

The tragedy of humanity's progressive deconstruction as the image of God is intentionally highlighted by the structural development of

---

1. Schaeffer, *Genesis*, 100.

Genesis. The major structural word of the book is the Hebrew *tôl^edôt*. While it is sometimes translated "generations," "histories," or simply "descendants," it is best understood as "this is what became of." The expression is very fitting, for apart from Genesis 1:1—2:3, *tôl^edôt* serves as a header for each major section of the book that details the tragedy of what became of mankind as he journeyed away from his Creator. So we have the *tôl^edôt* of the heavens and the earth (2:4—4:26); of Adam (5:1—6:8); of Noah (6:9—9:29); of Shem, Ham, and Japheth (10:1—11:26); and finally (for our purposes) of Terah (11:27—15:11).

It is not surprising that in these *tôl^edôt* we are reminded three times of humanity's identity as the image of God (Gen 1:26-27; 5:3; 9:6).[2] This is the high ground from which humanity fell. Then the downward trend of sin and death in each section quickly comes to the forefront. The tragedy of it all is highlighted by Nancy Pearcey when she writes:

> Our value and dignity are rooted in the fact that we are created in the image of God, with the high calling of being His representatives on earth. In fact, it is only *because* humans have such a high value that sin is so tragic. If we were worthless to begin with, then the Fall would be a trivial event. When a cheap trinket is broken, we toss it aside with a shrug. But when a priceless masterpiece is defaced, we are horrified. It is because humans are the masterpiece of God's creation that the destructiveness of sin produces such horror and sorrow.[3]

However, while each *tôl^edôt* is marked by the defacing of God's masterpiece, we also find in each tokens of grace and rays of hope inspiring confidence in the ultimate fulfillment of God's purposes. In the *tôl^edôt* of the heavens and the earth (2:4—4:26), God announces the great *protoevangelium* ("first gospel") of Genesis 3:15, and "men began to call on the name of the Lord" (Gen 4:26). In the *tôl^edôt* of Adam (5:1—6:8), "Enoch walked with God" (Gen 5:22). In the *tôl^edôt* of Noah (6:9—9:29), God promises to never again destroy humanity with a flood (8:21-22). In the *tôl^edôt* of Shem, Ham, and Japeth (10:1—11:26), God's grace is seen in preventing mankind from destroying himself through a makeshift uniformity as well as in specifying Shem as the line of blessing for all peoples. In the *tôl^edôt* of Terah (11:27—15:11), God's promise

---

2. While Genesis 1:26-27 does not formally fall within the first *tôl^edôt*, it nevertheless governs the more specific account of Genesis 2:4—4:26.

3. Pearcey, *Total Truth*, 87.

to bless all peoples of the earth is initiated in Abraham (11:31—12:3). Therefore, while we witness the progressive, inevitable deterioration and alienation of the Old Humanity, we simultaneously witness the eternally outgoing God of mission initiating his redemptive plan to birth a New Humanity. Through it all, man remains man. The image of God is marred and obscured, but happily never obliterated.

As we trace through each *tôlᵉdôt* of Genesis 1–11, we can observe the impact of sin on collective humanity as the image of God. What we discover is that each expression of mankind as the image of God—rule, resemblance, and relationship—is profoundly affected by the titanic booms of evil. Yet we also discover in each a ray of hope in view of the final establishment of the New Humanity, called the "new man" (Eph 2:15; 4:22–24; Col 3:9–11).

The *tôlᵉdôt* of the Heavens and the Earth (Gen 2:4—4:26)

The setting is idyllic. Man as the image of God stands in perfect harmony with his Creator, with fellow man (Eve), and with all of creation. No need is unmet. No want is unsatisfied. Man exists as the apex of all creation, a little lower than the angels, fulfilling his role as God's vice-regent of the earth (Ps 8). Moses reminds us in Genesis 2:15 that God "put" man in the Garden of Eden. The descriptive term speaks of rest, safety, and dedication in God's presence. Man's foremost responsibility is to worship and obey God. In this respect, the Garden of Eden is a "temple-garden" depicted in later Jewish history by the tabernacle.[4]

Man's divinely given mandate is to populate, subjugate, dominate, cultivate, and preserve the earth that God has placed under his care. Relationally, man as God's image is in harmony with himself, with his Creator, with fellow man, and with all of creation. Corporate humanity stands as God's official representative on the earth, signifying that the earth belongs to Him. Why and how could man wander from all of this?

Genesis 3 begins with three words, the significance of which have altered the course of human history: "Now the serpent." (Gen 3:1). The Scriptures leave an impenetrable veil over the origin of evil in the universe. The appearance of the serpent, clearly identified as Satan, is left unexplained. The reader must await further revelation before drawing conclusions as to the primeval angelic rebellion that certainly predates

---

4. Sailhamer, *Genesis Unbound*, 74.

the Fall of man. What is explicit, however, is that Satan attacks the very apex of creation. His entire strategy is a perversion of the image.

The immediate effects of sin on mankind were *theological* (Gen 3:7–10), touching on man's relationship *with* God and his resemblance *of* God. Self-sufficiency, alienation, and fear are expressions of man having become a sinner at heart. Adam and Eve realized they were naked. Suddenly the God-given garments of innocence, holiness, and perfect love were stripped away like one's clothes at the end of the day. Man immediately set out to develop his own humanly concocted strategy for dealing with the dilemma: "They sewed fig leaves together and made coverings for themselves" (Gen 3:7). They innately knew something was terribly wrong. Their hastily manufactured garments, however, proved useless before the searching eyes of an all-knowing God. "Where are you?" was God's rhetorical question, gently leading the couple to perceive the alienation that had now crept into their previously enjoyed intimacy with God. At that point, man's alienation gives way to fear: "I heard you in the garden, and I was afraid because I was naked; so I hid" (Gen 3:10). The shamelessness of nakedness had now disappeared, only to be replaced by the shame of sin and self-righteousness. So man hid. Transparency and trust had turned to fear and mistrust—both vertically with God and horizontally with fellow man. After all, harmony in creation is dependant upon harmony with God.

What was the response to God's question, "Where are you?" Man went "east." Apparently, Adam and Eve were expelled to the east of the garden (3:24). Later Cain went east "out from the Lord's presence" (Gen 4:16–17). Following the Ararat departure, the people migrated eastward in hopes of making a name for themselves (Gen 11:2). To go east is to move away from the presence of our Creator. To go east is part of the deconstruction of the image of God. East spells alienation.

The immediate effects of sin on mankind were also *sociological* (Gen 3:11–13, 16). The transparency and intimacy characteristic of mankind as the image of God have now degenerated into shame, alienation, and blame. Humanity is profoundly fractured at its very core. The assertion of self fails to alleviate man's anxiety and fear, both of which spring from his sin-induced insecurity. The human race begins to collect in cities for the purpose of power. Since alienation from God results in insecurity, man builds cities to overcome his fears and in the process further alienates himself from fellow man (Gen 4:17; 10:12; 11:4–5, 8).[5] Prior to sin's intrusion, collective humanity did not fear exploitation. All of mankind enjoyed the bliss of relational harmony. Now the blame game begins: "The woman you put here with me—*she* gave me some of the fruit of the tree, and I ate it" (Gen 3:12, emphasis mine). While human speech was given to enhance man's relational potential, it is now wielded as an instrument of divisiveness. What were divisive words between Adam and Eve later became a bold act of murder in their son Cain (Gen 4:1–8). Such discord is the expression of *death*; and for Adam, Eve, Cain, and Abel, as well as all of humanity, death was now a certainty (Gen 3:3).

The immediate effects of sin on mankind were also *ecological* (Gen 3:14–19). God raised man out of the dust to reign. Now to the dust man will return; not to reign, but to die. That very dust is now cursed on account of man: "Through painful toil you will eat of it all the days of your life" (Gen 3:17). Sin has tilted the cosmos. From that day forward, all of creation has been groaning (Rom 8:22).

"The superficiality of man is never so plain," writes G. C. Berkouwer, "as when he measures himself by his overt acts and ignores his being-a-sinner at heart."[6] The *tôlᵉdôt* of the heavens and the earth (2:4—4:26) leaves us in no doubt: man is a "sinner at heart." Sin is historical, not a mere social maladjustment that can be rectified over time. Furthermore, sin is abnormal. Its entrance into man's experience was never part of God's original intentions for humanity. Finally, sin is malignant, not benign. Once implanted into the heart of man, it relentlessly pervades every aspect of his existence. As the story of fallen humanity unfolds, it becomes evident that the cancer of sin is implanted deep in the human heart. Outward actions are merely symptomatic of a much deeper sickness that strikes at the very core of human existence.

According to Romans 5, the sin of Adam carried devastating consequences, not only for this primeval couple, but also for the entire human race. Just as a climber on a mountaintop can dislodge a pebble which in turn rolls and gathers others until a huge avalanche hurtles down the entire side of the mountain, so Adam's sin in the garden dislodged a

---

5. Throughout Genesis 1–11, the city is portrayed negatively. It is in the city that man seeks to find a place of refuge from his own insecurity, forgetting that God and God alone is man's security. For Israel, nation preceded city, for her sense of identity and security was to be in God alone. For the nations of the world, city preceded nation, for it was in the city that man sought to satisfy his quest for security.

6. Berkouwer, *Sin*, 317.

pebble of devastating consequences—spiritual death resulting in physical death and ultimately in eternal death—that as an avalanche has swept throughout the whole human race. When Adam disobeyed God, man fell from life to death, from grace to judgment, from heaven to hell.

This is what happened to the heavens and the earth. The image of God is obscured but not obliterated. Man is still man. In view of this, God immediately initiates his redemptive program with a promise as he speaks to the serpent: "And I will put enmity between you and the woman, and between your offspring and hers; he will crush your head, and you will strike his heel" (Gen 3:15). This promise, known as the *protoevangelium* ("first gospel"), reminds fallen man of the certain fulfillment of God's victory over evil. While the Old Humanity failed to exercise dominion, the New Humanity in Jesus Christ will ("crush your head;" cf. Rom 16:20; Heb 2:8–9).

The tôl^{e}dôt of Adam (Gen 5:1—6:8)

While at the end of the *tôl^{e}dôt* of the heavens and the earth "men began to call on the name of the Lord" (4:26), the situation quickly deteriorates again. Apart from Enoch (5:24), *no one on planet earth seeks after God*: "The LORD saw how great man's wickedness on the earth had become, and that every inclination of the thoughts of his heart was only evil all the time. The LORD was grieved that he had made man on the earth, and his heart was filled with pain" (Gen 6:5–7).

God had blessed humanity with the divine mandate to procreate and fill the earth. Paradoxically, man is filling the earth by promulgating violence. The result is death. In Genesis 3 we find the first obituary recorded in the Bible. The repeated refrain is not surprising: "and he died." That the world is one giant cemetery stands as a memorial to sin's devastating consequences. Nevertheless, for the second time we are reminded that humanity, as the likeness-image of God, stands as the capstone of God's creation (Gen 5:1–2). Against the backdrop of the separation of death, God takes one apart from death—Enoch. As the lone exception to the above obituary, Enoch stands as a reminder of the Creator's ultimate victory over that which symbolizes man's alienation. Divine desire will prevail.

The tôlᵉdôt of Noah (Gen 6:9—9:29)

Noah is described as "a righteous man, blameless among the people of his time" and as one who "walked with God" (Gen 6:9). His life stood in stark contrast to society as a whole: "Now the earth was corrupt in God's sight and was full of violence. God saw how corrupt the earth had become, for all the people on earth had corrupted their ways" (Gen 6:11–13). In view of such sin, judgment fell, and so did the rain, washing the earth clean in preparation for a new beginning. But "God remembered Noah" (8:1a).[7] Indeed, Noah is depicted in these verses as the Adam of the postdiluvian world. As Adam, he walks with God and is a righteous man (Gen 6:9). As Adam, he is the recipient of God's promissory blessing. As Adam, he is mandated as a caretaker of the renewed earth (Gen 9:1–4). As Adam, he is commissioned to be fruitful and to fill the earth (Gen 9:1). In many senses, Noah is a second Adam who heads a new family of humanity. So we find here for the third time the incessant reminder of man as the image of God (Gen 9:6).

Like the first Adam, Noah ends his life in disgrace. As Adam took of the fruit of the garden and became naked, so Noah took of the fruit of the vine and became naked. Also like Adam, Noah found grace (Gen 6:8). Here we find a word play in the Hebrew text. The consonants of Noah's name (*nh*) in the reverse order signify grace (*hn*). Noah became a recipient of grace. Once again, the image of God is obscured but never obliterated.

A TALE OF A TOWER AND TABLE:

The tôlᵉdôt of Shem, Ham, and Japeth (Gen 10:1—11:26)

"We have it in our power to begin the world over again," Thomas Paine once exclaimed. "A situation similar to the present has not happened since the days of Noah until now."[8]

For many, the American Revolution meant not only the elimination of a king, but also the beginning of a new world from scratch. Paine may not have stopped to think about the danger of associating the new world with the days of Noah. What went wrong following the founding

---

7. That is the focal point of this account. As so frequently in these early chapters of Genesis, the point of emphasis is highlighted by a literary chiasm that leaves the reader in no doubt about the central theme. Ross, *Creation and Blessing*, 191.

8. Cited in Pearcey, *Total Truth*, 279.

and independence of the colonies is not dissimilar to what went wrong subsequent to the universal flood: alienation. This is recorded in the *tôlᵉdôt* of Shem, Ham, and Japeth (Gen 10:1—11:26). It's the tale of a tower and a table.

As man attempts to become more than he is, he becomes less than he is. Not only is this true in the Garden of Eden but also in the plains of Shinar. "What the wicked dreads will overtake him," Solomon writes (Prov 10:24). "Overtake him" it does. Through a series of literary chiasms, antithetical parallelism, and subtle word plays, the author highlights in Genesis 10-11 the puzzling paradox of sin. Man never finds in sin that which he enters sin to find. What all the earth attempted to avoid actually happened: *dispersion*.

Through a skillful arrangement of narrative and genealogy, the author prepares us for the subsequent *tôlᵉdôt*, that of Terah (Gen 11:27—15:11). Here we find the breakthrough of God's promise to bless all peoples in his chosen one, Abraham (Gen 12:1-3). But who are these peoples? How did they spread out upon the face of the earth? What accounts for our distinct languages, cultures, ethnicities, and physical features? These are some of the "most profound and perplexing problems confronting contemporary anthropological, sociological, and biblical scholarship."[9] It is on these questions and others that the *tôlᵉdôt* of Shem, Ham, and Japeth (Gen 10:1—11:26) sheds some light.

The Table of the Nations

Genesis chapters 10 and 11 are inseparable. The latter explains the former. The Table of the Nations in chapter 10 is unexplainable apart from the interpretive insight of the Tower of Babel in chapter 11. The primary purpose of Genesis 10 detailing the Table of the Nations is to demonstrate that the human race, though originally united in origin, now becomes divided by language, territory, and politics. The literary bookends surrounding this table are found in Genesis 9:19 and 11:9:

> These were the three sons of Noah, and from them came the people who were scattered over the earth. (Gen 9:19)

> From there the LORD scattered them over the face of the whole earth. (Gen 11:9)

---

9. Merrill, "Peoples," 3.

As a result of this account of the dispersion of the nations, Israel would better grasp her own unique position as God's chosen nation and her calling to be a blessing to the nations scattered around her.

Genesis 10 contains one of the oldest ethnological tables in the literature of the ancient world and reveals a remarkable understanding of the ethnic and linguistic situation following the Flood. Many of the names in this chapter appear in subsequent books of the Old Testament and have been found in archaeological discoveries in the last century and a half.[10] The structure of this table is not based so much on physical descent as on territorial and geopolitical affiliations. These are described by such terms as "family"/"tribe"/"clan" (*mishpaḥâ*), "language" (*lāshôn*), "country"/"territory" (*'ereṣ*), and "nation" (*gôy*).

According to Genesis 10, all of post-flood humanity sprang from the three sons of Noah—Shem, Ham, and Japheth. Yet as we explore the content of this table, there is a remarkable absence of emphasis on ethnic distinctions in any scientific, technical sense.[11] Shem means "name," most likely a reference to the selection of the Shemites to be closely associated with "the Name," that is Yahweh. Ham's name is most likely related to a word meaning "hot" and may be connected to the region of Egypt (Ps 78:51; 106:22). Japheth, on the other hand, probably means "spacious," Noah himself having requested that the territory of Japheth might be "extended" (Gen 9:27). As this brief survey shows, the names of those from whom all the peoples of the earth descended have nothing to do with race or ethnicity. They are rather geographical terms, at least in the case of Ham and Japheth. Therefore, Genesis 10 is not an ethnic map for the purpose of tracing the development of three races, but rather a complex description of people group affiliations based largely on political and geographical associations.[12]

Upon closer examination, however, several clues in the text give some insight as to the development of the world's various ethnicities. For example, Shem's descendants are the Shemites, including both the Hebrews and Arabs (Gen 10:21–31). What is of particular importance here is the emphasis on Eber from whom come the Hebrew people. Eber's

---

10. Ross, "Table of Nations," 340–53.

11. Merrill, "Peoples," 7. Merrill states: "It is clearly not intended to be . . . a scientifically constructed analysis of the origin and development of races in the modern sense of that term."

12. Hays, *People and Nation*, 59–63.

two sons are Joktan and Peleg (Gen 10:25). It was during Peleg's time that humanity was divided following the debacle at the Tower of Babel. The Japhethites embrace what are normally classified as two "races," the Caucasian (Indo-European) and the Oriental, including East Asians, Indians, and Aryans (Gen 10:2–5). They are geographically spread out from Madai (Media) on the east to Javan (Greece), Tarshish (Spain), and Kittim (Crete) on the west.[13]

From the Hamites sprang not only the Canaanites but also those living in Egypt and Nubia (Gen 10:6–20). They are geographically spread out from Egypt to Lybia to Syria-Palestine. Of particular importance in the Hamitic line is Cush (Gen 10:6–8). The words "Cush" and "Cushite" occur more than fifty times in the Old Testament in reference to an ethnic entity and are nearly always associated with the country south of Egypt along the Nile. The prophet Jeremiah, referring to the black skin of the Cushite, asks, "Can the Ethiopian (*kûshî*) change his skin or the leopard his spots?" (Jer 13:23). Apparently, the statement had become proverbial, implying that "Cushites were known in Jeremiah's Jerusalem, that they were known for their dark skin color, and that they were known well enough that popular proverbs arose about their skin color."[14]

Some, of course, have suggested that the curse of Genesis 9:20–27 resulted in the descendants of Ham being inferior to others. This antiquated and unfounded argument suggests that such inferiority is symbolized by the black skin of Ham's descendants through Cush, but there are no grounds for such an ethic reading of the curse. The curse of Genesis 9 looks ahead to the social and religious life of Israel's ancient rival, Canaan, and specifically to the immorality of that people who threatened to compromise Israel's religious fidelity. It is not a question of the ethnicity of a people, but of the immorality of a people.[15] In contrast to such a pejorative reading of the curse, several passages that mention the Cushites speak of them in an extremely positive light. In Numbers

---

13. Merrill, "Peoples," 4–8. What is lacking mention, however, is any reference to East Asians (such as Chinese, Japanese, and Koreans), Inuits, Native Americans, Polynesians, Australian aboriginals, or even such influential shapers of ancient civilization as the Sumerians. The reason for this is that the Bible presents a theological history with a particular focus on Israel as God's chosen people and in no way purports to serve as an ethnological handbook. The Table of the Nations is rather "sacred history."

14. Hays, "The Cushites," 404.

15. See Robertson, "'Curse of Ham,'" 177–88; Mathews, *Genesis*, 423.

12:1, for example, Miriam and Aaron speak against Moses for marrying a Cushite woman. To get the point across, the passage states twice that she was a Cushite, a term that carried strong connotations of black ethnicity. While some have argued that this woman could not have been a black Cushite, the evidence points in the other direction.[16] As a result of Aaron's and Miriam's hostility—evidently racial in character—Miriam was struck with white, leprous skin. The whiteness of her leprous skin may have only accentuated God's disapproval of Miriam's prejudice against her black sister-in-law.[17]

Several other passages concerning the Cushites are prophetic (Isa 20:3–5; 45:15; Jer 46:9). Zephaniah 3:9–10 states: "Then will I purify the *lips* (*śāpâ*, speech; emphasis mine) of the peoples, that all of them may call on the name of the LORD and serve him shoulder to shoulder. From beyond the rivers of Cush my worshipers, my scattered people, will bring me offerings." As we will see, this statement is particularly relevant to Genesis 11 where, before the dispersion of the humanity, all mankind shared one "lip" (*śāpâ*, speech). Though confused at Babel, these same lips will be purified to worship the Lord. Here, those who will worship are not only from Cush, but even from beyond the rivers of Cush, which would be the heart of Africa!

From these passages and others, it is clear that the biblical story *is* multiethnic in background. Black people are not a late addendum to the story of mankind, nor are they despised or considered in any way inferior. Their story goes back to the earliest periods of human history. J. Daniel Hays states it well: "As a civilization, the Cushites, a black people, were not an obscure people who have appeared only in modern history, discovered when Europeans explored Africa. The ancient world in general and Israel in particular were aware of the antiquity of Cush."[18] They, along with all humanity, equally reflect the *imago Dei*.

---

16. For a complete overview of the various arguments, see Hays, "Cushites," 397–401. See also Adamo "African Wife of Moses," 230–37.

17. Hays, "Cushites," 399.

18. Ibid., 397. Eugene Merrill notes, "Race . . . is not fundamentally a matter of pigmentation but of ethnicity based on descent from the sons of Noah. How that played out in the connection between race and ethnicity seems to have been of little concern to the Bible or more importantly to the God of the Bible." Merrill, "Peoples," 22.

The Tower of Babel

The table of Genesis 10 details the dispersion at the tower of Babel in Genesis 11. The main emphasis in this section is not the building of the tower of Babel but the dispersion of the peoples. We clearly see this in the literary structure of Genesis 11:1–9:[19]

   A All the earth had one language (v. 1)
     B there (v. 2)
       C one to another (v. 3)
         D Come, let's make bricks (v. 3)
           E Let's make for ourselves (v. 4)
              F a city and a tower
                 G And the Lord came down to see (v. 5; cf. 8:1)
              F' the city and the tower (v. 5)
           E' that the humans built (v. 5)
         D' Come, let's confuse (v. 7)
       C' everyone the language of his neighbor (v. 7)
     B' from there (v. 8)
   A' (confused) the language of the whole earth (v. 9)

According to verse 5, these were the "children of Adam," all of whom had one "lip" (*śāpâ,* speech) and one "vocabulary" (*dᵉbārîm,* the content of what is said). Morris speculates that this was a Semitic language, possibly even Hebrew, as all the proper names of people and places in the pre-Babel period have meaning only in Hebrew and its cognate languages.[20] While this is speculation, what is clear is that mankind's determination to gather in one place and build was in direct disobedience to God's command to replenish and have dominion over the earth (Gen 1:26–27; 9:1–3). God's design for them was the systematic colonization and nurture of the entire earth, with each people group and consequent culture having a form of local government (Gen 1:28; 9:1). Man chose, however, to establish a strongly centralized government that would eventually result in the oppression of others, if not the entire world. Ravaged by the insecurity of sin, man demonstrated an unwillingness to fill the earth and subdue it. Could it be that mankind innately sensed the

---

19. Fokkelman, *Art in Genesis,* 22–23; Ross, *Creation and Blessing,* 235; Wenham, *Genesis,* 234–38.
20. Morris, *Genesis Record,* 267.

sociological axiom that social separation causes cultural differentiation and they rebelled against it? We do not know. What seems clear is that apart from the alienating influence of sin, diversity of culture would not *in itself* prove to be a dividing wall among the peoples of the earth.

Given the intrusion of sin, a multiplicity of nations carrying out their divinely given mandate to protect humanity as the image of God would be more viable and less destructive than collective humanity who is gathered in one place and who has one prideful intent. Man, however, pursued uniformity for the purpose of power and oppression. Consequently (and quite paradoxically), man's common language (v. 1) became a multiplicity of confused languages (v. 9), and man's place of unity (*šām*, "there" v. 2) became his place of disunity (*miššam*, "from there" v. 8).[21] The people arrogantly intended to "make . . . a name" for themselves (v. 4; cf. Ps 14:1). In doing so, they failed to realize that Yahweh is the only one who can make one's name great (Gen 12:2–3)!

Most likely, the entire account is a satire on the claims of Babylon to be the center of civilization and its temple tower to be the gate of heaven. Babel was notorious for its pride. The Babylonians called their city *Bâbili*, meaning in Akkadian "gate of gods." Here we see a polemical and phonetic word play: It was called "Babel" (*bābel*) for there the Lord "made a babble" (*bālal*).[22] Such is to be expected of humanity now alienated from his Creator. Man has once again gone east. The plain of Shinar, called the "valley of the world" in the Talmud, was located in the broad plain between the Tigris and Euphrates Rivers south of present-day Baghdad. Could they have thought that this region reminded them of their antediluvian home? Did they dream of restoring the conditions of Eden itself?

The Genesis account attributes to Nimrod the establishment of an immense political power centered in Babylon, Erich, Akkad, and Calneh (all of which are in Shinar), as well as at Ninevah, Rehoboth, Ir, Calah, and Resen (which are found in northern Mesopotamia).[23] Genesis 10:8 describes him as a "mighty hunter." In that day, kings demonstrated their authority to rule over others by their prowess over the animal kingdom. The cultural mandate of Genesis 1:26–27 was to rule over animals, but never to oppressively rule over other human beings. Whatever Nimrod's

21. Ross, *Creation and Blessing*, 247.
22. Wenham, *Genesis*, xlviii–xlix.
23. Merrill, "Peoples," 17.

motivations, it seems likely that humanity was driven by its innate survival impulse, which if carried out as planned, would have resulted in self-destruction. Reinhold Niebuhr has pointedly observed that racial prejudice is a form of irrationality nourished by such deep human impulses: "Racial prejudice is an inevitable concomitant of racial pride; and racial pride is an inevitable concomitant of the ethnic will to live. . . . There are spiritual elements in every human survival impulse; and the corruption of these elements is pride and the will-to-power."[24] Nimrod was driven, it seems, by such an "ethnic will to live."

Under Nimrod's leadership, the builders undoubtedly expected to ascend to heaven to meet God. Every city of importance was built with a step tower known as a ziggurat. In the Babylon of Nebuchadnezzar's day (sixth century BC), there was a seven-story tower with a temple at its apex. This temple was called *E-temen-anki*, meaning the "building which is the foundation of heaven and earth." It measured ninety meters by ninety meters at the base, was ninety meters high, and was considered one of the wonders of the world. It seems this tower and others like it drew their inspiration from the ancient tower of Babel.[25] Paradoxically, though Nimrod and his prideful cohorts intended to reach heaven, God has to descend just to see it!

The point of contrast is found between verse 3 "come, let us make bricks," and verse 7 "come, let us confuse." "The construction on earth is answered by the destruction from heaven."[26] Those who had said to one another "Come, let us make" and "Come, let us build" could now no longer do so. Their language was confused. Such direct intervention on God's part was not only punitive but also preventative. As we follow the narrative of Genesis 10–11, it becomes increasingly clear that God sovereignly uses nationalism as a deterrent to sin. Gerhard von Rad states it well: "God's eye already sees the end of the road upon which mankind has entered with this deed, the possibilities and temptations which such a massing of forces holds. . . . Therefore God resolved upon a punitive, but at the same time preventative act, so that he will not have to punish man more severely as his degeneration surely progresses."[27]

---

24. As cited by Visser 'T Hooft, *Ecumenical Movement*, 67.
25. Ross, *Creation and Blessing*, 238–39; Dyer, *Rise of Babylon*, 53.
26. Ross, *Creation and Blessing*, 236.
27. Rad, *Genesis*, 149.

It has been argued from the Babel account that God *willed* the separation and consequent alienation of the peoples of the earth. One church statement reads: "God willed separate races and nations, each with a different language, culture, etc., and therefore racial separation (even within the Christian Church) which will keep the races intact, is not only permissible, but a Christian duty."[28] Such a perspective, of course, could not be further from the truth. If Genesis 10–11 says anything, it is that alienation by language is a result of man's sin and not God's original design for mankind as the *imago Dei*.

Various theories have been proposed to explain how such a confusion of languages took place. One writer even proposes that lightning struck the tower of Babel and that the ensuing confusion of speech resulted from a scrambling of the electrical circuits in the brains of those struck![29] However the final imposition of language took place, the alienating effects of sin had already set the stage:

> If language is the audible expression of emotions, conceptions, and thoughts of the mind, the cause of the confusion or division of the one human language into different national dialects might be sought in an effect produced upon the human mind, by which the original unity of emotion, conception, thought, and will was broken up. This inward unity had no doubt been already disturbed by sin, but the disturbance had not yet mounted to a perfect breach.[30]

We simply cannot determine whether God immediately imposed a classification of languages or whether the classifications developed later by virtue of geographical and cultural isolation. It's quite possible the confusion (*bālal*) was simply and initially in the dialect. This would have led to misunderstanding and misapprehension and ultimately to separation. Once the separation took place, the influence of climate and customs as well as various other factors finally resulted in the development of substantially different languages. Furthermore, this may have happened rather quickly. Archeology has confirmed that civilization, along with its customs and languages, appeared more or less contemporaneously

---

28. Quotation from a South African Dutch Reformed statement cited by Visser 'T Hooft, *Ecumenical Movement*, 63. He adds: "The quotation . . . should not be taken as representative of all Dutch Reformed theology."

29. See Strickling, "Tower of Babel," 53–62.

30. Keil and Delitzsch, *Pentateuch*, 1:174–75.

throughout the world, and particularly in the Mesopotamian and Nile valleys.[31] In spite of the alienation brought about by the diversity of languages being imposed, humanity as the image of God was still one race.

What can be said of the ethnic and perceived ethnic distinctions that have developed throughout the world? Some believe the debacle of Babel also involved the implantation of these distinctions in humankind.[32] Others have suggested that Noah's three sons already represented racially distinct entities.[33] This is simply not realistic. Apart from supernatural genetic intervention, Noah could not have produced children with such distinctions. Another suggestion is that environmental factors triggered latent genetic distinctions that manifested themselves after the dispersion from Babel. However, there is no scientific or biblical support for such a thesis. For centuries people have lived in "nonnative" environments without this resulting in changes.[34]

A far better explanation is that, as each family and tribal unit spread out from Babel, they quickly developed distinct cultural as well as biological characteristics. The restrictions of separate languages severely limited communication between groups. As a result, inbreeding took place. In a relatively limited interbreeding population, the particular suit of genes, though recessive in the larger population, become dominant. As a result, distinctive characteristics such as skin color, hair texture, height, facial features, and temperament can become typical of particular tribes or people groups. All humans possess the same color, just different amounts of it.[35] We all descended from Noah and Adam. We all still remain the *imago Dei*, albeit deconstructed.

CONCLUSION

The titanic effects of sin have reverberated throughout the entire human race. A priceless masterpiece has been defaced. Defaced, but not destroyed. Obscured, but not obliterated. The devastating effects of sin have profoundly touched man as the *imago Dei*, compromising

---

31. Ross, *Creation and Blessing*, 246–47; Livingston, *Pentateuch*, 31.

32. See Merrill, "Peoples," 21.

33. Custance, *Noah's Three Sons*, 148–49.

34. Merrill, "Peoples," 21. The fact that the Hamites were dispersed from Nubia to Northern Mesopotamia suggests that skin color has little to do environmental factors.

35. Morris, *Genesis Record*, 276. See also Parker, *Creation Facts* for a more detailed explanation.

humanity's resemblance to his Creator, his relationship with both God and fellow man, as well as his mandate to rule as God's vice-regent over the earth. Prior to the entrance of sin, man reveled in the shamelessness of nakedness—a transparency and intimacy of relationship unequaled in human experience. Then man went east. Far east, away from the presence of his Creator. East spells alienation. In moving away from his Creator, mankind has moved away from himself. The transparency and trust so characteristic of that first primeval couple have now turned to fear, mistrust, and alienation. The judgment at Babel carried with it no hope for the future. "There is no clothing for the naked sinner, no protective mark for the fugitive, no rainbow in the dark sky."[36] We see only separation and further alienation of humanity as the image of God. Man as the image of God has been deconstructed.

God's purposes, however, will not be thwarted. In the confusion and scattering of the nations, God chooses a seed that will ultimately bring blessing to the peoples of the earth. This is the story of the *tôle dôt* of Terah (11:27—15:11). Out of the Old Humanity scattered at Babel, a New Humanity will be gathered at Pentecost. In some ways, Abraham as the father of many nations becomes himself a type of "second Adam" in whom all the peoples will be blessed. Thus, the arrangement of Genesis 11 and 12 is not accidental. The problem (Gen 11) and the solution (Gen 12) are brought into immediate juxtaposition. God chose Abraham as the microcosm to bring blessing to all of humanity as the macrocosm.[37]

In all of this, we must remember the tragic events on earth are a mere reflection of turmoil in the heavenlies. Not only is humanity fallen, the entire cosmos is tilted. Because of this, we cannot understand the alienation of ethnicities on earth apart from what the Bible says about the divisive influence of Satan and his demonic minions. Albeit fallen, such powers are nevertheless termed "sons of God" by the writers of Scripture. It is to this influence exerted by the sons of God on Adam's fallen race that we now turn.

---

36. Ross, *Creation and Blessing*, 242.
37. See Wenham, *Genesis*, 213.

4

Babel and the Sons of God

I do not know how to explain it; I can not tell how it is, but I believe angels have a great deal to do with the business of this world.

Charles H. Spurgeon

"Now the serpent..." (Gen 3:1).
The Bible teaches that the devil and his demons are fallen angels. Though few details are given, several passages indicate that certain angels fell from their original condition as members of God's heavenly council or angelic army.[1] Beyond this, next to nothing is said in Scripture about the origins of evil among the angelic hosts. While the Bible leaves an impenetrable veil over the origins of evil in the universe, it does shed some light on the identity of Satan and his demonic minions as well as their role in the progressive deconstruction of collective humanity as the *imago Dei*. This process of deconstruction has resulted in the dividing walls of ethnicity in both society and the church.

After Satan's sudden and pernicious intrusion into human experience and God's promise to eventually crush the head of the serpent (Gen 3:15), Satan recedes into the background. Following this frontal attack of Satan and his fallen angels (i.e. demons) on humanity to purposefully deface the image of God, we see no further *direct* mention of him in the

---

1. 2 Pet 2:4–5; Jude 6. For a detailed discussion of two Old Testament passages (Isa 14:4–20; Ezek 28:12–19) often interpreted as referring to the origin of cosmic evil, see Boyd, *God at War*, 157–62; Newsom, "Metaphors," 151–61; Jeppesen, "You are a Cherub," 83–94; Page, *Cosmic Rebellion*, 140–59.

successive *tôlᵉdôt* of Genesis. We might conclude the serpent and his horde of fallen angels have gone into hiding; but he is there, performing his insidious work. However, this demonic involvement in the alienation of the human race is difficult to understand apart from Scripture's explicit acceptance of the reality of angels and demons.

MATERIALIST OR MAGICIAN

When it comes to the topic of supernatural evil, no one has more concisely stated the potential of error than C. S. Lewis:

> There are two equal and opposite errors into which our race can fall about devils. One is to disbelieve in their existence. The other is to believe, and to feel an excessive and unhealthy interest in them. They themselves are equally pleased by both errors and hail a materialist or a magician with the same delight.[2]

"Materialist" or "magician." Neither of these approaches does justice to the clear, unequivocal language of the Old and New Testament. We need a balanced, biblical approach to understand the role of the "powers" in relation to the deconstruction of humanity as the *imago Dei*.

Particularly since the rise of modern critical approaches to the Scriptures, some dismiss outright the biblical *weltbild* that unabashedly affirms the existence of angelic and demonic powers. Rudolf Bultmann once wrote of the perceived paradox of anyone using what for his day was considered "advanced technology"—a light bulb or radio—and at the same time claiming to believe in the world of demons. Such an approach falls prey to Satan's greatest weapon, which is to convince the world that he doesn't exist. Indeed, "the modern world begins when one no longer believes in angels."[3]

Others subtly reinterpret the biblical references to demons and spiritual powers, largely divesting them of their supernatural character, yet attributing to them the more contemporary meaning of societal structures. Walter Wink, in his well known trilogy on the powers, concludes: "The powers that Paul was most concerned with did not

---

2. Lewis, *Screwtape*, 9.

3. "Le monde moderne commence quand on cesse de croire aux anges." Cited by Maldame, "Les anges," 121 (translation mine).

fly; they were carved in stone."[4] From this perspective, the powers are "demythologized."[5]

As for the Bible's teaching on Satan and his demons, we only have three options: dismiss what the Bible says as irrelevant for our day and culture, reinterpret the biblical teaching so that it is more palatable to our scientific mentality, or accept it as a true picture of reality. We must not be materialists or magicians when it comes to the influence of supernatural evil on humanity. If we are like the majority of believers in the Western world, however, we tend toward the extreme of naturalism. Even when it concerns the present day divisions in the church, we often fail to see the spiritual causes behind the sociological realities. The spiritual explanations we do propose often do not take into account the pernicious influence of the powers about which the Bible has so much to say. Apart from a biblical perspective on the powers, we will never properly understand the diabolical source of ethnic division in the world and in the church today. It is here that Moses' theological interpretation of the Tower of Babel in Deuteronomy 32:8 is insightful.

THE SONS OF GOD AND THE SONS OF MAN: DEUTERONOMY 32:8

The Song of Moses in Deuteronomy 32 is one of the most impressive poems of the entire Old Testament. The interest of this poem for our purposes is limited to the latter part of verse 8 and its immediate context. A rapid overview of several versions immediately brings to light one of the difficulties of the translation and interpretation of the text: "When the Most High gave the nations their inheritance, when he divided all mankind . . ." (NIV):

". . . he set up boundaries for the peoples
according to the number of the *sons of Israel*." (NIV)[6]

". . . he fixed the bounds of the peoples
according to the number of the *sons of God*." (RSV)[7]

---

4. Wink, *Naming the Powers*, 82. Wink's perspective will be addressed in greater detail in chapter 9.

5. The term "demythologize" does *not* imply that the biblical writers believed that the angelic powers were mythical. It rather describes the contemporary process of divesting the concept of the "powers" of any supernatural reality.

6. Emphasis mine in each case. This reading reflects the Masoretic Text (*bᵉnê yiśrā'ēl*).

7. This reading reflects the Hebrew designation *bᵉnê 'ĕlōhîm* ("sons of God").

"... one by one he fixed the folks,
each with its guardian angel." (Moffatt)[8]

The interpretation and implications of the readings are vastly different. The reading "sons of Israel" (NIV) seems to indicate that in some way the various peoples of the earth were separated so enough territory would be left for God's chosen people, Israel. On the other hand, the reading "sons of God" (RSV) or "each with its guardian angel" (Moffatt) seems to indicate that God somehow implicated angelic beings in the repartition of the peoples of the earth.

The interpretation of this verse largely depends on three factors: the textual criticism of the readings "sons of God" (or guardian angels) or "sons of Israel," the literary analysis of this portion of the song of Moses, and the broader theological context (Gen 11; Deut 4:19; 29:25). I have discussed elsewhere the details of each of these factors, so here I will simply give a brief overview of the key elements.[9]

As for the two readings "sons of Israel" or "sons of God," the textual evidence most certainly favors the latter. The reading "sons of God" is not only supported by the Greek Septuagint[10] as well as the relatively recent discoveries at Qumran,[11] but it is also the *lectio difficilior* that best explains the tendency to "correct" the text to read "sons of Israel." From the standpoint of textual criticism alone, the reading "sons of God" is to be favored over "sons of Israel."

The rhetorical analysis of the entire song (but specifically of verse 8) also favors the reading "sons of God." Here we have a remarkable example of contrastive parallelism. The literary clue is found in the final word and letter of each line in the Hebrew:

---

8. The Moffatt translation relies on the majority of the manuscripts of the LXX "according to the number of the angels of God" (*kata arithmon angelōn theou*).

9. For a detailed discussion of the textual and interpretive details as well as an extensive bibliography, see my unpublished doctoral dissertation in French "Les Anges des Nations." See also Stevens, "'Sons of God' or 'Sons of Israel,'" 13–41; "Territorial Spirits," 412, note 9; Heiser, "Sons of God," 52–74.

10. While two manuscripts of the LXX (mss 848 and 106c) read "sons of God", the majority read "angels of God." Nearly all of the apostolic fathers rely upon the translation of the LXX for this verse.

11. The Qumran fragments are 4Qdt j/q. See Tov, *Textual Criticism*, 269; Cross, *Qumran Cave 4*, 139.

> A When the Most High gave an inheritance to the *nations* (*gôyim*),
> B when he divided all *mankind* (*bᵉnê 'ādām*);
> C He set up boundaries for the *peoples* (*'ammîm*),
> D according to the number of the *sons of God* (*bᵉnê 'ĕlōhîm*).

With the reading "sons of God" (*bᵉnê 'ĕlōhîm*), not only does each line end with the Hebrew letter *m*, but there is also interplay between synonymous and contrastive parallelism. Whereas lines A and C are basically synonymous ("nations" // "peoples"), lines B and C mark a contrast between mortals and heavenly beings ("mankind" [lit."sons of Adam"] // "sons of God").[12] Interestingly, it is this same contrast ("sons of Adam" // "sons of God") that we find in Genesis 6 and that led God to take such drastic steps of judgment upon mankind while showing grace to Noah and his family. Furthermore, the reading "sons of God" rather than "sons of Israel" in verse 8 best highlights the uniqueness of Israel as God's precious possession. It is not that Israel benefits by having a territory sufficient for her needs, but rather that among all the nations placed under the intermediary governance of the sons of God, she alone is set apart for a unique, intimate relationship with the Creator.

What is most relevant to our discussion, however, is the broader theological context of this otherwise brief, passing remark by Moses. If we accept the reading stating that the peoples were separated "according to the number of the sons of God," several questions come to the forefront: Who are these sons of God? What are the implications of this for our understanding of the dispersion of the peoples of the earth at the Tower of Babel (Gen 11)? More importantly, what is the significance of such a perspective for the ethnic divides among the peoples of the world today? In other words, to what degree do these sons of God contribute to the deconstruction of the sons of Adam as the image of God?

The Identity of the Sons of God

The Hebrew expression "sons of God" (*bᵉnê 'ĕlōhîm*) occurs only here and in Genesis 6:2; Psalm 29:1; 89:7; Job 1:6; and 38:7. While it has been a matter of much debate, I am convinced that in *every* passage where this expression occurs, it refers not to *human* judges or princes, but to actual *heavenly* powers (whether they be angels or demons according

---

12. Geller, "Dynamics," 196.

to the context) or to *perceived* powers (i.e. pagan divinities; cf. Ps 29:1; 89:7).[13] As U. Cassuto summarizes: "In Hebrew the phrase 'sons of God' may refer to any being which is not man and is not God. The language is not precise."[14]

Beyond the *nature* of these sons of God, we must also mention their *role* in God's heavenly court.[15] Recently, numerous studies have drawn attention to the parallels of this biblical motif to those found in other documents of the Ancient Near East. As Theodore Mullen states, "The concept of the divine council, or the assembly of the gods, was a common religious motif in the cultures of Egypt, Mesopotamia, Canaan, Phoenicia, and Israel."[16] This in no way justifies the conclusion that the Old Testament merely adapts the myths of the surrounding nations to its own life and theology. The differences between the biblical literature and the other ancient Near Eastern documents on this topic are explicit. In the Old Testament, Yahweh is *always* differentiated from the other members of the heavenly court and depicted as the sovereign God and unique creator of the universe (Job 4:18; 15:15; Ps 103:19–20; 1 Kgs 22:19–22). While the angels are part of the celestial sphere, they *never* appear as equals to God. "For who in the skies above can compare with the LORD?" asks the psalmist. "Who is like the LORD among the heavenly beings?" (Ps 89:6). These celestial beings, including the sons of God, are only subjects and servants having no independent authority of their own.[17] As members of the heavenly court, they fulfill three principle roles: they report, deliberate, and execute (Job 1; 1 Kgs 22). As messengers, they carry out the orders of the Lord (Ps 103:20) who alone governs the universe from his throne.

---

13. Some commentators contend that the expression "sons of God" is also used as a description of those who are in an intimate relation with God (see Isa 43:6; Exod 4:22; Deut 14:1; Jer 31:9; Hos 2:1; cf. 1:10; 11:1). However, none of these passages use the exact expression "sons of God."

14. Cassuto, *Studies*, 309.

15. Several expressions are used in the Old Testament to refer to this assembly of celestial beings: "council of the holy ones" (Ps 89:7), the "great assembly . . . of the gods" (Ps 82:1), and "mount of assembly" (Isa 14:13).

16. Mullen, *Assembly*, 113.

17. It is this that differentiates angels from *perceived* pagan deities in the Bible. Cf. Boyd, *God at War*, 116, who says: "The gods are very powerful, but they all have their power on loan from the Creator God."

In summary, the expression "sons of God" speaks of a category of supraterrestrial beings all of whom belong to the heavenly council of Yahweh. While the Old Testament often terms these beings "sons of God," "holy ones," or simply "gods," the New Testament most often refers to them as "angels," "authorities," "rulers," and "powers."

The Separation of the Nations

Accepting the reading "sons of God" (i.e. angels) over "sons of Israel" in Deuteronomy 32:8, we still must ask: To what is Moses referring when he speaks of the separation of the nations according to the number of these celestial beings? When did this take place? Are these celestial beings angels, demons, or both?

Several indicators in the text of Deuteronomy 32:8 point clearly to the account of the Tower of Babel as the interpretive context. First, the structure of Deuteronomy 32:1–9 leads us to believe that Moses is appealing in poetic terms to an ancient tradition concerning the dividing of the peoples of the earth according to the number of the gods. Using the traditional literary structure termed *rîb*, Moses poses a rhetorical question in verse 6: "Is he not your Father, your Creator, who made you and formed you?" Rather than responding directly to the question, however, Moses cites an ancient tradition concerning the separation of the peoples of the earth (v. 8). He prefaces this with an appeal to "consider the days of old" and "consider the generations long past" (v. 7). Moses goes on to explain to the people that it is "your father" and "your elders" who can recount what took place at this momentous occasion of human history. Then in verse 8, Moses cites what appears to be a poetic adaptation of an ancient extra-biblical tradition concerning the repartition of the peoples of the earth.[18] However, in citing this ancient tradition, Moses *appropriates* and *reinterprets* it as a polemic against the idolatrous perspectives of the nations surrounding Israel. Norman Habel clarifies: "In this instance, then, the application of the ancient tradition cited is really a *reinterpretation and appropriation* of an important mythic truth from El theology that demanded attention within the Israelite

---

18. Such accounts were common among the nations surrounding Israel and especially at Ugarit. Of the 1,454 Ugaritic terms that describe the "gods" or the celestial sphere, 711 (or 49 percent) find parallels in the Old Testament. See DeMoor, "El, the Creator," 187.

community."[19] The concepts and terminology would most certainly have been recognizable in the ears of the Canaanites, but the message was divested of any hint of pagan polytheism. Evidently, both the structure and content of this poetic pericope point to a time in antiquity when God sovereignly divided the peoples of the earth.

A second indicator in Deuteronomy 32 that points to the separation of the peoples of the earth at the Tower of Babel is shared terminology. Five terms are shared in common between Genesis 10–11, and Deuteronomy 32:8: "peoples" (*'ammîm*), "boundaries" (*g^{e}bûlâh*), "nations" (*gôyîm*), "sons of Adam" (*b^{e}nê 'ādām*), and "divided" (*pârad*). Indeed, this emphasis on peoples, nations, and the sons of Adam rather than fixed territories stands in marked contrast to the Ugaritic literature of the day. As we will see, the powers of the Bible are always viewed in relation to *people* and their *sociopolitical structure* rather than their respective geographical territories.

Beyond shared terminology, we also see God's heavenly council in the two accounts. In Deuteronomy 32, this is limited to the invocation of heaven and earth (Deut 32:1–4) and the explicit mention of the sons of God in verse 8. In Genesis 10–11, however, the activity of the heavenly council seems to be highlighted in the plural: "Come, let *us* go down and confuse their language." (Gen 11:7; emphasis mine). As we have seen, the same plural is found in God's declaration of Genesis 1:26–27, "Let us make." The difference is that, while it is difficult to see angels involved directly in the act of creation, it is far more understandable to see them as God's executants in the repartition of the nations as described in Genesis 10–11. In fact, one of the intentions of the book of Genesis is to highlight divine providence in the separation of the peoples of the earth.[20]

What then do we make of the statement of Deuteronomy 32:8 indicating that the nations/ethnicities of the world were separated "according to the number of the sons of God?" How does this relate chronologically to the repartition of the peoples as described in Genesis 10–11? Daniel Block suggests the most likely chronological sequence is as follows: First, there is the prior existence of Yahweh's divine council consisting of the sons of God. Second, the Most High repartitions the sons of man according to peoples/nations, taking into account the number of the sons of God who are assigned the role as guardians of the

19. Habel, "Ancient Tradition," 257; Craigie, *Ugarit*, 79.
20. Morris, *Genesis*, 273; Boyd, *God at War*, 136.

nations.[21] Third, Israel, however, has the privileged position of belonging to Yahweh apart from any angelic intermediary. Fourth, Yahweh assigns a territory with its boundaries to each of the peoples of the earth.[22]

The Idolatry of the Nations

I do not believe we can understand this repartitioning of the nations according to the sons of God apart from the idolatry that incurred God's judgment at the Tower of Babel. As stated earlier, the judgment of the Tower of Babel was both punitive and preventative. It was punitive in that mankind as the *imago Dei* could no longer understand himself. The confusion of languages led to the further deconstruction of humanity. It was also preventative in the sense that *deconstruction* is better than *destruction*; man's separation was better than man's annihilation. The idolatrous intents of man's heart at Babel were such that, apart from such divinely imposed repartitioning of mankind, humanity would self-destruct.

It is in fact this same idolatrous tendency that Moses warns Israel about in Deuteronomy 4:19–20. Moses states:

> And when you look up to the sky and see the sun, the moon and the stars—all the heavenly array—do not be enticed into bowing down to them and worshiping *things the LORD your God has apportioned to all the nations under heaven*. But as for you, the LORD took you and brought you out of the iron-smelting furnace, out of Egypt, to be the people of his inheritance, as you now are (emphasis mine).

From a biblical perspective, the sun, moon, and stars (the "heavenly array") play at least two roles in Scripture: they are given for the welfare of man and nature (Ps 136:7–9; Gen 1:14–18) and they testify to the glory of God (Ps 19; cf. Acts 14:16–17; Rom 1:19–21). However, what was

---

21. The biblical revelation remains very discrete as to the exact relation between the number of nations/ethnicities dispersed throughout the earth and the number of the "sons of God." Of course, the literature of later Judaism did not hesitate to speculate, assigning precisely seventy angels to the seventy nations as delineated in Genesis 10 (cf. Sirach 17:17; 1 Enoch 89:59—90:27; 90:22–25; *Testament of Naphtali* 8:3—10:2). Yet in Deut 32:8 any mention of specific numbers of nations or angels is noticeably absent. In contrast to the Jewish rabbis, who so often speculated in their angelology concerning numbers and hierarchies, the biblical literature remains remarkably silent. See Edersheim, *Life and Times*, 748–63; Russell, *Jewish Apocalyptic*, 257.

22. Block, *Gods of the Nations*, 21–22.

originally intended for mankind's needs and enjoyment—the heavenly bodies given for "signs and seasons"—was usurped by fallen humanity as a vehicle of idolatrous worship.

It is well known that the worship of astral deities was a common practice at this time throughout the Ancient Near East.[23] The symbol of such idolatrous worship was the ziggurat (Akk. *ziqqurratu*) erected as early as the third millennium BC. This stepladder edifice made of mud and bricks was considered to be a stairway between the gods and earth (cf. Gen 28:12). At the pinnacle of the ziggurat was a temple area constructed as the supposed habitation of the god(s). The original pantheon of the Babylonians was the seedbed for the worship of the gods and goddesses of Rome, Greece, India, Egypt, as well as other nations. Furthermore, these pagan deities were closely associated with the stars and planets—the "host of heaven" of Deuteronomy 4:19–20. From this developed the zodiac with its numerous constellations. Henry Morris even suggests that "the zodiac system of constellations may originally have been devised by the antediluvian patriarchs. . . . If so, the subsequent system of astrology is a gross corruption of the original evangelical significance of the heavenly bodies, created originally to serve in part for 'signs and seasons.'"[24]

What then is the connection between the idolatry of the nations and the repartition of the peoples of the earth according to the number of the sons of God (Deut 32:8)? As an act of divine judgment, God not only confused the languages, but also handed the peoples of the earth over to angelic intermediaries, the sons of God. Such divine judgment is not unlike the "handing over" that Paul speaks of in Romans 1:18–32 (cf. Acts 7:42). Consequently, certain of these fallen sons of God incited the idolatrous worship of the creation rather than of the Creator. This too is part of the deconstruction of mankind as the *imago Dei*. Behind all of this lurked the fallen powers that were intent both on leading all mankind astray as well as alienating humanity from itself.

---

23. See McKay, *Religion in Judah*, 45–59; Craigie, *Deuteronomy*, 136–37.

24. Morris, *Genesis*, 264–65. Morris comments: "The Virgin, whose sign among the stars once reminded men of the promised Seed of the woman, began to assume the proportions of an actual Queen of Heaven; and Leo, the great sidereal lion at the other end of the zodiac, became a great spiritual King of Heaven. Soon the stars, the physical 'host of heaven,' were invested with the personalities of the angels, the invisible spiritual heavenly host" (271).

If this accurately represents the theological interpretation of Genesis 10–11 as given by Moses in Deuteronomy 32:8, then following the debacle of the Tower of Babel each nation/ethnicity of the world (with the exception of Israel) was assigned one or more members of the celestial court. The implications of such an assigning of the peoples of the earth to angelic beings—apparently both fallen and unfallen—cannot be overstated. Not only does such a conclusion shed light on God's governance of the world through angelic intermediaries, but it also hints at the spiritual powers that lie behind the ethnic strife in our present day world. Could it be that what happens on earth—wars, racism, ethnocentrism, and the like—are in some degree a reflection of what is taking place in the heavenly sphere among the sons of God? The following account of Daniel 10 leaves us in no doubt.

OF PRINCES AND PEOPLES: DANIEL 10

If Deuteronomy 32:8 teaches that the peoples of the world have been assigned to angelic powers, then the insightful account of Daniel 10 describes the implications of this both for understanding ethnic hatred as well as for calling believers to prayer. The key verses in question are Daniel 10:12–14. The angel Gabriel comes to Daniel and says:

> Do not be afraid, Daniel. Since the first day that you set your mind to gain understanding and to humble yourself before your God, your words were heard, and I have come in response to them. But the prince of the Persian kingdom resisted me twenty-one days. Then Michael, one of the chief princes, came to help me, because I was detained there with the king of Persia. Now I have come to explain to you what will happen to your people in the future, for the vision concerns a time yet to come.

Daniel 10 is the decisive Old Testament passage for the study of the cosmic powers that exert influence over the peoples of the earth. S. R. Driver, who does not hold to an angelic interpretation of Deuteronomy 32:8, affirms that the doctrine of tutelary angels set over the nations is found *explicitly* for the first time in this passage.[25] M. Delcor is of the same opinion: "This verse supposes, on the one hand—the notion of guardian angels over the nations—and on the other, the existence of an-

---

25. Driver, *Daniel*, 157. The angelic interpretation of verse 13 can be dated at least to the time of Origen (cf. *Homilies on Luke* 35).

gelic warfare in the heavens. For the first time the idea is expressed that each people has a protective angel."[26]

The Historical Setting

Daniel 10:1 specifies that Daniel received a prophetic revelation concerning a great war in the third year of Cyrus's reign as king of Persia. Apparently, this revelation led Daniel to mourn and fast for a period of three weeks (10:2). According to verse 3, this period of fasting ended on the "twenty-fourth day of the first month."

What opposition was Israel facing that led Daniel to such an intensive period of mourning and fasting? When the events are read in their historical context, it seems the reconstruction of the temple was the primary preoccupation of Daniel and his people (cf. Dan 9:25; Ezra 1–4). Though Cyrus had already allowed some of the Jewish exiles to return to their homeland, many were still dispersed in the Mesopotamian cities of Babylon, Persepolis, Susa, and Ecbatana.

The historical evidence points to the probability that Cambyses, son of Cyrus and crown prince, was primarily responsible for the opposition faced by the Jewish nation at this time. We do know the reconstruction of the temple was interrupted during the entire reign of Cambyses and not undertaken again until the more conciliatory reign of Darius 1 Hystaspes (521–486 BC). This is understakable in light of Cambyses's renowned and intense antagonism toward other religions and ethnicities.[27]

What is especially significant, however, is the correlation between one particular Ancient Near Eastern text describing Cambyses's enthronement as king of Babylon during the New Year's Festival[28] and the commencement of Daniel's three weeks of prayer and fasting. The historical evidence indicates that Daniel's three weeks of mourning and fasting ended on the twenty-fourth day of the first month (Dan 10:4), that is, Nisan 24 (= May 11), 535 BC. The parallels with the text describing Cambyses's enthronement are striking. William Shea summarizes:

26. Delcor, *Daniel*, 205 (translation mine).
27. Shea, "Prince of Persia," 233–39; Stevens, "Territorial Spirits," 423–25.
28. The text reads: "When, the 4th day, Cambyses, son of Cyrus, went to the temple . . . priest of Nebo . . . came (and) made the 'weaving' by means of the *handles* and when[he le]d the image of Ne[bo. . . . Nebo returned to Esagila, sheep-offerings in front of Bel and the god *Mâ[r]-b[iti]*." For the full text, see Oppenheim, *ANET*, 306.

What we find when these dates are compared is that the period of Daniel's mourning (during which also the angels wrestled with the prince of Persia)—twenty-one days—is the exact equivalent of the length of time between the date in Nisan on which Cambyses entered the temple during the New Year's festival, the 4th, and the date in Nisan on which the events of Dan 10 are described as occurring, the 24th. If the 24th of Nisan was the twenty-first day of Daniel's mourning, then by working backwards we find that the first day of Daniel's mourning was the 4th of Nisan, *the same day on which Cambyses entered the temple during the New Year's festival.*[29]

These observations point out the circumstances that *may* have provoked the prophet's three weeks of prayer and fasting. Given Cambyses's bellicose character, ethnocentricity, and hatred of foreign religions, it is understandable why Daniel would have devoted himself to prayer and fasting on behalf of his people and the project of reconstructing the temple already underway in Jerusalem. Cambyses's ascension to power compromised the more conciliatory stance toward the Jews demonstrated by his father, Cyrus. The likely parallel also highlights the close relationship between the celestial activity of angelic princes and the affairs of people, ethnicities, and kingdoms.

The Angelic Princes

While some have understood the "prince of Persia" in Daniel 10 to refer to one of the political authorities in Persia who opposed the Jews—even Cambyses himself—the choice of words and overall context clearly describe the prince of Persia as a supernatural demonic power. The common denominator in all the uses of the term "prince" (*śar*) is the concept of "one who commands."[30] Admittedly, the term often refers to *human* commanders or rulers in Daniel (1:7–11, 18; 9:6, 8; 11:5). Yet in at least three passages we find incontestable examples where the designation *śar* is applied to Michael the archangel (10:13, 21; 12:1), the "commander of the host" of heaven (8:11; cf. Josh 5:14–15), or to the Messiah himself ("prince of princes;" 8:25). Furthermore, the evident parallel between the prince of Persia and Michael, the guardian angel of Israel, must not be overlooked. This same parallel is found in verses 20–21 between the

29. Shea, "Prince of Persia," 245–46 (emphasis mine).
30. *HALOT*, 3:1350–53.

"prince of Greece" and "Michael, your prince." If the term *śar* refers (in a context of spiritual conflict) to the benevolent angel Michael who represented God's interests, it is not surprising to find the same term used to designate a malevolent angel (a demon) representing the interests of an earthly kingdom.

Without a doubt, this passage deals with mighty supernatural beings who are apparently engaged in spiritual conflict with one another. The princes of Persia and of Greece are demonic princes established over their respective nations. They are two of the sons of God referred to in Deuteronomy 32:8 who influence peoples and ethnicities. These are not mere human princes nor are they "territorial spirits"; rather, they are powerful national angels or "empire spirits" who oppose the accomplishment of God's purposes through His people Israel. They are two of the sons of God referred to in Deuteronomy 32:8 who influence peoples and ethnicities. In this case, their intentions are evil, standing in opposition to the angels Gabriel and Michael, the latter being one of the chief princes and the defender of the Jewish nation.

The Heavenly Battle

The account of Daniel 10 rends the skies and gives us a glimpse into the titanic battle taking place in the heavenly realms. The description is brief but profoundly insightful as to the influence of cosmic powers on nations, rulers, and political structures.

The angel Gabriel is sent to Daniel to strengthen the prophet (v. 12) and to convey the revelation of chapters 11 and 12. For twenty-one days, the demonic prince of Persia *resisted* the angel Gabriel. During this time, God's messenger angel was doing more than strengthening the prophet Daniel and conveying further revelation. He was engaged in spiritual warfare, opposing the malevolent influence of the demonic prince of Persia on human political authorities. The demonic prince of Persia, who in this case is working through the intermediary of the then ruling political authorities, must be countered in his destructive schemes against Israel. This is the first objective of Gabriel's mission. This seems to be confirmed by the clause "for I [Gabriel] had been left there with the kings of Persia" (v. 13).[31]

---

31. Translation mine. The phrase "kings of Persia" is problematic. For a full discussion of the details, see Stevens, "Territorial Spirits," 424–25.

Who are these human political authorities ("kings of Persia") through whom the demonic prince of Persia is at work? Given the above mentioned historical context, the designation refers to the two kings—Cambyses, the Babylonian head of state,[32] and Cyrus, the king of Persia. In the same way that Satan rose against Israel to incite King David to oppose the will of God (1 Chr 21:1), so this malevolent angelic "kingdom-prince" attempted to accomplish his evil intentions by the intermediary of two heads of state, Cyrus and his son Cambyses. The result was not only the obvious opposition to the fulfillment of God's purposes through Israel, but also the pitting of one ethnicity against another. As Gregory Boyd states, "What occurs on earth, again, is a replica and a mirror of what occurs in heaven. Indeed, it is a microcosmic example of the macrocosmic spiritual struggle."[33]

This intimate relationship between celestial and terrestrial activity is also indicated elsewhere in Daniel. For example, in Daniel 11:1 we read: "I [Gabriel] took my stand to support and protect him." To whom does "him" refer? Most certainly it refers to Michael, the archangel of the Jewish people. Michael, Israel's primary angelic defender, needed the help of Gabriel during the reign of Darius (Dan 6). Similarly, Gabriel, Israel's primary angelic messenger, called on Michael in his struggle against the prince of Persia (Dan 10). All of this affords us unusual insight into angelic activity in the heavenlies as it relates to the various ethnicities on earth.

The immediate context of Daniel 11:1 also addresses this intimate relationship between celestial activity and the terrestrial scene. Beginning in Daniel 10:21, a complex and intentional literary structure demonstrates that Daniel 11:1 is not an incidental phrase that needs to be reformulated or amended as some have claimed. Rather, the verse belongs to the central body of revelation that begins in 10:20. In this case, 10:20—11:1 and 12:1–3 form an inclusio frame around the revelation of 11:2–45.

> First, he [Gabriel] discloses to Daniel the heavenly battle that goes on behind the terrestrial scene: 10:13, 20–21; 11:1. Second, he reveals the historical consequences of the preceding

---

32. Whatever may have been the precise political position of Cambyses on May 11, 535 BC, the term "king" is quite adequate for describing the *role* of Cambyses and his father Cyrus. See Culver, *TWOT*, 1:507–10.

33. Boyd, *God at War*, 90.

> supra-historical battle: 11:2b–45. Lastly, he returns to the celestial scene and the vindication of his people: 12:1–3 . . . *the terrestrial struggle involving the accession into world power of a new kingdom bound to persecute Israel (11:2b–45) presumes a whole heavenly battle going on behind it.*[34]

While Daniel chapters 1–5 depicts the history of world empires, chapters 6–12 (and especially chapters 10–12) unfold the reality of the conflict that rages in the supraterrestrial sphere. As A. T. Lincoln states, these chapters depict "war in heaven between the angels of the nations which has its counterpart in the events on earth."[35]

Such a perspective, of course, carries important ramifications for our racialized society as well as for the dividing walls of ethnicity within the church. There is more to our segregation than meets the eye. Behind the divisions and resultant alienation—and even behind the sociological dynamics that contribute to the dividing walls—are the powers of the heavenly world that exert their malicious influence upon both society and church. R. H. Charles states it well when he writes:

> The presupposition of Old and New Testament apocalyptic is that the world's disorder and sin is only a part of the disorder and sin affecting the spiritual world. . . . The conflict is not limited to this earth or to this life. It is a warfare from which there is no discharge until the kingdom of this world is become the kingdom of the Lord and of His Christ.[36]

If we do not take this into consideration, then all of our sociological analysis will be of little help in addressing the root causes of our present day divisions. When we do take this into consideration, however, our first response should be that modeled by Daniel—fervent, intercessory prayer. In direct response to Daniel's prayer, God sent an angel to counteract the evil intentions of the prince of Persia and to reveal God's unfolding program to the prophet. While Cyrus and his son Cambyses opposed the reconstruction of the Jewish temple in the terrestrial sphere, spiritual warfare was being waged in the celestial sphere as the angel Gabriel countered the malevolent influence exerted by the angelic prince of Persia on the contemporary political situation on earth. In this celestial warfare, Daniel's prayer was not without significance. First, the

---

34. David, "A Late Gloss?" 509, 512 (emphasis mine).
35. Lincoln, "Liberation from the Powers," 350.
36. Charles, *APOT*, 1:298.

angel Gabriel was sent to Daniel in direct response to his prayer (v. 12). In addition, as a result of Daniel's intercession God unveiled in Daniel 11 his program for Israel's future. Most importantly, as he continued to pray, Daniel gained victory over the opposing prince of Persia, resulting in the eventual removal of the obstacles to the rebuilding of the temple.

It is important to observe that Daniel did not engage in aggressive prayer against such powers with the expectation of "binding" or "evicting" them. The prophet did not pray *against* cosmic powers but *for* the people of God and the fulfillment of God's redemptive purposes (cf. Eph 6:18–20). Apparently Daniel's focus in prayer was not on the celestial warfare in the heavenlies, but on the promises of God (Dan 10:12; cf. Jer 25:11; 29:10) and their fulfillment on the terrestrial scene. Indeed, these promises were fulfilled, but not immediately. Historically the immediate obstacles to the reconstruction of the temple were not overcome for another decade and a half. The prince of Persia continued to exert his influence for another two hundred years until the time of the Greek Empire. Such historical facts underscore the absolute sovereignty of God in the outworking of his purposes in response to the prayers of his people. Indeed, "he does as he pleases with the powers of heaven and the peoples of the earth" (Dan 4:35).

THE SUBJECTION OF THE WORLD

One passage in the New Testament brings further clarity to what we have seen so far. The writer to the Hebrews states: "It is not to angels that he has subjected the world to come, about which we are speaking" (Heb 2:5). The statement assumes that the present world *is* subjected to angels. From what we have seen, this was not God's original intention. Humanity as the *imago Dei* was created to rule over the inhabited earth as God's vice-regent. However, the destructive effects of sin deconstructed humanity as the image of God, compromising man's resemblance to his Creator as well as his relational capacities and representative role. It is the latter aspect of representation and dominion that the writer to the Hebrews describes when he affirms, "Yet at present we do not see everything subject to him" (Heb 2:8). Humanity's movement *east*—away from God—culminated in the dispersion of humanity and its subjection to angelic powers (Gen 11; Deut 32:8).

The similarity of vocabulary and concepts between Hebrews 2:5 and the Septuagint reading of Deuteronomy 32:8 is striking.

> It is not to *angels* that he has subjected the *world* to come. (Heb 2:5)

> He divided the *nations* according to the number of the *sons of God*. (Deut 32:8)

We notice in both passages a connection between the inhabited world and the angels. The term chosen by the writer to the Hebrews to denote the "world" (*oikoumenē*) has from its earliest usage always meant the *inhabited* world, populated by the sons of Adam.[37] As for Deuteronomy 32:8, the emphasis placed on the *inhabited* world is evident in the three terms: *nations* (*gôyim*), *mankind* (*bᵉnê 'ādām*), and *peoples* (*'ammîm*). According to Deuteronomy 32:8, it is the *peoples* of the earth (*not* geographical territories)—previously united but now dispersed—who have been placed under the tutelage of the sons of God.[38] Furthermore, the expression "sons of God" in Deuteronomy 32:8 finds its parallel in the term "angels" to which God has *not* subjected the world to come according to Hebrews 2:5. Finally, the designation "angels" certainly includes the "rulers," "authorities," and "powers" (1 Cor 15:24; Eph 1:20; 6:12) to which the peoples of the word are presently subjected. It is the author's use of Psalm 8 in Hebrews 2:6–9 that elucidates the subtle connection between all three passages:

> But there is a place where someone has testified: "What is man that you are mindful of him, the son of man that you care for him? You made him a little lower than the angels; you crowned him with glory and honor and put everything under his feet." In putting everything under him, God left nothing that is not subject to him. Yet at present we do not see everything subject to him. But we see Jesus, who was made a little lower than the angels, now crowned with glory and honor because he suffered death, so that by the grace of God he might taste death for everyone.

---

37. Michel, *TDNT* 5:157–59; Cf. LSJ, 1205.

38. This emphasis on the peoples of the earth and their sociopolitical structures is found throughout the Old Testament and distinguishes the biblical literature from the traditions of the surrounding nations. In pagan nations around Israel, the identity of a people was defined first in terms of a false god's relationship to his *territory*. These deities were depicted only secondarily with respect to the inhabitants of those areas. However, the biblical literature stands in contrast to such mythical and animistic notions. In contrast to this pagan concept (Judg 11:24; 1 Sam 26:19–20; 2 Kgs 3:27), the Old Testament never accepts such thinking as God's view. The emphasis is rather on the relationship between God (or the "gods") and the *peoples* of the earth. See Block, *Gods of the Nations*, 23–29.

The precise relationship between this eschatological dominion promised to the New Humanity and the spiritual powers that presently afflict all humanity is clarified as we compare the citation of Psalm 8 in Hebrews 2 with Deuteronomy 32:8, Daniel 10:12–21, 1 Corinthians 15:24–58, and Ephesians 1:20–22 . This can be depicted as follows:

DEUTERONOMY 32:8 DANIEL 10:12–21	HEBREWS 2:5–9 PSALM 8	EPHESIANS 1:20 1 CORINTHIANS 15:24
"Sons of God" = *angels* "prince of Persia" "prince of Greece"	The angels to whom the world is presently subjected	"rulers" "authorities" "powers"

In Psalm 8, the tension point is found in the fact that man *does not* presently exercise dominion over "all things," including the spiritual powers of this age (v. 8b, 14). However, this "already/but not yet" tension between mankind's present inherent role as the *imago Dei* and its yet future and complete realization is found at the end of verse 9: "But we see Jesus." There is, in fact, a profound continuity between the "world to come" (v. 5) and the created world as described in Psalm 8. According to verse 9, what is not yet fully realized in man's experience has been fully accomplished in Jesus, the "second man" (1 Cor 15:47), who came to "destroy him who holds the power of death—that is, the devil" (Heb 2:14). God's design for mankind is now accomplished in the person of Jesus whose name testifies to his complete identification with humanity and who is now exalted above every ruler, authority, and power (Eph 1:20; 1 Cor 15:24). As the "last Adam" (1 Cor 15:45), he definitively identified himself with fallen humanity so that he might lift it up again to a position of glory, magnificence, and dominion.

CONCLUSION

The prophet Isaiah reminds us, "In that day the Lord will punish the powers in the heavens above and the kings on the earth below" (Isa 24:21). As we have seen, what takes place on earth is to some degree a reflection of what is taking place in the heavenly sphere. The powers in the heavens and the kings on the earth are inseparable.

I have suggested that these powers are the sons of God described in Deuteronomy 32:8. According to Moses' interpretation of the separation of the nations at the Tower of Babel, the peoples of the earth have been placed under the governance of guardian angels. As an act of judgment in view of man's prideful arrogance, God "gave over" the ethnicities of the world to a form of intermediary, providential governance under the sons of God (cf. Rom 1:24, 26, 28; Acts 7:42). As we have seen in Daniel 10, the Scriptures give an unusual glimpse into the celestial sphere and the warfare that occurs between such sons of God. The guardian angel Michael and the messenger angel Gabriel engage the demonic princes of Persia and Greece, opposing them in their attempt to impede God's purposes through his people Israel.

Alienation, fear, mistrust, racism, hatred, and every form of evil that separates mankind from himself and from his Creator is incited, to one degree or another, by the demonic powers that have attached themselves to the various peoples of this world. These spiritual, intangible powers "hide" behind the more tangible societal and political structures that govern our everyday lives. Societal and political structures are *not* the powers themselves, but they can be controlled by the powers. The Bible never demythologizes the powers. The sons of God (whether good or evil in character) remain supranatural in essence. They are members of God's heavenly court and under his providential, sovereign directives.

The implications of this biblical view of reality must not be ignored when considering the present day ethnic divides both in society and in the church. All forms of racism, ethnic hatred, or the alienation of nations are ultimately incited by the very powers that seek to divide and deconstruct humanity as the *imago Dei*. As Paul reminds us, "Our struggle is not against flesh and blood, but against the rulers, against the authorities, against the powers of this dark world and against the spiritual forces of evil in the heavenly realms" (Eph 6:12). It is these very powers that the Son of Man came to destroy in his great redemptive act at the cross. There the Old Humanity, with his alienation, ethnocentrism, and divisiveness, was crucified (Rom 6:6). And there the New Humanity, marked by reconciliation, unity, and love, was created (Eph 2:15). This is the focus of our next chapter.

5

The New Humanity

The more genuine and the deeper our community becomes the more will everything between us recede, the more clearly and purely will Jesus and His work become the one and only thing that is vital between us.

Dietrich Bonhoeffer

IN THE BEGINNING OF the twentieth century, European and American scientists worked together to develop the field of eugenics. Frances Galton coined the term, defining it as "the study of the agencies under social contract that may improve or impair the racial qualities of future generations, either physically or mentally."[1] The philosophy behind eugenics was to regulate human breeding to improve the biological future of humanity. The vision was to create and assure the development of a pure race, a "new man." With this in view, they developed international scientific roundtables, held conferences, and reported to government agencies. However, the entire initiative was founded upon the fallacious assumption that societal ills were the result of biological deficiencies. They were convinced they could solve the societal problems of the world and create a new society through biological engineering. This, of course, was impossible. Not only was it impossible, but the very science behind eugenics eventually led to such human travesties as the Nazi experiments of the 1930s and 1940s. Many people here in America also

---

1. Meneses, "Science and The Myth," 41.

became enamored with eugenics. Between 1911 and 1930, twenty-four states had enacted sterilization laws for "social misfits" and "idiots." By 1941, thirty-six thousand people in America had been sterilized.[2]

Man innately recognizes that something is terribly wrong at the core of the human race, but his concocted attempts to salvage the situation and create a new society prove futile. Writing in 1875, Charles Darwin maintained that as social horizons widened, *simple common sense* would help man see that he should live in harmony with all of his fellow men. Obviously, Darwin's idealistic dream has not been realized.

On the other hand, God has done what no man can do. This is what Paul describes in Ephesians chapter 2. What the first man—Adam— erased, the second man—Christ—*more than* replaced.

> His purpose was to create in himself *one new man* out of the two, thus making peace, and in this one body to reconcile both of them to God through the cross, by which he put to death their hostility. (Eph 2:15b, emphasis mine)

The creation of the "one new man" is the *only* remedy to the segregation and alienation so characteristic of the human race. "God is the ultimate salvage artist," writes Randy Alcorn. "He loves to restore things to their original condition—and even make them better."[3] That is precisely what God has done in the creation of the one new man.

Just who is this "one new man?" What is the relation between this "man" and the original man of the creation account? More specifically, what is the relevance of this image to the dividing walls that fragment the church today? In this chapter, I will demonstrate that the one new man of Ephesians 2 is the New Humanity of which Christ, the second man, is the head. The New Humanity is God's redemptive answer to the deconstruction of humankind, the *imago Dei,* through sin. In stark contrast to the division and alienation of fallen Eden and Babel stands the New Humanity as the arena of peace, unity, and reconciliation.

One of the basic assumptions underlying New Testament theology is the existing disharmony between man and God, between man and fellow man, and ultimately between God and Satan. In essence, the unity of the world is broken. This radical alienation in each of these three spheres is graphically depicted in Ephesians 2, along with a focus

2. Ibid.
3. Alcorn, *Heaven,* 89.

on reconciliation in the former two. The creation of unity out of disunity—the creation of the one new man—is but the complementary New Testament answer to the most pressing Old Testament questions concerning man's relationship to his Creator and fellow man.

As we have already seen, man's relationship with his Creator was disrupted in Genesis 3 through his own self-assertive rebellion. Sin entered man's experience as a malignant, deadly abnormality, compromising humanity's divinely endowed role as God's image. Because of satanically inspired sin, collective mankind as God's likeness-image was marred, his representative role on earth was perverted, and he became alienated in his relationship with God and fellow man. This schism between peoples came to manifest itself especially in the chasm between God's covenant nation Israel and non-Israelites. However, the alienation between Israel and the Gentiles is merely in microcosm a reflection of the relational estrangement that perpetuates humanity's Babel experience to this very day. This is the dilemma posed in the Old Testament for which Paul's doctrine of the New Humanity offers the solution.

Our exploration, however, does not stop with mere interpretation. We must grasp the significance of this concept as it relates to the dividing walls that fragment the life of the contemporary church. Much of the doctrine of the New Testament relates to how we view ourselves as those who are *together* in Christ. This is the power of identity. The New Testament consistently moves us from doctrine to practice. Our collective biblical identity must shape our relational practice. When it comes to the segregation of the body of Christ along lines of color and culture (not to mention class, generational preferences, and other type of affinity groupings), there is no more potent remedy than a thorough understanding, appreciation, and application of the biblical teaching of our collective identity as the New Humanity.

GETTING THE BIG PICTURE: TOGETHERNESS

By AD 62, the year in which Paul most likely wrote his letter to the Ephesians,[4] the best years of the apostle's life had been expended trying to preserve unity between two conflicting elements in the church—Jew and Gentile. Now the apostle to the Gentiles was imprisoned in Rome

---

4. For a discussion of the date of this epistle, see Heibert, *Introduction*, 267; Barth, *Ephesians*, 1:51. Concerning authorship, see the detailed discussion in Hoehner, *Ephesians*, 2–61.

for his faithfulness in declaring to "both Jews and Gentiles that they must turn to God in repentance and have faith in our Lord Jesus" (Acts 20:21). Here, enjoying the relative freedom of his own hired quarters, Paul has ample opportunity to think, teach, and write (see Acts 28:3). After having addressed the pressing issues giving rise to the Epistle to the Colossians, the apostle's mind is "free for one supreme exposition, non-controversial, positive, fundamental, of the great doctrine of his life—that doctrine into which he had been advancing year by year under the discipline of his unique circumstances—the doctrine of the unity of mankind in Christ and of the purpose of God for the world through the Church."[5]

The controlling idea of Paul's letter to the Ephesians is the unity of the church. Paul argues profoundly and passionately that the reason we as believers are to live together in unity—inclusive of differences of ethnicity, background, and culture—is because God has graciously, through the sacrificial death of his Son, made Jew and Gentile one new man (Eph 2:15). In other words, *in reality* the dividing walls of ethnicity have been once and for all deconstructed (Eph 1–3). Therefore, *in our experience* we must deconstruct the walls, never allowing them to be reconstructed (Eph 4–6).

Paul initiates the theme of the epistle in chapter 1 with a hymn of praise to the triune God for having predestined, accomplished, and assured our inheritance as believers (1:3–14). From the outset, our attention is drawn to the non-homogeneous Three-in-One—Father (1:3–6), Son (1:7–13), and Holy Spirit (1:13b–14)—as the template of God's design for humanity. Even as Father, Son, and Holy Spirit exist and work *together*, so also the triune God's design is to bring "all things in heaven and on earth *together* under one head, even Christ" (1:10; emphasis mine). As Father, Son, and Holy Spirit are one, though each with his particular work to accomplish in the redemption of mankind, so also we, the redeemed from every ethnicity on earth, are to be brought *together* as God's purposes reach their fulfillment.

Following the prayer of 1:15–23, Paul then details in 2:1–10 the means by which God has accomplished this redemptive work for which he is praised. It is here we find once again this intentional emphasis on

---

5. Robinson, *Ephesians*, 10. For opposing viewpoints concerning the chronological priority of Colossians over Ephesians, see Lohse, *Epistles*, 4; Coutts, "Ephesians and Colossians," 201–7.

togetherness: "But God, who is rich in mercy, because of His great love with which He loved us, even when we were dead in trespasses, made us alive *together* with Christ (by grace you have been saved), and raised us up *together*, and made us sit *together* in the heavenly places in Christ Jesus" (Eph 2:4–6, NKJV [emphasis mine]). Then, as if Paul simply can't rid his mind of the concept of "togetherness," he describes the church as a building that is "joined *together*" in which we are "built *together*" to become God's habitation by his Spirit (2:21–22). It's unfortunate the full force of these descriptive statements is not brought out by many of the newer translations. Each of the verbs—"made alive," "raised up," and "seated" (as well as the "joined together" and "built together" of verses 21 and 22)—is preceded by the Greek suffix *syn*, meaning "together."

The backdrop for this focus on togetherness is established in Ephesians 2:1–3. There Paul characterizes the former life of *both* Gentile (2:1–2a) and Jewish (2:2b–3) believers as thoroughly marked by spiritual death. He begins by describing the Gentiles in verse 1: "*you* were dead in your transgressions and sins." However, in verse 3 he shifts to the first person plural and refers to Jews: "all of *us* also." Clearly the church of Ephesus as well as the surrounding churches who received this circular letter were comprised of *both* Jews and Gentiles, though Gentiles may have been in the majority (see Acts 19:10).[6]

In Paul's day, one of the most significant cultural divides that existed was between Jew and Gentile. They dressed differently, ate differently, worshiped differently, and thought differently. Such religious and cultural differences within Judaism eventually led to the establishment of separate Hebraic and Hellenistic synagogues (see Acts 6:9). However, in the one new man all of this has changed. These Jewish and Gentile believers now share one thing in common—they were *all* spiritually dead, but now they have *all* been *co-enlivened*, *co-raised*, and *co-seated* in Christ. Yes, Ephesians is all about *togetherness* among believing Jews and Gentiles from every ethnicity around the world. In these verses, the great Peacemaker, the Messiah, is seen to be the antidote to every type of ethnic estrangement.

---

6. For a discussion of the composition of the Ephesian church in the first century, see Tellbe, *Christ-Believers*, 75. It is estimated that the total population of Ephesus in the first century was about 200,000, of which about 10,000 to 25,000 were Jews.

Together. This truth defines our collective identity. Because of this, it is no longer "'me and my God,' but 'we and our God.'"[7] Furthermore, the "we" includes those of every ethnicity and culture that name the name of Christ.

"WALLING IN" AND "WALLING OUT"

Have you ever noticed how nearly every nationality or ethnicity tends to view the world in terms of "them" and "us"? To use Robert Frost's terms, we "wall in" and "wall out." This is the diversity in alienation that marks humanity since the Fall of Adam. Such an "us-them" polarity was prevalent among the Persians, who considered themselves at the very center of a concentric circle. Once the Greek empire came into supremacy, we discover the same phenomenon. The Greeks were the "civilized" and all others were considered barbarians, a description that comes from the word *barbar*, meaning to stammer or stutter like a child. Later when the Romans gained supremacy, they considered all others as barbarians. During the High Middle Ages, educated North Europeans viewed foreigners as "monsters," humanoids who lived in the forests and prairies as embodiments of evil forces. Such a worldview gave us the vocabulary of the *satyr* (those half human-half goat creatures) and the Old Norse *íviôr*, trolls living under bridges.[8] In our day, the Hutu of Rwanda considered the Tutsi an inferior people, calling them cockroaches and in need of extermination. An indigenous group in North Australia call themselves "Tiwi," meaning "we, the only people." They have various terms for outsiders, but consider no one but themselves to be fully human.

From the standpoint of the Old Testament and particularly later Judaism, there were the Jews, and then there was everyone else, called the Gentiles (or more literally, the *nations*; Gk. *ethnē*). The Gentiles came to be viewed as the "other," those on the periphery of human existence. The designation eventually became an ethnic slur, a pejorative ethnographic designation for non-Jews who lacked the sign of circumcision. Particularly after the fall of Northern Israel in 722 BC and of the Southern Kingdom in 586 BC, Israel began to define herself in terms of her relationship to the surrounding nations rather than in relation to God. Later, when the Romans took political control over

---

7. Bock, "New Man," 160.
8. Hiebert, "Western Images," 99.

Israel in 63 BC, the category *ethnē* became nuanced as referring to all those who are enemies of God, that is, the Gentiles. The previously mentioned social dynamics of boundaries and social solidarity were in full play. Therefore, the designation *ethnē* not only describes the Gentiles' otherness in relation to God's chosen; it further defines their otherness in relation to God himself.[9]

It is this insipid ethnocentrism that Paul dismantles in these verses. Before deconstructing such false thoughts, however, he first describes them. He knows we cannot fully appreciate what God has done to deconstruct the dividing walls unless we understand the nature of those walls in the first place. For this reason, the intense ostracism between Jew and Gentile is carefully described by Paul in these terms:

> Therefore, remember that formerly you who are Gentiles by birth and called "uncircumcised" by those who call themselves the "circumcision" (that done in the body by the hands of men)—remember that at that time you were separate from Christ, excluded from citizenship in Israel and foreigners to the covenants of the promise, without hope and without God in the world. (Eph 2:11–12)

In these verses, Paul specifies the major boundary markers that define Jewish and Gentile identity. He demonstrates that before the advent of the great Peacemaker, the Gentiles *as a people* lay outside the orbit of God's covenantal love and election. The Gentiles' condition of otherness in these verses has been well summarized as "Christless," "stateless," "friendless," "hopeless," and "Godless."[10] While it is true that in the pre-Christ era the Gentiles were spiritually disadvantaged, Paul's emphasis in these verses seems to be on ways in which the Gentiles were *religiously* and *ethnically* marginalized by the Jews. He does this by highlighting the alienation from a typical Jewish perspective. Paul's ultimate intention, however, is to eradicate spiritual as well as ethnic and cultural distance between Jew and Gentile. He wants to create a new "space" for those who otherwise had no space.

Paul does this by first reminding the Gentiles that they were formerly alienated from the nation of Israel. This alienation was nurtured particularly in later Israelite history by the issue of circumcision. Circumcision was intended as a sign of righteousness by faith in Yahweh's covenant

---

9. Yee, *Ethnic Reconciliation*, 74–77.
10. Hendriksen, *Ephesians*, 129–31.

promises; such faith would manifest itself in adherence to the law. So often, however, it was not representative of a true "circumcision of the heart" but was merely "handmade" (v. 11; cf. Rom 2:29; Col 2:11; Gal 5:6; 6:15). It soon became nothing more than the sign and seal of being with "our kind of people."

On the other hand, the Gentiles were derogatorily designated the "uncircumcision" (literally the "foreskin"). Such an appellation unequivocally classified the Gentiles as "outsiders" (Acts 11:2–3; Rom 2:26; 4:9; Gal 2:7–9). So these nicknames—"the circumcised" and "the uncircumcised"—became boundary marking terms designating the Jews as "insiders" and the Gentiles as "outsiders."[11]

Along with being ostracized by the circumcision, the Gentiles were excluded from the covenant blessings that were to culminate in the promised Messiah. That is why Paul describes them as being "separate from Christ." While individual Gentiles could become members of God's theocratic nation from its inception, as a whole they had no part in God's specific promises reserved for Israel. They were excluded from the spiritual privileges and rights of the Old Testament theocracy as well as from hope in God.

Paul uses two terms in Ephesians 2 that are helpful in understanding the profound alienation existing at this time between Jew and Gentile. For any strict Jew, dealings with the "foreigners" (2:12) and "aliens" (2:19) were a matter of great importance. Though contact between the elect nation and Gentiles was not forbidden, teaching was early formulated to regulate social interaction between the two. As a result, strict ethical demands were placed even upon resident aliens.[12] Later, far more gross and unbiblical distortions of the Jew-Gentile dichotomy developed as illustrated in the Mishnah and Talmud. Here we see the ethnocentrism of the Jewish nation taken to an extreme. The Jews viewed the Gentiles as "fuel for the fires of hell." It was considered unlawful to help a Gentile mother in the pangs of childbirth for that would result in bringing another Gentile into the world. If a Jewish boy married a Gentile girl or a Jewish girl married a Gentile boy, a funeral was performed indicating the death of that child. The Mishnah further states: "Cattle may not be left in the inns of the gentiles since they are suspected of bestiality; nor may a woman remain alone with them since they are suspected of

---

11. Yee, *Ethnic Reconciliation*, 77–83.
12. Davies, *Paul and Rabbinic Judaism*, 113–14.

lewdness; nor may a man remain alone with them since they are suspected of shedding blood."[13] Somehow Israel had forgotten that she had been established by God to be a blessing *to* the nations rather than to be isolated *from* the nations.

The epitome of this growing hostility was seen in the temple, constructed by Herod the Great. The temple itself was made up of three courts: the Court of the Priests, the Court of Israel, and the Court of the Women. Beyond this, however, was the Court of the Gentiles. To get to this court, one had to descend five steps from the temple itself to a wall. Then on the other side of the wall, one would descend fourteen more steps to another wall. Beyond that was the Court of the Gentiles. From here, Gentiles could look up and see the temple but were not allowed to approach it. They were separated by a one-and-a-half meter stone barricade. Along this barricade were various notices that read in Greek and Latin: "trespassers will be executed." Two of these notices have been discovered by archeologists in the last hundred years. On one of these the exact wording is: "Let no foreigner enter within the partition and enclosure surrounding the temple. Whoever is arrested will himself be responsible for his death which will follow."[14] The "dividing wall" in the Temple that separated Jew and Gentile was not historically broken down until the Roman legions under Titus destroyed the temple in AD 70. At the time that Paul wrote this epistle, the wall was still standing—literally, *but not spiritually.*

As we have already seen, such "walling in" and "walling out" is not uncommon today. It rarely takes the form of literal concrete walls such as the balustrade of Herod's Temple or the impenetrable wall that divided the church building I visited in southern France. *Our dividing walls are much more subtle and intangible.* It is precisely their subtle, intangible character that makes them so powerful. We allow color, culture, and class, as well as a whole array of human sociological determinants—individualism, status quo bias, and religious consumerism—to regulate the definition of "our kind of people." We certainly never put up a sign stating that trespassers will be executed. We don't need to. In far too many churches, our homogeneity of ethnicity already speaks clearly and loudly of who is "in" and who is "out." What other explanation can

---

13. ʿAbodah Zarah 2:1.
14. Deissmann, *Ancient East*, 80; cf. Josephus, *Jewish Antiquities*, 15:417.

account for the fact that today a mere 7.5 percent of Christian churches can be classified as ethnically mixed?

DECONSTRUCTING THE DIVIDING WALL

What brought about the spiritual deconstruction of the dividing wall separating the Jewish people from the nations of the world? What is the basis of our unity as believers today across lines of ethnicity? How can diversity in unity replace diversity in alienation? The answer is given by Paul in verses 13–15:

> But now in Christ Jesus you who once were far away have been brought near through the blood of Christ. For he himself is our peace, who has made the two one and has destroyed the barrier, the dividing wall of hostility, by abolishing in his flesh the law with its commandments and regulations.

Having established the fact of disunity, Paul now addresses in these verses the means by which those who are "far off" have been "brought near." He demonstrates unequivocally that the *pax Christi* is God's antidote to relational estrangement, whether between Jew and Gentile or between any ethnicity existing today. Christ the Peacemaker has resolved the hostility.

The basis for bringing near those far off (i.e. the *ethnē*) is described in the phrase "through the blood of Christ" (v. 13). This, of course, is Christ's sacrificial cross-work about which Paul now details three specific results. First, Christ established peace between Jew and Gentile by unifying them—"making the two one." As Jesus' Jewish body hung on the cross, he grasped believing Jews with one hand and believing Gentiles with the other and brought them together as one body. This is the *togetherness* about which Paul has already spoken so much.

Second, this reconciliatory act necessitated the tearing down of the "barrier, the dividing wall." More literally, this is the barrier *formed by* the dividing wall. This has been understood in several ways.[15] Some have understood it to signify the partition in the temple referred to above, which isolated the court of the Gentiles (cf. Acts 21:27). This is not likely, however, as this barrier still stood even as Paul penned these words.

---

15. A thorough discussion of the various interpretations is found in Yee, *Ethnic Reconciliation*, 144–54 and Hoehner, *Ephesians*, 368–70. For a history of interpretation of Eph 2 see Rader, *Racial Hostility*.

Others have suggested the expression refers to the veil separating the Holy and Most Holy places in the temple, but this veil spoke particularly of the separation of all people from God and not specifically of the separation between Israel and the nations. Certainly the barrier formed by the "dividing wall of hostility" is a figure of speech referring to the Mosaic law. However, it was not the law itself that was the alienating force. It was rather the *misunderstood* and *misused law* that epitomized the dividing wall between Israel and the nations. The law, good in and of itself (cf. Rom 3:31), had been misappropriated as an ethnic-defining boundary marker to consolidate Jewish identity.

The manner in which this wall was deconstructed is suggested by the third descriptive word, "abolishing" (*katargēsas*) in verse 15. Here, the word carries the idea of "rendering powerless" (cf. Heb 2:14). In his death, Christ rendered powerless the Mosaic law, consisting of various ordinances. Such "ordinances" were the "rules of the law" (or halakic rulings) governing the conduct of devout Jews.[16] The effect of such detailed and often misunderstood and misused ordinances was hostility between Israel and the nations of the earth (Eph 2:14, 16). This hostility was religious in nature, but it was more than that. It became social and ethnic.

In the Old Testament, God intended that Israel be a source of blessing to the nations. What was intended to be a source of blessing, however, became a source of alienation. The good news is that this hostility, too, was nullified. Essentially, Christ destroyed the fruit (hostility) by rendering powerless the root (the law). The New Living Translation states it concisely: "By his death he ended the whole system of Jewish law that excluded the Gentiles" (2:15). Christ "ended" the law by satisfying the law. Furthermore, all of this was accomplished "in his flesh." "By accepting death in his human Jewish circumcised body," writes J. Coutts, "he brought death to the enmity for which circumcision stood, and united Jew and Gentile."[17] The very hostility brought about by a sign in the flesh was nullified by Christ's death in the flesh. Jewish circumcision "in the flesh" was *exclusive*. But Christ's crucifixion "in the flesh" was *inclusive*! Amazingly, the very enmity that put Christ on the cross was abolished by the cross! He gave his Jewish body in sacrifice, and from his side came a new body, the New Humanity, the inclusive, multiethnic church.

16. Yee, *Ethnic Reconciliation*, 157.
17. Coutts, "Ephesians and Colossians," 206.

RECONSTRUCTING DIVERSITY IN UNITY

It is this positive aspect of uniting Jew and Gentile—as well as believers of *all* ethnicities—that Paul now discusses.

> His purpose was to create in himself *one new man* out of the two, thus making peace, and in this one body to reconcile both of them to God through the cross, by which he put to death their hostility. He came and preached peace to you who were far away and peace to those who were near. For through him we both have access to the Father by one Spirit. (Eph 2:15b–18; emphasis mine)

The precise identity of this "one new man" (Eph 2:15) is dependent on several factors besides the Jew-Gentile dichotomy already mentioned. Before addressing these issues, it would be well to note the wide diversity of opinion among interpreters as to the meaning of this expression "one new man." Many commentators either do not deal with the concept at all or hurriedly interpret it to be a "new creation," a man quite separate from the previous one, or "all post-cross humanity."[18] Among those who do attempt to interpret the concept, three basic views emerge. First, there are those who prefer even here an individualistic interpretation, asserting that Christ has given to *individual* Jews and Gentiles a new *nature*.[19] Others contend that the one new man is either Christ himself[20] or Christ *and* his body, the church.[21] The third interpretation is quite similar to the second except that the church alone (to be distinguished from its head, Christ) is the one new man.[22]

Any individualistic interpretation of the new man in Ephesians 2 must be rejected on at least two counts. First, those who argue for such an interpretation often begin with the mention of the new man in Ephesians 4:22–24 and Colossians 3:9–11 where an individual interpretation is assumed and then read this back into Ephesians 2:15. Second, an individualization of the one new man is simply not contextually congruent with the controlling idea of the pericope, which pertains first to peace between Jew and Gentile and then to the reconciliation of both to

---

18. See Lenski, *Interpretation*, 442; Abbot, *Epistles*, 65; Westcott, *Ephesians*, 38.
19. Needham, *Birthright*, 74–75, 83.
20. So Best, *One Body*, 153, who states that "the one new man is not a corporate personality but a genuine *individual*" (emphasis mine).
21. See Hanson, *Unity of the Church*, 80.
22. Barth, *Ephesians*, 1:309. See also the NEB—"new humanity."

The New Humanity

God. A further exploration of this text and context will help determine the precise identity of the one new man and its implications for the dividing walls of ethnicity in the church today.

The Genesis Link

We cannot understand who we are as the new man until we understand who we were as the old man. We also cannot understand our identity as the old man until we see its connection to the first man, Adam. Paul's use of the terms "create," "man," and "new" in these verses implies an interpretive link to the creation account of the first man in Genesis 1–2 as well as to the disruptive events to follow in Genesis 3. We can hardly read these words in Ephesians 2 without thinking of when God created the first man:

> Then God said, "Let us make man in our image." . . . So God created man in his image, in the image of God he created him, male and female he created them. (Gen 1:26–27)

Paul is very selective in his choice of words to describe the new man of Ephesians 2:15. His use of the word "create" (*ktizō*) presupposes the Old Testament doctrine of creation, strongly suggesting that the creation account of Genesis 1:26–27 is the interpretive link to understanding the creation of the one new man. Whatever the one new man is, he is not contrived or concocted by man, but created by God! No amount of biological engineering could ever bring this new man into existence.

Beyond this, Paul chooses the term "man" (*anthrōpos*) in describing this new entity rather than "people" (*laos*) or "nation" (*ethnos*), even though several Old Testament passages would favor using the latter two terms.[23] Just as for the Hebrew term *'ādām*, the basic underlying concept of *anthrōpos* is "generic man," the "human race," or "mankind." Aristotle brings out the corporate meaning of the term when he speaks of a multitude of citizens coming together to form "one man" and later Arrianus can term humanity "the ideal man."[24]

When we come to the New Testament, the term *anthrōpos* is consistently distinguished from *aner*, which can mean a man as contrasted to woman (Matt 14:21; 15:38); a husband (Matt 19:3, 9; Mark 10:2; Rom

---

23. See Ezek 37:15–28; especially verses 17, 19, 27, 28; cf. 2 Bar. 48:24; 85:14.
24. Aristotle, *Politica*, 3.6.4; Arrianus, *Epict.* 2.9.3; cf. MM, 43; Vorländer, *NIDNTT*, 562.

7:2); an adult male (1 Cor 13:11); manliness (Luke 23:59); or on occasion man, as genus (Luke 5:8). It is only in the latter sense that *aner* most nearly approximates the collective meaning of *anthrōpos*.[25] The point of these distinctions is this: the emphasis of the designation "one new man" is on the *solidarity* rather than the *individuality* of its constituents. Paul's choice of vocabulary is intentional. His emphasis is upon humanity viewed *collectively*, not individually.

Not only do the concepts of "creation" and "man" link the one new man to the account of beginnings in Genesis 1, but so also does the concept of "newness." The creation of the *new* man is the divine response to the corruption of the *old* man, birthed through the disruptive events of Genesis 3. The concept of "newness" appears in all but seven of the New Testament books. In the majority of cases, the term "new" (*kainos/neos*) carries a distinctly eschatological flavor. The transition from the old to the new is a transition to a "new order of life—the life order of the new creation, the new man."[26]

Paul's "Adam theology" has been the topic of much discussion in recent years, particularly as to the source of his thought. Apart from his firm rooting in Old Testament theology and the factor of direct revelation, it is quite possible that Paul drew to some degree upon the contemporary rabbinical teaching concerning Adam.[27] Though much of this Jewish speculation concerning Adam was extremely fanciful and not serious theology, it did serve one dominant interest—*it emphasized the unity of all mankind in Adam*. This of course is paralleled by Paul's teaching in such passages as Romans 5:19: "Through the disobedience of the one the many were made sinners." Paul's words to the Corinthians are similar: "For in Adam all die" (1 Cor 15:22). What is true of the one is true of the many. Moreover, in rabbinical thought, Adam was in some way a prototype of the eschatological man. In the same way, Paul views the second man, Christ, as not only historical and individual, but also eschatological and collective: "So also through

---

25. J. H. Moulton and G. Milligan note that "The New Testament has no trace of the curious misuse by which the principal difference between *anthropos* and *aner* is ignored." MM, 44.

26. Ridderbos, *Paul*, 63.

27. Scroggs, *Last Adam*, 32. It is true that most of the rabbinic logia about Adam are later than the first century AD. However, if one takes apocryphal, pseudepigraphal, and rabbinic thought together, it is fair to say that Jewish interest in Adam was high in the first to third centuries.

the obedience of the one man the many will be made righteous" (Rom 5:19). As Robin Scroggs notes, "Paul's Christology of the Last Adam is primarily directed toward illuminating and assuring the Christian's hope of eschatological humanity."[28]

Paul's consistency in contrasting Christ, the second man, to Adam, the first man (Rom 5:12, 21; 1 Cor 15:45, 47) is also evidenced in his contrast of the new man to the old man (Rom 6:1–15; Eph 4:22–24; Col 3:9–11). In keeping with Paul's interpretive distinctions, the new man stands in contrast *not* to Adam, the first man, but rather to Adam's fallen and corporately alienated progeny. "The contrast here is not Adam . . . but the 'old man,' man under the domination of sin, conceived as a kind of 'corporate personality.'"[29] This would also suggest that the one new man is best understood to be the corporately reconciled body of Christ, the church. While in intimate relation to its head, Christ, it is nevertheless distinct.

That this is the case is also confirmed by Paul's expression "in himself" (v.15) as the sphere in which this New Humanity is created. The expression "in himself" is simply the equivalent of the favorite Pauline expression "in Christ" (1:1, 3, 10, 12, 20; 2:6, 7, 10) that describes the identification of the church with Christ in his death, burial, and resurrection (see vv. 5–6, 10, 13). The expression can be compared to a very small key that opens a large door that leads into an expansive room or building. The phrase "in Christ" or its equivalent "in him" or "in whom"[30] is that small key to understanding Paul's grand theme of togetherness.

This collective identification with Christ is the basis for the characteristics of newness and unity expressed both in the term "new man" as well as in other Pauline passages such as Galatians 3:28—"for you are all one (Gk. *eis*—i.e. one "man") *in* Christ Jesus" (emphasis mine). This close relationship between Christ and his body is further amplified by the parallelism between "in himself" and "in one body" (*en eni sōmati*) in verse 16 (cf. Acts 9:4). However, this parallelism does *not* imply that the two are synonymous. While the one body is not independent of

28. Ibid., 59.

29. Dahl, "Christ, Creation and the Church," 436.

30. The references are as follows: "in Christ" (1:1, 3, 10, 12, 20; 2:6, 7, 10, 13; 3:6, 11, 21); "in him" (1:4, 9, 10; 2:15, 16); "in the beloved" (1:6); "in whom" (1:7, 11, 13 [bis]; 2:21, 22; 3:12); "in the Lord" (1:15; 2:21; 4:1); "in his blood" (2:13); "in his flesh" (2:14); "in Jesus" (4:21).

Christ, it is distinct from Christ as its head.[31] *This only confirms that the church, the body of Christ, is the one new man.* As such, the one new man—the New Humanity—is the sphere in which reconciliation of Jew and Gentile takes place and in which both together are reconciled to God. It is in the New Humanity that diversity in unity replaces diversity in alienation.

Two Men and Their "Girdle Strings"

Several years ago, I transplanted some lavender from one part of the yard to another. Not only did we prefer the new location for aesthetic purposes, but the soil and exposure to the sun were better suited for the shrub. Essentially we moved the plant from one soil and climate to another, which enhanced its growth. Likewise, those who are in Christ and members of the New Humanity have been "transplanted into a new soil and a new climate, and both soil and climate are Christ."[32] Paul also uses this image in writing to the Romans. He says, "If we have been united with him like this in his death, we will certainly also be united with him in his resurrection" (Rom 6:5). The expression "united with him" was used in the first century of trees planted *together* in the same bed and that grow *together* as one. Likewise all believers, regardless of color or culture, have been transplanted *together* into a new "soil" and a new "climate." Essentially, we have changed "geography" and have adopted a new shared identity. As to soil and climate, there are only two options: Adam and his corporately alienated humanity or Christ and his corporately reconciled humanity.

How can such solidarity exist among those in Adam and among those in Christ? To grasp what Paul is saying, we need to throw off for the moment the rugged individualism of our culture and look at what I termed in chapter 2 the "relational solidarity" of the human race. There I made reference to Henry Wheeler Robinson and his concept of "corporate personality." This collective perspective of unity allows any constituent member of a group to be addressed *as the whole* of the group. In turn, the whole group may be addressed *as a single entity*. Likewise, any constituent member of the group may speak *representing the whole*, or

---

31. Smith, "Two Made One," 52, note 74. Furthermore, in the New Testament and the apostolic fathers *en eni sōmati* ("in one body") and *en sōma* ("one body") always mean the church, with the one exception of 1 Cor 6:16.

32. J. S. Stewart cited by Ryrie, *Balancing*, 50.

the whole may speak *representing one of the members*.³³ One of the best New Testament examples is found in Hebrews 7:9–10: "One might even say that Levi, who collects the tenth, paid the tenth through Abraham, because when Melchizedek met Abraham, *Levi was still in the body of his ancestor*" (emphasis mine). Here we have Abraham paying a tithe to Melchizedek; but then, generations later, Levi and those of the tribe of Levi, are said to have paid the tithe "*in* Abraham" their ancestor!

We also have contemporary illustrations of this same truth. If your grandfather died at the age of three, where would you be today? Your experience is inevitably and inseparably bound up with his. In the same way, your spiritual experience is inevitably and inseparably bound up with Adam's. Each person reading these words has two parents, four grandparents, eight great-grandparents, and sixteen great-great grandparents. If you multiply by two for each generation, it's technically possible for you to have more than a million ancestors by going back only twenty generations. The whole mass of humanity is a mixture of distant cousins, and we are all bound together in the shared sinfulness of the human race.³⁴

From a biblical standpoint, the unity envisioned by Paul is not so much psychological (as implied by Robinson's term "corporate *personality*"), as it is covenantal, springing from a covenantal relationship with Yahweh. In view of this, the term "corporate solidarity" is to be preferred over "corporate personality." Paul views all mankind in a relationship of corporate solidarity with either the first man, Adam, or the second man, Christ. The Old Humanity, in relation to the first man, Adam, is under the rule of sin (Rom 5:12–14) and death (1 Cor 15:22) and is alienated from God (Eph 4:18) and from fellow man (Eph 2:11–13; see Gen 4:1–8). The New Humanity, in relation to the second man, Christ, experiences life (1 Cor 15:22), righteousness (Rom 5:19), and the restoration of relational unity (Eph 2:14–15; Col 3:11; Gal 3:17). "In God's sight there are two men—Adam and Christ—and these two men have all other men hanging at their girdle strings."³⁵

---

33. Robinson, *Corporate Personality*, 3.
34. Barnhouse, *Romans*, 229.
35. Thomas Goodwin cited by Bruce, *Romans*, 127.

THE MYSTERY OF THE NEW HUMANITY

I love mysteries. The gradual unfolding suspense of a well-written mystery can keep me riveted for hours. An experienced writer of thriller mysteries will often introduce various people and circumstances that at first appear obscure and unrelated, but then converge as the suspenseful plot unfolds. The often clandestine ambiance relentlessly engages me, spurring me to read on in hopes of unraveling the unexplained elements.

The world's *greatest* mystery, however, is something quite different. "Mystery" (*mystērion*) in the Bible doesn't mean that which is dark, obscure, occult, clandestine, or puzzling like a maze or labyrinth. The biblical idea of "mystery" means simply a truth previously concealed, but now revealed. It also carries the idea of something that is *impossible* for man to comprehend or penetrate on his own; it must be revealed by God. Divine revelation, not human speculation, unlocks the door of understanding the mystery of which the biblical writers speak.

In Ephesians 3:2–6 Paul explains the mystery of the New Humanity by the imagery of the body:

> Surely you have heard about the administration of God's grace that was given to me for you, that is, the *mystery* made known to me by revelation, as I have already written briefly. In reading this, then, you will be able to understand my insight into the *mystery* of Christ, which was not made known to men in other generations as it has now been revealed by the Spirit to God's holy apostles and prophets. This *mystery* is that through the gospel the Gentiles are heirs together with Israel, members together of one body, and sharers together in the promise in Christ Jesus. (emphasis mine)

What then is the "mystery" of which Paul speaks? Paul tells us in unmistakable "this is that" terms in verse 6: "This mystery is that through the gospel *the Gentiles are heirs together with Israel, members together of one body, and sharers together in the promise in Christ Jesus*" (Eph 3:6; emphasis mine). Paul uses three terms in this one verse that emphasize the essential nature of this mystery that we have already highlighted: "heirs together," "members together," and "sharers together." To be sure we get the point, the expression "members together" (*synsōma*) comes from an entirely new word coined by Paul and found in no other writer.

Togetherness in Christ's body. That is what the biblical mystery is all about. The mystery is this: *All who trust in Christ—whether Jews or*

Gentiles (i.e. all non-Jews)—enjoy equality and full privileges before God, having been united in this one organic body called the New Humanity. This truth is called a "mystery" because it was hidden in the Old Testament. To be sure, the idea that nations outside of Israel would experience salvation *is* made known in the Old Testament. God promised Abraham that in his descendants "all *nations* would be blessed" (Gen 12:3). However, the idea that God's chosen people would one day be *redefined* as an inclusive covenant community in which believers from non-Jewish nations would have full spiritual equality is a concept completely foreign to the Old Testament writers. In this sense, the church has not *replaced* Israel (Rom 9–11). What has been replaced is the covenantal ethnocentrism that came to characterize the people of God.[36] This is the mystery of togetherness of which Paul speaks. This is God's "secret wisdom" (1 Cor 2:7). It is wisdom for it is the antidote to the relational and ethnic estrangement characteristic of Babel and the Old Humanity. It is secret because, though now revealed, it was previously concealed.

The mystery of the New Humanity is sketched in Figure 5.1. It all began when the great Three-in-One—Father, Son, and Holy Spirit—created mankind as his image. As the *imago Dei*, humanity was created from the dust to rule as God's authoritative vice-regent over the earth (Gen 1:26, 27; 2:7). Furthermore, as God's likeness-image, man was created to resemble his Creator, sharing in such communicable divine attributes as "love," "righteousness," "goodness," "truth," and "relational oneness." Finally, humanity was created as a plurality (Adam/Eve), mirroring the diversity in unity characteristic of his Maker.

All of this was tragically compromised at the Fall. Through one act of disobedience (Rom 5:19), humanity's essence and role as the *imago Dei* was severely marred, giving birth to the Old Humanity characterized by divisiveness and death. The relational diversity in unity characteristic of humanity before the Fall became diversity in alienation after the Fall. Babel stands as the epitome of such relational estrangement, only to be later reflected in the growing hostility between Jew and Gentile. In

---

36. While the precise relationship between Israel and the church in the New Humanity is beyond the scope of this book, Franz Mussner's conclusion is accurate: "The Church is not the people of God which has taken the place of Israel, the Old Testament people of God. Rather, according to Rom 11:1, the Church is only 'the participant in the root' (Israel and its forefathers), the extended people of God who *together* with Israel form the one people of God." Mussner, *Tractate*, 9. See Blaising and Bock, *Dispensationalism*, 117–19 and *Progressive Dispensationalism*, 232–83.

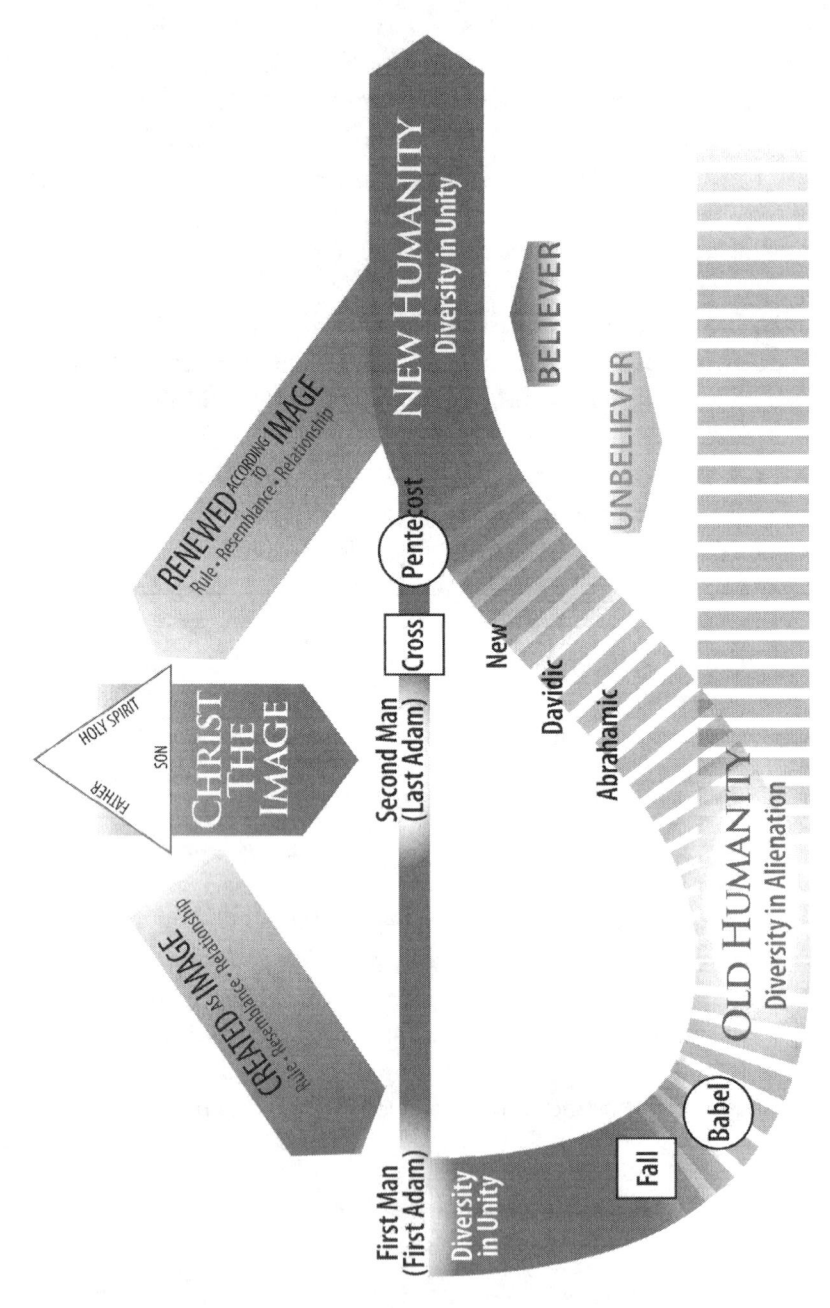

Figure 5.1

keeping with the *protoevangelium* of Genesis 3:15, however, God graciously intervened by means of three unconditional covenants that are *inclusive* in scope.

Following on the heels of Babel (Gen 10–11), God immediately enacted his covenant with Abraham promising that through him all peoples of the earth would be blessed (Gen 12:1–3; Gal 3:6–18). Later, God's promises became more precise in his covenant made with David (2 Sam 7; 1 Chr 17; Ps 89, 110, 132). This covenant provided the means by which the universal blessing of the Abrahamic covenant would be realized among the nations. Both the Abrahamic and Davidic covenant find their ultimate fulfillment in the new covenant made at the cross (Matt 26:28; Luke 22:20; 1 Cor 11:25). This covenant promised a heart regenerated and indwelt by God's Spirit, the forgiveness of sin, and the resurrection unto eternal life (Isa 55:3–5; Jer 31:33–34; Ezek 36:27). Furthermore, it provided the promise of reconciliation among the nations (Isa 51:4–5; 60:16–17).

The fulfillment of these three unconditional covenants is ultimately realized in the person and work of the second man, the last Adam, Jesus Christ. As the *very* image of God (1 Cor 11:7; 2 Cor 4:4; Col 1:15), he is the head of a new progeny, the New Humanity, composed of all who believe. The New Humanity was conceived at the cross and born at Pentecost. What the first man, Adam, failed to accomplish, the second man, Christ, fully accomplished. The cross is God's remedy to the Fall; Pentecost is God's remedy to Babel. Both the cross and Pentecost are foundational to the present and future aspects of the promised new covenant blessings.

As we await the full realization of these blessings, the New Humanity lives in the present tension of the already/but not yet. Believers of every ethnicity are *already* made alive *together*, raised *together*, and seated *together* in the heavenly realms in Christ (Eph 2:5–6). In this sense, we already experience partially that which one day we will experience fully. Our present vocation as the New Humanity is to live in accordance with our true identity. To the degree that we do, we are renewed according the image of our Creator in precisely the three areas so profoundly marred by man's sinful rebellion—rule, resemblance, and relationship (Eph 4:23–24; Col 3:10–11). This will be the topic of chapter 8.

We must not overlook the *newness* of the New Humanity.[37] Once again, Paul's choice of vocabulary is intentional, highlighting several key elements intrinsic to the New Testament concept of newness. First, there is the aspect of *contrast*. This is particularly seen in Paul's well-known words of 2 Corinthians 5:17—"Therefore, if anyone is in Christ he is a new creation; the old has gone, the new has come." A marked contrast is drawn between the characteristics of the past (i.e. sin and relational disharmony) and the fresh qualities intrinsic to the new (i.e. righteousness and relational harmony). This same contrast is highlighted in Paul's juxtaposition of the *new* man of Ephesians 2:15 with the *old* man of Romans 6:6, Ephesians 4:22, and Colossians 3:9. While the old man is characterized by disharmony and alienation, the new man is the arena of peace and reconciliation (Eph 2:15–16). We will never be all we were meant to be until we realize that we are no longer who we used to be.

The implications of this for the church today are obvious, speaking directly to our complacency vis-à-vis the dividing walls that fragment the body of Christ. The segregation of the church along lines of ethnicity—or any other contrived boundary markers (worship style, affinity groups, socioeconomic class)—is a distinctive feature of the old rather than the new. It is a return to Babel. It must be identified for what it is and "put off" (Eph 4:22–24; Col 3:9–11) as we strive to live out our true identity as the one new man.

In contrasting the new to the old, Paul is *not* talking about a leveling of ethnic differences. He is rather addressing a prevalent ethnocentric perspective that deems such differences as grounds for segregation. The peace and reconciliation characteristic of the New Humanity does *not* lead to a homogeneous solidarity in which ethnic identity or distinctiveness is lost.[38] In the New Humanity, distinctions are not abolished

---

37. Of two choices, Paul selects the term *kainos* over *neos* to express the newness of this "man." A study of the two terms from their classical usage up through New Testament times indicates that while *neos* carries most frequently a temporal nuance, the term *kainos* as used to describe the "one new man" includes both aspects of time and quality. There is a distinction between the terms, but not one that is best described as temporal verses qualitative (contra. Trench, *Synonyms*, 219–24). Rather, *kainos* looks backward while *neos* looks forward. The term *kainos* has the sense of "not yet having been" and can have a temporal focus (what is new in that it has not previously existed) or a qualitative focus (that which takes the place of what previously existed). On the other hand, *neos* describes quite consistently something as "not having been long" and looks forward. See Cremer, *BTL*, 32; Behm, *TDNT*, 3:447–48; Lightfoot, *Epistles*, 215; Harrisville, *Newness*, 11, 73–74.

38. Rom 1:16; 9:24; 1 Cor 1:24; 12:13; Gal 2:14–15.

or ignored. Distinctions still exist, but *evaluations* based on ethnicity or any other boundary markers do not. In light of this, I believe Ernest Best misses the point entirely when he states:

> There are Jews and there are Gentiles; but the Jews that become Christians *lose their* Jewishness and are not Jewish Christians, and the Gentiles that become Christians *lose their* Gentile-ness and are not Gentile Christians; both are simply Christians—a third and new type of man distinct from the twofold classification of Jew and Gentile. There are now three races of men, Jews, Gentiles, and Christians.[39]

In the New Humanity, the two are made one, *but this does not abolish or minimize distinctions between ethnic groups*. They all remain mutually dependent, yet ethnically distinct. Jews do *not* become Gentiles and Gentiles do *not* become Jews. The deconstruction of the dividing wall was not intended to make Africans more American or Koreans more Kurdish. No, in the New Humanity, differences are not abolished or ignored, but appreciated and included as vital to defining our collective identity in Christ and manifesting the same diversity in unity characteristic of the Trinity. This new race, the New Humanity, is raceless only in the sense that ethnicity must never be the criteria for determining fellowship with God or with fellow believers. In other words, ethnic identity should no longer be a boundary marker for determining group identity, including the group identity of the local church. In the New Humanity, the only boundary marker is Christ. *The determining factor of commonality is no longer ethnicity, affinity, or cultural and sociological allegiances or preferences, but Christ* (Col 3:11). C. S. Lewis states it well: "The church is not a human society of people united by their natural affinities, but the Body of Christ, in which all members, however different (and he rejoices in their differences and by no means wishes to iron them out) must share the common life."[40]

A second feature of newness is its *dynamic character*. This builds on the aspect of "contrast" in that the new actually asserts itself over the old and crowds it out of existence. That seems to be a specific nuance characterizing the New Humanity of Ephesians 2:15 and 4:24. There is an

---

39. Best, *One Body*, 154. Some critics of the early Christians referred to them as a *tertium genus*, a "third race." For a detailed discussion of the expression, see Wright, "A Race Apart," 134–37; Yee, *Ethnic Reconciliation*, 166, note 151

40. Lewis, *Letters*, 7 December 1950.

intentional exclusion of that which was particularly characteristic of the past. As will be seen, this is Paul's emphasis throughout Ephesians 4–6. The appeal of our newfound collective identity in Christ is to live consistently with who we truly are. In other words, the previously mentioned radical individualism and status quo bias that keep us bound in the shackles of a sociologically determined homogeneity must now be put off, for these are the sin tattered clothes that belong to the corporately alienated Old Humanity. In the New Humanity, the segregationist divisions of the past are thrown off and the reconciliatory unity of the present is put on!

Finally, the *eschatological implications* of newness suggest that this is God's final period in redemptive history. It is the moment of the already/but not yet. We are already *together* in Christ—regardless of culture, ethnicity, or socioeconomic status—seated *together* in the heavenly realms. Moreover, the presence of diverse ethnicities and cultures no longer compromises our togetherness; to the contrary, it enriches our togetherness. In the present, however, we experience only partially that which some day we will know fully. Much is yet to be literally fulfilled; nevertheless, the superior coming age has already dawned and the future can to some extent be experienced in the present! René Padilla writes: "That purpose is yet to be consummated. But *already*, in anticipation of the end, a new humanity has been created in Jesus Christ, and those who are incorporated in him form a unity wherein all the divisions that separate people in the old humanity are done away with. The original unity of the human race is thus restored; God's purpose of unity in Jesus Christ is thus made historically visible."[41]

Meditate on this mystery. At creation, God breathed into the first man's nostrils and he became a living soul. God then caused a deep sleep to fall upon Adam, during which time God opened his side, took one of his ribs, and fashioned a woman who was to be his bride and partner. Eve was the only woman in the history of mankind taken from her husband's body before being his bride. She was bone of his bone and flesh of his flesh.

In a similar way, the second man, Christ, was led to the cross and into the sleep of death. His side was pierced, and the blood that flowed from his wound gave birth to the New Humanity—"bone of his bone and flesh of his flesh." Then once again the great Three-in-One breathed and the New Humanity became a living organism.

The New Humanity, even as Eve, is both body and bride—one flesh with the Head and bride of the Head. As Eve had no existence apart from

---

41. Padilla, "Unity of the Church," 287.

Adam, so the church, the New Humanity, has no existence apart from Christ. The Old Humanity with Adam as its head has now been superseded by the New Humanity with Christ as its head. Both at the cross and Pentecost, Jesus more than replaced what Adam erased. The ecstasy of community has been restored, and the Trinity rejoices!

CONCLUSION

Where there is revelation, there is also responsibility. If, by God's grace, Paul received this revelation of the mystery, it is also God's grace that commissioned Paul to the ministry: "I became a servant of this gospel by the gift of God's grace given me through the working of his power" (Eph 3:7).

The mystery is truth revealed *to* Paul; the gospel is truth preached *by* Paul.[42] But the mystery and the gospel are one in the same. The mystery of Jew and Gentile being united into one new, living organism called the New Humanity is what Paul preached, and he was willing to die for this message. That is why he tells his readers not to be discouraged by his sufferings: "I ask you, therefore, not to be discouraged because of my sufferings for you, which are your glory" (Eph 3:13; cf. Col 1:24). For Paul, suffering on behalf of the church and its growth in unity was a privilege. Because of his understanding of the crucial role of the church in God's program, Paul was willing to suffer intensely for the establishment and ongoing unity of Christ's church. This included not only being in prison, but also suffering from and persevering through misunderstandings, divisions, and even verbal attacks from other believers. Why? Because he knew he had been entrusted with the stewardship of the mystery, the truth of all peoples being united in God's New Humanity.

This is now our privilege. In the following chapters we will discover the same diversity in unity that characterizes the universal New Humanity was not only *permitted* but also intentionally *nurtured* in the geographical expressions of the New Humanity—local churches. This was the high road, and the high road was not the easy road. It would have been much easier to allow believers to group themselves according to their natural affinities as determined by color, culture, and class, but to do so would compromise the mystery of the gospel. The same holds true today.

---

42. Stott, *God's New Society*, 118.

6

Babel Reversed

> *The Jerusalem Decree also cries aloud at every attempt to solve the conflicts arising out of cultural differences among Christians by resorting to the formation of separate congregations, each representing a different homogeneous unit.*
>
> René Padilla

BOTH AT THE CROSS and at Pentecost, Jesus replaced what Adam erased. One is incomplete without the other. Conception and birth go hand in hand. If the cross brought about the conception of the New Humanity, Pentecost brought about the birth of the New Humanity. Just as a child is conceived and then born, so also the New Humanity is conceived (Eph 2) and then birthed into this world (Acts 2). At Pentecost, the *mystery* of the New Humanity became the *reality* of the New Humanity.

The entire account is well-known but deserves to be read again with fresh eyes:

> When the day of Pentecost came, they were all together in one place. Suddenly a sound like the blowing of a violent wind came from heaven and filled the whole house where they were sitting. They saw what seemed to be tongues of fire that separated and came to rest on each of them. All of them were filled with the Holy Spirit and began to speak in other tongues as the Spirit enabled them. Now there were staying in Jerusalem God-fearing Jews from every nation under heaven. When they heard this sound, a crowd came together in bewilderment, because each one

heard them speaking in his own language. Utterly amazed, they asked: "Are not all these men who are speaking Galileans? Then how is it that each of us hears them in his own native language? Parthians, Medes and Elamites; residents of Mesopotamia, Judea and Cappadocia, Pontus and Asia, Phrygia and Pamphylia, Egypt and the parts of Libya near Cyrene; visitors from Rome (both Jews and converts to Judaism); Cretans and Arabs—we hear them declaring the wonders of God in our own tongues!" Amazed and perplexed, they asked one another, "What does this mean?" (Acts 2:1–12)

According to the most reliable calculations, the events recorded here by Luke took place on Sunday, May 24, AD 33.[1] On this day, the multinational, multilingual, multiethnic organism called the church officially moved out of its period of gestation and into the world for all to see. As God breathed into the first man and he became a living being, so God now breathes into the new man and he too becomes a living organism. What is conceived at the cross is now animated at Pentecost. The New Humanity is born.

A body without breath is a corpse. An individual or a church without the Holy Spirit is spiritually dead. A. W. Tozer once said, "If the Holy Spirit was withdrawn from the church today, 95 percent of what we do would go on and *no one* would know the difference." But then he adds: "If the Holy Spirit had been withdrawn from the New Testament church, 95 percent of what they did would stop, and *everybody* would know the difference."[2] As we will see, apart from the supernatural, unifying work of God's Spirit, any attempt to live out our true identity as God's New Humanity will prove futile. Only as we discover the reality of our oneness sourced in the Holy Spirit can we live out an authentic diversity in unity in the body of Christ. Such unity is a supernatural experience and can never be contrived or manufactured or organized by mere human effort. This is the message of Pentecost.

PENTECOST: BABEL REVERSED

Luke begins his story by stating, "When the day of Pentecost came" (2:1). Pentecost was one of seven important feasts celebrated by the Jews. Each of these feasts was a divinely purposed illustration prefiguring a

1. Hoehner, *Chronological Aspects*, 143.
2. Original source unknown.

corresponding spiritual reality. Three of these feasts were celebrated in the Jewish month of Nisan (our March/April):

- Passover: illustrating *redemption in* Christ (fourteenth day of the month)
- Unleavened Bread: illustrating *communion with* Christ (fifteenth day of the month)
- Firstfruits: illustrating the *resurrection of* Christ (sixteenth day of the month)

Fifty days following the festival of Firstfruits came Pentecost, meaning "fiftieth" (*pentēkostos*). The Old Testament explanation of this festival is found in Leviticus 23:15–21. Verses 16–17 of that chapter speak of the importance of what Luke describes for us in Acts 2:

> Count off fifty days up to the day after the seventh Sabbath, and then present an *offering of new grain* to the LORD. From wherever you live, bring *two loaves* made of two-tenths of an ephah of fine flour, baked with yeast, as a wave offering of firstfruits to the LORD. (emphasis mine)[3]

For Israel, Pentecost was a time of *harvest*. They presented an "offering of new grain" to the Lord. For the church also Pentecost was a time of great harvest, not agriculturally, but spiritually. According to Luke, on this day alone more than 3,000 people came to faith in Jesus Christ (Acts 2:41; cf. John 14:12–14). Such harvest is but the firstfruits of the rich blessing upon all nations promised to Abraham.

Pentecost was also a time of *unity*. Later in Israel's history, it became one of the great pilgrimage feasts when Jews scattered throughout the Roman world would return to Jerusalem (Acts 20:16). In fact, such unity is already implied in the offering of the "two loaves" of bread. The New Testament tells us those two loaves are both Jew and Gentile now bound together in one body and given the same Holy Spirit. Jesus said to his disciples, "I have other sheep that are not of this sheep pen. I must bring them also. They too will listen to my voice, and there shall be one flock and one shepherd" (John 10:16). Furthermore, Paul writes to the Corinthians, "Because there is one loaf, we, who are many, are one body, for we all partake of the one loaf" (1 Cor 10:17).

---

3. Amazingly, this is the only offering to have yeast, possibly implying that what is born will be far from perfect.

On this particular day, the disciples—about 120 of them we are told in Acts 1:15—were gathered in one place. They had been told by Jesus himself to wait. "Do not leave Jerusalem, but wait for the gift my Father promised, which you have heard me speak about. For John baptized with water, but in a few days you will be baptized with the Holy Spirit" (Acts 1:4–5). Before the message could progress, the men (the missionaries) had to be prepared. They're simply doing what Jesus told them to do; they're staying in Jerusalem and waiting . . . and praying.

This is where the story gets exciting. Suddenly, there is supernatural *sound, sight,* and *speech*. The *sound* is like the "blowing of a violent wind." Moses tells us that God breathed into the first man's nostrils and he became a living soul (Gen 2:7). Jesus tells us: "The wind blows wherever it pleases. You hear its sound, but you cannot tell where it comes from or where it is going. So is everyone who is born of the Spirit" (John 3:8). The Spirit is like a wind, bringing life. Here, as in the creation account, the great Three-in-One breathes, bringing life to the New Humanity already conceived at the cross.

Then there is the *sight* of "what seemed to be tongues of fire." If the wind speaks of life and power, then the tongues speak of passion and purity (Deut 5:4). In Exodus 19, God descends on Mount Sinai in fire and smoke as the Ten Commandments are given to Moses, marking the birth of the nation of Israel. Here, tongues of fire descend on the disciples, marking the birth of the church. As Moses came down from Mount Sinai with "tables of stone, written with the finger of God" (Exod 31:18), so at Pentecost the Spirit of God comes down from heaven, taking the law of God and writing it on human hearts (Heb 8:10; 10:16).

Finally, we see the disciples *speaking* in other tongues. No question here of incoherent utterances or mere ecstatic groans. That these tongues are real languages and *not* inarticulate babbling or unintelligible sounds is clear from what follows. More than fifteen different nationalities and dialects (listed in verses 5–12) make up the crowd of people witnessing this phenomenon. They all hear the disciples speaking the wonders of God *in their own language*!

What we have here is nothing less than a reversal of the experience of the Tower of Babel (Gen 11), a truth noted by commentators since the early church fathers. Think of it. At Babel, humanity arrogantly ascends toward heaven, attempting to restore on its own terms relationship with God and fellow man. The initiative proves disastrous.

At Pentecost, heaven humbly yet powerfully descends to man in the third person of the Trinity, reconciling the irreconcilable. At Babel, the languages are confused and the people dispersed. At Pentecost, the languages are understood and the people unified. At Babel, the people are scattered as an act of judgment. Following Pentecost, the people are also eventually scattered, preaching God's blessing upon the nations (Acts 8:4). While Babel depicts earth's divided nations, Pentecost is God's "United Nations."

To drive this point home, Luke goes out of his way to note that those witnessing this phenomenon were "from every nation under heaven" (Acts 2:5). This was not uncommon for the feast of Pentecost, which typically drew thousands to Jerusalem. According to Josephus, the city of Jerusalem, which normally had a population of about fifty thousand, would swell to nearly one million during the holy time between Passover and Pentecost. Though largely composed of God-fearing Jews, the majority of these visitors came from the dispersion. While many were Jews or Jewish proselytes, they nevertheless functioned as representatives of their homelands. Obviously, something spectacular is about to take place in fulfillment of God's promise to bring blessing to the very nations dispersed at the Tower of Babel.

Luke, of course, is speaking from his own worldview in reference to "every nation under heaven," referring specifically to the Greco-Roman world around the Mediterranean basin. What is striking, however, is not those omitted from his list (for example, Native Americans and Australian aboriginals), but those mentioned in his list. He describes five major people groups, apparently moving from east to west:

- Peoples from the Caspian Sea westward (v. 9a): Parthians, Medes, Elamites, and residents of Mesopatamia. Many of these were descended from the Jewish exiles displaced there in the eighth and sixth centuries BC.

- Peoples of Asia Minor or Turkey (vv. 9b–10a): Cappadocia (east), Pontus (north), Asia (west), and Phrygia and Pamphylia (south).

- Peoples of North Africa (v. 10b): Egypt and the parts of Libya near Cyrene.

- Visitors from Rome across the Mediterranean (vv. 10c–11a): This would include both Jews and converts to Judaism.

- Cretans from the island of Crete and Arabs who lived east of Palestine between the Red Sea and the Euphrates River (v. 11b).[4]

Interestingly, the cosmopolitan character of the crowd included representatives of all three of the principal divisions of humanity mentioned in Genesis 10: Shem, Ham, and Japheth. Those previously divided by language were now hearing the gospel of reconciliation *in their own language* as the incontestable sign of the dramatic reversal of Babel. If they didn't speak Aramaic, they would have known Greek so technically there was no need for such a display of languages. Yet *each* heard the good news in the heart language from where he had come.

Those are the hearers, but what about the speakers? Luke points out that they were "Galileans" (Acts 2:7). Galilee was noted for its diverse mix of ethnicities. Assyrians, Babylonians, Egyptians, Macedonians, Persians, Romans, Syrians, and indigenous Canaanites were part of the multicultural mosaic of this region. Galileans were also known for their lack of culture and intellectual astuteness (John 1:46; 7:52). Recognized by their difficulty in articulating gutturals and their habit of swallowing syllables, those of the metropolis of Jerusalem viewed them as provincial.[5] Once again, the allusion to Babel is striking. In contrast to the arrogant pride of Nimrod and his Babylonian followers, God now works through humble Galileans—those outside the heart of cultural and religious Judaism—to declare the wonders of God in a multiplicity of tongues.

This is the message of Pentecost. The deconstruction of the Old Humanity has now been superseded by the creation and birth of the New Humanity. The alienation of Babel is now replaced by the reconciliation of Pentecost. The determining factor of "sameness" is no longer ethnicity, cultural affinity, personal preferences, or even denominational affiliation. It is Christ alone (Gal 3:28). The corporate solidarity of the New Humanity is realized by the presence of the Holy Spirit indwelling *each and every* member of the body of Christ. It is this truth that both Peter and Paul explain more fully.

---

4. This summary is adapted from Stott, *Spirit, Church and World*, 63–65.
5. Ibid., 65.

PENTECOST EXPLAINED BY PETER AND PAUL

Starting in verse 14, Peter stands up to speak, saying, "Let me explain this to you; listen carefully to what I say." After dismissing the ridiculous notion that these men are drunk, he quotes from Joel 2:28–29.

> In the last days, God says, I will pour out my Spirit *on all people.* Your sons and daughters will prophesy, your young men will see visions, your old men will dream dreams. Even on my servants, both men and women, I will pour out my Spirit in those days, and they will prophesy. (emphasis mine)

Peter makes it explicitly clear: The sounds, sight, and speech the crowds have just witnessed is in fulfillment of what the prophet Joel promised long ago. It isn't contrived, it isn't staged, and these people certainly aren't drunk. After all, who gets drunk at nine o'clock in the morning? No, what all have seen and heard is the sure sign that the Spirit of God has come as promised.

The Spirit is a going-away present from Jesus, his ascension gift to his disciples. Here, Jesus is saying, "I will now exchange my physical presence for my omnipresence." God's people, whether under the old covenant or the new, are known as the "people of the Presence" (i.e. God's presence). While in the Old Testament, the Spirit was at times *with* believers and *on* believers—empowering them to do God's will—he now at Pentecost comes to live permanently *in* believers. Pentecost is the fulfillment of God's promise to live *in* his people by his Holy Spirit.

The striking feature of Joel's statement as well as Peter's citation of it is that God's Spirit would be poured out on *all* people. The immediate context clearly indicates that here Joel is speaking of all the inhabitants of Judah (cf. Ezek 39:29; Zech 12:10). Yet in its broader context, the benefits of this blessing extends even to those who are "far off" (Acts 2:39; cf. Eph 2:13). While applicable first of all to the Jews and Jewish proselytes present in Jerusalem for the occasion of Pentecost, the universal tone of Peter's message cannot be denied: "for *all* whom the Lord our God will call" (Acts 2:39). This includes men and women, young and old of every nationality on the face of the earth. On this occasion, it most certainly included those who believed among the more than fifteen different nationalities delineated by Luke.

This same inclusive emphasis is seen also in Paul's explanation of the event of Pentecost. He writes to the Corinthian church fractured by competing parties: "For we were *all* baptized by one Spirit into one body—whether Jews or Greeks, slave or free—and we were *all* given the one Spirit to drink" (1 Cor 12:13; emphasis mine). Apparently, part of the solution to a fragmented church is to recognize the miracle that took place at Pentecost, at which moment *all* true believers—irrespective of ethnicity, socioeconomic status, culture, gender, or language—were placed by one Spirit into one body. This is the bedrock foundation for unity both in the universal and local church. Any local church that defines for itself criteria of membership or participation other than membership by the Spirit in God's universal body is in danger of compromising the very nature of the church.

The church in Corinth was amazingly diverse. Both Jews and Gentiles had heard the message of the gospel while they were *together* in the synagogue (Acts 18:4). As a result, the Corinthian church included God-fearing Gentiles like Gaius (a Roman citizen), Titius Justus (Acts 18:7; 1 Cor 1:14) and Stephanas and his household. It also included Jews like Crispus, the ruler of the synagogue and his household (Acts 18:8; 1 Cor 1:14). Gaius's house was located next to the synagogue (Acts 18:7) and later became the meeting place of the "whole church," which consisted of such Jews as Lucius, Jason, and Sosipater, as well as Gentiles such as Erastus, the city treasurer (cf. Rom 16:23), and Quartus (Rom 16:21, 23). Some in the Corinthian church were slaves, while others were free (1 Cor 7:21–22).

It may well be this very diversity of the Corinthian church that presented certain challenges to its unity (1 Cor 1:10–12). It would seem that those following Peter were Jewish believers who insisted on the food regulations implemented by the Jerusalem council (1 Cor 8:1ff; 10:25ff). The "Christ party" may have been made up of Gentile believers who considered themselves spiritually free and more mature. In response to such divisions, however, Paul asks a rhetorical question: "Is Christ divided?" (1 Cor 1:13). The expected reply is that Christ is *not* divided; therefore, his church must not be either. In fact, Christ and his church are one in the same way that you and your physical body are one. What makes this a reality is the shared Spirit of God who himself is the "bond of peace" (Eph 4:3). Again, it is the diversity in unity given by the Spirit that must characterize the New Humanity, rather than homogeneity of ethnicity, socioeconomic status, age, gender, language, or cultural background. This is as true for local churches as it is for the universal church.

Only as we recognize this can we begin to experience the authentic community that was a by-product of Pentecost.

AUTHENTIC COMMUNITY

In recent years, the expression "authentic community" has become a buzz word in the emerging church. Somewhat in reaction to the structure and organization of the mega-church movement of the 1980s and 1990s, a refreshing call has been issued to experience the genuine community that characterizes the Jerusalem church in Acts 2. The togetherness stressed in the creation of the New Humanity in Ephesians 2 is equally present in the birth of the New Humanity in Acts 2. Luke describes this togetherness as *fellowship*. Acts 2:42 says, "They devoted themselves . . . to the fellowship." However, just what *is* the fellowship or authentic community to which these believers were devoted as a result of Pentecost?

As we have seen, God has infused into the very soul of each of us a longing for belonging. We were created for relationship—first with God and then with one another. This is intrinsic to who we are as the *imago Dei*. Fellowship is God's answer to our longing for belonging. Like so many words, however, this word "fellowship" is rusty, dusty, and worn with time. It suffers from misuse, stereotypes, and caricatures.

Our English word "fellowship" comes from that well-known Greek word *koinōnia*. It is used about twenty times in the New Testament and is translated as "communion," "partnership," or "community." In fact, the word is derived from a similar term used in Acts 2:44—"All the believers were together and had everything *in common*" (emphasis mine). Fellowship means basically to "share in common with others."

How could more than three thousand people, representing such a diversity of nationalities and languages, suddenly experience the profound communion and partnership described in Acts 2:42–47? Such fellowship was certainly not founded on affinity of culture, preferences of worship style, or social stratification. Nor was skin color an issue as those present and responsive to Peter's message certainly included black people from Egypt and parts of Libya. Apparently, the individualism, consumerism, and status quo bias that so fragments the evangelical church in America were not a predominate factor in this early community of believers. Birds of a feather *do* flock together. In this case, the "feather" is the shared experience of Spirit baptism. He alone is the "bond of peace." Such fellowship is supernatural, not natural. It is not contrived, but Spirit-birthed.

It quickly becomes apparent that any unity or sense of community founded upon *natural* factors such as ethnicity, culture, language, or socioeconomic conditions rather than the *supernatural* ingredient of God's indwelling Spirit falls short of true biblical community. Such is a return to Babel with its man-contrived uniformity rather than the experience of Pentecost with its God-given diversity in unity. It is the Spirit-given diversity in unity that we are now to strive to maintain at all cost. As Paul reminds us: "Make every effort to keep the unity of the Spirit through the bond of peace. There is one body and one Spirit—just as you were called to one hope when you were called—one Lord, one faith, one baptism; one God and Father of all, who is over all and through all and in all" (Eph 4:3–6).

While such unity cannot be *created* by us, it can and must be *maintained* by us. Indeed, it must be maintained as intentionally and passionately as we preach the forgiveness of our individual sins. As Gregory Boyd states:

> If Christ on the cross has in fact torn down the racial wall of separation that divided people-groups (Eph. 2:11–22), and if his Spirit now seeks to manifest this by reversing the effects of the catastrophe at the tower of Babel (Acts 2:5–12), then the church has no choice but to seek to manifest this reality as intensely as we have sought to manifest the reality that the forgiveness for our individual sins was purchased at the cross. In other words, that racism has ended ought to be as demonstrable in the church—to our culture and in the face of the (now defeated) spiritual powers of racism—as is the gospel truth that personal condemnation has ended.[6]

PENTECOST AND THE POWERS

I began this chapter by stating that the cross and Pentecost are inseparable. Apart from the cross, there could be no Pentecost. Apart from the conception of the New Humanity, there could be no birth of the New Humanity. The reverse is also true—apart from Pentecost, the New Humanity remains an inanimate creation, a theological construct, void of the life-giving Spirit. At Pentecost, the full significance of Christ's

---

6. Boyd, *God at War*, 254.

atoning death and defeat of the powers is made real in the experience of each and every believer who together comprises the New Humanity.

That this is true is seen in Peter's words to the multitude:

> Exalted to the right hand of God, he has received from the Father the promised Holy Spirit and has poured out what you now see and hear. For David did not ascend to heaven, and yet he said, "The Lord said to my Lord: 'Sit at my right hand until I make your enemies a footstool for your feet.'" (Acts 2:33–35)

If at Babel the peoples were divided and delivered over to the powers (Gen 11; Deut 32:8), then at Pentecost those who believe of every nation and ethnicity are united and delivered from those very same powers. This seems to be Peter's point in quoting Psalm 110, the most frequently cited passage in the New Testament. Oscar Cullman points out the significance of this passage when he states: "Nothing shows more clearly how the concept of the present Lordship of Christ and also of his consequent victory over the angel powers stands at the very center of early Christian thought than the frequent citation of Ps. 110:1, not only in isolated books, but in the entire New Testament."[7]

When Jesus was resurrected from the dead and exalted to the right hand of God the Father, he inherited all the rights and authority of his position as God's Son. According to Romans 1:4, it was at the resurrection that Jesus was publicly declared the Son of God with power. It was also because Jesus was raised and ascended into heaven that the Spirit of God could descend bringing birth to the New Humanity (John 16:6). It is only by being incorporated into Christ and the New Humanity that we share in this cosmic victory over the divisive powers of darkness.

In his first epistle, Peter says essentially the same thing. He argues that baptism now saves us. It is not the literal water that saves us, for this only removes dirt from the body. It is rather "the pledge of a good conscience toward God," that is, our faith. However, this faith is instrumental to the degree that it is placed in the resurrection of Christ, "who has gone into heaven and is at God's right hand—*with angels, authorities and powers in submission to him*" (1 Pet 3:21–22; emphasis mine). In other words, our association with Christ in his cross work is also our association with Christ in his cosmic work in defeating the divisive,

---

7. Cullman, *Christ and Time*, 193.

self-serving, consumerist powers that alienate humanity and constantly seek to segregate the church.

THE EXAMPLE OF THE EARLY CHURCH

In Christ, the spiritual powers of racism and ethnocentrism have been defeated. Was this evident in the life of the first-century church? Without a doubt, the world of the early church was extremely diverse. The Roman world at this time has been described as "a proper melting pot." Yet it is not clear just how much melting really took place. In any case, it is certain that Greco-Roman cities were severely disrupted by ethnic strife leading to widespread riots.[8] David Rhoads notes:

> The region around the Mediterranean Sea was multilingual, multiracial, and multiethnic, with many different religions and philosophies. These Jewish groups and Gentile nations comprised the multiplicity of cultures that Christianity sought to address and to embrace. In this multicultural arena, the diversity of early Christianity took shape.[9]

The Church in Jerusalem

Take the church in Jerusalem, for example. Peter Wagner contends that the church of Jerusalem *was* divided along homogeneous lines with separate house churches for the educated and less educated, for the rich and the poor, for Palestinian Jews and those who were "Hellenized."[10] Yet there is absolutely no evidence to indicate this was the case. In fact, the contrary is true. Luke's intention is to underscore that the believers of the early church in Jerusalem were "together" (Acts 2:44) and had "all things in common" (Acts 2:44; 4:32). They were indeed of "one heart and soul" (Acts 4:32). There is absolutely nothing in Luke's description of the early church to support the idea that the "mixed church in Jerusalem divided along homogeneous unit lines."[11]

The Jerusalem church was largely composed of second-class Galilean Jews and migrant Hellenized Jews from the Diaspora. Peter and John themselves were considered "unschooled, ordinary men" (Acts

---

8. Stark, *The Rise of Christianity*, 158.
9. Rhoads, *The Challenge of Diversity*, 2.
10. Wagner, *Our Kind of People*, 114.
11. Ibid., 122–23.

4:13). Later in Acts 6:7, Luke mentions more mainstream Jews who become members of the Jerusalem congregation ("a great many priests became obedient to the faith"). There were also Aramaic-speaking Jews alongside of Greek-speaking Hellenists (Acts 6:1ff), including at least one Gentile from Syrian Antioch (Acts 6:5).[12] On a socioeconomic level, the Jerusalem church was comprised of the poor who were in need of assistance alongside wealthy landlords (Acts 2:44–45; 4:32–37).

Such diversity was not without its problems. In Acts 6, we see the Grecian Jews began to complain against the Hebraic Jews because their widows were being overlooked in the daily distribution of food. The pragmatic solution in this case—and the one likely preferred by the majority of homogeneous church growth advocates today—would have been to create two distinct denominations rather than deal with the difficulties of working across ethnic and socioeconomic lines. This had been their experience as Jews *before* their conversion. The Hellenists would attend synagogues where their worship was expressed in their own language and culture. In fact, one of those is mentioned in this very context—the Synagogue of the Freedmen (Acts 6:9). On the other hand, Hebraic Jews maintained their own synagogues where the Scriptures were read and worship was conducted in Hebrew (or Aramaic).[13] Therefore, it would have been quite natural for these Grecian Jews to have reasoned, "We can get along better and be more productive if we were meeting as our own ethnic church!" They could have also reasoned, "It's too difficult trying to live in community with these Hebraic Jews. If we form our own homogeneous group, the gospel might grow even faster!" That might appear to be the wisest thing to do from a merely human perspective.

God, however, had other plans. His desire is for the unity of the New Humanity across ethnic lines. He wants his church to be one, not just *theologically*, but *experientially*; not just *universally*, but *locally*. The leadership of the early church wisely recognized that too much was at stake. God's purposes of spiritual unity must become a tangible reality. The prayer of Jesus for oneness would be answered even in the more mundane aspects of the life of the local church. Rather than opt for pragmatic solutions, the Jerusalem congregation "faced head-on the challenges posed by diversity with action that was prayerful, immediate,

---

12. Padilla, "Unity of the Church," 148.
13. Bruce, *Acts of the Apostles*, 181.

The Church in Antioch

One of the most notable churches in the New Testament world was the church of Antioch. Antioch was the third-largest city in the then known world, boasting a population of nearly half a million people. As a major cosmopolitan center, it was the home of many cults and mystery religions. It's cultural and ethnic diversity was also noteworthy. Antioch was the home to Syrians, Romans, Greeks, Arabs, Persians, Armenians, Parthians, Cappadocians, and Jews.[15] The church at Antioch was founded when those who had been scattered by persecution came to this metropolitan area to preach the gospel. Men from Cyprus and Cyrene preached, not only to Jews, but also to Greeks, and many turned to the Lord (Acts 11:19–20). Soon after, Barnabas, a Levite and a native of Cyprus (Acts 4:36), was sent by the Jerusalem church to provide leadership and establish a link with the church in Jerusalem (Acts 11:24). He then recruited Saul to help in the establishment of this local church. Both Saul and Barnabas were bilingual, speaking Greek and Aramaic. Both were Jews immersed in Greek culture.

It is not surprising, then, that the leadership of the church at Antioch was just as diverse as its surrounding community. Luke writes in Acts 13:1, "In the church at Antioch there were prophets and teachers: Barnabas, Simeon called Niger, Lucius of Cyrene, Manaen (who had been brought up with Herod the tetrarch) and Saul." The prophet/teacher Simeon has the Latin surname of Niger, which means "black."[16] Niger was a country located in the sub-Saharan West Africa, as it is today. Luke had already shown how the gospel went to an Ethiopian eunuch, a black (Acts 13). Now a black African is part of the leadership team of this thriving community. It is quite possible that this was the same Simeon who carried the cross for Jesus (Luke 23:36) and whose sons, Alexander and Rufus, were known in the Christian community (Mark 15:21; cf. Rom 16:13).

---

14. DeYoung et al., *United by Faith*, 24.
15. Ibid., 27; Stark, *The Rise of Christianity*, 156–58.
16. See the discussion in Hays, *From Every People and Nation*, 177.

Lucius was most likely a Gentile, a native of the African city of Cyrene. Cyrene was located near the northern coast of Africa in the modern day country of Libya. He was probably one of the original evangelists mentioned in Acts 11:20 who was bold enough to cross cultural frontiers and preach the gospel to the Gentiles. Manaen was a "foster-brother" to Herod Antipas, the tetrarch of Galilee, with whom he had been raised. This being the case, he was most likely from somewhere in Palestine since the Herodian dynasty ruled over this area from approximately 65 BC to 90 AD. Having been raised in the household of a king, he had a cultured background and represented the higher class of society.[17] Saul, of course, was an ex-Pharisee, a "Hebrew of Hebrews," but also a Roman citizen from the city of Tarsus, located in Asia Minor (Acts 9:11). Of those mentioned by Luke, two were from Africa, one from the Mediterranean, one from the Middle East, and one from Asia Minor. It is little wonder, then, that the believers at Antioch were called "Christians" or "Christ-followers" (Acts 11:26). The term comes from the title *Christos* and the colloquial suffix *–ianos*, which denoted ownership. Christians "belonged" to the Messiah.[18] That was their allegiance beyond any particular nationalistic or ethnic adherence. Their one particularity was their loyalty to the "man for all nations," Jesus Christ. As Mark DeYmaz states, "In the church at Antioch, we see the fulfillment of all that was anticipated by Christ in his prayer, as both Jews and Gentiles came to know the Father's love through the unity of his children."[19]

Other New Testament churches also reflected this commitment to diversity in unity, yet not without difficulty.

The Church in Rome

Without a doubt, the church in Rome was as diverse as any New Testament church. Paul appealed to both Jews (Rom 2:17) and Gentiles (Rom 11:13). He made it explicitly clear that the church was composed of both Jew and Gentile alike (Rom 9:24). Furthermore, the listing of Romans 16 includes Greek, Latin, and Roman names. There even seemed to be "country folk" and "city folk" in the same community. In

---

17. F. F. Bruce suggests that Manaen may well have been Luke's informant, conveying to the evangelist the latest news of Herod's court and family. See Bruce, *Acts of the Apostles*, 216.

18. Strauss, "Significance of Acts 11:26," 284–95.

19. DeYmaz, *Multi-Ethnic Church*, 22.

Romans 16:9, Paul refers to Stachys, whose name literally means "ear of corn." Yet he is part of a small house church with Urbanus, meaning "city bred." We obviously cannot draw too much from this observation, but it's worthy of note.

In spite of this, it does seem that various groups of believers had formed in Rome based more or less on homogeneous distinctions. Even F. F. Bruce concludes: "Perhaps some local groups consisted of Jewish Christians and others of Gentile Christians, and there were few, if any, in which Jewish and Gentile Christians met together."[20] Whether this was the case or not, it is clear that Paul's desire is for these believers to manifest in tangible ways their oneness in Christ. So he urges them: "May the God who gives endurance and encouragement give you a spirit of unity among yourselves as you follow Christ Jesus, so that with one heart and mouth you may glorify the God and Father of our Lord Jesus Christ" (Rom 15:5–6). Evidently, one of Paul's purposes in writing this epistle was that "a larger number of segregated house churches would at last be able to worship together—Jews praising God among the Gentiles and Gentiles praising God with his people."[21]

Among all the New Testament churches, there were clashes of culture. One of the most difficult revolved around the issues discussed in the Jerusalem council described in Acts 15. The question of circumcision as a requirement of salvation was not merely theological; it was also cultural. It threatened to once-and-for-all divide the early church, separating Jewish from Gentile believers. Such may have been the pragmatic route. Just as many local churches today are segregated by ethnicity, culture, or preferred styles of worship, the apostles could have proposed a programmed segregation in the early churches as a means of relieving the tension. Instead, the apostles were extremely careful not to let this happen. As René Padilla states, "The Jerusalem Decree also cries aloud at every attempt to solve the conflicts arising out of cultural differences among Christians by resorting to the formation of separate congregations, each representing a different homogeneous unit."[22]

---

20. Bruce, *New Testament History*, 394.
21. Minear, *Obedience of the Faith*, 16–17.
22. Padilla, "Unity of the Church," 295.

CONCLUSION

The cross and Pentecost are inseparable, together forming the basis of the creation and birth of the New Humanity. If the New Humanity was created at the cross (Eph 2), he was born at Pentecost (Acts 2). A body without breath is a corpse; so the New Humanity without the breath of God's Spirit remains an inanimate creation.

Pentecost is a reminder of the diversity in unity that should characterize the church. The "sameness" brought to us by the gospel is divine in nature, not socially or humanly acquired. The unity of the New Humanity is not based on ethnicity, phenotype, language, culture, or socioeconomic class. It is not determined by personal likes and dislikes. It transcends color, culture, and class, as well as both denominational ties and generational distinctions. The unity of the church is derived from the Spirit-given "bond of peace" (Eph 4:3) and is founded firmly and uniquely on who we are together as the "one new man" in Jesus Christ (Eph 2:11–22). At Pentecost, the Spirit of the triune God united into one living organism people of multiple cultures, ethnicities, and nationalities. The truth that peace has now been made between Jew and Gentile, that we share the "same Holy Spirit" (Eph 2:18) and are carefully joined together as a dwelling of the non-homogeneous God—Father, Son, and Holy Spirit (Eph 1:3–14; 2:19–22)—*this truth must be the one and only criteria that determines local church identity in the body of Christ.* Anything less than this is a return to Babel rather than an expression of Pentecost.

For the church to truly be the church, "my kind of people" must no longer be those who look like, talk like, worship like, or necessarily think like I do. The ecstasy of true community is discovered when we put off the old clothes of individualism, consumerism, competition, and status quo bias and put on the new clothes of sacrificial love, reconciliation, and unity (Eph 4:22–24). This is the *koinōnia* to which we should be devoted as believers (Acts 2:42). This is a supernatural experience and can never be contrived or manufactured or organized by mere human effort. Only as we walk in the Spirit can we live out the diversity in unity to which we are called. Quite frankly, until we do this, what Francis Schaeffer called the "final apologetic" of the church in society will never be realized. This is the message of Pentecost.

7

The New Humanity as *Ekklēsia*

> *The fact that the church is the body of Christ means that Christ receives a body, a form or shape, and becomes visible and real in the world.... And when theologians say that what is meant here is the "invisible Christ," they are simply demonstrating the nonsense of which only theologians are capable.*
>
> Eberhard Arnold

IT'S SO OBVIOUS THAT it can easily be passed over. The most basic and fundamental name given to the New Humanity is *ekklēsia*, the church. Here, however, a thorny question presents itself. Just what is the church? What do we mean when we speak of the "universal" church or the "local" church and what is the precise connection between the two? The question is extremely relevant to the issues of diversity and multiethnicity in the New Humanity. For if the *ekklēsia* of God consists of nothing more than ad hoc groups of Christians who gather informally or web-based interchanges from the comfort of one's home, then how will the multicolored beauty of the New Humanity be tangibly seen by the world? In other words, what did Jesus mean when he prayed that we all might be one? Was he speaking of a mere ephemeral spiritual unity that would rarely, if ever, display itself in palpable, tangible ways? Are the characteristics of diversity in unity—and specifically multiethnicity—that characterize the universal New Humanity also to characterize local expressions of the New Humanity?

My thesis as set forth in this chapter can be summarized in three affirmations. First, an inseparable link exists between the universal church and the local church—the local church is in microcosm what the universal church is in macrocosm. Second, this inseparable link between the universal and local church indicates that the diversity in unity that characterizes the former should also be intentionally nurtured and ultimately reflected in the latter. Finally, to the degree that such diversity in unity is nurtured and reflected in and among local churches, we fulfill Jesus' prayer that his followers may be brought to complete unity (John 17:23).

Many, however, would not agree.

REVOLUTION!

George Barna, in his groundbreaking book *Revolution*, sketches a picture of the spiritual landscape of America in the first quarter of the twenty-first century. His book not only informs us of the radical changes reshaping the church, but also describes what he terms the new "revolutionaries" who are increasingly finding their source of spiritual nurture and expression *outside* the sphere of what is traditionally known as the local church.

From the outset, Barna clarifies what he believes to be the distinction between the Church (uppercase C) and the church (lowercase c). According to Barna, the Church with an uppercase C is comprised of *all* believers connected by their shared faith in Jesus Christ. The Church with an uppercase C is what has been normally termed the "universal" church. On the other hand, Barna defines the church with a lowercase c as "the congregation-based faith experience, which involves a formal structure, a hierarchy of leadership, and a specific group of believers." The church with a lowercase c is what has been normally termed the "local" church. According to Barna, the purpose of the "revolution" is "to advance the Church and to *redefine* the church."[1]

His interesting and realistic analysis looks at where Americans find their primary means of spiritual experience and expression. He classifies these among four basic alternatives: the local church, alternative faith-based communities, family, and various cultural expressions including the media and arts. Barna goes on to project that by the year 2025 the

---

1. Barna, *Revolution*, x (emphasis mine).

spiritual profile of our nation will be radically different than it is today. According to Barna, only about one-third of the spiritually-minded population will look to the local church as the primary or exclusive means of expressing their faith. Another one-third will pursue their spiritual interests through alternative forms of faith-based community, such as the homeschooling movement, biblical worldview groups, various marketplace ministries, and spiritual discipline networks. And a final one-third will express their faith experience through various cultural mediums such as the arts and media. As for the family, it will remain only a "blip on the radar screen" in terms of being a viable expression of faith experience and community. Barna sums it all up when he states: "Ultimately, we expect to see believers choosing from a proliferation of options, weaving together a set of favored alternatives into a unique tapestry that constitutes the personal 'church' of the *individual*." The bottom line is that *if we place our hope in the local church, our hope is misplaced*.[2]

To the contrary, I insist that true revolutionaries refuse to be driven by the insipid and pervasive individualism of our culture that dilutes the dynamics of accountability and responsibility most effectively lived out in the local church. In other words, they are committed to both the Church (uppercase C) and the church (lowercase c). Furthermore, true revolutionaries strive to nurture local New Humanity churches in which the characteristic of diversity in unity is tangibly demonstrated. Finally, true revolutionaries believe that as they do this, Jesus' prayer for authentic unity is realized and the Trinity rejoices!

THE PROBLEM OF LANGUAGE

Language can often be misleading. Part of the problem is the evolution that occurs in the meaning of words over a period of time. For example, the word "gay" today has implications that were never attached to the word only fifty years ago. Or take the word "hussy," which any English dictionary defines as a worthless, ill-behaved women or girl. Yet the word originally comes from *huswife*, meaning "housewife." The original meaning of our English word "cute" was "bow-legged." In the thirteenth century, our word "nice" meant "foolish" or "stupid."

The same phenomenon is true when it comes to words used in the Bible. Over time they take on linguistic baggage that necessitates getting

---

2. Ibid., 49, 66, 36 (emphasis mine).

back to the original meanings used by the biblical writers. Not only do we need to understand the words the first-century writers used, but also the biblical, cultural, and historical context of these words.

This is equally true for understanding the biblical word *ekklēsia*, translated (somewhat unfortunately) as "church" in our English Bibles. Much of our confusion about the nature of the church comes not only from misunderstanding the biblical term *ekklēsia*, but also from stereotypes of the English term "church." To the average English speaker the word "church" denotes everything from a denomination or hierarchy of ordained ministers to a particular building up the street. The word "church," then, carries a heavy institutional nuance. Even Webster's defines the church as "a building for public and especially Christian worship."[3] However, a remark such as "I pass the church every day on my way to work" would have been unintelligible to Christians in Paul's day. It seems to be this institutional, structural view of the local church to which Barna reacts so strongly—and with good reason. This problem is partially explained by the translation history of the word "church."

Surprisingly, our English word "church" does not find its source in the Greek word *ekklēsia*. Linguistically, it is derived from a different Greek word (*kyriakos*), meaning "belonging to the Lord." This Greek word (*kyriakos*) is used only twice in the New Testament and surprisingly *never in reference to the church*.[4] This certainly explains why William Tyndale's English translation of the New Testament (AD 1525) completely avoided the use of the English word "church" as a translation of the Greek *ekklēsia*. Tyndale preferred the word "congregation." This latter term appropriately places emphasis on the *people* who gather together rather than on the *place* where they meet. However, later translations ignored Tyndale's precision, rather loosely and unfortunately substituting the word "church" for "congregation."[5]

---

3. *Webster's*, s.v. "church."

4. In 1 Cor 11:20, the term refers to the Lord's Supper: *kyriakon deipnon*. In Rev 1:10, the term refers to the Lord's Day: *kyriakē hēmera*.

5. Tyndale did use the English word "church" in Acts 19:37, which he translated as "robbers of heathen churches." Later translations more appropriately rendered the phrase, "robbers of temples." Several European languages more appropriately derive their word for "church" directly from the Greek: *église* (French), *eglwys* (Welsh), and *Gemeinde* (German). Luther used the latter term to refer to the church composed of true believers as opposed to *Kirche* (derived from the Greek *kyriakos*). Griffiths, *Cinderella*, 11–12.

The New Humanity as Ekklēsia 141

Due to the subsequent development of the English language, the usage of the term "church" as a translation of *ekklēsia* led to such an unfortunate building-centered concept of the church. It may be that if Tyndale's translation of "congregation" had been retained, emphasizing those who assemble together, British and American church history would have been quite different.

ASSEMBLY . . . COMPANY . . . MULTITUDE

What then does the New Testament word *ekklēsia* mean? This New Testament noun comes from the verb *kaleō* meaning to "call or summon" and the prefix *ek* meaning "out of." So inherent to the word *ekklēsia* is the idea "to call out." Contrary to the opinion of some, however, the word does not emphasize the idea of separation *from* something. The focus is rather on being summoned or called *to* something.

In most of its earliest usages (classical period), the word *ekklēsia* referred to people called out from their homes into a legislative assembly. Often these citizens would be summoned by the town crier. In time, however, the word came to refer simply to any assembly, regardless of how they were summoned or why they were gathered.[6]

In the Greek Old Testament, we have some insightful examples of how this word is used.[7] It can refer to: people *convened* for evil counsel (Gen 49:6), individuals *assembled* for civil affairs (Prov 5:14), those *gathered together* for war (Num 22:4), a *company* of returning exiles (Jer 31:8), Israelites *gathered* for religious purposes (Deut 4:19), a *community gathered* in Jerusalem (Ezra 10:12), even a *council* of angels (Ps 89:6).

From all the occurrences of the word in both classical and Old Testament usage, we can draw at least three observations. First, there is always a *physical gathering* for the assembly to exist. Second, each assembly has some *deliberative purpose* for the gathering. Finally, each assembly is *autonomous*.[8] As for the first requirement, the Jews who prepared the Septuagint never thought of the *ekklēsia* as an abstract unity linking people who did not actually meet together. Rather, the people formed an assembly only when they met. We can see here the implications of these

---

6. Robertson, *Grammar*, 174.

7. The term occurs in the LXX 103 times in seventy-seven passages. The word *ekklēsia* always translates the Hebrew *qāhāl* in the Old Testament, meaning "assembly, congregation, convocation."

8. Radmacher, *Church*, 122.

initial conclusions for those who feel they can love God with all their heart, soul, and mind apart from the physical gathering of the *ekklēsia*. We can also conclude that whatever characterizes the *ekklēsia* is manifested in a very local, physical sense. However, do these tentative conclusions carry over to the way the word was used in the New Testament?

THE *COMMUNION SANCTORUM*

In the Greek of Christ's day, the word *ekklēsia* could be used for any gathering of people, not just specifically the church. For example, in Acts 7:38 Stephen calls the assembly of Israel in the wilderness an *ekklēsia* (cf. Heb 2:12). In Acts 19:32, 39, and 41, the word refers to an unruly mob and a lawful assembly, both of which are secular in nature. In literary terms, this is called the *non-technical* usage of the word "church." However, even here (as in the classical and Old Testament usage) the people were physically gathered together.

This broad, generic usage of the word explains why, in Paul's earliest letters, he felt it necessary to specify of what *ekklēsia* he was speaking. After all, other assemblies of all types existed in cities throughout the Roman world. Those of which Paul is specifically speaking are "in Christ": "To the *church* of the Thessalonians *in God the Father* and *the Lord Jesus Christ* (1 Thess 1:1); "For you, brothers, became imitators of God's *churches* in Judea, *which are in Christ Jesus*" (1 Thess 2:14); "To the *church* of the Thessalonians *in God our Father* and *the Lord Jesus Christ*" (2 Thess 1:1); "Therefore, among *God's churches* we boast about your perseverance" (2 Thess 1:4).[9]

We find, then, that in the New Testament the additional characteristic of *spiritual unity* is added to the previous emphasis on *physical presence*. "Here was a new kind of *ekklēsia*—a Christian *ekklēsia*—and it was distinct from every other *ekklēsia* because it had the content that Jesus Christ gave it. This Christian *ekklēsia* may be defined, then, as a local assembly spiritually united in Christ with an autonomous nature."[10] In fact, it is this understanding of *ekklēsia* that is reflected in the vast majority of the uses of the term in the New Testament. Of the 114 times the word *ekklēsia* is used, ninety speak of the local church rather than the universal church.

---

9. Emphasis mine in each case.
10. Radmacher, *Church*, 130.

Interestingly, however, the extensive descriptions seen in the above verses specifying of what church Paul is speaking are no longer seen as necessary in the letters written after these earlier epistles. Though a few add the simple description "of God,"[11] the vast majority of epistles speak simply of the church or churches in a specific house, city, or region. Apparently, the word became so identified with a new kind of assembly—one marked by *both* physical and spiritual unity—that it was no longer necessary to specify its Christian character. In literary terms, this is called the *technical* usage of the word "church."

The development of the word "church" in the New Testament does not stop, however, with the technical use. A gradual, nearly imperceptible development takes the reader toward a *metaphorical* use of the word. In this sense, the word "church" refers not only to the gathered assembly marked by physical and spiritual unity (the local church), but also to the people who make up the assembly whether or not they are physically gathered together (the universal church). One of the best examples of this is found in Acts 8:1–3 where Luke describes the persecution that broke out against the church in Jerusalem:

> And Saul was there, giving approval to his death. On that day a great persecution broke out against the church (*ekklēsia*) at Jerusalem, and all except the apostles were scattered throughout Judea and Samaria. Godly men buried Stephen and mourned deeply for him. But Saul began to destroy the church (*ekklēsia*). Going from house to house, he dragged off men and women and put them in prison.

Here, the members of the church constitute the *ekklēsia*, even when they are living in their personal houses ("going from house to house"). When Luke says that "all . . . were scattered," he is referring to the "church at Jerusalem." Amazingly, though scattered, they did not cease to be the church. For in Acts 9:31 Luke adds, "Then the *church* throughout Judea, Galilee and Samaria enjoyed a time of peace. It was strengthened; and encouraged by the Holy Spirit, it grew in numbers, living in the fear of the Lord" (emphasis mine). In other words, those scattered continued to be the church regardless of the fact that they were now dispersed

---

11. In eleven cases we find the simple description "of God" added to the word "church" to define the spiritual nature of the assembly (Acts 20:28; 1 Cor 1:2; 10:32; 11:16, 22; 15:9; 2 Cor 1:1; Gal 1:13; 1 Tim 3:15; 1 Thess 2:14; 2 Thess 1:4). Again, the majority of these are in the earlier letters of the New Testament.

throughout Judea, Galilee, and Samaria. These believers became an "unassembled assembly."[12]

In summary, we have what we call the *non-technical* use of the word "church," referring to any assembly of people, such as in Acts 19:32–41. The focus is on the assembly itself and the characteristic of physical proximity is evident. This usage gradually gives way to a *technical* use of the word, referring specifically to an assembly of Christians. In these cases, there is not merely physical unity, but also a profound spiritual unity derived from being in Christ. Finally we discover the *metaphorical* use of the word "church," stressing the spiritual unity of all believers, irrespective of location or physical proximity. This is the universal New Humanity. Here the church gathered (local) has become the church scattered (universal).[13] Figure 7.1 depicts this development:

Non-Technical	Technical	Metaphorical
ekklēsia = any assembly ⇨	*ekklēsia* = assembly of Christians ⇨	*ekklēsia* = all Christians
physical unity	physical + spiritual unity	spiritual unity

Figure 7.1

Such fluid movement between the technical and metaphorical usage of the word "church" is seen on the lips of Jesus himself. In Matthew 16:18 he says to Peter, "I will build my church," obviously referring to the universal body of believers. This is the metaphorical use of the word "church." However, later when addressing the issue of discipline within the local congregation, Jesus uses the more technical nuance referring to a specific group of Christians located in a particular area: "If he refuses to listen to them, tell it to the *church*; and if he refuses to listen even to the *church*, treat him as you would a pagan or a tax collector" (Matt 18:17; emphasis mine).

---

12. See also 1 Cor 15:9, Gal 1:13, and Phil 3:6. Robertson, *Word Pictures*, 1:101.

13. Some refer to this as the "ideal," "universal," "spiritual," or "invisible" church. From a literary viewpoint, the word is used metaphorically. The strictly metaphorical uses of the word "church" are found in Matt 16:18; 1 Cor 12:28; Eph 1:22; 3:10; 3:21; 5:23–25, 27, 29, 32; Col 1:18, 24; Heb 12:23.

This use of the word *ekklēsia* in its metaphorical sense reaches its pinnacle in Paul's letters to the Ephesians and the Colossians. The following examples demonstrate this:[14]

> And God placed all things under his feet and appointed him to be head over everything for the *church*, which is his body, the fullness of him who fills everything in every way. (Eph 1:22–23)

> And he is the head of the body, the *church*; he is the beginning and the firstborn from among the dead, so that in everything he might have the supremacy.... Now I rejoice in what was suffered for you, and I fill up in my flesh what is still lacking in regard to Christ's afflictions, for the sake of his body, which is the church. (Col 1:18, 24)

Since the church is the fulfillment of God's covenant with Abraham promising that in him all nations would be blessed (see Gen 12:1–3; 28:3; 35:11; 48:4–5), it makes sense that in some cases the New Testament word refers to the universal New Humanity composed of believers from a variety of cultures, languages, and nations. All true believers share a corporate identity and solidarity not founded on physical proximity or a particular ethnicity, but on the spiritual reality of oneness in Christ. Believers have confessed from the earliest creeds onward to be part of one holy, *catholic*, apostolic church. Catholic in this sense means simply "according to the whole" (*kata* "according to" + *holos* "the whole").[15] This is the universal church, the New Humanity. As such, whether gathered or scattered, all believers make up the *communion sanctorum*, the communion of the saints.

To summarize, then, the word *ekklēsia* in the New Testament most frequently refers to two basic ideas. There is the local church referring to an autonomous group of believers united both physically (in the same locality and gathering) and spiritually (in Christ). There is also the universal church referring to believers united spiritually in Christ without necessarily sharing physical proximity. Yet several questions remain: What is the relation between the two? Does the New Testament

---

14. Emphasis mine. In these two Pauline epistles the word *ekklēsia* is used thirteen times. Only twice (Col 4:15–16) does it refer to the local church.

15. Ignatius (second century AD) was probably the first to use the term "catholic church" to refer to the universal church. "Wherever the bishop shall appear, there let the multitude of the people also be; even as, wherever Jesus Christ is, there is the Catholic Church" (*Epistle to the Smyrnaeans*, I).

ever conceive of a believer being part of the universal church without associating with a local church? Beyond that, how do we define the local church? More importantly for our purposes, is the multiethnicity of the New Humanity also to be expressed in the local church?

THE VISIBILITY OF THE INVISIBLE

Some years ago, I was walking with my youngest son, Justin, in our neighborhood on a clear, summer night. As he looked at the sky, he remarked, "How awesome, Dad! Look at the moon." I immediately looked up, but saw only a thin, crescent moon. That the entire orb was not visible in no way hindered Justin from identifying what he saw as "the moon." What he saw *was* genuine moon and fully united with the rest of the moon that wasn't visible at the time. Similarly, each local congregation under Christ *is genuine church* and intended to be a replica in miniature of the universal New Humanity. In the local church, the intangible becomes tangible and the invisible becomes visible. At least, that's the way it was meant to be!

Because of the emphasis in a few New Testament passages on the universal church, some Christians are content to remain relatively isolated from its specific geographical manifestation, the local *ekklēsia*. In fact, recent studies show that six out of ten Americans having no association with a local church consider themselves to be Christian.[16] In this sense, they are "invisible," leading to the characterization of the universal church as the invisible church. According to the Bible, however, while the church is universal and *indivisible,* it must never remain *invisible.*

Barna, in his book *Revolution,* seems to argue for this priority of the universal church over any local church:

> Revolutionaries realize—sometimes very reluctantly—that the core issue isn't whether or not one is involved in a local church, but whether or not one is connected to the body of believers in the pursuit of godliness and worship. . . . You see, it's not about *church.* It's about *the Church*—that is, the people who actively participate in the intentional advancement of God's Kingdom in partnership with the Holy Spirit and other believers.[17]

---

16. Barna Group Update, 2006.
17. Barna, *Revolution*, 38.

As Barna argues, is it only about the universal Church (uppercase C) and not about the local church (lowercase c)? From the standpoint of the New Testament, just as the church (*ekklēsia*) is *never* associated with a building, so also it is *never* disassociated from the local church (lowercase c). The universal church of the New Testament *always* met in visible, local assemblies. For example, in Paul's letter to the Colossians he takes us from the height of theological insight regarding the universal church right down to tangible boundaries that help in defining further the local church:

> The universal church: And he is the head of the body, the church (*ekklēsia*); he is the beginning and the firstborn from among the dead, so that in everything he might have the supremacy. (Col 1:18–19)

> The local church: Give my greetings to the brothers at Laodicea, and to Nympha and the church (*ekklēsia*) in her house. (Col 4:15)

What are these tangible boundaries? We can start with the three observations drawn from the use of the term *ekklēsia* in the Old Testament—physical presence, deliberative purpose, and autonomy—all of which seem to be carried over in how the word is used in its technical sense in the New Testament. For example, the early believers of the local church in Jerusalem met together with a *deliberative purpose* in Acts 2:41–47. We later see that each local church was *autonomous*, being responsible for its own functioning and discipline (1 Cor 14:40; Matt 18:17).[18] We should particularly note, however, the characteristic of *physical presence* or proximity; that is, the believers actually gathered together to be a local church.

The contemporary idea of being part of the universal church but not associating with a local church was completely foreign to the New Testament writers. For example, in the passage cited above there is physical presence among the believers who meet in the house of Nympha. The churches of Judea (Gal 1:22–23) appear to be composed of Christians who met regularly. In fact, it would be impossible for Paul to refer to the

---

18. Many New Testament passages stress the autonomous nature of local churches. For example, each church (1) can judge its own members (1 Cor 5:13); (2) has authority to appoint its own leaders (Acts 6:1–6); (3) has authority to settle its own internal disputes (1 Cor 6:1–5); and (4) has authority in matters concerning interchurch relations (Acts 15:1–2, 22, 23, 25, 30).

churches of a locality unless the gathering of these believers was a regular occurrence. Beyond this, the many "one another" commands addressed to local churches in the New Testament assume physical proximity and personal presence in the local gatherings, which allowed such concrete expressions of love.[19] When Paul, Silas, and Timothy write to the church of the Thessalonians, they recommend that this letter be read to all the brethren, greeting them with a holy kiss (1 Thess 5:26–27). Such tender expressions of affection are not sent at a distance, but necessitate physical proximity and presence. The obvious implication is that the church of the Thessalonians was a community of believers who gathered on a regular basis. The indisputable emphasis in each of these passages is on a visible, gathered community in a local circumscription. In other words, the universal New Humanity expressed itself in local New Humanity churches.

All of these gatherings as the local *ekklēsia* are different from the regularly held political councils of the day, for these believers are the church "in God the Father" (1 Thess 1:1). They are also different than the weekly synagogue meetings familiar to the Jews since it is a gathering of those "in the Lord Jesus Christ." However, it cannot be denied that this universal *communion sanctorum* "in God the Father and in the Lord Jesus Christ" was tangibly and necessarily expressed in local gatherings. In other words, *the invisible spiritual realities of the universal New Humanity are to be concretely and visibly manifested in the local New Humanity*. The two are inseparable. The church scattered (universal) must also be the church gathered (local).

THE CHURCH AS THE CHURCH

Based on the above, it could still be argued that whenever members of the universal church gather, there we have a local church. After all, Jesus does say, "For where two or three gather together because they are mine, I am there among them" (Matt 18:20). So when believers connect via diverse marketplace ministries, the Internet, spiritual discipline networks, or as a family unit, do we not there have a local church? According to Barna and many Christians today, any ad hoc gathering of believers qualifies as what God intends the church to be in its local manifestation.

---

19. Rom 12:10, 16; 13:8; 14:13; 15:7, 14; 16:16; 1 Cor 1:10; 16:20; 2 Cor 13:12; Gal 5:13; Eph 4:2, 32; 5:19, 21; Col 3:13, 16; 1 Thess 5:11; Heb 3:13; 10:24; Jas 4:11; 1 Pet 1:22; 3:8; 4:9; 5:5, 14; 1 John 1:7; 3:11, 23; 4:7, 11–12; 2 John 5.

Rather paradoxically, it is just prior to the above well-known words of Jesus that we find the most helpful passage in distinguishing between an ad hoc group of believers and the local church:

> If your brother sins against you, go and show him his fault, just between the two of you. If he listens to you, you have won your brother over. But if he will not listen, take one or two others along, so that "every matter may be established by the testimony of two or three witnesses." If he refuses to listen to them, tell it to the *church*; and if he refuses to listen even to the *church*, treat him as you would a pagan or a tax collector. (Mat 18:15–17; emphasis mine)

According to Jesus, two or three witnesses—albeit believers among whom Christ is present (verse 20)—are clearly differentiated from the church. Though part of the church universal, the church local is more than an event, a conversation, a spontaneous gathering, or an ill-defined relational web of believers.[20]

What then does define the local church? We have already mentioned four important criteria that seem to characterize the use of the word *ekklēsia* in its technical sense (i.e. the local church): (1) spiritual unity, (2) physical presence, (3) autonomous character, and (4) deliberative purpose. However, as we take the New Testament as a whole, we can add to these criteria several indispensable characteristics. For example, there is also the element of authority and accountability. This is assumed in Jesus' words in Matthew 18:15–17, for it is the church that takes the initiative to exercise discipline in the case of an erring brother. Apparently, Jesus' seminal teaching on this topic was further developed by Paul in his dealings with the Corinthian believers. As a local church ("assembled in the name of the Lord Jesus"), they also were to encourage the twin dynamics of accountability and responsibility among believers by exercising their authority in correcting a member of their assembly (1 Cor 5:1–5).

Where is such authority invested? The New Testament writers clearly place it at the feet of the elders appointed in each local church. Luke underscores this in Acts 14:21–23 as he recounts Paul's first missionary journey.

---

20. Another example of this is found in Acts 15:2–4. Here the apostolic missionary team is distinct from the *church* that sends them.

> They preached the good news in that city and won a large number of disciples. Then they returned to Lystra, Iconium and Antioch, strengthening the disciples and encouraging them to remain true to the faith. "We must go through many hardships to enter the kingdom of God," they said. Paul and Barnabas appointed elders for them in each church and, with prayer and fasting, committed them to the Lord, in whom they had put their trust.

During Paul's first missionary journey he "made disciples" (Matt 28:19–20) in Derbe, Lystra, Iconium, and Antioch. Paul's ministry in each location probably transpired over several months as his entire first missionary journey lasted between one to two years. The gospel was preached, people believed, and converts were organized into local churches with recognized leadership (cf. Titus 1:5). Apparently, the apostles believed that structured leadership was vital in any concept of the local church.

There is a final element that seems to be a nonnegotiable for defining the local church, thus distinguishing it from various spontaneous ad hoc gatherings of believers. For the universal church to be the local church, there must be the regular practice of the two ordinances of baptism and the Lord's Supper (Matt 28:19, 20; 1 Cor 11:18–34). While the Lord's Supper speaks of our redemption from sin, baptism speaks of our incorporation into Christ's body. Both are tangible, identifiable practices designed to be experienced in the orderly, defined context of the local *ekklēsia*. This is not to say that the New Testament prohibits the practice of either of these in more spontaneous, impromptu gatherings of believers. However, it does indicate that for a group of local believers to be a local church, these elements must be present as a regular occurrence.

I would agree with Barna on one point: "The Bible does not *rigidly* define the corporate practices, rituals, or structures that must be embraced to have a local church."[21] But it *does* define them. When the Church (uppercase C) is the church (lowercase c), the invisible and universal become visible and local. The local church is *not* defined by tradition, buildings, institutional bureaucracy, or finely tuned programs. But it *is* defined by seven nonnegotiables clearly laid out in the New Testament:

- Spiritual unity

---

21. Barna, *Revolution*, 37.

- Physical presence (proximity)
- Deliberative purpose
- Autonomous character
- Spiritual accountability
- Recognized leadership
- The ordinances of baptism and the Lord's Supper

The point here, however, is that the local church is not merely a marketplace ministry, a parachurch association, a homeschooling movement, or a spiritual formation network. Nor is it simply an ad hoc group of two or three believers (members of the universal church) who gather for prayer and fellowship. On the other hand, the local church is not a building or an institution. It is rather a group of believers who regularly assemble and are characterized by the above seven marks of what a local church is all about.

Is it really not about the church (lowercase c) but only about the Church (uppercase C)? Can you be a revolutionary follower of Jesus Christ and remain disassociated from the local church? I'll let the pen of Robert Saucy answer the question: "As for membership in an invisible church without fellowship with any local assembly, this concept is never contemplated in the New Testament. *The universal church was the universal fellowship of believers who met visibly in local assemblies.*"[22] According to the New Testament, the New Humanity scattered must be the New Humanity gathered!

What is it that has led to this unbiblical emphasis on the universal church to the neglect of the local church? While I was writing this chapter, a homeless man stopped by our church office. He had Bible in hand, so I assumed he claimed to be a Christ-follower. After he expressed his need for help in finding a shelter, I asked if he was already a member of a local church in the area. His response was quite typical: "No, they are all hypocrites." I immediately shared my own need to be more Christlike, an admission (coming from a pastor) that seemed to startle this man. While insisting he was part of the universal body of believers, he had dismissed any local church as hypocritical and not worthy of his personal involvement.

---

22. Saucy, *Church*, 7.

We all have our ideal images of our favorite company of friends, or preferred job, or choice church. When these disappoint (as they inevitably do), we pull away and once again enter the pursuit of the next ideal. Like a young child imagining his fantasy group of special friends, we paint in our minds a picture of the ideal church. When this doesn't measure up, we fall back on our connection to the "invisible" church. Here we can exercise the control that we so desire. Leslie Newbigen describes it well when he states:

> The idea of the invisible church, in its popular use, derives its main attraction—unless I am mistaken—from the fact that each of us can determine its membership as he will. It is *our* ideal Church, containing the people whom we—in our present stage of spiritual development—would regard as fit members. . . . The congregation of God is something quite different. It is the company of people whom it has pleased God to call into the fellowship of his Son. *Its members are chosen by him, not by us, and we have to accept them whether we like them or not.* It is not a segregation but a congregation and the power by which it is constituted is the divine love which loves even the unlovely and reaches out to save all men.[23]

LIVING LOCALLY AS THE NEW HUMANITY

Thus far I have contended that the true revolutionaries are those who recognize that the dividing walls of ethnicity have been deconstructed in the supernatural creation of the New Humanity, the universal church. More than this, they also believe and are committed to living and nurturing such diversity in unity in local New Humanity churches that are visible, geographical expressions of the diversity in unity characteristic of the New Humanity.

The New Humanity scattered must be the New Humanity gathered according to the New Testament model of local churches. True revolutionaries could not disagree more with Barna's thesis that if we "place our hope in the local church, our hope is misplaced." Our hope in the local church is not misplaced; it is firmly placed in Christ as both head and cornerstone (Col 1:18; 1 Pet 2:6). Christ has promised, "I will build my church and the gates of Hades will not overcome it" (Matt 16:18). As

---

23. Newbigin, *Household*, 22–23 (emphasis mine).

the New Testament unfolds, it becomes clear that the Church with an uppercase C is inseparable from its local manifestation with a lowercase c.

On one occasion, I had lunch with a friend who was quite cynical about the local church. He had visited our church family on a couple of occasions, but he seemed to have difficulty connecting. Wondering whether the problem lay with our church members, my friend, or a little of both, I decided we should get together and talk. Our exchange was candid. The typical arguments for not associating with a local church body were revisited and debated. I believe the exchange was beneficial for both of us. A few days later, I received this e-mail in return:

> As I have said more than a few times before . . . I have not been able to bring myself to the place in my thinking that I can abide the thought of joining and being involved in another Christian fellowship, a "church." . . . And I am not totally off the hook with God because he says in His Word that we are not to forsake the gathering together for worship and etc., but I am a member of "the mystical body of believers," The Church of Jesus. I have trod this difficult and lonely road away from vibrant official Church fellowship for about five years now. But, you know, there wasn't much of it there when I was there, so I am saying two things: First, I am away from mainstream local church fellowship. Second, one of the reasons is the fact that what's there is not so hot anyway. Be in touch with your thoughts and feedback. May God always bless, make wise, and protect those who are Heaven-bound![24]

Maybe you have heard similar attitudes expressed. Or maybe this reflects how *you* feel about the local church—"What's there is not so hot anyway." Like many, you may have concluded that the spiritual and relational disfigurement of many local churches—not to speak of the ethnic and cultural homogeneity that characterizes the vast majority—must be explained away and replaced by new, fresh forms. As a result, the proverbial "throw out the baby with the bathwater" kicks into play leading far too many Christ-followers into an isolationism that is not only spiritually unhealthy but also ignores the inseparable connection between the universal and local church. Undoubtedly, many cultural shifts—such as what Barna terms the "niching" of society—help to explain such trends. I believe, however, a more important factor is the typical Christian's lack of understanding of what the New Testament says about the vital,

---

24. Used with permission.

indispensable role of the local church. For all of its flaws and failures, God has not given up on the local church and we shouldn't either.

It is precisely this inseparable relationship between the universal and local church that strongly argues for the intentional nurturing of diversity and multiethnicity in the local congregation. Some, of course, argue against this. Peter Wagner, a strong proponent of the homogeneous principle of church growth states: "Whenever Paul speaks of Christian believers being 'all one in Christ,' he is referring not to a normative pattern for local congregations, but rather to a supracongregational relationship of believers in the total Christian body over which Christ himself is the head."[25] Such a conclusion, however, ignores not only the inseparable link between the local and universal expressions of Christ's body, but also the intimate link between both and Christ himself.

Indeed, when it comes to Jesus' prayer that his disciples might be "brought to complete unity" (John 17:23), it is nonsense to interpret this in mere spiritual, universal terms. How will the world see in any tangible, meaningful sense the unity of believers from different ethnicities and cultures if it is not expressed in and among local churches? The "supracongregational relationship of believers in the total Christian body" means little to my next door neighbor or colleague at work. It could be understood as little more than a Platonic ideal. It is rather the supernatural demonstration of unity among believers who come from various walks of life, background, ethnicity, and culture that speaks of the power of the gospel.

CONCLUSION

I have argued in this chapter that the New Humanity is the *ekklēsia* of God. While the Scriptures do speak of the universal church, the vast majority of usages of the term *ekklēsia* refer to the local expression of the New Humanity. Furthermore, an inseparable link exists between the universal church and the local church. The local church is in microcosm what the universal church is in macrocosm. This inseparable link between the universal and local expressions of the New Humanity suggests that what characterizes the former should be intentionally nurtured and ultimately reflected in the latter. In other words, local churches should become New Humanity churches. In chapter 11,

---

25. Wagner, *Our Kind of People*, 132.

I will address how to approach situations in which the surrounding community is largely homogeneous in terms of ethnicity. In principle, however, the diversity in unity that marks the universal church should also be nurtured and expressed in the local church. Such diversity in unity would most certainly include diversity of ethnicity. However, it should also include other expressions of diversity—age, culture, worship styles, and of course, gender.

If these conclusions are correct (and I am convinced they are), *we simply do not have biblical justification for the intentional establishment of homogeneous local churches*. While particular ethnicities, cultures, ages, and even genders may be the focus of evangelistic initiatives (cf. 1 Cor 9:20–23) or initial discipleship, immediate steps must be taken to help these young believers understand their New Humanity identity and associate with a local church that embraces such diversity in unity. Such local churches cut across all lines of affinity and ethnicity. While such local churches may not be the most comfortable place to be, they will in the long term best reflect the beauty and unity for which Christ prayed (John 17:23). This is how we become true revolutionaries!

8

A Change of Clothes for the Church

Every trait of the Old Man's behavior is putrid, crumbling, or inflated like rotting waste or cadavers, stinking, ripe for being disposed of and forgotten.

Marcus Barth

IN *THE VOYAGE OF the Dawn Treader,* C. S. Lewis tells of a young boy named Eustace who, motivated by his greed, steals a gold armband. When he puts it on, however, he discovers that his greed turns him into a dragon. To make matters worse, the armband becomes painfully tight on his dragon foot.

One night, Eustace the dragon encounters a huge lion who offers a solution to his predicament. The lion tells Eustace to follow him to a high mountain well resembling a round bath. Upon arriving, Eustace longs to bath his aching foot in the crystal clear water, but the lion tells Eustace that he must first undress. At first, Eustace objects, reasoning that dragons don't wear clothes. Then he remembers that dragons—being "snaky sort of things"—shed their skins.

As Eustace starts scratching, the scales tumble to the ground. Like the peeling of a banana, the dragon's whole outer skin falls away. When he puts his foot into the water, however, he observes that it is just as tough, wrinkled, and scaly as before. So he continues scratching at the skin underneath only to realize that there is yet another layer of skin underlying that one. Finally the lion, named Aslan, says, "You will have to let me undress you."

Though fearful of the lion's claws, Eustace is desperate to be free from his dragon character. As Aslan begins to peel away the skin, layer by layer, Eustace feels as though he is about to die. Finally, with the thick, gnarled mess of dragon skin lying on the ground, Aslan takes hold of Eustace and throws him into the crystal clear water. Initially, the water stings; but it soon becomes perfectly delectable. Eustace begins to swim, splash, and laugh without pain. Eustace is a boy again!

In this story, Lewis vividly and masterfully illustrates the profound theological lessons concerning the New Humanity as described in Ephesians 4:22–24 and Colossians 3:9–11. Like it did for Eustace, the deceit of sin led humanity to a lifestyle of self-serving and divisive behavior. The Old Humanity became a "dragon" of sorts. Mankind's privileged role as God's image on earth was compromised. Humanity's representative role as God's vice-regent was perverted, his resemblance to his Creator was tarnished, and his relationships with fellow humans were deconstructed. Man discovered his nakedness and hid (Gen 3:10), attempting to conceal his shame from an all-knowing God. The effort proved futile. Makeshift garments were put on as an attempt to regain some measure of respectability and righteousness. This too proved to be inadequate. The transparency and intimacy initially characteristic of humankind as the image of God degenerated into shame, alienation, and blame. Humanity is in need of a change of clothes.

THE IDENTITY OF THE "OLD/NEW MAN"

The apostle Paul describes such a change of clothes in Ephesians 4:22–24 and Colossians 3:9–11. As you read these verses, notice the parallels with what we have already discovered about the New Humanity in Ephesians 2:15.

> . . . that you put off, concerning your former conduct, the *old man* which grows corrupt according to the deceitful lusts, and be renewed in the spirit of your mind, and that you put on the *new man* which was *created* according to God, in true righteousness and holiness. (Eph 4:22–24 [NKJV]; emphasis mine)

> Do not lie to one another, since you have put off the *old man* with his deeds, and have put on the *new man* who is renewed in knowledge according to the image of Him who *created* him,

where there is neither Greek nor Jew, circumcised nor uncircumcised, barbarian, Scythian, slave nor free, but Christ is all and in all. (Col 3:9–11 [NKJV]; emphasis mine)

Nowhere else does Paul give such an in-depth description of the "old/new man" as in these verses (cf. Rom 6:6). Nevertheless, as for the one new man of Ephesians 2, commentators are in sharp disagreement as to the identity of this "man." The vast majority individualize the term "man" (*anthrōpos*) in these verses, interpreting it as the *nature* of the individual believer.[1] Among those who interpret "man" as an old/new nature, some assert that while the believer has received a new nature, the old nature is still retained.[2] This has unfortunately led to somewhat of a schizophrenic view of the Christian life, in which a royal battle rages between the old self and the new self, both of which are vying for control of the believer's life. Others understand the expression to indicate that a radical inward change has taken place so that the old man (cf. Rom 6:6) no longer exists and the individual believer is now an entirely new being.[3] Both of these perspectives view the terms in the sense of the *ordo salutis*, referring specifically to the believer's personal conversion experience. The distinctive feature of both interpretations is their *individualistic* emphasis.

On the other hand, a few have seen the main emphasis of the old/new man motif to indicate, not so much inward transformation, but rather a "new mode of existence" or eschatological lifestyle that should characterize the individual believer.[4] A change has taken place for the believer transferring him from the old "aeon" or dominion to the new "aeon." The distinctive feature of this viewpoint is its *eschatological* emphasis.

For others, Paul's Adam theology (1 Cor 15; Rom 5) takes a prominent role in interpreting the "new man" references. As Markus Barth states: "The 'New Man' is most likely Christ himself, understood as the

---

1. Allan, *Ephesians*, 87; Bullinger, *Figures*, 569. This view is reflected in some of our more current translations. The RSV speaks of the "old nature" and "new nature" in both Eph 4 and Col 3. The NASB and the NRSV use the expressions "old self" and "new self."

2. Ryrie, *Balancing*, 35; Chafer, *Spiritual*, 112–14; Pentecost, *Pattern*, 99; Berkhof, *Systematic Theology*, 533.

3. Needham, *Birthright*, 74–75, 83; Murray, *Principles*, 218.

4. Roon, *Authenticity*, 336; Tannehill, *Dying and Rising*, 15. See also the J. B. Phillips translation: "the old way of living, the new life."

head, the epitome, the reality, the standard, the representative of the new 'creation' (Eph 2:10; 2 Cor 5:17; Gal 6:15)."[5] While this is also true to some degree for the ecclesiological view (below) as well as the eschatological view (above), the focus on Christ himself as the "new man" is more restrictive. The distinctive feature of this interpretation is its *christological* emphasis.

A final view, though often ignored by much popular teaching on these passages, understands the "old/new man" concept in a corporate sense, having reference to the New Humanity of which Christ, the last Adam, is the source and head.[6] The expressions "the old man" (*ton palaion anthrōpon*) and "the new man" (*ton kainon anthrōpon*) in these verses speak not of "a change that comes about in the way of faith and conversion in the life of the individual Christian, but of that which once took place in Christ and *in which his people had part in him in the corporate sense.*"[7] In this sense, Paul's references to the old/new man cannot be disassociated from the "one new man" concept of Ephesians 2. The distinctive feature of this interpretation is its *ecclesiological* emphasis.

It is my conviction that the collective nuance of the New Humanity in Ephesians 2:15 must govern our understanding of the old/new man as described in Ephesians 4 and Colossians 3. For far too long the "old/new man" terminology has been read through the individualized lenses of western culture. As a result, we have missed not only the intended meaning of Paul's precise terminology in these passages, but also the relevance of these texts for the dividing walls that piecemeal the landscape of the contemporary church.

Immediately, we see several parallels between Paul's teaching concerning the New Humanity in Ephesians 2 and similar terminology describing the old/new man in Ephesians 4 and Colossians 3. For example, in both Ephesians 4 and Colossians 3, Paul's teaching concerns an old/new *man* (*anthrōpos*) just as in Ephesians 2:15—"one new *man*" (*anthrōpos*). As already demonstrated, the terminology is *collective* in nuance referring to the solidarity of humanity in connection with either Adam, the first man, or Christ, the second man. Paul had at his disposal a wide range of vocabulary to choose from if his intent was to convey the idea of an "old nature" resident in individual believers.

---

5. Barth, *Ephesians*, 2:539.
6. Gutherie, *Theology*, 657–59; Westcott, *Ephesians*, 38; Bock, "New Man," 157–67.
7. Ridderbos, *Paul*, 63 (emphasis mine).

For example, he could have chosen the term "flesh" (*sarx*), which is often rendered "nature" in contemporary translations (cf. Rom 8:3–9; Gal 5:17; Eph 2:3). Or he could have employed the expression "body of sin" (*sōma tēs hamartias*) as found in Romans 6:6, a term nearly synonymous with "flesh." Finally, he could possibly have chosen the term "nature" (*physis*), an expression he has already used earlier in this epistle (Eph 2:3). However, Paul chose none of these terms that would indicate an individualized interpretation of the "old/new man" concept. Instead, he chose the designation "man" (*anthrōpos*), which clearly carries corporate overtones, speaking frequently of humankind in a generic sense. Therefore, the old/new man of Ephesians 4 and Colossians 3 seems to emphasize the corporate solidarity of the Old/New Humanity as it does in Ephesians 2.

The creation motif is another factor linking the old/new man of Ephesians 4 and Colossians 3 to the one new man of Ephesians 2. In all three passages (Eph 2:15; 4:24; Col 3:10), the new man is "created" (*ktisis*) even as Adam was created. In stark contrast to the old man who is being corrupted because of evil desires, the new man has been created "to be like God in true righteousness and holiness" (Eph 4:24). Furthermore, this new man is now being renewed "in knowledge in the image of its Creator" (Col 3:10). While the creation motif in these passages argues against identifying the new man as Christ himself,[8] it does link both references to Ephesians 2:15 as well as to the creation account of Genesis 1:26–27. In light of this, the parallels are between Adam, the first man, and Christ, the second man, as well as between Adam's collective progeny, the old man, and Christ's collective progeny, the new man. Christ, the image of God and the last Adam, initiated through his redemptive work the grand opportunity for alienated humanity to experience reconciliation and the hope of once again fulfilling his ordained role as the image of the heavenly man (1 Cor 15:45–49).

Given these parallels with the one new man of Ephesians 2 and the creation account of Genesis 1:26–27, it seems best to understand

---

8. It seems clear that (as in Eph 2:15) the new man cannot be synonymous with Christ. Christ and his cross-work are foundational to the new man but not equivalent to this man. To say that the new man was created *in* Christ (Eph 2:15; 4:24) is quite different from saying that the new man *is* Christ. The christological interpretation of the new man is usually supported by such references as Gal 3:27 and Rom 13:14, but these references do not necessitate this interpretation and the above mentioned considerations rule against it.

the "old/new man" terminology of Ephesians 4 and Colossians 3 as referring to the Old/New Humanity. This interpretation is confirmed by Paul's description of the new man in Colossians 3:11. Here the new man is described as the *place*[9] where there is "*no* Greek or Jew, circumcised or uncircumcised, barbarian, Scythian, slave or free, but Christ is all, and is in all" (emphasis mine). Paul's statement begins with a strong negation—a negation of *even the possibility*[10] that in this new man such preferential distinctions could exist. To reduce Paul's understanding of the old/new man to an individualistic nature renders this affirmation in verse 11 nonsensical. It is inconceivable that such a statement of relational diversity in unity could be described as a reality in the new nature of an individual. No, the relational affirmations of this verse are a reality *in* the new man as a *collective* entity for whom Christ is all and in all (cf. Gal 3:28)!

To sum up, the old man of Ephesians 4:22 and Colossians 3:9 is to be identified with the old man of Romans 6:6. The old man is the entirety of humanity alienated from God and within itself. As we have already seen, Paul's terminology refers to the corporate solidarity of the Old Humanity in connection with Adam as its head. The good news of Romans 6:6 is that, by means of the once-for-all death of the "one man, Jesus Christ" (Rom 5:15), the believer's connection with the Old Humanity has been definitively broken. Just as the old man is the entirety of humanity alienated from God and within itself (i.e. the Old Humanity), the new man is the entirety of humanity reconciled to God and within itself (i.e. the New Humanity). Through the redemptive-historical cross-work of Jesus, the second man and last Adam, believers of all ethnicities have now been identified *together* as those comprising the new man. Therefore, just as the one new man of Ephesians 2, the new man of Ephesians 4 and Colossians 3 is to be identified as the New Humanity, the church.[11]

---

9. The Greek particle *hopou* denotes "place" and is in reference to the new man of verse 10. See Robertson, *Grammar*, 712; BAG, 579.

10. Blass and DeBrunner, *Grammar*, §98; Lightfoot, *Colossians*, 216.

11. As I will demonstrate, this does not exclude individual implications for those who belong to the New Humanity. Some of the same terminology is applied elsewhere with more of an emphasis on the individual. In 2 Cor 4:16, Paul speaks of the renewal of the "inner man." Then in Eph 3:16, Paul prays for believers to be strengthened with God's Spirit in the "inner man" (cf. Rom 7:22). Furthermore, the renewal of each individual believer is foundational to the renewal of the collective whole (Eph 4:23).

UNDRESSING THE OLD AND DRESSING THE NEW

This being the case, what could Paul possibly mean by his characteristic "put off/put on" terminology? How can an individual or a group put off/put on something that is collective in meaning? Furthermore, how can those who are part of the New Humanity put on what they already are? Finally, do the put off/put on imperatives refer to the past one-time act of conversion or baptism or to ever new acts of ethical decision in the life of the believer?

The Old/New Humanity as a Lifestyle

In an attempt to answer these questions, several observations can be made. First, in Ephesians 4:22 Paul urges believers to put off the old man, describing such action as "with regard to your former way of life." Though grammatically connected to the command to "put off," this phrase nevertheless sheds light on Paul's understanding of the old/new man in these verses. The "former way of life" describes the Old Humanity *as it concretely manifested itself in the believers' former lifestyle*. In other words, Paul is speaking of the relational ethics characteristic of the Old Humanity. Therefore, the designation "old man" is to be understood as a figure of speech referring to the divisive behavior of their former life as described in verses Ephesians 4:17–19 (cf. Col 3:5–9).[12] Furthermore, if the descriptive designation "old man" is a figurative term for the corporately alienated lifestyle of the Old Humanity, we could conclude that the counterpart expression "new man" in these passages is equally a reference to the corporately reconciled lifestyle of the New Humanity as described in Ephesians 4:25–32 (cf. Col 3:12–25). Therefore, in both Ephesians 4 and Colossians 3, Paul is describing the old/new man in ethical terms.

In Romans, Paul views the old man *anthropologically*, describing unregenerate humanity's relation to Adam (Rom 5:12–21) as well as regenerate humanity's relation to the last Adam, Christ (Rom 6:1–23). In Ephesians 2, Paul views the new man *ecclesiologically*, describing the uniting of Jew and Gentile into one body, the church. However in

---

12. More specifically, the figure of speech is a metonymy of subject in which the noun ("man") is used for the actions associated with the "man." Furthermore, the translation "*your* former manner of life" (NIV, NASB) must supply the possessive pronoun. Its absence may indicate that the phrase is better translated "*the* former manner of life," referring to the pre-cross era.

Ephesians 4 and Colossians 3, Paul views the old/new man *ethically*, describing the lifestyle characteristic of each and what must now be put off/ put on by the believer. From all three perspectives, the man described *is a collective entity* (i.e. the Old/New Humanity), though viewed in each context through a different lens.[13]

Putting Off and Putting On

A second observation pertains to *when* this action of putting off/putting on takes place? Is it at the point of conversion or is it a daily occurrence in the life of the church? How do both of these relate to the redemptive-historical crucifixion of the old man (Rom 6) and creation of the new man (Eph 2)?

Whatever may be the temporal significance of putting off/putting on the old/new man, Paul views the redemptive-historical crucifixion of the Old Humanity and creation of the New Humanity as foundational to such action. That is why he affirms in Ephesians 4:21 that believers were taught to carry out this ethical change of clothes "just as truth is *in Jesus*." Nowhere else in this epistle does Paul use the name "Jesus" by itself. Rarely does the designation occur alone, but when it does there is generally an express reference to the historical Jesus with particular emphasis on his death and resurrection.[14] Viewed from a redemptive-historical viewpoint, *Christ's death, burial, and resurrection initiated the history of which believers of all ethnicities become a part at the point of conversion.* In other words, the crucifixion of the Old Humanity (Rom 6:6) and the creation of the New Humanity (Eph 2:15) are both redemptive-historical. However, the change of clothes (put off/put on) of which Paul now speaks is ethical and experiential. The order is of vital importance. The redemptive-historical crucifixion of the Old Humanity and creation of the New Humanity are foundational to any ethical change of clothes in the present. Just as for Eustace, the old man is to be undressed and the new man is to be dressed. Also like Eustace, *we cannot do it on our own*. The more we scratch and attempt to shed in our own strength the relational alienation of the Old Humanity, the more we discover our inadequacy.

---

13. See Hoch, "New Man," 117–19.
14. See 1 Thess 1:10; 4:14; Rom 8:11; 2 Cor 4:10, 11, 14.

Yes, dragon skins are not easily discarded. The only remedy is the crucifixion of the old and the creation of the new on the cross. For this reason we are *never* told in Scripture to crucify the old man.[15] That is why Paul affirms elsewhere: "I *am* crucified with Christ, and it is no longer I who live, but Christ who lives in me" (Gal 2:20; emphasis mine). Such crucifixion of the old and consequent creation of the new already took place historically and definitively at the cross. Any action of putting off the old and putting on the new is founded upon this fact rooted in salvation history.

There is, however, a personal sense in which believers have put off the Old Humanity and put on the New Humanity. Such a change of clothes took place at the point of conversion as depicted in baptism. Like Eustace, we can attempt in our own strength to shed (like an old, discarded skin) the shame-ridden fig leaves of the Old Humanity and put on the garments of justice and reconciliation that characterize the New Humanity—only to discover our inadequacy. We scratch and peel away the old without ever discovering the new. We are as rough and scaly as before. Finally, Jesus says, "You will have to let me undress you!" That he does—*when we embrace the cross*. The process is painful. The layers of sinful self-righteousness and divisiveness are only stripped away by a "circumcision done by Christ" (Col 2:11). Such "undressing" is penetrating and profoundly transforming. It strips off the gnarled mess of the Old Humanity and makes all things new (2 Cor 5:17). Now, "buried with him in baptism and raised with him through . . . faith" (Col 2:12), we discover ourselves fully human once again.

This seems to be the emphasis of Paul's "put off/put on" terminology in Colossians 3:9–11, which is grammatically placed in the indicative rather than the imperative: "*Since you have put off* the old man with his deeds, and *have put on* the new man" (NKJV; emphasis mine). No doubt, Paul is referring to believers' conversion and subsequent baptism into Christ (1 Cor 12:13; Rom 6:3; Gal 3:27). Here, the new man is the New Humanity conceived at the cross, born at Pentecost, and with which believers become identified at the point of conversion. When one becomes part of the New Humanity, the historic death, burial, and resurrection of Christ are no longer external events of the past, but that which initiated the history of which the believer is now a part. That is why Paul

---

15. Compare Gal 5:24 where in the NIV "sinful nature" is best translated "flesh" (*sarx*).

writes earlier in this same chapter: "Since, then, you have been raised with Christ, set your hearts on things above, where Christ is seated at the right hand of God. Set your minds on things above, not on earthly things. For you died, and your life is now hidden with Christ in God" (Col 3:1–3).

Baptism, of course, depicts this reality as well as the "put off/put on" imagery of Ephesians 4 and Colossians 3. The candidate would approach the water wearing an old garment, which would then be stripped off as he entered the waters of baptism. Upon coming up out of the water, the believer would put on a new suit of clothes, usually a white robe.[16] At the point of conversion as symbolized by baptism, the believer's connection to the Old Humanity with its relational *exclusivism* is definitively put off and his connection to the New Humanity with its relational *inclusivism* is definitively put on. It is this relational inclusivism of which Paul writes to the Corinthian believers: "For we were *all* baptized by one Spirit into one body—whether Jews or Greeks, slave or free—and we were *all* given the one Spirit to drink" (1 Cor 12:13; emphasis mine). Baptism is the decisive, initial act that must now be followed by an obedient lifestyle. In the "put off/put on" terminology of Colossians 3 Paul is saying, "Let them now adorn their baptism profession of faith with a godly life."[17]

It is this godly, relationally reconciled life of the New Humanity that must now be put on daily. While the "put off/put on" imagery of Colossians 3 is in the indicative (taking place at the point of conversion/baptism), the same clothing imagery of Ephesians 4 is in the imperative: believers are taught to put off/put on as an ongoing process.[18] Daily, based on our New Humanity identity, we must *deconstruct* the ways of the old life and *construct* the ways of the new life. In Christ, the dirty, tattered clothes of the past *have been* put off and the fresh, clean clothes of unity and purity *have been* put on. This must now be seen in the lifestyle of the local church. As S. Lewis Johnson writes, "Clothes do not make the man, but a man is often reflected in his clothes, and Paul would have

---

16. For a discussion of first-century baptismal practices, see Beasley-Murray, *Baptism*, 149–50.

17. Hendriksen, *Colossians*, 149.

18. The aorist infinitives "put off" (*apothesthai*) and "put on" (*endysasthai*) are governed by the present infinitive "be renewed" (*ananeousthai*).

the new man reflected in a new moral attire after the image of him that created him."[19]

New Clothes for the New Humanity

What is the "moral attire" that we as believers are to put off and put on? Moreover, *how* are we to do this? One cannot read Ephesians 4 or Colossians 3 without observing the *relational* character of Paul's imperatives. By means of a series of second-person plurals, Paul defines the societal ethics of the Old/New Humanity. Paul specifies that we are first to put off the divisive moral attire characteristic of the Old Humanity that is being "corrupted by its deceitful desires" (Eph 4:22). Having urged us to be who we are (4:1–6) and to remember who we were (4:17–19), Paul then exhorts us not to be who we once were (4:20–22). We do this by putting off falsehood (v. 25), because "we are all members of one body" (v. 25). Furthermore, we do this by laying aside anger (v. 26), thievery (v. 28), unwholesome speech (v. 29), bitterness (v.31), brawling and slander (v. 31), along with "every form of malice" (v. 31).

As for the description of the clothes of the Old Humanity in Colossians 3, Paul lists such vices as "anger, rage, malice, slander, and filthy language from your lips" (v. 8) and then exhorts us to "not lie to each other" (v. 9) since we have already put off the Old Humanity. Yes, caught in his own deceitful web of self-centeredness, the existence of the Old Humanity is transitory and his destiny is dim.

In contrast to the old man who is "being corrupted" (Eph 4:22), the new man has "been created" (Eph 4:24). Therefore, not only are we to shed the lifestyle characteristics that once marked our existence as those belonging to the Old Humanity, but we also are to wear the new moral attire characteristic of our new identity as part of the New Humanity. We are to "speak truthfully" to our neighbor, for we are "all members of one body" (v. 25). As members of the New Humanity, we are to "speak

---

19. Johnson, "Christian Apparel," 23. Some have interpreted Paul's "put off/put on" terminology in light of the mystery religions, Gnosticism, or Greek and Hellenistic Jewish literature (see Lohse, *Epistles*, 141; Horst, "Observations," 181–82). However, the most likely background for Paul's imagery is the Old Testament. Here we find many examples of being clothed with such moral qualities as "strength" (Isa 51:9; 52:1), "righteousness" (Ps 132:9; Job 39:14), "salvation" (2 Chr 6:41), and "splendor" and "majesty" (Ps 104:1). A particularly helpful parallel is found in Ps 132:9 where being "clothed with righteousness" is similar to "putting on the new man" who is righteous (Eph 4:24). New Testament references include 1 Thess 5:8; Gal 3:27; Rom 13:12, 14; 2 Cor 5:2–4.

A Change of Clothes for the Church 167

the truth, the whole truth, and nothing but the truth." Furthermore, we are to "share with those in need" (v. 28). As for our speech, we are to express only that which is "helpful for building others up according to their needs" (v. 29). And we are to be "kind and compassionate to one another, forgiving each other, just as in Christ God forgave" us (v. 32).

Paul's words to the Colossians echo the same relational refrain. Recognizing our corporate identity as "God's chosen people" and as those who are "holy and dearly loved," we are to clothe ourselves "with compassion, kindness, humility, gentleness and patience" (v. 12). Furthermore, we are to "bear with each other and forgive whatever grievances you may have against one another" (v. 13). We are to forgive others as the Lord forgave us (v. 13). And over and beyond all these moral virtues characteristic of the New Humanity, we are to "put on love, which binds them all together in perfect unity" (v. 14). As we do this the "peace of Christ" will "rule" in our hearts, for as members of the New Humanity we are "called to peace" (v. 15).

In both Ephesians and Colossians, one can't help but notice the emphasis on *love* as both the motivation for and manifestation of such a change of clothes. In Paul's letter to the Ephesians, love is referred to no less than sixteen times. While in chapters 1–3 there are no commands to love, we do find affirmations of the love of the Father for the Son and for believers (1:6; 2:4). Such affirmations prepare us for Paul's prayer of Ephesians 3:17–19 where he requests that we, "being rooted and established in *love*, may have power, together with all the saints, to grasp how wide and long and high and deep is the *love* of Christ, and to know this *love* that surpasses knowledge—that you may be filled to the measure of all the fullness of God" (emphasis mine). Paul clarifies that the love of God is too large to be confined or defined by any geometrical measurements. It is not three-dimensional, but four-dimensional! It has breadth, length, height, and depth. It is "broad" enough to reach the whole world and beyond (1:9–10, 20). It is "long" enough to stretch from eternity to eternity (1:4–6, 18; 3:9). It is "high" enough to raise all who believe in Christ to heavenly places (1:13; 2:6). It is "deep" enough to rescue people from sin's depravity and even from the grip of Satan himself (2:1–5; 6:11–12). Christ's love is as unknowable (v. 19) as his riches are unfathomable (v. 8).

Only as the New Humanity is impacted by such profound love are we motivated to obey the exhortations of chapters 4–6 that are summed up in Ephesians 5:1–2: "as dearly loved children . . . live a life of love, just as Christ loved us." This same emphasis is also evident in Paul's words to the Colossian believers. Only as we grasp that we are "dearly loved" (3:12) can we effectively "put on love" (3:14) as our new moral attire. These words remind us that understanding our new identity is more than a "mind" thing; rather, it touches the deepest recesses of our emotional and volitional being. It is more than intellectual understanding; it is feeling and responding to the eternal love expressed to us by the Father, Son, and Holy Spirit (Eph 1:3–14). Essentially, both Jesus and Paul prayed the same thing—that the love expressed in the Trinity might be demonstrated in the New Humanity (John 17:21–26).

It is explicitly clear that, in giving these highly relational commands that are best summed up by love, Paul is *not* speaking of a mystical, universal, or spiritual community. Admittedly, it is in Ephesians and Colossians more than in any other of his epistles that Paul speaks of the church in its universal dimensions. Nevertheless, when he moves from the indicative (who we are) to the imperative (what we are to do), he relates positional truth to the practical realities of life in community. Paul is addressing the *local* church, the New Humanity as expressed in a specific, geographically defined area, consisting of Jews and Gentiles, slaves and free, men and women, young and old, all of whom were living and worshiping in proximity to one another. Furthermore, while these Spirit-produced virtues of "compassion," "kindness," "forgiveness," "love," "humility," and "patience" are essential for any group of Christ-followers, they are especially tested and refined in the context of ethnic and cultural diversity. This was true when Paul wrote these words, addressed to a context of tension between Jew and Gentile. This is equally true today in the multiethnic church. A Japanese member of the church I pastor recently wrote me these words concerning the growing number of ethnicities reflected in our congregation: "The unconditional love of Jesus will have plenty of opportunity to become central at Central Bible Church! I also happen to believe that by pursuing this (i.e. multiethnicity) we will have the greatest chance to discover for ourselves how much God has loved us who are so unlike him."

Living the Death of Jesus

It is evident that a life of relational unity in the context of ethnic diversity cannot be realized apart from the cross. The unity of the New Humanity created *at* the cross is maintained *by* the cross. The dividing walls that piecemeal the church today can be deconstructed only as we take up the cross in our daily lives. As Klyne Snodgrass observes, "This means that we do not leave our cocrucifixion behind. We stay crucified. It is a reality that stamps our lives."[20] If we have already been crucified *together*, buried *together*, and raised *together* (Rom 6:6; Eph 2:5-6), what prevents us from living *together*, worshiping *together*, and serving *together*? Today, the body of Christ is broken because individual Christians are not. Dietrich Bonhoeffer once said, "When Christ calls a man, he bids him come and die." Paul can say, "I die every day" (1 Cor 15:31), and elsewhere, "I am always carrying in the body the dying of Jesus" (2 Cor 4:10-11). It was also this perspective that enabled him to say, "I fill up in my flesh what is still lacking in regard to Christ's afflictions, for the sake of his body, which is the church" (Col 1:24). Paul so identified with the God-inspired vision of diversity in unity in the New Humanity that he was willing to endure the same suffering that Christ endured in order to see such oneness become a reality. Are we?

RENEWAL ACCORDING TO THE IMAGE

In Jesus' high priestly prayer on the night he was betrayed, he requested of the Father that his followers might "be brought to complete unity" (John 17:23). Could Jesus' prayer have been in the mind of Paul as he wrote of the New Humanity to the Ephesian and Colossian believers? It seems likely. For in both passages (Eph 4:22-24; Col 3:9-11) we find a detailed exposition of *how* we are brought to complete unity. We are brought to complete unity by putting off the divisive behavior of the Old Humanity and by putting on the reconciliatory behavior of the New Humanity. Such a change of moral clothes, however, involves a profound process of renewal.

Paul says in Colossians 3:10 that the New Humanity is "being renewed in knowledge in the image of its Creator." Furthermore, in Ephesians 4:23 he urges: "Be made new in the attitude of your minds." Paul obviously highlights the importance of this renewal, mentioning it in both passages that address our change of moral attire. The process of personal and corporate renewal is foundational and indispensable to any action of putting off and putting on in the life of the church. Apart from

---

20. Snodgrass, "Identity," 264.

such profound renewal—individually and collectively—any perceived change of clothes is superficial and contrived. Whatever this renewal consists of, Paul's words are a timely reminder that we must never settle for humanly contrived means of making the church be what it is called to be. While outward organization, targeted initiatives, and cooperative attempts to nurture the diversity in unity that is the hallmark of the New Humanity may all have their place, little genuine and lasting change will be made apart from the renewal of which Paul speaks.

The Renewal

What *does* this renewal consist of? A helpful starting point is to recall the aspects intrinsic to the Pauline concept of newness highlighted in chapter 5.[21] Our renewal can be viewed with respect to our past, present, and future. With regard to the past, the renewal of the New Humanity implies a stark contrast with the lifestyle of the Old Humanity. Such a distinct difference exists between the new and the old that the two are mutually exclusive. As previously noted, the new actually asserts itself over the old and crowds it out of existence. While our actions are so much a part of our person as to be called a "man," our New Humanity lifestyle must be so completely foreign to our previous behavior as to be called a *new* man. If the Old Humanity is characterized by disharmony and segregation, the renewal of the New Humanity suggests that the church is progressively characterized as the arena of peace and reconciliation. As such, the renewal that Paul describes *is* in direct answer to Jesus' prayer that his followers might be brought to *complete* unity (John 17:23). In this renewal, *nothing* that hints of the divisive behavior of the Old Humanity must be allowed to exist in the experience of the New Humanity.[22]

As to the future, participants in the New Humanity live in the realm of the already/but not yet. Today we experience partially what one day we will experience fully. Jesus' prayer hints of this same tension between earthly and heavenly realities: "I am in them and you in me. May they be

---

21. The verbs describing the renewal process, *anakainoō* (Col 3:10) and *ananeoō* (Eph 4:23), are formed from the adjectives *kainos/neos*, which describe the *new* man in Eph 2:15.

22. This may explain why the "put off" terminology is nearly always associated with "all" or "everything" as in Col 3:8, Heb 12:1, Jas 1:21, and 1 Pet 2:1. The object of "putting off" is always designated as a totality.

brought to *complete* unity." We are *already* one with the Father and Son, but have *not yet* experienced the complete unity for which Jesus prays. However, the process of renewal Paul describes relentlessly pushes the church forward with Jesus' prayer on her lips: "Thy kingdom come, they will be done, on earth as it is in heaven." When properly understood, this eschatological aspect of finality provokes a holy discontent with things as they are. Having glimpsed and tasted what we will someday be, we are not content to remain as we are. This perspective effectively dispels any status quo bias that passively accepts the present day ethnic divides in the church, all of which blatantly contradict our collective identity as the New Humanity.

As to the present, the renewal of the New Humanity is dynamic in nature. As in Jesus' prayer, the descriptions of renewal in both Ephesians 4:23 and Colossians 3:10 are in the passive voice. This indicates that *the renewal springs from the very nature of who the church is as the New Humanity.* The same Spirit that gave birth to the New Humanity now dynamically renews the New Humanity according to the image of his Creator. Our responsibility is to cooperate with what the Spirit is doing to help us become what we were meant to be. This, of course, implies a process—one that bring the lifestyle of the church into harmony with its true identity.

Each of these aspects of the renewal of the New Humanity is grounded in an understanding and growing appreciation of our new identity. In Ephesians 4:23 this renewal takes place "in the attitude of your minds," whereas in Colossians 3:10 this same renewal is "in knowledge." In the former passage, Paul uses the term "mind" (*nous*), speaking of the "inner direction of their thought and will and the orientation of their moral consciousness."[23] In the latter passage, the term "knowledge" (*epinōsis*) speaks of learning that results in behavioral change.[24] A survey of these two terms here and elsewhere indicate the degree to which both speak of a profound, inner change of perspective and orientation resulting in a corresponding change of behavior. Furthermore, such change of perspective must take place *both* individually and corporately. In Ephesians 4, Paul emphasizes the individual aspect—"in the attitude of your minds" (v. 23)—whereas in Colossians 3:10 the renewal described is in direct relation to the collective New Humanity. If the church is to be

23. Behm, *TDNT*, 4:958.
24. Bultmann, *TDNT*, 1:708. Cf. Col 1:9; Phil 1:9–11.

renewed *collectively* and *relationally* as the New Humanity, each believer must experience *personally* and *inwardly* a renewal of biblical proportions influencing how he/she views others within the body of Christ. Paul writes to the Corinthian believers, "So from now on we regard no one from a worldly point of view" (2 Cor 5:16). For Paul, this change of perspective was the result of a change of identity (2 Cor 5:17).

Any attempt to put off and put on certain behavior apart from a profound renewal that affects our individual and collective identity is a step toward legalism. On the other hand, when we embrace our New Humanity identity, we also embrace the relational ethics motivated by love that accompany this identity. In this sense, the clothing imagery in these passages begins in our minds and hearts before it begins in our behavior. Our identity as the New Humanity is foundational to our behavior as the New Humanity. We must put on a new way of thinking before we can put on a new way of acting. Again, any lasting change of clothes for the church must begin here. Only as our *minds* are renewed with a growing *knowledge* of our individual and collective identity in Christ will we be able to effectively live out our vocation as the New Humanity.

The Image

Our vocation as the New Humanity is to represent the Thee-in-One as his image. All humanity was created and continues to exist *as* the image of God. However, for all who are part of the New Humanity, a renewal takes place that is *in accordance with*[25] the image of our Creator.[26] While touching each individual member of the New Humanity, this renewal *according to* the Creator's image has in view the church as a corporate entity. Just as Adam *alone* was not the full image of God apart from Eve, so in the New Humanity no one individual *alone* (or one local church alone) stands as the full image of God apart from others. We all—red, yellow, black, or white—desperately need one another for this renewal to take place. As the New Humanity experiences this collective renewal, which crowds out the divisiveness of the past and pushes us toward the complete diversity in unity of the future, the three characteristics

---

25. Paul intentionally chooses his vocabulary to convey the distinction between all humanity *as* the image of God and the New Humanity which is now being renewed *according to* (*kata*) the image.

26. The reference is certainly to Christ, who created "in himself" the New Humanity (Eph 2:15) and is the perfect image of God (2 Cor 4:4; Col 1:15).

intrinsic to humanity's representative role as image are restored (see Figure 5.1, page 102).

First, the New Humanity is being renewed to *rule*. Our identity as the New Humanity reminds us that we were originally created (Gen 1) and then recreated (Eph 2) as God's official representatives, entrusted with the vocation of being God's vice-regent in this otherwise alienated world (Ps 8; Heb 2:5–9). What the Old Humanity failed to do, the New Humanity has been created and empowered to do. The vocation of ruling would certainly include the original cultural mandate given to the first man—to fill and subdue the earth (Gen 1:28). This—God's *Magna Carta*—entrusted to the original humanity is no less the responsibility of the New Humanity. "When we obey the Cultural Mandate," Nancy Pearcey writes, "We participate in the work of God Himself, as agents of His common grace." Understanding this helps us "move beyond *criticizing* culture to *creating* culture."[27] Unfortunately, many evangelicals today have forgotten the implications of our mandate to rule, confusing the mandates of our culture for the mandates of the gospel.

As the scriptural story of humanity unfolds we see that our mandate to rule extends far beyond our relationship to this earth and its culture. As the New Humanity, we are called to have dominion in our conflict with evil. It is in the New Humanity, with the authority given by our Head, that sin is mastered (Col 3:5) and Satan is crushed (Rom 16:20). We rule by putting off the old and putting on the new. We rule by living according to kingdom culture rather than fallen culture. We also rule by exercising our authority over the demonic powers that seek to reconstruct the walls that have been torn down through Christ's cross work. Jesus promised to build his church and that the gates of hell itself would not prevail against it (Matt 16:18). At present, we do not see all things in subjection to mankind as God originally intended (Heb 2:8). *However, we see Jesus*, the ideal man who guarantees our future rule (Rev 5:10; 11:15; 20:6; 22:5).

Second, the New Humanity is being renewed to *resemble* its Creator. Just as the original humanity was created as the likeness-image of God (Gen 1:26), so the New Humanity is being renewed into the likeness of its Creator, Jesus Christ. The New Humanity, the church, was chosen in Christ to be "holy and blameless in his sight" (Eph 1:4) and is presently being cleansed by "the washing with water through the word"

27. Pearcey, *Total Truth*, 49, 58.

(Eph 5:26). While we were never created *as* gods, we were designed to be *like* God—to individually and collectively share in his communicable attributes such as "justice," "love," "peace," and "mercy."

This points us to the third aspect of our renewal as the New Humanity—*relationship*. As the New Humanity, we faithfully resemble our Creator to the degree that we reflect in our relationships the unity of Father, Son, and Holy Spirit who together provide the template for the renewal of redeemed humanity. Thus "the Church as a whole is an icon of God the Trinity, reproducing on earth the mystery of unity in diversity."[28] We reproduce this mystery to the degree that the human boundary markers of color, culture, and class are no longer the criteria of determining our associations within the body of Christ. When we clothe ourselves with the New Humanity, we clothe ourselves with the reality that "there is no Greek or Jew, circumcised or uncircumcised, barbarian, Scythian, slave or free, but Christ is all, and is in all" (Col 3:11; cf. Gal 3:28).

In this one verse, Paul mentions religious, cultural, and social boundary markers that characterize and accentuate the segregationist tendencies of the Old Humanity. He first mentions the Jew/Gentile divide, employing the term "Greek" rather than "Gentile." The Greeks were considered the epitome of Gentile culture, in whose eyes all others were barbarians. Paul further mentions the semantically loaded boundary markers "circumcised/ uncircumcised" that we have already discussed. As for the slave in the culture of that day, Aristotle remarked that he was merely a "living tool." Finally, on the bottom of the social rung were the Scythians whom Josephus describes as "little better than wild beasts."[29]

Distinctions and Boundaries

What could Paul possibly mean when he states that in the New Humanity these religious, cultural, and social distinctions no longer exist? Does the renewal of the New Humanity result in a leveling of ethnic and cultural identity? Is Paul encouraging a type of amalgamation in which believers of various ethnicities—not to mention cultures, backgrounds, generations, or class—lose their personal identity in favor of becoming something entirely different, a type of "third race"?

---

28. Ware, *Orthodox Church*, 240.
29. O'Brien, *Colossians*, 193; Josephus, *Against Apion* 2.269.

In answering these questions, it is helpful to distinguish between the concept of "distinctions" and "boundaries." Distinctions are those factors—whether ethnic, cultural, or otherwise—that contribute to determining individual or group identity. I am an American. Even after spending many years in France and after acquiring the language and the culture to a great extent, I was considered by many in that country as "the American." The fact that I was born and raised in America made me *distinct* from those born and raised in France. As applied to Colossians 3:11, Paul is obviously not arguing for a leveling of *distinctions*. Greeks remain Greeks and Jews remain Jews. Such distinctions exist intrinsically and are invariable. I cannot change where I was born or the color of my skin. Other distinctions are somewhat variable—"slave or free." Yet even here, Paul is not too concerned with any change of situation (1 Cor 7:21–22).

Boundaries, on the other hand, are created when distinctions begin to have primary defining force in the life of a person or group. Boundaries are symbolic and variable; they help a group distinguish itself from other groups. When a group identifies who it is by defining who it is not, greater solidarity and group homogeneity are the result. This also results, however, in the fragmentation of the larger whole into "in-groups" and "out-groups." In some spheres of life, ethnic boundaries may be acceptable and needed. Paul is arguing, however, that in the New Humanity, ethnic (Greek/Jew), social (slave/free), and religious (circumcised/uncircumcised) distinctions *must no longer have primary defining force*. When they do, they become boundary markers that fragment the larger whole—the body of Christ.

From this perspective, Paul is *not* arguing for a leveling of distinctions in the New Humanity. As we have seen, the creation of the one new man does *not* constitute the denial of differences between Jew and Gentile, or between any other ethnicity represented in the New Humanity. Christ calls us *past* our ethnicity, but not *out of* our ethnicity. Furthermore, the renewal of the New Humanity is not *irrespective* of differences of ethnicity and culture, but *inclusive* of such differences. The unity of the New Humanity is not "color blind." We are not collectively renewed as the New Humanity by superficially ignoring our differences of color and culture, but by profoundly appreciating our differences. Distinctions still exist within the body of Christ, but evaluations based on those distinctions must be deconstructed. Distinctions still exist, but they no longer have primary defining force. Paul is saying that in the non-homogeneous New Humanity such distinctions must *never* be the basis of defining our primary identity or determining our unity. Such boundary markers have been replaced by Christ "who is all, and is in all" (Col 3:11).

CONCLUSION: A CHANGE OF CLOTHES FOR TODAY

When I got up this morning, I put on my clothes. You most likely did also. As mentioned earlier, clothes do not make the individual; but an individual is often reflected in his or her clothes. Like believers down through the centuries, the church today is in need of a change of clothes. To strip off the old and put on the new, however, requires a profound *change of identity*. In fact, such putting off and putting on *is* the very change of identity that Paul is speaking of in the passages we have examined. No amount of reorganization, "ten easy steps," churchwide campaigns, urgent appeals, or faddish trends will suffice in helping the church live out its God given vocation. No, we must be touched at our very core—our understanding, conviction, and appreciation of who we truly are as God's New Humanity. Nothing less will do.

From Paul's clothing metaphors of Ephesians 4 and Colossians 3, we have discovered that the new man in these passages is to be equated with the one new man of Ephesians 2:15. In all three passages, Paul is speaking of the New Humanity—created at the cross (Eph 2:15), embraced at conversion (Col 3:10), and practiced as a lifestyle (Eph 4:24). Furthermore, the New Humanity is continually being renewed according to the image of its Creator, reflecting the same diversity in unity characteristic of Father, Son, and Holy Spirit.

While ethnic *distinctions* continue to exist in the New Humanity, ethnic *boundaries* must not. This is what Paul means when he declares that in the New Humanity there "is no Greek or Jew, circumcised or uncircumcised, barbarian, Scythian, slave or free" (Col 3:11). Ethnic distinctions are God given; ethnic boundaries are man-made. Distinctions of ethnicity enrich the life of the New Humanity in both its universal and local expressions; ethnic boundaries fragment the church, leading to homogeneous subgroups in which ethnicity often becomes the primary defining force of identity.

The contemporary phenomenon of churches splintered along lines of ethnicity (not to mention class, generational preferences, secondary doctrines, and worship styles) is—at its very core—a problem of *identity*. We all, churches included, function out of identity. We must ask ourselves: *Which identity will we adopt?* Which set of clothes will we put on? Will it be the homogeneity of our ethnicity, which is most likely where we will feel the most comfortable? Or will it be the diversity in unity of our New Humanity identity? Based on the biblical evidence, the local church should intentionally nurture the diversity in unity that characterizes both our Creator and his creation—the New Humanity.

9

The Powers That Divide

I know there is a God because in Rwanda I shook hands with the devil. I have seen him, I have smelled him and I have touched him. I know the devil exists, and therefore I know there is a God.

Lieutenant General Roméo Dallaire

THROUGH THE OPEN WINDOW I hear the rhythmic music of joyful believers. The harmony of their voices and the movement of their bodies remind me that I'm in Africa. The vibrant sound of praise continues for hours, reverberating throughout the surrounding neighborhoods. The joy in the believers' faces and the hope of which they sing seem to push back the otherwise overwhelming stench of urine and garbage in the streets.

The 1994 genocide in Rwanda, Africa, claimed the lives of nearly a million of its citizens. The horror of the massacre is beyond description. Entire families were annihilated simply because they belonged to a particular tribe. Those who survived carry the deep physical and emotional scars of a tragedy the world must never forget.

Today, the country is still reeling from the impact of the devastation. Bodies are still being uncovered where they had been ruthlessly buried in mass graves. Erected on many of these sites are small memorials declaring "Never Again!" Others have simply passed into oblivion and will never be found.

During a recent visit, one pastor recounted to me his story of survival. For days he hid in a damp, reeking hole in the ground. A compassionate colleague managed to bring him enough food for survival. From the very beginning of the genocide, he was separated from most of his family members, never to see them again. Only he, his wife, and one son survived. Emmanuel Sitaki is another survivor of the genocide. He is a close, personal friend and served as an elder for several years in our local church. Emmanuel lost more than thirty members of his extended family during that atrocious massacre. The remains of one family member were only recently found.

It is estimated that more than 25 percent of the entire population of eight million in Rwanda today are orphans. The ravages of the genocide and HIV/AIDS have left an even greater proportion of widows.

What happened in Rwanda between two indigenous tribes, Tutsi and Hutu, is obviously an extreme example of what Michael Emerson and Christian Smith term "racialization." However, it is more. Behind the racialization leading to such human atrocities is a demonization of ethnicities. Lieutenant General Roméo Dallaire, in charge of the United Nations peacekeeping troops at the time, "watched as the devil took control of paradise on earth and fed on the blood of the people."[1] Satan did this by pitting one ethnicity against another and fueling the fires of hatred, all of which led to the ruthless massacre of hundreds of thousands. Throughout history, whether it be Cain against Abel, the Babylonians against the Israelites, the Hutu against Tutsi, or white against black, Satan has taken control and "fed on the blood of the people."

THE REALITY OF OUR ENEMY

If Satan feeds on the blood of the people in society in general, he does even more so within the church. The devil is a destroyer, as indicated by his name "Apollyon" (Rev 9:11). As the *protoevangelium* of Genesis 3:15 so graphically describes, he is intent on striking at the heel of Christ. The apostle Paul knew this. That is why he concludes his letter to the Ephesians with an exposé of the enemy's ruthless strategies to divide and ultimately destroy the New Humanity. As Satan did at Babel, so he does in the body of Christ today. If Pentecost is the reversal of Babel, Satan's

---

1. Dallaire, *Shake Hands*, jacket.

intent is to *reverse the reversed*. In Ephesians 6:10–12, Paul describes in startling detail just what the church at large is up against:

> Finally, be strong in the Lord and in his mighty power. Put on the full armor of God so that you can take your stand against the devil's schemes. For our struggle is not against flesh and blood, but against the rulers, against the authorities, against the powers of this dark world and against the spiritual forces of evil in the heavenly realms.

The apostle Paul was neither a materialist nor a magician. He was guided by the Holy Spirit to give us penetrating insight into the reality of the spirit world and the adversary's incessant attacks against the church, the New Humanity. In no other passage of Scripture do we find such a detailed listing of the formidable forces of evil against which the New Humanity must take its stand.[2] The author of these verses makes it explicitly clear—the adversary wants to dismember the New Humanity, for in dismembering the New Humanity he launches a frontal attack on the head of the church, Christ himself.

These final words of Paul to the Ephesian believers have often been referred to as *the* manual of spiritual warfare. Throughout the history of the church, believers have turned to this passage for encouragement and wisdom in opposing the forces of darkness. This text certainly does not touch on all the Bible has to say about the church's titanic struggle against intelligent evil, but it amazingly and concisely pulls together the essential truths about our enemy, our New Humanity identity, and the powerful resources available to us in Christ. Paul's words are a clarion call to fight the *right* battle with the *right* resources.

More often than not, Paul's words here (as well as throughout his letter to the Ephesians) are interpreted from the standpoint of our western individualistic mindset. We talk about the *individual* believer's battle and the *individual* believer's armor. While not denying the need for individual obedience to Paul's commands, the entire thrust of this passage has in view the community of believers as a whole. As we have seen, Paul's letter to the Ephesians is all about *togetherness* as the New Humanity. The New Humanity, as the arena of diversity in unity, is God's redemptive answer to the diversity in alienation of the Old Humanity through sin and satanic assault. Whatever Paul says in this exposé on

---

2. In verses 10–16, Paul employs nine different terms for power encompassing six different word groups. Arnold, *Power and Magic*, 103.

spiritual warfare must be interpreted in the light of his emphasis on the community of believers.

Paul begins this important section by saying, "Finally, be strong in the Lord." In view of all he has said up to this point about who we *are* together in Christ (Eph 1–3) and how we are to *live* together as believers (Eph 4:1—6:9), we are now to *arm* ourselves for the spiritual battle we will inevitably face as the New Humanity (Eph 6:10–20). More often than not, that warfare will be experienced in Satan's pernicious and unrelenting attempts to tear apart our togetherness. He does this by attempting to reconstruct the dividing walls that have already been deconstructed in Christ (Eph 2:15).

Paul reminds us that our real battle is *not* against "flesh and blood," which was a well known Jewish expression for humanity.[3] We do not have the energy to waste fighting among ourselves. Our real battle is elsewhere. Essentially Paul is saying: "In all the relationships that I have just spoken of—between husbands and wives; between children and parents; between employers and employees; or between ethnicities, cultures, socioeconomic classes, and even different age groups—our real struggle is *not* against these people or groups of people, but against the spiritual powers of darkness that are intent on working havoc in the New Humanity." In reality, the dividing walls have been once-and-for-all deconstructed (Eph 1–3). Therefore, experientially we must deconstruct the walls and never allow them to be reconstructed (Eph 4–6). When there is segregation and conflict in the New Humanity, our focus must not be on flesh and blood, the "in-group" or the "out-group," or even merely on the sociological tendencies that push us toward a fragmentation of the body of Christ. Rather, we must remember the reality of the Babel-like powers that inspire such divisiveness and lay hold of the resources God places at our disposal to counteract such disunity.

SATAN'S GENERAL HEADQUARTERS

In any war, an efficient intelligence agency is important if successful warfare is to be waged. If we underestimate the enemy, we'll go out to battle unarmed and unprepared.

---

3. Sirach 14:18; *1 Enoch* 15:4; Matt 16:17; 18:23; 1 Cor 15:50; Gal 1:16; Heb 2:14. See Yee, *Ethnic Reconciliation*, 45.

Here in Ephesians 6:10–12, Paul paints a graphic picture of the enemy's general headquarters or command center. This is Satan's "boardroom of hell." Paul first mentions the devil in verse 11 whom he also terms the "evil one" in verse 16. The designation "devil" (*diabolos*) means "false accuser." As the commander in chief of a vast horde of satanic allies, he is elsewhere called the "prince of this world" (John 12:31; 14:30; 16:11).

Paul then proceeds to mention in verse 12 various diabolical beings in league with the devil, using a variety of terms: "rulers" (*archai*), "authorities" (*exousia*), "powers of this dark world" (*kosmokratores tou skotous toutou*), and "spiritual forces of evil" (*pneumatika tēs ponērias*) in the heavenly realms. Elsewhere he adds to these terms other classifications such as "dominions" (*kyriotētes*), "thrones" (*thronoi*), "lords" (*kyrioi*), as well as the much debated expression "the basic principles of the world" (*ta stoicheia tou kosmou*).[4] Beyond these terms, the Gospels in particular add the more generic designation of "demons." All of these diabolical beings scheme together in a worldwide program of seduction aimed at the destruction of both the Old and the New Humanity.

At first glance, such descriptive titles paint a picture of grotesque spiritual beings à la Darth Vader in *Star Wars* or the evil forces of Saruman in *The Lord of the Rings*. Who are these beings? Why does Paul mention so many different categories of supernatural powers? Does this imply a sort of demonic hierarchy? Are these powers to be identified with the demons who frequently afflicted individuals in the Gospel accounts? What is the relation between these powers and those we have already discussed in chapter 4 (Deut 32:8; Dan 10)? Finally, are these powers to be identified with or differentiated from societal and institutional structures?

Whatever the answer to these questions, some of which are beyond the scope of this book, it is clear that these powers played an extremely important role in the teaching of primitive Christianity. It is also evident that the apostle was speaking of certain spiritual powers with which his readers were familiar. Already in their Septuagint version of the Old Testament, they had associated such terms as *archōn* ("ruler" in Dan 10:13), *dynameis* ("hosts of heaven" in Ps 148:2; 2 Kgs 17:16), and *exousiai* ("rulers" in Dan 7:27; cf. 2 Macc 3:24) with the heavenly powers.

---

4. For a detailed discussion of each of these terms, see Arnold, *Power and Magic*, 4–102; Stevens, "Les Anges des Nations," 167–213; "Territorial Spirits," 413–18.

Furthermore, the apocalyptic literature of late Judaism, the discoveries at Qumran, as well as the Greek magical papyri of the day are replete with references to the powers, providing a backdrop against which the New Testament terminology can best be interpreted. Any attempt to understand Paul's extensive vocabulary of the powers must take into account these potential background sources. Walter Wink correctly concludes: "If our goal is to understand the New Testament's conception of the Powers, we cannot do so simply by applying our own modern sociological categories of power. We must instead attend carefully to the unique vocabulary and conceptions of the first century and try to grasp what the people of that time might have meant by power, within the linguistic field of their own worldview and mythic systems."[5]

THE POWERS "DEMYTHOLOGIZED"?

What *did* Paul and the people of his day mean by the nomenclature "power"? After all, our understanding of the warfare of the New Humanity is dependent on our answer to that question. C. B. Caird has pointed out that the vast majority of theologians and commentators prior to the 1930s either completely avoided this aspect of Paul's teaching or gave it the "niggardly acknowledgment" of a few pages.[6] Since that time, however, the majority opinion has favored the tendency to "demythologize" the powers to one degree or another. The champion of such an approach was Rudolph Bultmann who argued that we must speak of "the unworldly as worldly, the gods as human."[7] Following Bultmann's directive, a variety of interpretations have been proposed. Gordon Rupp, writing as a historian between the two World Wars, seems at first to acknowledge a vast hierarchy of personal demonic beings, but later speaks of them in purely social, political, and economic terms.[8] Along these same lines, G. H. C. MacGregor believes they are best understood as

---

5. Wink, *Naming the Powers*, 4.

6. Caird, *Principalities and Powers*, viii. Interestingly, C. B. Caird's vocabulary employs the kind of racial slur the powers relish. Two exceptions to Caird's conclusion are Otto Everling (*Die paulinische Angelologie und Dämanologie*, 1888) and Martin Dibelius (*Die Geisterwelt in Glauben des Paulus*, 1909).

7. Bultmann, *Mythology*, 10.

8. Rupp, *Principalities and Powers*, 2, 9–11, 83. More recently, A. T. Lincoln takes a similar approach. Lincoln, "Liberation," 348–49.

"national necessity," "economic determinism," or "military expediency."[9] Hendrik Berkhof goes so far as to state: "One can even doubt whether Paul conceived of the Powers as personal beings. In any case this aspect is so secondary that it makes little difference whether he did or not."[10]

Certainly the most monumental work in recent years on the powers is the well-known Powers trilogy by Wink—*Naming the Powers, Unmasking the Powers,* and *Engaging the Powers.* Wink explains that his trilogy was written during his extended stay in Latin America where he witnessed the oppression of social injustice. Wink's exegesis of the biblical text, which is highly influenced by his Jungian analysis of society, led him to conclude that the powers are neither celestial beings nor simple personifications of evil. They are rather the interior and subjective aspect of the more objective societal structures (i.e. institutions and governments). Wink writes:

> As the inner aspect they are the spirituality of institutions, the "within" of corporate structures and systems, the inner essence of outer organizations of power. As the outer aspect they are political systems, appointed officials, the "chair" of an organization, laws—in short, all the tangible manifestations which power takes. Every Power tends to have a visible pole, an outer form—be it a church, a nation, or an economy—and an invisible pole, an inner spirit or driving force that animates, legitimates, and regulates its physical manifestation in the world. Neither pole is the cause of the other. Both come into existence together and cease to exist together. When a particular Power becomes idolatrous, placing itself above God's purposes for the good of the whole, then that Power becomes demonic. The church's task is to unmask this idolatry and recall the Powers to their created purposes in the world—"so that the Sovereignties and Powers should learn only now, through the Church, how comprehensive God's wisdom really is."[11]

---

9. MacGregor, *Cosmic Background,* 27.

10. Berkhof, *Christ and the Powers,* 23–24.

11. Walter Wink adds: "What is needed is an interpretive framework that can do justice to the loose way the ancients could refer to these powers as now human, now structural, now heavenly, without feeling any apparent need to indicate specifically which they had in mind." Wink, *Naming the Powers,* 15. This hermeneutical approach has already influenced more recent commentators. See, for example, Goldingay, *Daniel,* 313–16.

Wink is evidently trying to find a balance between the reductionism of liberation theology (powers = societal structures) and the more traditional evangelical interpretation (powers = spiritual beings). In the process, however, he has essentially "exorcised" the powers from the Scriptures. In redefining and reducing them to the subjective "driving force" or the "within" of corporate structures and systems, we are delivered forever from their *supernatural* influence. If this is the case, our battle truly is against flesh and blood. In other words, "We lose the demons and gain the structures, for the principalities and powers are structures in disguise!"[12]

We are all more or less influenced by our own *weltbild* ("worldview"). This is certainly evident in Wink's Powers trilogy. At the very outset he states:

> We moderns cannot bring ourselves by any feat of will or imagination to believe in the real existence of these mythological entities that traditionally have been lumped under the general category "principalities and powers." . . . It is as impossible for most of us to believe in the real existence of demonic or angelic powers as it is to believe in dragons, or elves, or a flat world.[13]

There is no doubt, however, that the New Testament writers considered these powers to be personal, cosmic beings that inhabited the heavenly realms. Without losing their identity as personal, spiritual beings, they were and are actively involved in every aspect of human existence (culture, institutions, societal structures, church) as they carry out their destructive purposes. This has already been evidenced in the malevolent influence of the prince of Persia on the political figure Cambyses, son of Cyrus (Dan 10). From a biblical world view, the true "myth" is the sophisticated modern man who, due to certain humanistic presuppositions, cannot bring himself to accept the plain language of the New Testament. As Clinton Arnold concludes:

> If Paul wished to make himself understood to his readers (even if he was somehow enlightened about the myth of the "powers"), he would certainly not speak of the "powers" as social structures when his readers would think of evil spiritual beings. He would leave his readers confused and bewildered. . . . On this basis we

---

12. Stott, *God's New Society*, 271.
13. Wink, *Naming the Powers*, 4. For a helpful critique of Wink's presuppositions, see Arnold, *Powers of Darkness*, 177–82.

have every reason to suppose that when the author of Ephesians spoke of the "principalities, powers, authorities," his readers would naturally think of the demonic "powers" they feared.[14]

We find another problem in the tendency to demythologize the powers, reducing them to signify societal structures or institutional evil. It is what James Barr has termed "illegitimate totality transfer."[15] This is done by attributing to a specific term in a specific context all the meanings that this same term can have in other contexts. While it is true that nearly all of the terms for the powers are borrowed from the sphere of human government and are often used elsewhere in the Bible to refer to civil authorities and rulers, this does not justify applying to *every* usage of the term that same meaning. Take, for example, the term "ruler" (*archōn*), which refers twenty-four times in the New Testament to "human rulers."[16] Yet in at least nine instances, this same term designates "spiritual powers."[17] However, the term *archōn* cannot signify *at the same time* both human *and* spiritual powers, given that the two do not share the same nature.[18]

Finally, to interpret the heavenly powers as equivalent to earthly structures (or even to the spiritual dimension of those structures) not only misinterprets the term's contextual meaning, but also divests the powers of their true "power." *The principalities and powers are able to exert influence over the more objective, tangible societal structures (including the church) precisely because they transcend these structures.*[19]

THE BOARDROOM OF HELL

Recognizing the supernatural and personal nature of these powers, we might ask if there is a specific role that each of these powers plays in the

---

14. Arnold, *Power and Magic*, 50–51.

15. Barr, *Semantics*, 217–18.

16. Matt 9:18, 23; 20:25; cf. Mark.10:42; Luke 22:25; 8:41; 12:58; 14:1; 18:18; 23:13, 35; 24:20; John 3:1; 7:26, 48; 12:42; Acts 3:17; 4:5, 8, 26; 7.27, 35; 13:27; 14.5; 16.19; 23.5; Rom 13:3; 1 Cor 2:6–8.

17. Matt 9:34; 12:24; Mark 3:22; Luke 11:15; John 12:31; 14:30; 16:11; Eph 2:2; Rev 1:5.

18. Cf. Oscar Cullman's "double interpretation" of the New Testament powers (particularly in 1 Cor 2:6–8 and Rom 13:1–7) as detailed in *The State in the New Testament*, 95–114.

19. Boyd, *God at War*, 60.

enemy's warfare against the Old and New Humanity. Does Paul describe here a type of hierarchical command center? Do the various descriptive names given to the powers indicate a specific role or mandate carried out by each?

This topic has spawned much speculation over the years. The apocalyptic literature of late Judaism was renowned for its near obsession with the names and roles of both angels and demonic powers.[20] Much more recently, the spiritual warfare movement of the 1990s placed an unwarranted emphasis on the importance of identifying and naming the powers over particular nations or people groups or on the territorial association of these powers.[21] However, a detailed study of Paul's terminology suggests that Paul avoided such speculative assigning of hierarchical roles, specific mandates, or territorial emphases.

That being said, the usage of several of Paul's designations both contextually in the New Testament as well as in certain of the background sources mentioned above leads to several tentative conclusions. For example, the term "rulers" (*archai*) speaks of the authority of these powers over the peoples of the world. The same term is used in the Septuagint version of Daniel 10 to describe the national influence of the demonic prince of Persia and of Greece (Dan 10:13, 20). The vocabulary indicates that such rulers exert their influence *directly* over the inhabited world rather than over other spiritual powers.[22] Without a doubt, these are the angels of the nations. The term "authorities" (*exousiai*), on the other hand, seems to place a particular emphasis on the intimate tie between these supernatural powers and their earthly governmental counterparts—the kings and rulers of this world. In this case, the *exousiai* exert their influence in sphere of sociopolitical structures.

Paul's unique expression "the powers of this dark world" (*kosmokratores tou skotous toutou*) makes use of a term already prevalent in the magical and astrological literature of the first century—*kosmokratōr*. As this term was often used in reference to pagan deities, the apostle may well have had in mind the deceptive idolatrous influence of the mystery religions of his day. Contemporary parallels may

---

20. For examples, see Stevens, "Territorial Spirits," 418, n. 31.

21. Ibid., 410–11 for an extensive bibliography.

22. If the author wanted to emphasize the idea of ruling over other supernatural powers, the term *archontes* would be employed. See Delling, *TDNT*, 1.483.

include any false religious or ideological system that blinds humanity to the truth of the gospel. Paul also mentions the "spiritual forces of evil in the heavenly realms," a designation that seems to emphasize both the evil character of these powers as well as their opposition to the New Humanity who himself is also "in the heavenly realms" (Eph 1:3, 20; 2:6, 19).

Though not mentioned in Ephesians 6, another designation for the powers that holds particular interest for our discussion is the term "principles" (*stoicheia*) found in Galatians 4:3, 9 and Colossians 2:8, 20. Arnold describes these powers as "an integral part of the present evil age. They function as masters and overlords of unredeemed humanity working through various means—including the Jewish law and pagan religions—to hold their subjects in bondage."[23]

From this brief survey, it is evident that one does not need to demythologize the powers to make them relevant to contemporary life and society. Whether it be the rulers that directly influence the inhabited world, the authorities that work through political structures, the powers of this dark world that delight in false ideology, the spiritual forces of evil that oppose all that is good, or the enslaving principles that hold in bondage the human mind and soul—all of these scheme together to enslave the Old and New Humanity alike. But what form does their opposition take?

SATAN'S SCHEMES

Coming from the Southeast, I'm particularly intrigued by anything relating to the Civil War. The Battle of Antietam in 1862 lasted for only twelve hours, but ranks as the bloodiest days of the Civil War. Though militarily a draw, Major General George McClellan was able to hold off General Robert E. Lee's thrust into Maryland, forcing him to retire across the Potomoc. McClellan had the opportunity, however, to defeat Lee decisively. Two Union soldiers discovered a mislaid copy of Lee's battle plans wrapped around three cigars. The plans revealed that Lee had divided his army, making the dispersed regiments extremely vulnerable to attack. Unfortunately, McClellan didn't move quickly enough and squandered his opportunity of procuring a decisive victory.

---

23. Arnold, *Colossian Syncretism*, 194.

Our enemy's battle plans have fallen into our hands (2 Cor 2:11), but we must act. Paul tells us to "put on the full armor of God, that you may take your stand against the devil's *schemes*" (Eph 6:11, emphasis mine). The word is *methodeia* from which we derive our English word "method." His schemes are his crafty methods, maneuvers, and strategies in order to deceive, defraud, and destroy. Satan obviously carries out his pernicious schemes in society as a whole, promoting individual and structural evil worldwide. Contextually, however, Paul's concern in these verses is not so much with the battle *outside* the church, but the one *inside* the church. All the while recognizing the influence of the powers upon society as a whole, Paul here focuses on their ruthless influence upon the church as the New Humanity. The very powers that tighten their grip on the minds and hearts of the various ethnicities of the world—inciting division, hatred, and conflict—refuse to relinquish their grip even after one becomes a member of the New Humanity. To the contrary, Satan's hellish and frontal attacks become all the more brutal and deceitful.

The Adversary's utmost priority is to fragment and segregate the New Humanity so that the church's witness both to people (John 17:20) and to the powers (Eph 3:10) is diminished. I am convinced that the powers adapt their malicious strategies to the specific culture in question. While in Paul's day they "fed" on the rampant occultism and religious idolatry so characteristic of that society, today these same pernicious powers promote ethnic hatred, materialism, structural racism, and oppressive ideologies. In their assault on the New Humanity, they infiltrate the ranks, promoting a heightened sense of individualism and consumerism within the church, both of which lead to further ethnic segregation among believers.

We will never get to the source of our segregationist tendencies until we face their demonic character. We must come face-to-face with the demonic source of divisiveness within the body of Christ and call it for what it is. We can no longer sit back and complacently acquiesce to the natural sociological dynamics that fragment the New Humanity by pushing us into affinity groups determined by ethnicity, age, generational preferences, and class. The fact that eleven o'clock on Sunday morning remains the most segregated hour in American culture cannot be lightly explained away as a mere sociological phenomenon. No, spiritual dynamics are at play. The powers are reveling in their success (albeit limited) in fragmenting the New Humanity into self-interest groups. If they cannot divide the church through such overt maneuvers as racial prejudice and lack of forgiveness, then they will rely upon more covert sociological currents to segregate the church. They particularly relish the contemporary church's insatiable desire for numerical growth at the expense of qualitative unity and reconciliation. Paul Louis Metzger states it well when he writes: "Church growth strategies that emphasize quantitative over qualitative enlargement and cater to consumer choice and personal preference whet the appetites of the demonic powers as malevolent consumers and breed disunity."[24] The widespread divisions in the church today—whether socioeconomic, generational, or ethnic in character—are merely the rotten fruit of the adversary at work sowing seeds of individualism, consumerism, and ethnocentrism. All of these divisive manifestations fly in the face of our true identity as God's New Humanity.

OUR STANCE

Because our enemy schemes, we must stand! And stand we can. "Finally, be strong in Lord," Paul tells us. Literally, he says, "Be strengthened!" Paul's command is in the passive voice. It is not something we can do ourselves (like "pull yourself together" or "get with it!"), but something we allow Christ to do for us. That's why Paul adds, *"in the Lord."* Only as we find our strength in our collective identity in Christ will we be able to effectively resist the divisive strategies of the adversary. It is this same strengthening for which Paul prays in Ephesians 3:16–17: "I pray that out of his glorious riches he may strengthen you with power through his Spirit in your inner being, so that Christ may dwell in your hearts through faith."

Being strengthened, we must stand (Eph 6:14). This is the chief admonition of the passage upon which hangs each of the six following commands in verses 14–18. "Being strengthened" means to draw up in military formation for combat. We do this by putting on the splendid armor that God has made available to the New Humanity.

PUTTING ON THE ARMOR

During Nero's reign, Paul arrived in Rome and was placed under house arrest (cf. Acts 28:11–16). Luke tells us the apostle was allowed to stay by himself in rented quarters, along with the soldier who was guarding him.

---

24. Metzger, *Consuming Jesus*, 80–81.

There was a steady stream of visitors, like the fugitive slave Onesimus who was converted under Paul's ministry. While waiting for his hearing, Paul was under the watchful eye of the *stratopedarchēs* (Acts 28:16), likely to be identified with the prefect (commander) of the Praetorian (imperial) Guard. It is probable this commander had charge of several imperial soldiers who guarded Paul and who relieved one another in steady succession. If so, they most certainly heard the life transforming testimony of the apostle. Being chained to one of these guards, Paul had the opportunity to observe up close their royal military attire (Acts 28:20). Could it have been this experience that inspired the illustration of the church's spiritual armor that we find in Ephesians 6:10–18? I believe it is likely.

Paul tells us twice in these verses to put on the *full armor* of God (Eph 6:11, 13). The expression (*panoplia*) emphasizes not only the completeness of the armor (there must not be one piece missing), but also the quality of the armor (the various pieces are fully capable of protecting against the enemy). The protective quality of this armor is highlighted by the fact that Paul draws some of his imagery from the armor put on by the Messiah himself (cf. Isa 11:5; 59:17). It is therefore the divine armor of the Messiah that the community of believes is to take up and put on. Furthermore, each piece of armor seems to speak of both positional and practical truth. From this perspective, each piece of armor indicates what we already have in Christ (truth, righteousness, peace, etc.) as well as how we are to now live with other believers (truthfully, righteously, peacefully, etc.).

There has been much discussion over the years as to whether these weapons are defensive or offensive in nature. In reading Paul's description, one cannot avoid the conclusion that they are both. As Wink observes, "It is humorous to watch the statement bob from scholar to scholar that the weapons listed here are all 'defensive.'. . . The Pentagon says the same about nuclear missiles. . . . The terms employed are taken straight from the legionnaire's equipment and the metaphor is of the church like the Roman wedge, the most efficient and terrifying military formation known up to that time and for some thousand years after."[25]

What is often ignored in many popular treatments of this passage is that Paul is describing the armor of the New Humanity rather than the armor of the individual Christian. Each individual believer, of course,

25. Wink, *Naming the Powers*, 86.

has his role to play in this spiritual battle. Paul's primary concern in these verses, however, is the debilitating effect that Satan's pernicious assault can have on the *church as a whole*. By taking up the various pieces of spiritual armor, we collectively oppose the adversary's attempt to divide and ultimately defeat the New Humanity.

The Belt of Truth

The first piece of armor the New Humanity is to put on is the belt of truth. Paul says in verse 14, "Stand firm, then, with the belt of truth buckled about your waist." Here, Paul's words come from Isaiah 11:5 where the prophet is describing the future righteous rule of the humble shoot that would sprout from Jesse's family tree: "Righteousness will be his belt and faithfulness the sash around his waist." The prophet foresees that truth and faithfulness to God would be the outstanding characteristics of the coming Messiah. The inevitable result is that people would live in peace (Isa 11:6–9).

Three different belts were worn by Roman soldiers. Paul seems to be speaking here of a special belt or sash worn by military nobility, such as an officer or high official. This belt was often highly ornamented, complete with pockets for carrying writing instruments, money, even a pipe![26]

This belt speaks of *nobility*. The members of Christ's church are all, without exception, enrobed in the military apparel of nobility. Together we form an army. In this battle, each member of the New Humanity—regardless of color, culture, or class—bears the insignia of military nobility. No distinction exists between officers and privates, between captains and enlisted men, between the weak and the strong, between the support personnel in the rear and the heroic fighters on the front lines. We are all officers in God's army and are corporately and individually invested with all the spiritual authority and nobility that this rank implies.

Not only does this belt speak of nobility, but also of *liberty*. This particular belt worn by the Roman soldier kept the various pieces of the armor in place, giving the legionnaire liberty in his movement. It makes sense, then, that Paul calls this the belt of *truth*. As Jesus said, "You will know the truth, and the truth will set you free" (John 8:32). When it

---

26. The two other belts were a leather apron designed to protect the lower abdomen and a type of sword-belt. Barth, *Ephesians*, 2:766–67.

comes to the ethnic divides in the church today, only the truth of our New Humanity identity will free us to be all we were meant to be.

Both the nobility and liberty of this belt find their source in its nature—*truth*. Paul has already spoken of truth five times in this letter (1:13; 4:15, 21, 25; 5:9). Our authority over the enemy flows out of the truth of our shared identity. This truth is first of all doctrinal—what we are to believe. Satan's most effective and divisive strategy is to keep the church from understanding and experiencing her true identity as the New Humanity. Authentic diversity in unity in the body of Christ can only flow out of a renewed understanding of the truth of our collective identity in Christ. As we have seen, the process of putting off the Old Humanity and putting on the New Humanity can only be done in accordance with the *truth* that is in Jesus (Eph 4:21). Furthermore, the very identity that we are to put on has been "created in *true* righteousness and holiness" (Eph 4:24; emphasis mine). Therefore, any attempt to nurture diversity in unity within the universal or local manifestation of the New Humanity must begin with the truth of this change of identity.

Believing the truth profoundly transforms our identity; behaving truthfully radically enhances our community. Both our belief and our behavior explain what it means to put on the belt of truth. This belt is not only doctrinal truth—what we are to believe about ourselves (Eph 1–3). It is also ethical truth—how we are to behave toward others in love (Eph 4–6). We belong to each other as members of his body, the church. We are already dressed with the noble attire of the belt of truth that is now to be tangibly expressed in our speech, lifestyle, and motives. In other words, we take up the belt of truth by speaking and living truthfully with all people and particularly with our spiritual siblings in Christ.

The Breastplate of Righteousness

The breastplate of the Roman soldier was originally a sleeveless jacket made of leather or linen, called a *cuirass*. It later developed into a type of metal breastplate that protected the soldier's chest and (contrary to what many have thought) even his back. A later development was mail armor, formed of plates of brass, laid one upon another, like the scales of a fish.[27] All of these were designed to protect the soldier at his most vulnerable point—his heart.

---

27. Ibid., 769.

The righteousness that Paul is speaking about is first of all our right standing with God. In Isaiah 59:17, the Messiah is described as one who "put on righteousness as his breastplate." Having clothed ourselves with Christ (Gal 3:27), *all* who are part of the New Humanity share that same righteousness. "God made him who knew no sin to be sin for us, so that in him we might become the righteousness of Christ" (2 Cor 5:21; cf. Zech 3:1–5).

Like the belt of truth, the breastplate of righteousness not only speaks of our *position* of righteousness in Christ, but also of our *practice* of righteousness as believers. We take up the breastplate of righteousness by living righteously. More often than not, living righteously is demonstrated in our relationships with others. For most of us, our greatest battles are relational. Were it not for other people, the Christian life would be relatively easy. The well-known axiom proves true: "To live above with saints we love, that will be glory; to live below with saints we know; well, that's another story!" We know that one day we will worship with others of every ethnicity, color, and language on the face of the earth, but somehow the "story" here below doesn't work out that way. The litmus test of righteous living is seen in how we relate to those who are different from us within the church.

The Sandals of Peace

Members of the New Humanity are also to have their "feet fitted with the readiness that comes from the gospel of peace" (Eph 6:15; cf. Isa 52:7). In the Roman Empire, ordinary people would often walk about barefoot. Roman soldiers, however, were equipped with a type of half boot made of leather and tied to the ankles with ornamental leather straps. These boot shoes were studded with nails giving the soldier a firm, solid stance that kept him from sliding.[28]

It's rather paradoxical that Paul speaks of peace in a context of warfare! Then again, it all makes sense. This is the very peace that Satan wants to destroy in the New Humanity. Though Satan's attacks are relentless, these sandals of peace give us a firm footing enabling us to stand.

While the Bible speaks of the peace *with* God (Rom 5:1) as well as the peace *of* God (Phil 4:6–7), here Paul is speaking more specifically of the peace we already have with one another—irrespective of color,

---

28. Ibid., 798–99.

culture, or class—because of Christ. It is the same peace of which Paul says: "For he himself is our peace, who has made the two one and has destroyed the barrier, the dividing wall of hostility.... His purpose was to create in himself one new man out of the two, thus making peace" (Eph 2:14–15). This peace is doctrinal—a truth to be believed and appropriated by the church—but it is also practical. This peace is to be maintained at all costs: "Make every effort to keep the unity of the Spirit through the bond of *peace*" (Eph 4:3; emphasis mine).

The legacy left to us by Jesus and the apostles is a pair of shoes that speak of peace. "If it is possible, as far as it depends on you," Paul tells us, "live at *peace* with everyone." (Rom 12:18) As he closes that same epistle, Paul reminds us, "The God of *peace* will soon crush Satan under your feet" (Rom 16:20).

The Shield of Faith

The next piece of armor Paul tells us to put on is the shield of faith: "In addition to all this, take up the shield of faith, with which you can extinguish all the flaming arrows of the evil one" (v. 16). For the Roman soldier, this was a large, vaulted shield, about two and one-half feet wide and four and one-half feet high. It was made of wood, covered with leather, and often dipped in water before the battle. Two-thirds of this shield covered the legionnaire's body, and one-third covered his comrade to his left. This encouraged tight ranks and a sense of interdependence among the troops. This interconnectedness formed the famed Roman wedge that was the "centerpiece of the Roman army's devastating military efficiency."[29]

Such "tight ranks" and a "sense of interdependence" are needed among the troops of the New Humanity. We simply do not realize the degree to which we need one another in this conflict. In Paul's day, Jewish believes needed Gentile believers and Gentile believers needed Jewish believers. They both needed the overlap of their shields providing mutual protection. The same holds true today. Whether African American, Hispanic, Swedish, or Native American, our faith needs the mutual strengthening experienced when believers of diverse ethnicities learn to live, worship, and serve together.

---

29. Wink, *Naming the Powers*, 86–87.

This shield is the shield of *faith*. The enemy's strategy is to promote doubt, suspicion, and fear when it comes to those who are different from us. God's strategy is a strategy of faith. Contextually, this would be faith in God's purposes for his church, faith that the powers of darkness have been actually defeated at the cross, faith in God's revealed truth about our core identity as the New Humanity. Such faith will result in faithfulness as we live in view of our promised inheritance.

The Helmet of Salvation

As was true for all of the pieces of armor mentioned here, the helmet of the Roman soldier became progressively elaborate over time. By the first century, the helmet worn by Roman soldiers was so solid that nothing short of an ax or hammer could pierce its solid protection.[30]

Isaiah 59:17 tells us that the Messiah put on the helmet of salvation: "He put on righteousness as his breastplate, and the helmet of salvation on his head." In writing to the Thessalonian believers, Paul says, "But since we belong to the day, let us be self-controlled, putting on faith and love as a breastplate, and the hope of salvation as a helmet" (1 Thess 5:8).

The helmet protects the head. Satan will attack our *mind* to reach our *emotions* and our *will* (Phil 4:8; Rom 12:2). If the brain is injured or fails, the other organs will soon begin to fail also. In speaking of the New Humanity, Paul has already underscored the importance of the renewing of our *minds* (Eph 4:23). The helmet of salvation is essential to identity formation among believers—understanding and appropriating who we are as God's New Humanity. As the church, we must constantly reaffirm who we are and the salvation that we share *together* in Christ.

This seems to be Paul's emphasis in writing to the Corinthians: "For though we live in the world, we do not wage war as the world does. The weapons we fight with are not the weapons of the world. On the contrary, they have divine power to demolish strongholds. We demolish arguments and every pretension that sets itself up against the knowledge of God, and we take captive every thought to make it obedient to Christ" (2 Cor 10:3–5). Dividing walls exist within and among local churches to the degree that "strongholds" and "arguments" *in our minds* have not been taken captive and demolished. In the very next chapter, Paul expresses his concern that Satan might lead these believers' "minds" astray

---

30. Barth, *Ephesians*, 2:775.

from a pure devotion to Christ (2 Cor 11:3). Among the Corinthians, this resulted not only in being led astray by false teachers, but also in the fracturing of Christ's church (1 Cor 1:12). "Is Christ divided?" Paul asks (1 Cor 1:13). The antidote to segregation in the body of Christ begins with understanding, affirming, and deeply experiencing our collective identity in Christ.

The Sword of the Spirit

Finally, Paul tells us to take "the sword of the Spirit, which is the word of God." The sword mentioned here (*maxaira*) is a short sword, like a dagger, a knife, or even a type of surgical scalpel.[31] This short sword was more handy and aggressive than the long sword. As part of our spiritual equipment, this sword is given to us by the Spirit of God and consists of the word of God. In referring to the *word* of God, Paul uses a term (*rhēma*) that means specific Scripture spoken for a particular occasion. It is the word of truth that the Ephesians believed resulting in their salvation (Eph 1:13). It is the word that sanctifies and cleanses the New Humanity as the bride of Christ (Eph 5:26). It is the "one little word" that Luther referred to in his well known hymn, "A Mighty Fortress is our God":

> And though this world with devils filled, Should threaten to undo us,
> We will not fear for God has willed, His truth to triumph through us.
> The prince of darkness grim, We tremble not for him.
> His rage we can endure, For lo, his doom is sure:
> One little word shall fell him.

In Ephesians 6, the *rhēma* refers to specific Scripture that counters Satan's attacks aimed at the unity of the church. This would certainly include the many references in Scripture that speak of our identity as God's people. If one of the primary concerns of the biblical authors is identity formation, Satan's primary concern is identity deconstruction. It is the *rhēma* of God that can help the people of God both understand and stand strong in their New Humanity identity.

THE POWER THAT UNITES

Paul's letter to the Ephesians has more to say about the powers than any other New Testament book. This is understandable. Before coming

---

31. The same word describes the sword Peter used when he cut off the ear of the High Priest's servant in John 18:10.

to Christ, these Ephesian believers' lives were marked by much anxiety about their "fate," thought to be determined by the stars and cosmic powers. Even a cursory reading of Acts 19, which tells of the conversion of many of these believers, clues us into the sorcery and magic that influenced their lives and worldview. In Ephesus, the great goddess Diana, also known as Artemis, was worshipped as supreme in divine power and position. The signs of the zodiac around her neck assured the devotee that she possessed authority superior to that of astrological fate.[32]

In stark contrast to such supposed power, nothing is like the divine power that raised Christ from the dead and made Jew and Gentile—including believers of every ethnicity throughout the world—one New Humanity in Christ. In Ephesians 1:15–18, Paul prays that members of the New Humanity might know God's "incomparably great power" made available to those who believe. He then states that this "power is like the working of his mighty strength, which he exerted in Christ when he raised him from the dead and seated him at his right hand in the heavenly realms" (vv. 19–20).

As the New Humanity, we fight from the high ground—from the "heavenly realms" (1:3, 20; 2:6; 3:10; 6:12). What are the heavenly realms? It is the realm in which Christ reigns (1:20) and where his people are blessed and reign together with him (1:3; 2:6). The heavenly realms is that sphere of reality in which the multiethnic New Humanity lives as a result of being enlivened *together*, raised *together*, and seated *together* in Christ (2:5–6). In Ephesians, the heavenly realms are not described in contrast to the earth; rather, they encompass our every day lives on this earth. To live in the heavenly realms is to engage in a process of identity formation. Paul is referring to the inner realities of our lives: our thought life, our attitudes, our way of viewing ourselves and others. Such is not without opposition, however, for the heavenly realms are also the sphere in which the powers operate (3:10; 6:12), opposing God's work in and through the New Humanity. With the exception of Ephesians 1:3, the powers are mentioned in the immediate context of each passage that refers to this sphere called the heavenly realms. The implication is that the powers will staunchly oppose any attempt by believers to discover and live out their true identity.

---

32. Arnold, *Power and Magic*, 20–28.

The New Humanity is not only in the heavenly realms, but we also are *in Christ* in the heavenly realms. Christ is "far above all rule and authority, power and dominion, and every title that can be given, not only in the present age but also in the one to come" (1:21–22). God's power gave Christ the seat of kingly authority at his right hand (v. 20). In this position, every demonic power that could possibly come against Christ or against the New Humanity, threatening our unity and sowing divisiveness, has been placed under Christ's authority. Our intimate union with Jesus in his death, burial, and resurrection has invested us with great authority over the divisive powers of this age. Christ's resounding "It is finished!" once-and-for-all changed our spiritual status and stance. For this reason we are told to resist the enemy, rather than attack the enemy. Resistance and defense do *not* imply spiritual passivity, but the assurance of long-term victory. Everything in the universe will be ultimately subject to Christ. In these verses Paul makes allusion to Psalm 8 and Psalm 110 that look forward to Christ's ultimate rule over the earth and universe. As the writer to the Hebrews says, "At present we do not see everything subject to him" (Heb 2:8). Someday, however, we will. A lethal leash has been placed around the neck of the adversary and his ultimate doom is guaranteed. Though at times that leash appears long if not loosed, nevertheless it is there. We can therefore take up our spiritual armor with confidence.

At 8:32 a.m. on May 18, 1980, Mount St. Helens exploded with what is one of the most visible indications of the power of nature that the modern world has ever seen. The explosion ripped off thirteen hundred feet of the mountain with a force of ten million tons of TNT, or the rough equivalent of 500 Hiroshimas. A blast of 300-degree heat traveling at two hundred miles an hour killed sixty people, some as far as sixteen miles away. The blast leveled one-hundred-fifty-foot Douglas firs as far as seventeen miles away, destroying a total of 3.2 billion feet of lumber, enough to build 200,000 three-bedroom homes.[33] That's power, but nothing compared to the far superior power of God demonstrated in Christ's resurrection. It is that same power that has raised *together* Jew and Gentile alike—along with all those who believe from the multiple ethnicities around the world—and has seated them *together* in the heavenly realms. The power that unites us is far greater than the powers that

---

33. See Findley, "Mountain with a Death Wish," para. 7–8.

would divide us. Furthermore, *the power that raised us together is more than sufficient to bring us together and to keep us together.*

As the New Humanity is brought together and kept together, overcoming the demonic divisiveness that would pull us apart, a powerful proclamation takes place in the heavenly realms. Paul states in Ephesians 3:10: "His intent was that now, through the church, the manifold wisdom of God should be made known to the rulers and authorities in the heavenly realms." What could Paul possibly mean by such a statement?

The Scriptures teach that both good and evil powers need enlightenment concerning the depths of the gospel (cf. 1 Pet 1:12). To the degree that Paul is speaking of fallen angels, they also stand behind the ethnic hatred and hostility we witness. No doubt, these rulers and authorities are the same powers that were operative in the Garden of Eden and that led man into the disastrous decision to disobey God. They are the same powers that were implicated in the division of humanity at the Tower of Babel and in the ethnic hatred demonstrated toward Israel through Cambyses in the days of Daniel. They are also, however, the same divisive powers over which Christ was seated in the heavenly realms according to Ephesians 1:20–23.

In contrast to such satanically inspired division, the New Humanity stands as an ongoing testimony of God's *manifold* wisdom in providing reconciliation with God and fellow man. The descriptive term "manifold" was used in Paul's day to describe flowers and beautifully woven carpets. It is also found in the Septuagint as a description of Joseph's coat of many colors (Gen 37:3, 23, 32). This is what the New Humanity is—a multicultural, multiethnic tapestry that stands as a living testimony of God's reconciling grace. As the church grows and spreads throughout the world, it is as if a great drama is being enacted before the very spiritual powers that oppose such diversity in unity. We are not called in this verse to "preach" to the spiritual powers in the same way that we preach the gospel to those without Christ. The very fact of our spiritual unity in Christ *is* preaching to these powers (cf. 1 Pet 1:12). Furthermore, *to the degree that the New Humanity experientially nurtures and maintains the diversity in unity to which we have been called (Eph 4:1–6), the proclamation of Christ's reconciliatory work to the powers is reinforced.*

CONCLUSION

As the New Humanity, we stand against the adversary not only by *putting on* each piece of the armor, but also by *praying for* one another. Prayer is not merely the seventh piece of armor mentioned in this passage; it is the *means of deploying* all the other pieces of armor. No wonder Paul devotes four entire verses in Ephesians 6 to the subject of prayer.

> And pray in the Spirit on all occasions with all kinds of prayers and requests. With this in mind, be alert and always keep on praying for all the saints. Pray also for me, that whenever I open my mouth, words may be given me so that I will fearlessly make known the mystery of the gospel, for which I am an ambassador in chains. Pray that I may declare it fearlessly, as I should.
> Ephesians 6:18–20

Four times he repeats the command to pray: "And pray in the Spirit" (v.18), "keep on praying" (v. 20), "pray also for me" (v. 19), and "pray that I may declare" (v. 20). Four times Paul uses the adjective "all" (*pas*): "all occasions," "all kinds," "always keep on praying," and "all the saints." Paul leaves the distinct impression that prayer is indispensable for effectively wielding these pieces of spiritual armor. Prayer enables us to effectively put on each piece of our much needed armor as well as to remain in intimate contact with our Commander and Chief, listening to his directives.

Paul tells us to pray, and then twice in this epistle he models a pattern of prayer for the people of God (Eph 1:15–22; 3:14–21). After reminding us of our shared salvation planned by the Father (1:3–6), purchased by the Son (1:7–12), and protected by the Spirit (1:13–14), he then prays that we might have a spirit of "wisdom and revelation" to fully grasp the implications of our new identity (1:15–23). Similarly, in Ephesians 3:14–19, he prays that we might together with *all* believers comprehend the full-orbed dimensions of the love of Christ. Evidently, prayer is indispensable, not only for putting on the armor, but also for growing in our experiential understanding of our shared identity as the New Humanity in Christ. The more we *pray for* one another, the less we will *prey upon* one another.

Just before Jesus prays that his followers might be one even as he and the Father are one, he leaves his disciples a remarkable promise concerning prayer. It's found in John 14:12–13. Jesus says: "The truth is, anyone who believes in me will do the same works I have done, and even greater works, because I am going to be with the Father. You can ask for anything in my name, and I will do it, because the work of the Son brings glory to the Father" (NLT). In these two verses, Jesus tells us the "greater works" of the risen Christ are accomplished by the power of the Holy Spirit in direct response to believing prayer. These greater works would certainly include the unity of all believers, which Jesus also prayed for during this last meal with his disciples (John 17:20–23). Furthermore, it is clear that these greater works can only be realized by the powerful intervention of the Holy Spirit. This seems to be the meaning of Jesus' words "because I am going to the Father." Only as Jesus goes up can the Holy Spirit come down to indwell and empower those who believe (John 16:7). What releases this convicting and empowering work of the Holy Spirit in and through those who believe? It is prayer. That is why immediately after Jesus speaks of these greater works that are accomplished by the Holy Spirit he assures us: "You can ask for anything in my name, and I will do it." Apparently, prayer in the name of Jesus—that is, according to his will—releases the work of the Spirit who accomplishes these supernatural, greater works of Christ.

It is true. The power that raised us together *is* more than sufficient to bring us together and to keep us together, but it is concerted, believing prayer on the part of God's people that releases this power. New Humanity churches employ each piece of the splendid armor that God has provided his people. However, they also recognize that only through prayer can we effectively put on this armor and stand against the powers that divide.

10

The End of the Story

> *If you read history, you will find that the Christians who did most for the present world were just those who thought most of the next. . . . It is since Christians have largely ceased to think of the other world that they have become so ineffective in this. Aim at Heaven and you will get earth 'thrown in': aim at earth and you will get neither.*
>
> C. S. Lewis

TO GRASP THE STORY line of the Old and New Humanity, we must see the beginning, the end, and everything in between. Having looked at the beginning (chapter 2) and explored the in between (chapters 3–9), we now turn to the end of the story. For the New Humanity, the end of the story (which is actually only an eternal beginning!) is graphically described by the prophet-seer John in Revelation 21:1-4.

> Then I saw a new heaven and a new earth, for the first heaven and the first earth had passed away, and there was no longer any sea. I saw the Holy City, the new Jerusalem, coming down out of heaven from God, prepared as a bride beautifully dressed for her husband. And I heard a loud voice from the throne saying, "Now the dwelling of God is with men, and he will live with them. They will be his people, and God himself will be with them and be their God. 'He will wipe every tear from their eyes. There will be no more death' or mourning or crying or pain, for the old order of things has passed away."

BEGIN WITH END IN MIND

Stephen Covey, in his well-known book *The Seven Habits of Highly Effective People,* talks about seven key habits that characterize people of accomplishment. The second habit he addresses is this: *begin with the end in mind.*[1] For the New Humanity, this means to live the "already" in light of the "not yet." However, it is more. It also means to view God's description of the future as our model for the present. It is to incessantly pray, "Thy kingdom come, thy will be done, on earth as it is in heaven." Yes, as C. S. Lewis affirms, "It is since Christians have largely ceased to think of the other world that they have become so ineffective in this."[2]

Throughout the Bible, we are exhorted to do just that—to begin with the end in mind, to think of the other world, to allow our final destiny and God's design for history to shape our life in the present. "We do not need Christ to tell us that the world is full of troubles. But we do need His explanation of history if its troubles are not to be meaningless."[3] Or as Jonathan Edwards remarks: "It becomes us to spend this life only as a journey toward heaven . . . to which we should subordinate all other concerns of life. Why should we labor for or set our hearts on anything else, but that which is our proper end and true happiness?"[4] After all, we cannot understand who we are or what we are called to do apart from understanding what we will ultimately be.

The "proper end and true happiness" of the New Humanity and what we will ultimately be is graphically detailed in the final book of the Bible—Revelation. The parallels between that book and the original creation account in Genesis highlight God's intentionality throughout history.

> In Genesis, God plants the Garden on Earth; in Revelation, he brings down the New Jerusalem, with a garden at its center, to the New Earth. In Eden, there's no sin, death, or Curse; on the New Earth, there's no *more* sin, death, or Curse. In Genesis, the Redeemer is promised; in Revelation, the Redeemer returns. Genesis tells the story of Paradise lost; Revelation tells the story of Paradise regained. In Genesis, humanity's stewardship

---

1. Covey, *Seven Habits,* 96.
2. Lewis, *Chrisitian Behaviour,* 55.
3. Wilcock, *Heaven Opened,* 69.
4. Winslow, *Jonathan Edwards,* 142.

is squandered; in Revelation, humanity's stewardship is triumphant, empowered by the human and divine King Jesus.[5]

It is the picture of paradise regained that the prophet-seer John describes for us in the climactic account of Revelation 21:1–4. From the beginning of time, God's design has been to exist in harmonious relationship with humanity as well as with all of creation. We know, however, that the willful intrusion of sin worked havoc not only with mankind's relationship to God and with fellow man, but also with the entire balance of the cosmos. While through the prophecies of the Old Testament and its sacrificial system we catch glimpses of God's ultimate plan to redeem his creation, we are left with many unanswered questions. Our present experience, however, is *not* the final chapter in this unfolding mystery of God's will. That chapter will be written when all things are brought under the authority of Christ.

It is precisely the reconciliation of heaven and earth under the authority of Christ that John describes in the final chapters of his Apocalypse. Yet his descriptive terminology is couched in the language of romance. The new Jerusalem, up until this moment separated from earth in the intermediate heaven (Heb 12:22–23), now descends to the new earth "as a bride beautifully dressed for her husband" (Rev 21:2). This is not the first reference to the New Humanity as the bride of Christ in this unfolding revelation. Already in Revelation 19:6–9 we read:

> Then I heard what sounded like a great multitude, like the roar of rushing waters and like loud peals of thunder, shouting: "Hallelujah! For our Lord God Almighty reigns. Let us rejoice and be glad and give him glory! *For the wedding of the Lamb has come, and his bride has made herself ready.* Fine linen, bright and clean, was given her to wear." . . . Then the angel said to me, "Write: Blessed are those who are invited to the wedding supper of the Lamb." (emphasis mine)

Often in Scripture, God is viewed as a suitor looking for a wife. In fact, this romantic story of the universe begins with a man and a woman (Gen 1:27) and will end with a Man and his bride (Rev 21:2, 9). The Father signed the marital contract in ages past (Eph 1:3–6) and the Son paid the "bride price" (Eph 1:7–8). The betrothal of the church—the New Humanity—to Christ is a display of lavish love beyond human

---

5. Alcorn, *Heaven*, 85.

comprehension. It is a bold love that seeks out the unworthy. It is a love that extends itself to you and me, not because we are lovable, but to make us so. It is a love not merely in word, but in act—leading Christ to give himself up for us in a selfless step of unimaginable sacrifice.

ROMANCE AT THE HEART OF THE UNIVERSE

I can think of no more exhilarating moment in my life than when I stood in the front of a small country church, with groomsmen at my side, anticipating the entry of my bride.

Suddenly she appeared. Robed in white and clasping the arm of her dad, she began that traditional march down the aisle. The people stood, the music played, and my own heart raced like a strong stallion leading the pack. Before I knew it, we had said our vows, gave the customary kiss, and were officially declared husband and wife.

In all, that ceremony lasted no more than forty-five minutes; but it was the culmination of a process of communication, preparation, and deepening love that took place over months preceding the wedding itself.

We followed the classic process. We dated, I proposed (after seeking her dad's approval), she accepted, and we then began making preparations for the big day. When that much anticipated moment came, we said those affirmative words "I do" and lived happily ever after . . . at least on most days!

It's an awesome thing how God designed the institution of marriage—the monogamous relationship of one man and one woman—to illustrate the deeper reality of Christ's relationship to the New Humanity. In the Old Testament, we find the colorful image of a people in a marital relationship with God. The prophet Isaiah in speaking to Israel says, "As a bridegroom rejoices over his bride, so will your God rejoice over you" (Isa 62:5). Israel, however, was flagrantly unfaithful in her marriage to Yahweh. The prophet Jeremiah states it in these terms: "'Return, faithless people,' declares the LORD, 'for I am your husband. I will choose you . . . and bring you to Zion'" (Jer 3:14).

Hosea, a prophet who symbolized God's love for his people by marrying a prostitute and loving her unconditionally, paints this image as he speaks on God's behalf: "I will betroth you to me forever; I will betroth you in righteousness and justice, in love and compassion. I will betroth you in faithfulness, and you will acknowledge the LORD" (Hos 2:19–20; cf. Isa 49:18; Jer 3:1, 20; Ezek 16:1–59). God's marriage relationship with those under the old covenant has not ended, but its "vows" have been redefined. What was previously a marriage covenant with one specific people—the Jewish nation—now has universal implications touching all nations and peoples of the earth.

GOD'S WEDDING CALENDAR

Every reference in Scripture to the New Humanity as a bride refers to one of three phases in the Jewish marriage customs. There is first the *betrothal* ("Christ loved the church and gave himself up for her"; Eph 5:25), followed by a period of *preparation* (". . . to make her holy, cleansing her by the washing with water through the word"; Eph 5:26), both of which culminate in the *wedding* itself (". . . to present her to himself as a radiant church, without stain or wrinkle or any other blemish, but holy and blameless"; Eph 5:27). It is the invitation to the wedding that John describes in Revelation 19:6–9.

In Jewish culture, the period of preparation was followed by the procession of the bridegroom to the home of the bride and then back again. This often took place late at night, as seen in the parable of the ten virgins of Matthew 25. The bridegroom, accompanied by his friends, would be dressed in fine clothes as he made his way to the home of the bride (cf. Isa 61:10). He meets his bride, whose face is covered by a veil (Gen 29:25). He then begins to lead her back to his home, now accompanied by their friends and children (cf. Judg 14:11). The way is lit by torches. Nuts, oil, and wine are distributed to the guests and festive music is played along the way. Once at the home of the bridegroom, there is feasting with music and songs (Jer 24:8; 34:16). Finally, a formula is pronounced, such as "Take her, according to the Law of Moses and of Israel," and the wedding supper begins.[6]

This same spirit of festivity permeates the account of the wedding of the Lamb as described by John: "Let us rejoice and be glad and give him glory! For the wedding of the Lamb has come" (Rev 19:7). At this climatic moment, "the Beauty-Specialist will have put his final touch to the church, the massaging will have been so perfect that there will not be a single wrinkle left. She will look young, and in the bloom of youth,

---

6. See Yamauchi, "Cultural Aspects of Marriage," 241–52.

with color in her cheeks, with her skin perfect, without any spots or wrinkles. And she will remain like that for ever and ever!"[7]

THE NEW HUMANITY AS IMAGE

As the bride of Christ, the New Humanity is the new Eve destined to be married throughout eternity to the last Adam. As such, the New Humanity exists as the recreated and renewed image of God. In the culmination of time, the three aspects integral to humanity's representative role as the *imago Dei*—rule, resemblance, and relationship—will be fully restored.

Rule

We must catch the "significance of an all-inclusive drama of a cosmic struggle, in which is involved not only man in his sin and lost condition, but in which are also related the heavens and the earth, angels and demons, and the goal of which is to bring back the entire created cosmos under God's dominion and rule."[8] All of history is moving toward the ultimate goal of a restored and reconciled universe. Such was already the certain expectation of the Old Testament promises. Solomon declares, "He will rule from sea to sea and from the River to the ends of the earth. All kings will bow down to him and all nations will serve him" (Ps 72:8–11). The most explicit passage, however, is found in Daniel 7:13–14, which forms the backdrop for so much of the revelation given to the seer-prophet John. Employing the same universal terminology, Daniel describes generally what John describes specifically:

> In my vision at night I looked, and there before me was one like a son of man, coming with the clouds of heaven. He approached the Ancient of Days and was led into his presence. He was given authority, glory and sovereign power; all peoples, nations and men of every language worshiped him. His dominion is an everlasting dominion that will not pass away, and his kingdom is one that will never be destroyed.

David MacLeod summarizes succinctly this emphasis on dominion throughout the Bible:

> This inheritance of dominion is one of the great themes of the Bible, a theme that helps answer questions people have about the

---

7. Lloyd-Jones, *Life in the Spirit*, 175–76.
8. Ridderbos, *Paul and Jesus*, 77.

meaning of life and history. Genesis 1:27–30 records the fact that *dominion* or an *inheritance was given* to the human race. "Fill the earth," the Lord said, "and subdue it" (Gen. 1:28). In Psalm 8 . . . *dominion is celebrated.* "What is man," the psalmist asked, whom You crowned "with glory and majesty?" (v. 5). Genesis 3 gives the tragic record of *dominion lost* or the *inheritance forfeited.* Adam and Eve sinned and lost their royal status. In Jesus' temptation by Satan *dominion was usurped* (Luke 4:6) in that the devil offered to give Jesus worldwide dominion if He would fall down at his feet ("for it has been handed over to me, and I give it to whomever I wish"). In Jesus' preaching *dominion* was *announced* or the *inheritance reoffered* (Matt. 4:17). Christ said, "Repent, for the kingdom of heaven is at hand." Following the death, resurrection, and exaltation of Jesus, *dominion is decreed* or the *inheritance insured.* God the Father said to His victorious Son, "Ask of Me, and I will surely give the nations as Your inheritance" (Ps. 2:8). And here in Revelation 5 (looking on toward the Second Coming), *dominion is taken* or the *inheritance conferred.* The Son of Man will be presented before the Ancient of Days, and to Him will be "given dominion, glory and a kingdom." (Dan 7:14)[9]

This is nothing less than the fulfillment of God's purpose "to bring all things in heaven and on earth together under one head, even Christ" (Eph 1:10; cf. Col 1:20). Here, Paul depicts Christ as *above* all things. When the Greeks would add numbers, they would list them in a column as we do today. Then, rather than writing the sum of the numbers *under* the column, they would draw a line at the top of the column and above that line place the sum of the numbers. They "summed up" rather than "summed down." In Ephesians 1:10, Christ is pictured at the *top* of the column of all things. While in Colossians 3:11 he is *in* all, here he is *above* all. He is above the summation line of all things.[10] When will this take place? "When the kingdoms of this world have become the kingdom of our Lord and of his Christ" (Rev 11:15).

Not only will Christ rule, but the New Humanity will also rule with Christ. This will be the antithesis of the debacle of Babel. While the cross and Pentecost are the *foundation* of the reversal of Babel, the new heavens and earth will be the *culmination* of the reversal of Babel. In Genesis 11, the Old Humanity attempted to connect earth to heaven. In Revelation 21, God brings heaven down to earth. At Babel, the Old

9. MacLeod, "The Lion Who is a Lamb," 330.
10. Milne, *Dynamic Diversity,* 17; cf. MM, 342; LSJ, 944–45.

Humanity built a city for its own glory. At the consummation of time, the New Humanity will inherit a city designed for God's glory.

I previously pointed out that the judgment of Babel was both punitive and preventative in nature. It was punitive in the sense that humanity experienced God's judgment upon his obstinate rebellion. In attempting to become more than he is, humanity became less than he is. God's design for humanity was dominion—the systematic colonization and nurture of the entire earth. Humanity refused God's plan, choosing rather to establish a strongly centralized government that would eventually result in the oppression of others. Desirous of "making a name" for himself (Gen 11:4), humankind pursued uniformity for the purpose of power and oppression. God saw that "nothing they planned to do will be impossible for them" (Gen 11:6), so he took preventative measures. The dispersion of the peoples along with the subsequent development of nationalism proved to be a deterrent to sin. Apart from such dispersion, humanity would self-destruct. God's design, however, will not be frustrated. Humanity's original mandate—to exercise dominion over the whole earth—will be fulfilled. Humanity was created from the dust to rule. John's revelation affirms this truth time and again:

> To him who overcomes and does my will to the end, I will give authority over the nations—"He will rule them with an iron scepter; he will dash them to pieces like pottery." (Rev 2:26–27)

> You have made them to be a kingdom and priests to serve our God, and they will reign on the earth. (Rev 5:10)

> The throne of God and of the Lamb will be in the city, and his servants will serve him. . . . And they will reign for ever and ever. (Rev 22:3–5)

This dominion will be exercised over the earth as well as over the powers that divide. Indeed, the "all things" of Ephesians 1:10 include the heavenly powers. As we have seen, humanity's primeval rebellion eventually resulted in God assigning the nations of the world to the tutelage of angelic powers (Deut 32:8; Dan 10:12–21). Therefore, Christ's redemptive work in the world not only delivers the New Humanity from sin, but also from Satan.

The New Testament makes much of this perspective, which is often called *Christus Victor*.[11] Why else would Jesus tell Peter, "On this rock I will build my church, and the gates of Hades will not overcome it" (Matt 16:18). Paul, in looking back on Christ's redemptive work, states, "And having disarmed the powers and authorities, he made a public spectacle of them, triumphing over them by the cross" (Col 2:15). Finally, the seer-prophet John says without equivocation, "The reason the Son of God appeared was to destroy the devil's work" (1 John 3:8).

In Revelation 12:7–9, John describes the beginning of the end for Satan and his angels.

> And there was war in heaven. Michael and his angels fought against the dragon, and the dragon and his angels fought back. But he was not strong enough, and they lost their place in heaven. The great dragon was hurled down—that ancient serpent called the devil, or Satan, who leads the whole world astray. He was hurled to the earth, and his angels with him.

Here we find "one of the most picturesque figurative depictions of spiritual conflict found in the biblical canon."[12] John first refers to Michael, the guardian angel of God's people (Dan 10:13; 12:1). In contrast to his protective role over Israel in the Old Testament, he is here described as protecting—along with his angels—all of God's elect. In Revelation 13:4, the unbelieving humanity worships the beast, asking, "Who is like the beast? Who can make war against him?" In response, there is only one—Michael—whose name means "Who is like God?" His name underscores the incomparable nature of God, assuring victory in this titanic conflict with the "dragon and his angels." He is also described in Daniel 10 as "one of the chief princes." (Dan 10:13). As guardian angel of the New Humanity, Michael wins the victory over Satan.

Satan is also described in these verses as the "great dragon" and the "one who leads the whole *world* astray." The specific term is *oikoumenē*, referring to the inhabited earth and comprising the various ethnicities of the world. The expression undoubtedly includes the sons of Adam (*bᵉnê 'ādām*), the nations (*gôyim*), and the peoples (*'ammîm*) specifically mentioned in Deuteronomy 32:8. Just as the angelic princes of Persia and Greece, these powerful demonic emissaries hold under their

---

11. For further discussion, see Boyd, *God at War*, 238–68.
12. Kirk, *Angelology*, 191.

sway kings and nations, being the celestial counterpart of the beast and the kings of the earth (Rev 13:2; 16:13–14; 17:11). Here again we notice this undeniable rapport between angelic powers and the peoples of the earth. However, the cause and effect relationship appears to be reversed. As Walter Wink observes: "The usual causal sequence ('as above, so below') is here reversed, breaking the heavenly deadlock. Now 'as below, so above'; the suffering of Christ and the martyrs makes possible the expulsion of Satan from heaven."[13]

From heaven to earth and from earth to hell—that is the fate of Satan and his angels. After a moment of brief reprisal, the one who deceives the nations is ultimately "thrown into the lake of burning sulfur" and "tormented day and night for ever and ever" (Rev 20:10). End of story for the powers that divide. The leash placed on Satan at the cross has led him straight to hell.

Resemblance

As the restored image of the *imago Dei*, the New Humanity is not only destined to *rule* over the new earth, but also to *resemble* his Creator. Humanity was originally created as the likeness-image of God, and it is to the likeness-image of God that the New Humanity is finally restored. While never created to *be* gods, humanity was created to *be like* God. As we have seen, to be like God is often described in the Bible as putting on a new set of clothes.

Throughout the Bible, a great emphasis is placed on what we are wearing as our moral attire. Righteousness is frequently depicted as a garment. In Genesis, Adam and his wife were clothed in three different garments. There are the original clothes they were given at creation—the clothes of innocence. When sin entered, however, their garments of innocence disappeared and they were naked. This nakedness was certainly the absence of the original innocence they enjoyed before their alienation from God and one another. Man then did an interesting thing. He manufactured a cheap substitute garment. He sewed together fig leaves and designed makeshift garments, symbolizing his own self-effort to remedy his tragic situation. However, this symbol of good works would never do. Consequently, God provided the promise of a Savior, a

---

13. Wink, *Naming the Powers*, 34.

Redeemer, by shedding the blood of animals and by clothing Adam and Eve with the skins of this sacrifice.

Quite appropriately, the story line of the New Humanity ends with this same image of having on the right set of clothes. In Revelation 7:9–14, we see John looking out on a vast crowd too great to count, with representatives from every nation and tribe and people and language, standing in front of the throne and before the Lamb. They are clothed in white robes and hold palm branches in their hands as they sing, "Salvation comes from our God on the throne and from the Lamb!" While in this passage white robes most likely refer to the imputed righteousness of Christ lovingly and graciously given to this bride at the moment of betrothal (Eph 5:26), it is later stated that the "fine linen, bright and clean" given to the bride stands for the "righteous acts of the saints" (Rev 19:7–8). In other words, it is by putting off the old and putting on the new that the New Humanity resembles her head and makes herself ready for the wedding of the Lamb. As a result, she will be "prepared as a bride beautifully dressed for her husband" (Rev 21:2).

Relationship

We resemble our Three-in-One Creator to the degree that we relate to him and others in love. Jesus said, "Love the Lord your God with all your heart and with all your soul and with all your mind." He also said, "Love your neighbor as yourself" (Matt 22:37–38).

In the New Humanity, our vertical relationship with God is foundational to our horizontal relationships with others. The two aspects are inseparable and mutually dependent. John Calvin was certainly mistaken when he wrote: "To be in Paradise and live with God is not to speak to each other and be heard by each other, but is only to enjoy God, to feel his good will, and rest in him."[14] No! Who we are as the image of God and as the bride of Christ speaks of *relationship*. As the eternal Three-in-One enjoys relationship between Father, Son, and Holy Spirit from eternity past to eternity future, so the New Humanity as his image and bride was created for relationship. This was true in Eden, it is true today, and it will be true throughout eternity.

---

14. Cited by McDannel and Lang, *History*, 155.

The diversity in unity that characterizes the Trinity as well as the New Humanity will certainly not be obliterated in either the intermediate[15] or eternal heaven. The diversity and universal inclusivism of the heavenly New Humanity is explicitly described in the words of the new song vocalized by the heavenly choir in Revelation 5:9–10.

> And they sang a new song: "You are worthy to take the scroll and to open its seals, because you were slain, and with your blood you purchased men for God *from every tribe and language and people and nation*. You have made them to be a kingdom and priests to serve our God, and they will reign on the earth." (emphasis mine)

This passage is one of the greatest scenes of universal and multiethnic adoration recorded anywhere in Scripture. In this cacophony of praise, the Lamb is worshiped as the *only* one worthy to open the seals of the scroll, having purchased through his sacrificial death people from every "tribe" and "language" and "people" and "nation." By using a rhetorical device called "polysyndeton," the author lists in close succession one descriptive designation upon another to accentuate the idea of diversity and universality.[16] Such lists appear seven times in Revelation (5:9; 7:9; 10:11; 11:9; 13:7; 14:6; 17:15) and echo the Table of the Nations described in Genesis 10. Furthermore, each passage describes a distinct aspect of the spiritual conflict leading to Christ's promised rule in direct fulfillment of Daniel 7:14—"He was given authority, glory and sovereign power; all peoples, nations and men of every language worshiped him."[17]

Of the four terms mentioned in Revelation 5:9, "nation" (*ethnos*) is the most general, indicating the natural cohesion of a people united by kinship, culture, and common traditions.[18] On the other hand, the word "tribe" (*phylē*) describes people as a national unity of common descent[19] or a "subgroup of a nation characterized by a distinctive blood line."[20] Most references in the New Testament are to the tribes of Israel,

---

15. The expression "intermediate heaven" refers to the dwelling place of believers who have died (Luke 23:43; 2 Cor 5:8) prior to the establishment of Christ's earthly reign (Rev 20) and the new heavens and earth (Rev 21).

16. Blass and Debrunner, *Greek Grammar*, §460.3; Aune, *Revelation 1–5*, 361.

17. Cf. Dan 3:4, 7; 5:19; 6:25; Isa 66:18; Zech 8:22; Josephus, *Jewish Antiquities*, 7:356–57.

18. Schmidt, *TDNT*, 2:369; BAG, 276.

19. Maurer, *TDNT*, 9:245–50.

20. BAG, 1069.

though here the word is inclusive of the Gentile world. The term "people" (*laos*) speaks of people as a political unity with a common history and constitution.²¹ Finally, "language" (*glōssa*) refers to people united by a common language.²² John emphatically states that representatives from *every* nationality, ethnicity, language, and culture will be part of the New Humanity in this eternal kingdom.

In Revelation 7:9–10, John gives us another glimpse into the intermediate heaven as he describes the worship of the New Humanity now before the throne:

> After this I looked and there before me was a great multitude that no one could count, *from every nation, tribe, people and language*, standing before the throne and in front of the Lamb. They were wearing white robes and were holding palm branches in their hands. And they cried out in a loud voice: "Salvation belongs to our God, who sits on the throne, and to the Lamb." (emphasis mine)

Here John repeats the categories mentioned in Revelation 5:9, but he alters the order. There is diversity—individuals forming a great multitude from *every* nation, tribe, people, and language. There is also unity—they are standing *together* "before the throne and in front of the Lamb." This distinctive characteristic of diversity in unity of the heavenly New Humanity is also seen in that they cry out together in a "loud voice" in worship to God and to the Lamb.

This scene of such exultant, multiethnic worship must be interpreted against the backdrop of Babel in Genesis 11. As we have seen in chapter 3, the "children of Adam" were all of one "lip" (*śāpâ*, speech) and one "vocabulary" (*dᵉbārîm*, the content of what is said) as they arrogantly conspired to unite earth with heaven. Though confused at Babel, these same lips will be purified to worship the Lord. Zephaniah 3:9–10 states: "Then will I purify the *lips* (*śāpâ*, speech; emphasis mine) of the peoples, that all of them may call on the name of the LORD and serve him shoulder to shoulder. From beyond the rivers of Cush my worshipers, my scattered people, will bring me offerings." The worship of the New Humanity in Revelation 7:9–10 is in direct fulfillment of Zephaniah's prophecy. The babble of Babel has become the beauty and purity of multiethnic worship before the Lamb of God.

21. Strathmann, *TDNT*, 4:33, 51–52; Schmidt, *TDNT*, 2:369.
22. Behm, *TDNT*, 1:722.

Will this culmination of the reversal of Babel include the reestablishment of a common language? It is quite possible. Apparently, those who worship are united by a shared language.[23] Randy Alcorn suggests that this may be a trade language, heaven's equivalent to Swahili or English, both of which are often used as second languages to facilitate communication across linguistic boundaries. This could also be concluded from Revelation 5:10 where the redeemed are described as "a kingdom." One kingdom, one world, and one government may imply one shared language. Based on the biblical evidence, Alcorn speculates:

> Nonetheless, it seems likely that in addition to our common language, we will maintain our current languages. Although the confusion of languages at Babel was originally a curse, the gatherings in Heaven of people of every nation, tribe, and language show that God will unite forever the people divided at Babel—not by eliminating their differences, but by eliminating the sin, suspicion, and hostility.... We won't be omniscient, so it's doubtful we'll know all languages. But certainly we could learn them much faster. Those of us who aren't naturally gifted in languages may be amazed at our abilities.[24]

During my early years in France, worship in that language was difficult. Initially, it was a babble that was incomprehensible. I did not understand others and others did not understand me. Fortunately God understood us both! However, as I acquired the language and continued to use it as a medium of expressing my praise to God, it became *in that context* my preferred language of worship. Today when I hear worship in the French language, it often brings tears to my eyes. I would not find it at all strange that the heavenly New Humanity will share a type of heavenly language without abolishing the specific language of each ethnicity. Such heavenly language *in that context* may well be worship from "purified lips" expressing the diversity in unity that God desires. If on this side of heaven we can acquire a new language to the point of genuinely expressing our worship to God, so much more in the world to come. Can you even begin to imagine what it will be like to hear and see Americans, French, Brazilians, Kenyans, Indians, Britons, Rwandans, Germans, Italians, Filipinos, Koreans, Chinese, Egyptians, Germans, Swedes, Irish,

---

23. Smalley, *Revelation*, 191.
24. Alcorn, *Heaven*, 364–65.

and people of every nation and ethnicity of the world worshiping the King of kings with one voice?

While the discussion of various eschatological schemes pertaining to the period of tribulation and the millennial reign of Christ is beyond the scope of this book, it is clear that in Revelation 21–22 John's focus moves from the intermediate heaven to the eternal state—the new heaven and earth. Here we continue to see the diversity in unity of the New Humanity. As time reaches its culmination, the image of the New Humanity as bride once again comes to the forefront. Following the angelic announcement of the wedding supper of the Lamb (Rev 19:7–9) and a description of the millennial reign of Christ (Rev 20), John sees the new Jerusalem descending from heaven "prepared as a bride beautifully dressed for her husband." While some question the direct correlation between the new Jerusalem and the bride, verse 9–10 make the connection explicit: "'Come, I will show you the bride, the wife of the Lamb.' And he . . . showed me the Holy City, Jerusalem, coming down out of heaven from God." As the dwelling place of the New Humanity and capital city of the new earth, the new Jerusalem is described as the "bride, the wife of the Lamb." The imagery of the New Humanity as bride is itself a collective idea. We are not *individually* the bride of Christ, but *collectively* the bride of Christ. Alcorn states it well: "Christ is not a polygamist. He will be married to one bride, not millions. We belong to each other and need each other."[25] This was true at the moment of our betrothal to Christ as his bride, during this present period of preparation as his bride, and throughout eternity.

As the eternal home of the New Humanity, the new Jerusalem will be a mosaic of ethnic diversity. This eternal city is further described as the "dwelling of God with men" who will be his "people" (Rev 21:3). The term "people" is plural ("peoples"; *laoi*) in keeping with the universal, multiethnic character of this city. While the new Jerusalem includes the names of the "twelve tribes of Israel" inscribed on each gate (Rev 21:12), the wall of the city has twelve foundations on which are inscribed "the names of the twelve apostles" (Rev 21:14). This is the New Humanity, inclusive of *both* Jew and Gentile without amalgamating their distinctiveness. More specifically, the new Jerusalem has twelve gates—"three gates on the east, three on the north, three on the south and three on the west"—through which the kings of the earth "bring their splendor"

---

25. Alcorn, *Heaven*, 193.

(Rev 21:13, 26). Certainly, the "splendor" of which John speaks includes the beauty of the diverse cultures and ethnicities represented by their respective leaders. Not only will we have resurrected bodies in the new earth, but there will also be resurrected cultures. As we have seen, God is not interested in abolishing our differences, but in helping us appreciate our differences as we find our ultimate sense of security and identity in Christ. In the new heaven and earth, there is no fear of being absorbed into the "All" of Buddhism or of becoming like a mere raindrop in a nebulous ocean as taught by Hinduism. No, there will be no loss of personal or ethnic identity in the new heaven and earth. John's description reminds us that "nothing of the diversity of the nations and peoples, their cultural products, languages, arts, sciences, literature, and technology—so far as these are good and excellent—will be lost upon life in the new creation."[26]

Just as the Magi traveled from afar to the old city of Jerusalem, seeking the Messiah King, so those who comprise the universal, multi-ethnic New Humanity will humbly and regularly journey to the capital city of the new earth—the new Jerusalem—offering worship to the King of kings. The kings of the earth will humbly submit to the authority and power of the Lamb. There will be no "racism" in heaven. The diverse ethnicities of the world will no longer be in competition with each other. Rather, each and every ethnicity will harmoniously contribute to life and culture on the new earth. All will have equal access to the holy city and to the King!

CONCLUSION: HOMESICK FOR EDEN

The setting of the original Garden of Eden was idyllic. Humanity—created as the image of God—experienced perfect harmony with his Creator, with fellow man (Eve), and with all of creation. His representative mandate as God's vice-regent was to rule over the earth, resemble his Maker, and relate harmoniously with fellow man. Humanity existed as the apex of all creation, secure and safe in Eden, the temple-garden that God had prepared.

Then tragedy struck. Humanity's rebellion had consequences of cosmic proportions. Alienated from God and within itself, the Old

---

26. Cornelius Venema as cited by Alcorn, *Heaven*, 365.

Humanity became notorious for its ethnic strife. The beauty of harmony so characteristic of Eden degenerated into the wilderness of this world.

Thankfully, as we have seen, this is *not* the end of the story. Christ Jesus, the second man and last Adam, conquered sin and Satan at the cross and gave birth to the New Humanity. As God's New Humanity, we await a "second Eden," the transformation of this earthly wilderness into the beauty of the new heaven and earth.

That is precisely how John describes the new Jerusalem. In stark contrast to the Babylon of the Old Humanity (Rev 17–18), the new Jerusalem is the restored Eden of God's new creation. A river filled with the water of life flows through the middle of this heavenly city. On each side of the river stands the tree of life, producing twelve kinds of fruit—a ripe fruit each month (Rev 22:1–2). The leaves of this tree are for the healing of the nations.

As the new Jerusalem is the second Eden, so the New Humanity is the second Eve to be married to the last Adam. Having been freed through death from our previous husband, we have now been betrothed to our new husband, Christ. As our loving husband and faithful head, he is preparing the church—the New Humanity—for the long anticipated wedding feast. This wedding will initiate eternity spent in the presence of the King.

Until then, we are homesick for Eden. "For here we do not have an enduring city, but we are looking for the city that is to come" (Heb 13:14). This, too, was the longing of those faithful who have preceded us: "Instead, they were longing for a better country—a heavenly one. Therefore God is not ashamed to be called their God, for he has prepared a city for them" (Heb 11:16).

Engraved on our oldest son's tombstone are these words: "When we see Christ, we will see you again." This, too, is an expression of our longing for Eden. Restored rule—even over death. Restored resemblance—perfect conformity to the image of Christ. Restored relationship—with those we love and those who love the Savior of humanity.

11

On Earth as It Is in Heaven

Our Father in heaven, hallowed be your name.
Your Kingdom come, your will be done on earth as it is in heaven.

Jesus Christ

WHEN JESUS TAUGHT HIS disciples to pray, he requested of the Father that the realities of heaven become realities on earth—"Your will be done *on earth* as it is *in heaven.*" Randy Alcorn correctly observes, "We tend to start with Earth and reason up toward Heaven, when instead we should start with Heaven and reason down toward Earth."[1] The perennial question must be asked—*If the kingdom of heaven is not segregated, why on earth is the church?*

In the preceding chapters, we have explored some of the answers to that question as well as some of the biblical solutions. Our focus has been on biblical prescription rather than cultural description. It has been observed that "the church in the United States reflects a social reality rather than promoting a theological vision."[2] To the degree that local churches are driven by the sociological currents of our culture, we will continue to establish our boundaries in very predictable ways. On the other hand, rather than acquiesce to the predictable, we *can* and *must* set forth a "theological vision" for diversity in unity in and among local churches.

1. Alcorn, *Heaven*, 54.
2. DeYoung, et al., *United by Faith*, 131.

While the preceding chapters have set forth the biblical-theological vision, my intent in this chapter is to synthesize our discoveries and propose several directives as a starting point for implementing in and among local churches our New Humanity identity. In other words, what do New Humanity churches look like? What values shape their life in community and ministry? In what specific ways do they implement the biblical principles we have discussed thus far? While undoubtedly they will have different names, different emphases, as well as different degrees and types of diversity (for example, diversity of ethnicity, age, socioeconomic class, etc.), New Humanity churches are committed to nurturing several core values that will help us in experiencing on earth the realities of heaven.

IDENTITY FORMATION: TRANSFORMATION OF CORE BELIEFS

I keep on my desk an analytical balance. It's the old fashioned kind, with a weighing pan suspended from each arm of the scales. These balances have been used for centuries to determine precision mass measurement. A known weight is placed in one pan, which is then compared to an unknown sample placed in the other pan. The objective is to tip the scales, bringing the two objects into balance.

The apostle Paul may well have had in mind such an analytical balance when he wrote these words to the Ephesian believers: "I urge you to live a life *worthy* of the calling you have received" (Eph 4:1, emphasis mine). The term "worthy" (*axios*) literally means "bringing up the other beam of the scales."[3] Paul is telling us that our *lifestyle* (practice) as the New Humanity (Eph 4–6) is to be brought into balance with our *identity* (position) as the New Humanity (Eph 1–3). We do not deserve our New Humanity identity in Christ; this is given by grace. However, we are called to understand how much our New Humanity identity deserves from us; this is motivated by grace. To the degree that we do, we will "tip the scales," bringing our earthly experience as the church into balance with our heavenly vocation.

What does our New Humanity identity deserve from us? The answer to that question begins with *knowing* who we really are and *considering* it to be true (cf. Rom 6:1–14). As already stated, *we must*

---

3. Foerster, *TDNT*, 1:379; Hoehner, *Ephesians*, 504.

understand and help others understand who we are as the New Humanity and the implications of our collective identity for the life of the church. This is "identity formation."[4] The present day phenomenon of widespread segregation in the church along lines of color, culture, and class is at its very core a problem of identity. It is this crisis of identity that I spoke of in the introduction to this book and that continues to be the "unsolved problem" of the church today. What comes to *your* mind when you hear the word "church"? The answer to that question is largely shaped by what you believe the church to be in the first place. Furthermore, what we *believe about* the church profoundly influences how we *behave in* the church and in the world. Charles Colson reminds us that "the challenge for today's church is not so much convincing skeptics of the truth of the gospel as it is really believing it ourselves. Believing it in the radical way that compels us to be the Body of Christ, undeniably alive in the midst of death and destruction."[5]

Paradigm Shift

Yes, to become New Humanity churches we need a massive "paradigm shift" in how we think about the church. The concept of "paradigm shift" finds its origin in the early 1960s in Thomas Kuhn's groundbreaking book *The Structure of Scientific Revolutions*.[6] Kuhn effectively demonstrates that release from tradition or old ways of thinking is the seedbed of nearly every worthwhile breakthrough or discovery. Stephen Covey puts it this way: "Paradigm shifts move us from one way of seeing the world to another. And those shifts can create powerful change. Our paradigms, whether correct or incorrect, are the sources of our attitudes and behaviors."[7] Apart from a similar paradigm shift in our understanding of our collective identity as the New Humanity—an *experiential understanding* that touches us at the core of our being—our attempts to nurture diversity in unity across ethnic, generational, and socioeconomic lines will prove superficial. On the other hand, a growing understanding

---

4. Several recent works on identity formation in the church that are noteworthy include William Campbell, *Creation of Christian Identity*; Klyne Snodgrass, "Hermeneutics of Identity"; "Jesus and Identity"; "Paul's Focus on Identity"; "Pauline Perspectives"; and Mikael Tellbe, *Christ-Believers*.

5. Colson and Vaughn, *Being the Body*, xxix.

6. Kuhn, *Structure*, 18–34, 111–35.

7. Covey, *Seven Habits*, 29.

and appreciation of our New Humanity identity provides a trustworthy foundation and motivation for implementing lasting change.

In the movie *Bourne Identity*, Matt Damon plays Jason Bourne—a CIA agent who has suffered amnesia and is trying to figure out his true identity. While in Switzerland, he hitches a ride to Germany with a young woman named Marie. He's running from the police, but he's not even sure why. He tries to keep quiet about his situation until the frustration overwhelms him. Finally, in response to a simple question, he turns to Marie and says desperately, "I don't know who I am or where I am going." It then takes three feature-length movies before he finally discovers—or rediscovers—who he really is!

As individuals, whether believer or unbeliever, the single most important element in our emotional and mental health is a sane self-image. This includes a proper understanding of who we are as the image of God. Whatever may be your strengths or weaknesses, your positive personality traits or handicaps, you are of eternal value in God's eyes—created to rule on this earth, to resemble your Maker, and to enjoy harmonious relationship with God and with fellow humans. Likewise, individually as believers and collectively as the church, the single most important factor in our spiritual and relational health is a biblical understanding and appreciation of who we are *together* in Christ. Understanding who we are and where we are going as the New Humanity is foundational and indispensable to nurturing New Humanity churches. The answer to our segregational tendencies is found in a revival of our corporate identity. Authentic diversity in unity flows out of a healthy collective identity.

If we are to live out in the church the diversity in unity that characterizes Father, Son, and Holy Spirit—the template for our life in community—we must believe and behave according to our "born identity." As those dearly loved and born of God, we must allow the eternal love relationship between Father, Son, and Holy Spirit—as well as his "unknowable" love for us (Eph 3:19)—to become both the model and motivation for our interactions with others. As previously observed, this is not a mere intellectual exercise; it touches the inner recesses of our being. This involves a transformation of our core beliefs. A core belief is a "worldview that has deepened to a nonnegotiable *attitude* and *attribute*."[8] Obviously, the diversity in unity that characterizes the New Humanity as described on the pages of Scripture is *not* a core belief of

---

8. DeYoung et al., *United by Faith*, 158 (emphasis mine).

the majority of believers in America today as seen in the fact that 90 percent of worshippers attend ethnically homogeneous congregations. Paradoxically, the church should be setting the pace in this area. To do so, we must undergo a foundational identity overhaul. This will involve a paradigm shift—deconstructing certain deeply ingrained, taken-for-granted ideas as well as reconstructing our core identity as defined in Scripture. We need a "hermeneutics of identity."[9]

Hermeneutics of Identity

Hermeneutics can be defined as "the deciphering of life in the mirror of the text."[10] James speaks of a man who "looks at his face in a mirror," but then walks away and does nothing about what he sees (Jas 1:23–24). Such a person fails to allow the text of Scripture to be the determining factor in the deciphering of life. If hermeneutics is the deciphering of life in the mirror of the text, then a hermeneutics of identity means to allow the plethora of identity affirmations in Scripture to be our guide in deciphering what to believe and how to behave as the New Humanity.

Our greatest challenge as a church in developing such a biblical hermeneutics of identity is the present day cultural captivity of the church. In far too many cases, our tendency is to allow the surrounding culture, rather than Scripture, to define our identity. Whether it be the pragmatism of the Homogeneous Unit Principle, the relativism that subtly influences certain portions of the emerging church, or the religious consumerism that drives so much of American Christianity, we are so easily "tossed back and forth by the waves, and blown here and there" (Eph 4:14) by contemporary cultural currents. According to Martin Marty, "Evangelicals, for all the cultural bogeys, have chosen to adapt more to the mainlines of American life than most other groups."[11] The foundational problem is that we don't know who we are as the church. The biblical remedy is a hermeneutics of identity.

Admittedly, this word "identity" does not appear in most translations of the Bible. In a quick search, I found the term only in The Living

---

9. For the term I am indebted to Snodgrass, "Hermeneutics," 3–19. Snodgrass defines identity as "that sense of being and self-understanding that frames our actions, communicates to others who we are, and sets the agenda for our acts. We live out of a sense of identity" (p. 9).

10. Ricoeur, "Preface to Bultmann," 53.

11. Marty, "At the Crossroads," 39.

Bible and the New Living Translation in Ezekiel 17:14 and Acts 7:13. Nevertheless, the concept is there. In fact, Scripture is all about identity formation.[12] The constant appeal of the New Testament writers is, "Be who you are in Christ!" The ancient philosophical world also makes its contribution to the importance of this concept. Epictetus (ca. AD 55–ca. 135) writes, "In the first place, know who you are and then adorn yourself appropriately. You are a human being."[13] That is essentially the call of Scripture—"learn who you are" and then "adorn yourself"! This is the process of identity formation. Apart from this, we will continue to establish our boundaries in very predictable ways, being driven by the sociological and ideological currents of our culture.

Our "Identity Manual"

If identity formation is so crucial to nurturing New Humanity churches, then what can be done on a practical level to facilitate such training? The most obvious answer to that question is to bathe ourselves in our "identity manual"—God's Word—and in turn teach others what the Scriptures say about our collective identity as the people of God. The goal of this teaching is that each believer may no longer view himself or others "from a worldly point of view" (2 Cor 5:16).

Over the years, I have preached numerous messages (often as a series) that touch on this topic of identity. A starting point for such teaching would be to take the chapters of this book and develop a series on humanity as the *imago Dei*, touching on the beginning, the end, and everything in between. I would also suggest teaching a series on the many images of the church that are found in the New Testament—such as the church as body (1 Cor 12), building (Eph 2:21), or temple (2 Cor 6:16)—and draw out applications for how we are to believe and behave as the New Humanity.[14] I recently did a series in my own church, entitled *Discover the Real You*, in which I focused for three weeks on Romans 6, a key New Testament text relating to identity formation. Presently, I am teaching in our church a two-year course in Ephesians. This study has

---

12. Cf. Gen 1:26–27; 12:1–3; Exod 19:6; Ps 73; 139; Matt 5:13; Rom 1:7; 1 Cor 1:2; 6:11; Gal 5:13; Eph 5:8; Col 3:1–3; 1 Pet 2:9; Rev 21:1–4.

13. Epictetus, *Discourses*, 3.1.25.

14. A helpful tool for the preparation of such a series is Paul Minear's book, *Images of the Church*.

served as the biblical underpinnings for merging Oromo speaking and Romanian speaking fellowships into our larger church family.

Instruction concerning our New Humanity identity is certainly not limited to the New Testament epistles. The Gospels are also identity documents, focusing not only on Christ's identity but also on our identity in relationship to him. However the teaching is approached, we must help believers understand our collective identity in Christ, for this determines our commitments and boundaries. "If one is in Christ, the commitments of Christ expressed in His Word and His commands become the commitments of that person, and Christ's approach to boundaries—both boundaries rejected and boundaries not violated—become the approach of the person as well."[15]

Upon taking steps to focus on biblical identity formation, you may encounter resistance. I find that so many in our churches today want immediate short-term answers to their pressing problems. We want to be "fixed." Identity formation, on the other hand, focuses on shaping perspectives rather than offering pragmatic solutions. The goal of identity formation is to establish a biblical-theological foundation from which believers can learn to decipher their lives in the mirror of the text. It is teaching someone to fish rather than handing someone a fish. Such an approach is *far better* than pragmatic solutions.

The Symbols of our Identity

Beyond the verbal communication of truth, the Scriptures leave us two visual illustrations of truth that serve as powerful reminders of our New Humanity identity. These are baptism and the Lord's Supper. Both are identity shaping experiences that remind us of who we are. Over the centuries, the church has placed great emphasis on the imagery of baptism as a tool of identity formation. This can be seen, for example, in the cross-shaped baptisteries that were used in the Mediterranean basin, especially from the fourth to the sixth centuries. Other baptisteries shaped as niches in a tomb visually expressed the same truth of intimate association with Christ in his death, burial, and resurrection.[16]

Baptism speaks of more than *my* identification with Christ; it speaks of *our* identification with Christ. David Wright reminds us that

---

15. Snodgrass, "Jesus and Identity," 144.
16. Snodgrass, "Paul's Focus," 271.

for the early Christians "baptism was a single gate for all; it was a great leveler."[17] Whether rich or poor, Jew or Gentile, black or white, African or European, young or old—all who believe are to pass by this humbling, enduring sign of identification with Christ. Baptism reminds us that we were *co*-enlivened, *co*-raised, and *co*-seated with Christ. In view of this, is it not strange that we proclaim in baptism our collective identity in Christ, but then go our separate ways to worship in largely homogeneous, segregated congregations? We are baptized in the name of the Father, Son, and Holy Spirit—the non-homogeneous Three-in-One— but see little connection between that truth and our fragmentation as the body of Christ along lines of color, culture, and class.

One recent baptismal service at Central Bible Church where I pastor left an indelible impression on my mind. Those who testified to their faith before being baptized represented a diverse array of ethnicity and age. One woman was a refugee from the Republic of the Congo. Having fled that country during a time of tribal warfare, she found refuge in Gabon and eventually in the United States. Her testimony was translated from French into English. Another was a seventeen-year-old boy who had met Christ only several months prior to his baptism. He came to faith rather dramatically out of a context of drugs and teenage rebellion. Two were teenage girls raised in Christian homes. They testified of the impact the gospel had on their lives from an early age. One man was more than seventy years old with tattoos over most of his arms and back. He had been a professional boxer for some years in Portland, Oregon. Another woman, an African American, though not baptized that morning, gave testimony of how God had touched her life several years before. As this diverse group of believers passed through the waters of baptism, it served as a visual symbol to our congregation of the diversity in unity that is ours in Christ.

In a similar way, the Lord's Supper is also an identity shaping act in the life of the church. The Lord's Supper is *always* depicted as a community affair in the New Testament. It's not only about you and your relationship with Christ, but it's also about your relationship with other members of the New Humanity. That is why Paul writes to the severely divided Corinthian church—"Because there is one loaf, we, who are many, are one body, for we all partake of the one loaf" (1 Cor 10:17). Essentially, Paul is reminding this fragmented church that their

17. Wright, "A Race Apart?" 133.

divisiveness is blatantly inconsistent with their identity as "one body." Each time they participated in this identity shaping experience—the Lord's Supper—they were confronted with the truth of who they were together as illustrated by the "one loaf." So it should be for us. Is it not ironic that, as we share this one loaf that speaks of our indivisible unity as the New Humanity, 92.5 percent of our churches in America are segregated along lines of ethnicity?

At Central Bible Church, we will often highlight this truth of diversity in unity around the "one loaf" by having people of various ethnicities and ages serve the elements of the Lord's Supper to the congregation. One Sunday, more than ten different ethnicities (of the seventeen or so represented in the church) participated in serving the elements. It was an identity creating experience. The congregation not only heard the truth of their shared identity in Christ, but also visually saw this truth illustrated as African American, Japanese, Egyptian, Kenyan, Swedish, Filipino, Caucasian, Rwandan, and others served the bread and cup to the church family.

As for the Corinthians, the identity shaping power of the Lord's Supper speaks directly to our divisiveness as well as to the religious consumerism that lies behind so much of it. Paul says to the Corinthian believers: "Your meetings do more harm than good. . . . There are divisions among you" (1 Cor 11:17–18). Some in the Corinthian church were more concerned about feeding their belly then feeding their soul (vv. 17–22). In many churches today, the coffee table has replaced the Lord's Table. Niche marketing, polished performances, and luxurious buildings have, in some cases, taken the place of the simplicity and humility represented in the bread and cup. To counteract these tendencies, the Lord's Supper was instituted as an occasion of personal and corporate evaluation. That is why Paul explains:

> Therefore, whoever eats the bread or drinks the cup of the Lord in an unworthy manner will be guilty of sinning against the body and blood of the Lord. A man ought to examine himself before he eats of the bread and drinks of the cup. For anyone who eats and drinks without recognizing the body of the Lord eats and drinks judgment on himself. That is why many among you are weak and sick, and a number of you have fallen asleep. But if we judged ourselves, we would not come under judgment. When we are judged by the Lord, we are being disciplined so that we will not be condemned with the world. (1 Cor 11:27–32)

The examination to which we are called doesn't have to do with whether or not we are worthy to partake of these elements. The fact is, none of us are worthy. This table is reserved for sinners. Indeed, the Lord's Supper is a feast for sinners! If you don't fit that category, you're excluded. Rather, the examination has to do with our attitude and actions in approaching the Lord's Supper. Paul's reference to "recognizing the body of the Lord" is probably a *double entendre* referring to both the body of Jesus sacrificially offered (symbolized by the bread and wine) as well as the body of Christ, the church. As we have seen, the two are inseparable; out of the pierced side of Jesus' Jewish body came the New Humanity. Therefore, as we celebrate this feast for sinners, we cannot ignore the implications of its identity shaping truth for the church. We must examine ourselves, asking if our experiences of community reflect the selfless and sacrificial lifestyle Christ intends for his church. Are we actively moving across the lines of ethnicity that have been established in our surrounding community? Are we demonstrating in our lifestyle the radical inclusivism of the cross? Or are we passively promoting the ethnic divide by our practices of homogenous worship?

Such personal and collective examination should lead the church to humble sorrow and then to repentance. Paul writes to the Corinthians: "Godly sorrow brings repentance that leads to salvation and leaves no regret" (2 Cor 7:10). For true repentance to take place, there must first be "godly sorrow." The Corinthian church had "mourned" (v. 7, *odyrmos*) their situation, a term indicating deep sorrow. We too must be moved to profound sorrow over the ways in which we have attempted to respond in merely human terms to our longing for meaning and belonging. We must be brought to the point of godly sorrow over our individualism, religious consumerism, and competition between churches, all of which contribute to the present segregation of the Christ's body. We must be deeply moved by the degree to which such segregation grieves the heart of Christ, the head of the New Humanity. We must sorrow over the fact that such disunity is an affront to the very prayer of Jesus Christ that we be perfected in the diversity in unity characteristic of our Creator.

Throughout this book I have focused on the dividing walls of ethnicity in general terms. However, I believe that here in the United States there are at least two ethnic divides about which we must deeply grieve. The first divide—and the one foundational to all the others here in America—is the black/white divide. Tony Evans is correct in concluding: "Given the length and volatile history of this divide, if we can ever get this right, we will have developed a template for addressing wherever else this evil shows up in the culture."[18] A second divide that is both historical and long-standing is the white/Native American divide. I believe that in both of these areas it is the responsibility of Caucasian Christian leaders to take the lead in calling the church to "godly sorrow" for the ways we have and continue to contribute to these divides.

However, our sorrow must be "as God intended" leading, not to regret, but to repentance (vv. 9–10). To repent means to have a change of mind resulting in a change of behavior. It is to turn from any attitudes or actions that are vestiges of the Old Humanity lifestyle and to embrace the attitudes and actions that are in keeping with our New Humanity identity. Repentance is not only spiritual and emotional, it is also volitional. Genuine repentance manifests itself in a change of behavior. We cannot effectively deconstruct the walls that presently fragment the body of Christ apart from some serious housecleaning. Any genuine repentance over the ethnic divide in society—and particularly the black/white divide in America—must begin with the church (1 Pet 4:17). Even as Jesus expelled the consumers from the temple, we also must take inventory of our consumerist ways that have contributed to the present day dividing walls throughout Christ's body. We must accept responsibility for our attitudes and actions, and move in a positive direction in keeping with our New Humanity identity. We must intentionally and continually lay aside the diversity in disunity of Babel and embrace the diversity in unity of Pentecost.

Such godly sorrow that brings repentance "leads to salvation and leaves no regret" (v. 10). As for the Corinthians, the "salvation" of which Paul speaks means deliverance from our present situation. He is speaking of temporal deliverance rather than eternal deliverance. When we as a church sorrow over our present state of divisiveness and genuinely repent of the ways in which *we* have constructed the dividing walls that separate us, *God will intervene and deliver*. The promise of God to his people in the Old Testament holds true for his people today: "If my people, who are called by my name, will humble themselves and pray and seek my face and turn from their wicked ways, then will I hear from heaven and will forgive their sin" (2 Chr 7:14). This promise and hope should inspire within us the same "earnestness," "longing,"

---

18. Evans, *Embracing Oneness*, 17–18.

"concern," and "readiness to see justice done" that it did among the Corinthians (2 Cor 7:11).

Such earnestness and readiness to see justice done was modeled on one occasion in the life of General Robert E. Lee. His actions modeled the identity shaping power of the Lord's Supper. On Sundays, Lee attended services at St. Paul's Episcopal Church in Richmond, Virginia. The church was known for its long history and distinguished membership. On a warm Sunday in June 1865, Lee sat in his normal pew on the left side of the aisle. As the Lord's Supper was about to be served, a black man rose from his seat and made his way to the communion table. The congregation was frozen with shock. There was a section in the western gallery that was reserved for blacks. If they wished to receive communion, they would come forward only after all the whites had returned from the altar to their pews. Yet this black man dared to come to the altar first as if he were a social equal. If this had taken place only months before, he may have been hustled from the church, jailed for disturbing the peace, or even flogged. The minister and congregation were dumbfounded. No one moved, except Lee. He rose in his usual dignified manner, walked down the aisle, knelt down by the black man, and took communion. Seeing Lee's example, the other members of the congregation came forward together, black and white, to enjoy the Lord's Supper.[19]

IDENTITY, DISTINCTIONS, AND BOUNDARIES

When our identity is reframed, our relationships are reoriented. Distinctions are acknowledged and valued, but boundaries of color, culture, and class are obliterated.

I have argued that our identity as the New Humanity—not ethnicity, culture, class, or generational preferences—is that which should have ultimate defining force in determining our group boundaries within the body of Christ. Far too often, however, this is not the case. As Figure 11.1 illustrates, when we attribute primary defining force to such distinctions as color, culture, and class—all of which make up the diversity of the body of Christ and can potentially enrich our experience of community—these distinctions subtly (and often unconsciously) become boundary markers determining group identity. This movement toward

---

19. Flood, *Last Years*, 65–66.

232 GOD'S NEW HUMANITY

fragmentation is often fueled by the sociocultural factors we have already discussed—individualism, religious consumerism, marketplace mentality, and status quo bias. Simply put, color, culture, and class (as well as all the other distinctions that begin to have defining force in our lives) become the determinants of local church identity rather than Christ. The result is segregation in and among local churches—thus blacks tend to worship with blacks, whites with whites, Korean Americans with Korean Americans, baby boomers with baby boomers, millennials with millennials, *ad infinitum*. From a sociological perspective, we have become very predictable.

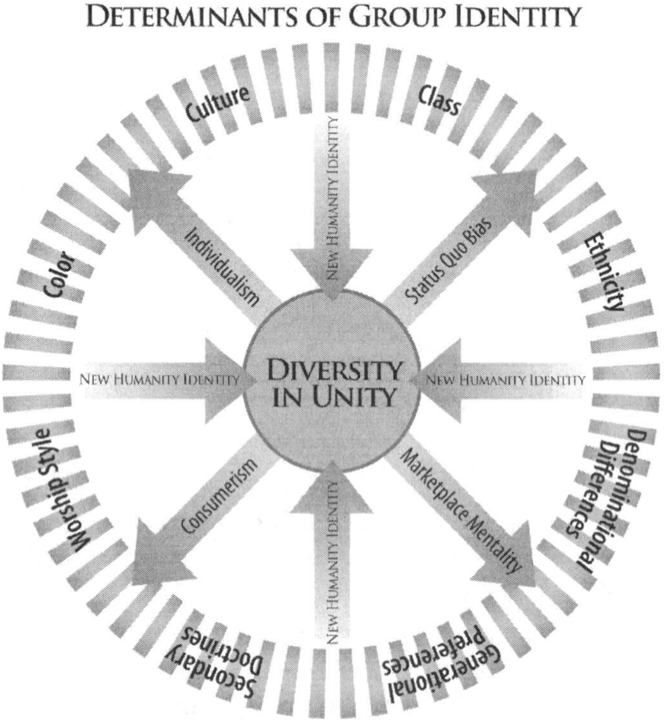

DETERMINANTS OF GROUP IDENTITY

Diagram showing a central circle labeled "DIVERSITY IN UNITY" with arrows labeled "NEW HUMANITY IDENTITY" pointing outward, surrounded by determinants: Culture, Class, Ethnicity, Denominational Differences, Generational Preferences, Secondary Doctrines, Consumerism, Worship Style, Color, Individualism, Status Quo Bias, Marketplace Mentality.

Figure 11.1

On the other hand, when believers experience a renewal of their New Humanity identity with its radical inclusivism, they begin to boldly move into environments marked by diversity in unity. Here such distinctions as color, culture, and class are appreciated, *but no longer have primary defining force in determining group identity*. Rather, such distinctions are made subservient to our collective core identity as the New Humanity where "Christ is all, and is in all." Our New Humanity identity is never "color blind"; it never merely overlooks distinctions of color, culture, or class within the church, but values such distinctions. It does, however, redefine our boundaries by doing away with *preferential evaluations* based upon those distinctions. Our boundaries become intentionally inclusive, rather than exclusive, pushing us toward the diversity in unity that reflects God's intentions for his church. In their study of multiethnic churches, Michael Emerson and Rodney Woo have concluded:

> The experience of being with people of a variety of backgrounds thus helps lead those in multiracial congregations to place a positive value on people's distinctiveness; to use those differences as part of the process of working toward a higher goal; to desire the differences, too, as a way of enriching themselves; and under healthy conditions . . . to learn how to live in a multiracial and multicultural group. In this sense, far from integration leading to assimilation . . . *integration helped people grow more secure in and proud of their cultural identities.*[20]

I have found this to be true our own church. I recently took a quick survey asking people to briefly respond to the question, "What have you most appreciated about our church becoming more multiethnic?"[21] The responses included the following:

- "I get to learn first hand from our many different nationalities some of their different cultures, habits, and ways of life."
- "My husband and I are different races so ethnic diversity helps us feel more 'at home.'"
- "I love meeting people of other cultures. . . . They enrich my life."
- "As a Caucasian, I see the need to inter-mingle with people of color and to broaden my perspective on faith and cultural diversity. The cocoon needs to fall away."
- "I am able to be challenged and stretched out of my comfort zone from my white, suburban background."
- "Getting to know believers from Guatamala, Rwanda, Japan, Romania and other far flung places. . . . Prejudice can be overcome,

---

20. Emerson with Woo, *People of the Dream*, 119.
21. Survey taken at Central Bible Church on two consecutive Sundays, August 21 and 28, 2011.

- one friendship at a time. One generation at a time."
- "As we become more ethnically diverse, we are more and more a reflection of God's purpose for the whole world."

While such testimonies are positive and encouraging, there are many challenges to face as a church becomes more multiethnic. This is partly because the local church is a more intimate sphere of life where open, transparent relationships are encouraged. Integration seems to be the strongest in the least intimate spheres of life, such as the shopping mall or the interstate that passes through your city. In the more intermediate spheres of intimacy, such as the workplace or school, a fair degree of integration also exists. In the more intimate spheres of life, however—such as marriage, the neighborhood, and the local church—our tendency is to segregate.[22] In the survey mentioned above, one respondent wrote: "People still do not go out of their way to integrate and try to converse with the diverse members of our congregation." Sometimes this is due to a fear of being misunderstood. Another church member wrote: "I'm 'afraid' of making a cultural blunder . . . in my 'all-American' approach to greeting and meeting people." This is certainly understandable, for in the more intimate spheres of life—such as the local church—diversity *can* accentuate the potential for conflict.

Potential for conflict, yes; but with it, we also find the greatest potential for authentic and enriching community. What often hinders us, however, are the unintentional, unconscious dynamics that push us toward homogeneity rather than enriched experiences of diversity in unity. This is our status quo bias. As already observed, few (if any) churches today would *reject* a fellow believer of a different ethnicity who desired to associate with that particular fellowship. Few churches, however, are conscious of the status quo biases that keep us comfortable with believers of the same ethnic or cultural "feather" and consequently take the initiative to intentionally nurture diversity in unity within their local fellowship or to become part of a local church where the majority is of a different ethnicity. After all, to do so can be quite uncomfortable, demanding sacrifice on our part. It will also require a fundamental shift in our belief systems and organizational practices as local churches. This is because genuine community reaches past human affinity to discover the shared life of Christ in the different "other." Henri Nouwen describes

---

22. See Paris, "Race," 27.

such community as "the place where the person you least want to live with always lives."[23] Admittedly, this is not comfortable. As Michael Emerson and Christian Smith observe, "If we accept the reasonable proposition that most people seek the greatest benefit for the least cost, they will seek meaning and belonging with the least change possible. Thus, if they can go to either the Church of Meaning and Belonging, or the Church of Sacrifice for Meaning and Belonging, most people choose the former."[24] *We must, however, learn to be comfortable with being uncomfortable if we are to live out our calling as the New Humanity.* Only then will the local church become the visible arena where the gospel is incarnated for the world to see.

For this reason, natural affinity should never be the *primary* criteria for building biblical community. Admittedly, natural affinity is the comfortable way to group ourselves. Nothing is wrong with being with people like you. When you encounter others, it is quite natural to ask, "Who here is like me? Do they speak my language? Do they share my culture, my background? Are they my age?" These are very *natural* questions to ask. The New Humanity, however, is not *natural*, it is *supernatural*. When God breaks through and makes spiritually dead people alive, our previous criteria for defining "togetherness" are radically transformed. We no longer allow similarities of color, culture, or class to define the boundaries of our relationships. We now have something much deeper, much more real and profound that links us with other believers. It is the fact that we were once dead but have now been made alive *together* in Jesus Christ.

When confronted by the uncomfortable nature of ethnic diversity in unity in the church, the natural tendency is to take the path of least resistance. That is why so many have chosen to do what the apostles in Acts 6 refused to do: establish homogeneous ethnic specific churches in a multiethnic society. As we have seen, when the Grecian Jews began to complain against the Hebraic Jews, the pragmatic solution would have been to create two distinct denominations—or at least, to start a second service!—where each ethnic group could be with their own kind. *But they did not.* They chose rather to immediately address with prayerful action the problems posed by cultural diversity. In doing so, they maintained the diversity in unity intrinsic to the New Humanity.

23. Nouwen, "Community," 83.
24. Emerson and Smith, *Divided by Faith*, 164.

Is there ever justification for *not* moving toward greater multiethnicity in a local church? Woo suggests four reasons why a church may choose not to nurture such ethnic diversity in the congregation.[25] First, it may be that your church is not located in an area where the demographics are multiethnic. However, while this may be true today, it may not be true in the near future. As we have seen, our society is changing rapidly and we must be prepared for these changes. Furthermore, even if the demographics of your area are relatively homogeneous, it is often possible to collaborate with other churches of another ethnicity outside of your immediate area to expose your people to the rich diversity of Christ's body. Such approaches as "pulpit exchanges" (i.e. pastors exchanging pulpits on a given Sunday), "pew exchanges" (i.e. several members of one church together attend another church of a different ethnicity and vice versa), or interchurch prayer gatherings that bring believers together across ethnic lines can be helpful. Though far more difficult, another possibility is to consider creating a multiethnic church by merging two or more ethnic specific congregations.[26] Since churches today remain ten times more segregated than the neighborhoods in which they are located and twenty times more segregated than nearby public schools, there remains much work to be done.

Second, it may be that the ethnicities represented in your area lack a common language. Admittedly, it is difficult to worship together apart from a shared language. While this problem may be resolved in heaven, we still face the practical challenges of language differences here on earth. However, the technological advancements of recent years allowing simultaneous translation into multiple languages largely discount this excuse. I recently preached a message for our congregation that was translated into two other languages, Romanian and Oromo. Since at the time we did not have the equipment necessary for simultaneous translation via headsets, the Romanian and Oromo translators stood to my right and left before the congregation and translated phrase by phrase. Obviously, a normal thirty-minute message was lengthened to about fifty minutes! While such an approach may not the most efficient, I have found it deeply impresses upon the congregation the beauty of the diversity in unity of Christ's church. Following that service, one of our

---

25. Woo, *Color of Church*, 262; cf. *United by Faith*, 143.

26. For a realistic appraisal of this approach, see Derek Chinn, "Creating a Multiracial Church."

members wrote: "It makes us more aware of other cultures and it shows us all kinds of people worship God and *it can be done in all languages and can be done together*" (emphasis mine).

Third, it could be argued that the unique circumstances of first-generation immigrants necessitate the development of ethnic specific churches rather than multiethnic churches. I and many others have found, however, that not only do such ethnic specific churches continue to fracture the body of Christ, but also that the "unique circumstances" of first-generation immigrants in the long term can best be met in a multiethnic church. Not only do first-generation immigrants need (for purposes of adaptation and enculturation) the broader body of Christ with all of its diversity, but the broader body of Christ also needs these immigrants *among* them rather than separated *from* them. Only in this way can we be a church *of* the nations and *for* the nations. In this way, the church truly can become a community in transformation rather than a community in segregation.

Finally, Woo suggests that for some congregations, such a move toward multiethnicity may prove to be destructive. If pursued without the proper preparation and identity formation that we have discussed, I would agree. For any church, identity formation precedes community transformation. Doing flows out of being. It is here that an extra dose of sanctified patience is required among church leaders. Part of experiencing what is "lacking in regard to Christ's afflictions, for the sake of his body" (Col 1:24) is the willingness to persevere and minister in view of the long term objective. We are engaged in a marathon, not a sprint!

In light of what the New Testament both describes and prescribes, I am convinced that to plant and nurture independent homogeneous ethnic specific churches in an increasingly multiethnic environment will inevitably compromise the process of renewal of which Paul speaks in Colossians 3:11. The same holds true for the planting and development of niche churches that attribute primary defining force to such factors as generational preferences, worship style, or class distinctions. While initially such churches may be a noble attempt to contextualize the gospel in the language and culture of those being reached, far too many become independent, homogeneous units that ultimately fragment the body of Christ. As for ethnic specific churches, some begin to exist for the express purpose of keeping a language and culture alive in an artificial manner, whereas what is needed is the adoption of a more widely used language and integration into a wider cultural context.[27]

What then is the solution? At Central Bible Church, we have moved toward an approach that Mark DeYmaz terms "graduated inclusion."[28] As I previously mentioned, we have about seventeen ethnicities represented in the Central Bible Church family. Of these, two in particular—a group of Oromo speaking believers (mainly from Kenya and Ethiopia) and a group of Romanian speaking believers—also gather each week as a language specific group. We recognize that some—particularly first-generation internationals—find it difficult to immediately integrate into and worship with the larger church family that is so immersed in North American culture. We nevertheless view these specific language groups as integral to Central Bible Church and as an evangelistic outreach to other Romanian and Oromo speaking people in our city. The shepherd-elder (a Kenyan) responsible for the Oromo believers is also part of our larger elder team. Though the Romanian believers are relatively new to our church family, we are working together on the same process of graduated inclusion. Furthermore, we encourage regular joint worship services that help facilitate the process of inclusion into the larger church family. Even all of this, however, is not a matter of *assimilation* (adopting our culture or norms) or of *accommodation* (superficially adjusting to their culture or norms), but of *inclusion* (all adopting the biblical norms of diversity in unity) as we strive by God's grace to become a healthy multiethnic church.

THE LOCAL CHURCH AS "PLAUSIBILITY STRUCTURE"

Among sociologists, the practical context in which ideas are fleshed out is termed a "plausibility structure." A plausibility structure provides a

---

27. Visser 'T Hooft, *Ecumenical Movement*, 65–66. He goes on to state: "The formation of special ethnic Churches must never be considered as more than a very provisional solution of the problem of nation and race in the Christian Church. The clear purpose must always be to arrive as soon as possible at the creation of supra-ethnic, supra-racial churches. In this matter the sociological pattern of the environment is in no sense a decisive argument against advance along this line, for the mission of the Church is to point the way towards unrestricted fellowship between men and women of all nations and races."

28. DeYmaz, *Ethnic Blends*, 100–11. See also his recent e-book *Should Pastors Accept or Reject the Homogenous Unit Principle?* available online.

concrete illustration of an abstract idea.[29] For many in our increasingly pluralistic society, Christianity no longer *seems* true. If the claims of Christ are to be understood and seen for what they are, society is in need of concrete illustrations of the reality of the gospel. That is precisely the role of the local church. Just as humanity was originally created as the representative image of God on earth, so the New Humanity was created to faithfully represent the diversity in unity of Father, Son, and Holy Spirit in this world. The local New Humanity—whether gathered or scattered—is a plausibility structure for the gospel. Though Jesus never used that terminology, that's exactly what he meant when he prayed that "all of them might be one, Father, ... so that the world might believe that you have sent me" (John 17:21). Then, to be sure the disciples got the point, Jesus repeated it again, "May they be brought to complete unity to let the world know that you sent me" (v. 23). In other words, the more abstract idea of the reality of the gospel is to be concretely illustrated in the church. The world must not only hear the words of the gospel, but also see the beauty of the gospel tangibly demonstrated in local New Humanity churches. "Like Israel of old," writes Joe Aldrich, "the quality of our corporate life is the key to the evangelization of our communities and of the world."[30]

The prayer of Jesus Christ for such palpable manifestations of diversity in unity among his followers will only be fulfilled to the degree that we maintain an unswerving commitment to the biblical priority given to the local church. This will not be easy. As demonstrated in chapter 7, such commitment goes countercurrent to the trends of the day that minimize or abandon all together the concept of the local congregation. Jesus promised, however, that he would build his church (Matt 16:18). In promising this, he was not merely thinking of the supracongregational relationship of believers worldwide, but also of the tangible, concrete manifestation of the New Humanity in local congregations. René Padilla expresses it well: "Unity in Christ is far more than a unity occasionally expressed at the level of 'the supracongregational relationship of believers in the total Christian body'; it is the unity of the members of Christ's body, to be made visible in the common life of local congregations."[31]

---

29. See Pearcey, *Total Truth*, 355.
30. Aldrich, *Prayer Summits*, 101.
31. Padilla, "Unity of the Church," 295.

Having served as both a pastor and missionary for nearly thirty years, I have experienced times when I felt like giving up on the local church. I have been disillusioned by the consumerism, individualism, market place mentality, and consequent fragmentation that I have witnessed. More importantly, I have been deeply disappointed by expressions of these same "demons" (as well as a whole host of others) that I see in my own life at times. How easy it is to begin to measure the "success" of a local church or other ministry according to human criteria, counting the number of heads present rather than the number of hearts changed. At my lowest moments, I have considered—as have so many pastors—throwing in the towel and giving up on this divine enterprise called the local church.

I am thankful that by God's grace I have not. God *is* building his church and his primary strategy is the local church. "For the Lord esteems the communion of his church so highly," John Calvin wrote, "that he counts as a traitor and apostate from Christianity anyone who arrogantly leaves any Christian society, provided it cherishes the true ministry of the Word and sacraments."[32] That is why Zane Hodges concludes, "To abandon the assembly is to abandon discipleship."[33] We must *never* give up on the local church, for it is particularly as the New Humanity is gathered in local congregations that the world will witness the diversity in unity for which Jesus prayed. That is why Paul was willing to suffer intensely on behalf of the local churches to which he ministered, for he was "completing what remains of Christ's suffering for his body, the church" (Col 1:24).

In this sense, the local church is not only a plausibility structure, attesting to the reality and power of the gospel, but it is also intended to be a type of "dynamic equivalence" translation of the essence of the gospel. Just as a good Bible translation faithfully represents in our contemporary language and culture the meaning of the original, so also the local New Humanity is to express in relevant terms the inherent quality of ethnic diversity in unity characteristic of the universal church. The local multiethnic church reflects the intent of the gospel as seen from the *protoevangelium* of Genesis 3:15 to the closing chapters of Revelation. On the other hand, as long as the vast majority of churches remain segregated by ethnicity, we say by our actions that color, culture, and

---

32. Calvin, *Institutes*, 2:1024

33. Hodges, "Notes," 52.

class are more important than the centrality of Christ. In an increasingly multiethnic society, people will no longer find credible the message of God's love for the ethnicities of the world when it is proclaimed from segregated congregations.

The concept of the local church as a plausibility structure refers to each individual congregation within a community or city, as well to all the local churches *together* in the same locality. The vast majority of references to the local church in the New Testament speak of believers within a particular city: "To all in Rome who are loved by God and called to be saints" (Rom 1:7), "To the church of God in Corinth" (1 Cor 1:2), "To all the saints in Christ Jesus at Philippi" (Phil 1:1), "To the holy and faithful brothers in Christ at Colosse" (Col 1:2), and "To the church of the Thessalonians in God the Father and the Lord Jesus Christ" (1 Thess 1:1). On a few occasions, believers in a wider geographical area are addressed: "To the churches in Galatia" (Gal 1:2) and "To God's elect, strangers in the world, scattered throughout Pontus, Galatia, Cappadocia, Asia and Bithynia" (1 Pet 1:1–2). While in the vast majority of cases these believers met in house churches scattered throughout the city, they nevertheless viewed themselves *together* as the local manifestation of Christ's church. This localized view of the church is crucial in nurturing New Humanity churches. Today there are far too many individual Christians and small, fragmented groups of Christians trying to do *independently* what can best be accomplished *interdependently*. A more biblical perspective of the church of the city (or of the region) can help counteract such an independent, disconnected approach to ministry.

Viewing ourselves as the New Humanity in a specific locality is also helpful in nurturing the diversity in unity that God intends for his church. Just as each individual member of the New Humanity is in need of the other members (1 Cor 12:14–27), so each local church is in need of the other churches in any given locality. Here in Portland, Oregon, my good friend Paul Metzger recently initiated the "John 17:23 Network," which exists "to encourage, exhort, and equip the multi-ethnic Body of Christ in the greater Portland area to fulfill Jesus' prayer in our midst that we might all be one." We have held several discussion forums as well as corporate prayer gatherings that bring together believers and churches of diverse ethnic backgrounds. Such gatherings have identity shaping value. They help equip believers for multiethnic ministry and serve as a springboard for collaborative outreach together.

LEADERS AS EQUIPPERS

I believe the first step in helping believers in our churches choose the church of "sacrifice for meaning and belonging" is identity formation. Identity formation is one of the primary responsibilities of local church leadership. DeYmaz states, "The job of local church leaders is to align the church with the will of God in spite of what is in line with our own will or the conventional wisdom of people."[34] It is crucial that church leaders understand our New Humanity identity and both teach and model this identity before the congregation.

In his book, *Not I, But Christ,* Stephen Olford tells of his experience at the beginning of his ministry as pastor of a well-known church in New York City. One of his first and biggest battles was over the issue of racial integration. Prior to his coming as senior pastor, almost 85 percent of the church had voted against allowing blacks to be members of the church. Olford pulled aside the church leadership and told them, "I want to make a statement. I am going to preach God's Word. I am going to believe God to send revival among us. I am going to pray unceasingly that this situation changes. *But* if we do not become an integrated church within two years, I will no longer be the pastor. This is not a threat; this is a divine mandate." Some time after this, a black federal judge came to speak with Olford. Olford shared his convictions about racial diversity with this man. More than that, he invited him to stay in the church-owned hotel. The judge was amazed, particularly when offered the best room in the hotel.

At the business meeting the church convened to discuss this issue, Olford preached the message he had prepared on the subject of racism and then fielded questions. There was intense opposition, and several verbally attacked Olford. Finally, a vote was taken. Only eleven voted against integration; of those, seven later came to Olford and confessed their sinful attitudes and actions. Of the remaining four, every one died within a year![35]

In the very context where Paul speaks of putting off the Old Humanity and putting on the New Humanity, he also instructs us about the indispensable role of church leaders in equipping the body of Christ:

---

34. DeYmaz, *Ethnic Blends*, 59.
35. Olford, *Not I, But Christ*, 120–21.

> It was he who gave some to be apostles, some to be prophets, some to be evangelists, and some to be pastors and teachers, to prepare God's people for works of service, so that the body of Christ may be built up until we all reach unity in the faith and in the knowledge of the Son of God and become mature, attaining to the whole measure of the fullness of Christ. (Eph 4:11–13)

These verses speak of a chain reaction sequence. Church leaders—here specified as apostles, prophets, evangelists, pastors, and teachers—prepare God's people for ministry. As God's people do that ministry, the body of Christ is edified and attains the "whole measure of the fullness of Christ." Such fullness is the maturity and community that God intends for the New Humanity. This maturity and community is possible only as spiritual leaders *equip* (*katartizō*; in NIV "prepare") the members of their churches. The word carries both the idea of *repairing* and *preparing*. The same word is used in Mark 1:19 to describe the mending of nets. A key role of church leaders who are nurturing multiethnicity in the local church is the pastoral mending of broken lives (cf. 2 Cor 13:11; Gal 6:1). Believers, as all humans, are looking for meaning and belonging. However, the sinful vestiges of alienation, fear, shame, and mistrust handicap that quest to the degree that we do not believe and appropriate our individual and collective identity in Christ.

I think of one refugee who for a time was part of our local church. She had passed through multiple African refugee camps before arriving in the States. In addition to being HIV positive, she faced the long, tedious immigration process in view of remaining here as a US citizen. The brokenness of her life and family led to some rather eccentric behavior during our worship gatherings. Since her actions were increasingly becoming a distraction to our corporate worship, two of our elders (one from Africa himself) lovingly confronted her. Unfortunately, she did not respond positively and left our church. What I want to underscore, however, is the responsibility we have as church leaders to pastorally "repair" those who are suffering, often due to prior identity abuse in their own lives. Some will respond positively, others may not. Nevertheless, our pastoral responsibility remains the same.

Not only are church leaders to equip by repairing, but also by preparing. The term *katartizō* also referred in Paul's day to outfitting an army with full provision for battle.[36] We, too, are in a titanic battle

---

36. LSJ, 910.

against the powers who would seek to divide and conquer by pitting one ethnicity against another within the local church. To counteract such opposition, we must engage our congregations in an ongoing process of biblical identity formation. This would include extensive teaching on our New Humanity identity, instruction related to ethnic and cultural differences, as well as training in how to sensitively consider others as more important than yourself (Phil 2:3). "The challenge of the next evangelicalism," writes Soong-Chan Rah, "is to empower the marginalized to recognize the gift that is the cultural mandate—that their culture is an expression of being made in the image of God and must be represented at the table of believers."[37] This begins with church leaders fulfilling their role as equippers.

Leaders equip best as they model the values they are seeking to instill. That is why a diverse leadership team is essential to nurturing multiethnicity in the local church. Congregants follow what they see modeled more than what they hear preached. Admittedly, this process of diversifying leadership takes time and prayerful attention. However, even when the paid staff is not as diversified as one might wish, there are other ways to lead by example. At Central Bible Church, while we do not yet have an ethnically diverse pastoral team, we have taken steps to diversify our elder team. We are also encouraging members of our congregation from various walks of life to lead in worship, serve the Lord's Supper, serve as greeters, preach on occasion, or serve in other leadership roles. The advice of one member of our church who is from a biracial family is a pertinent reminder:

> In the process of developing a multicultural dimension to our congregation, we must be led in doing so by those of a minority background. We will have to invite those of other cultures . . . to teach and lead worship with us and for us. We can't do it ourselves. We may have to be open to certain rituals, or to louder or quieter worship. We'll have to enjoy different foods at potlucks, and be willing to sit under the authority of those different from us whose teaching may be harder for us to relate to. We may have to have more messy discussions abut all these things, and compromise on the peripheral stuff more than we have had to so far.

---

37. Rah, *Next Evangelicalism*, 139.

SPIRITUAL WARFARE

In J. R. R. Tolkien's *The Fellowship of the Ring*, a surprisingly diverse group of crusaders band together for a common cause. Overcoming insurmountable odds, they persevere in their mission—to destroy the power of the Dark Lord lodged in his ring. They differ in so many ways—racially, physically, temperamentally—yet remain surprisingly united in their quest. At one point, however, a heated conflict breaks out among the crusaders. Anger surges. Harsh words are spoken. Axes are drawn and bows bent. Their close knit fellowship is on the verge of disbanding. When peace at last prevails, one wise counselor observes, "Indeed in nothing is the power of the Dark Lord more clearly shown than in the estrangement that divides all those who still oppose him."

We have seen that the "Dark Lord" of this world exerts a malicious multifaceted influence in the lives of believers and unbelievers alike. His ultimate objective is to destroy and alienate mankind—the *imago Dei*—from his Creator. On a macro scale, Satan and his allies exert a cultural and sociopolitical influence in the world. As already pointed out, such terms as "rulers" and "authorities" that denote *spiritual* powers are also often used in the Bible to refer to *civil* authorities and rulers. This seems to indicate an intimate connection between the invisible world and earthly society. The prophet Isaiah tells us: "In that day the LORD will punish the *powers* in the heavens above and the *kings* on the earth below" (Isa 24:21; emphasis mine). In a sense that we cannot fully understand, fallen spiritual powers "hide" behind earthly governmental authorities and societal structures in their pernicious attempts to carry out the devil's schemes. Does this not explain why Satan can offer to Jesus the power and glory of the kingdoms of the world? Satan's proposition is justified: the kingdoms of this earth *are* under his temporary control and influence.[38] Likewise John writes: "We know that we are children of God and that the whole world is under the control of the evil one" (1 John 5:19–20).

It is vital that we take seriously the reality of this spiritual conflict in our attempts to address the ethnic divides both in society and within the church. Gregory Boyd has highlighted the fact that one of the characteristics of Western thought is to view evil almost uniquely from an

---

38. John 12:31; 14:30; 16:11; Matt 9:34; 12:14; Mark 3:22; Luke 11:15.

anthropocentric and individualistic perspective.[39] I believe that this has handicapped us in our efforts to address issues of ethnic reconciliation. We fail to grasp the reality of spiritual, cosmic powers that exert their malicious, divisive influence on the ethnicities of the world as well as on societal structures. Again, all forms of racism, ethnic hatred, or the alienation of the nations are ultimately incited by the very powers that seek to divide and deconstruct humanity as the *imago Dei*.

The influence of Satan and his demons is not merely cultural and sociopolitical in nature, pitting one ethnicity against another. His hellish fury is particularly aimed at the church, the New Humanity. *He wants to divide all those who oppose him.* Jesus told Peter: "Satan has asked to have *you* that he might sift you as wheat" (Luke 22:31, emphasis mine). The "you" is plural, referring not only to Peter, but also to *all* the disciples who together comprised in embryonic form the New Humanity. Obviously, Peter got the point. A little more than thirty years later, Peter writes: "Be self-controlled and alert. Your enemy the devil prowls around like a roaring lion looking for someone to devour. Resist him, standing firm in the faith, because you know that your brothers throughout the world are undergoing the same kind of sufferings" (1 Pet 5:8–9). Satan desires to destroy the New Humanity by devouring individual Christians and local churches. Little wonder that the chief of staff of the hellish forces in Milton's *Paradise Lost* is called "pan-*demon*-ium." The New Humanity is the bull's-eye of Satan's target. One of his foremost strategies in hitting the bull's-eye is by working spiritual and relational pandemonium in the New Humanity as well as in its geographical manifestation, the local church.

We must recognize that the principalities and powers accommodate themselves to the psychology, mentality, and societal norms of the culture. G. W. Peters affirms this: "I am inclined to believe that both the divine as well as the evil, God as well as Satan, are accommodating themselves to . . . the world and life view of the people and are operating within the milieu as it is."[40] The powers, therefore, are quite content to allow natural sociological processes to segregate the New Humanity into homogeneous units defined by color of skin, language, age, culture, and socioeconomic status. In this, the power of the Dark Lord is clearly seen.

---

39. Boyd, *God at War*, 241.
40. Peters, "Demonology," 192.

What should be our response? We have already examined our manual of spiritual warfare as outlined in Ephesians 6:10–20. Here I would like to give further emphasis to the role of prayer in and among local churches as the *means* of putting on the armor of God. In their book *United by Faith*, DeYoung et al. urge, "Find out what is dividing your church and your community and knock it down."[41] Recognizing that it is not merely the sociological currents of the day but also the spiritual powers at play that are dividing our churches and community, we must devote ourselves to prayer. Change swings on the hinge of prayer. It is through prayer—individually and collectively—that we deploy our spiritual armor and "knock down" what is dividing our churches and community. It is through prayer that we demolish "strongholds," "arguments," and "every pretension" that oppose the will of God (2 Cor 10:3–5). Prayer is the starting point for bringing heavenly realities into our earthly experience. We can do more than pray *after* praying, but we can never do more than pray *before* praying. The deconstruction of the dividing walls must start here.

As did Martin Luther King, my own father had a dream. I mentioned earlier that, during the 1950s and 1960s, my dad was pastor of a church in the racially divided city of Chattanooga, Tennessee. He longed to see the day when white and black pastors would come together across ethnic and denominational lines and knock down through corporate, unified prayer what was dividing their churches and city. That finally happened in a first-ever pastors' prayer summit held in February 1999. For several years, my dad had worked hard to unite black and white leaders in Chattanooga, mobilizing them for such a summit. Just weeks before that historic first prayer summit began, my dad was diagnosed with acute leukemia. Though Dad died on the first day of the prayer summit he had worked so hard to prepare, he lived long enough to see his dream fulfilled.

I believe such gatherings for corporate prayer—both within and among local churches—are vital to the tearing down of the spiritual strongholds that paralyze the body of Christ today. You cannot read the story line of the phenomenal growth of the multiethnic church as described in Acts without observing the priority of corporate prayer among God's people. God's missional strategy was then and is today to transform his church into a "house of prayer for all nations" (Matt 21:13).

---

41. DeYoung et al., *United by Faith*, 74.

In Christ's day, the temple had to be cleansed from the consumerism of those who had forgotten what God's house was all about. God's house had been hijacked by the consumerist marketers of the day. The same can happen today. The power of intercession must be our first response to rampant segregation.

It is said that in 1952 a doctoral student at Princeton University asked the visiting lecturer, Albert Einstein, "What is there left in the world for original dissertation research?" Einstein replied, "Find out about prayer. Somebody must find out about prayer." The Scriptures describe prayer as God's favored vehicle for associating the New Humanity with the accomplishment of his purposes in this world. While the interplay of God's sovereignty and human responsibility remain intact, prayer nevertheless engages believers in both facilitating and accelerating the accomplishment of God's will "on earth as it is in heaven." That is why the prayers that honor God are in the name of Jesus, for the fame of Jesus, and toward the reign of Jesus. Indeed, we *can* and *must* pray in those terms when it comes to the diversity in unity that God most certainly wills for the New Humanity.

GOD'S NEW HUMANITY ON MISSION

Throughout our church auditorium hang thirty-six flags representing thirty-six nations of the world. At present, only about seventeen of those nations are represented by members of our church family. I dream of the day, however, when all thirty-six nations will be seen in living color in Central Bible Church. The flags are a regular reminder of our calling to be a church *of* the nations and *for* the nations.

One of those flags is the national flag of Iran. Each time I see it, I think of a young Iranian who first visited our church as a cultural experience. He had just arrived from Tehran to study at the University of Portland. Before arriving in America, his mother had already pricked his interest in Christianity by encouraging him to read the Bible. When he heard that we offered the opportunity to observe a worship service and afterward to share an international meal with others who desired to improve their English, he decided to attend. After several months of exposure to the gospel and interaction with other believing internationals, he placed his faith in Christ and was baptized. Each week, as this Muslum-background believer and those of other nationalities gather with our church family, they are a living testimony of our missional vocation to be a church *of* the nations and *for* the nations.

We have already seen that the church at Antioch was a church of the nations and for the nations (Acts 11:19–26; 13:1–3). The church at Antioch cared about the world because the church at Antioch reflected the world. Even the core leadership of the church was composed of two men from Africa, one from the Mediterranean, one from the Middle East, and one from Asia Minor (Acts 13:1). In this sense, the church at Antioch was a fulfillment of Jesus' prayer that his followers might be one even as the Father and Son are one.

Our mission as the New Humanity is integral to the renewal of our identity according to the *imago Dei*. We have seen that the three aspects intrinsic to humanity's role as the image of God—rule, resemblance, and relationship—were severely compromised in the Fall. Mankind's rule over the earth, resemblance to his Creator, and relational harmony with God and fellow mankind were *deconstructed*. In the New Humanity, however, each of these aspects is being restored according to God's original intentions.

It is specifically the aspect of *ruling* that pertains to our mission as the New Humanity. As already observed, the New Humanity will ultimately rule with Christ in the "summing up of all things" (Eph 1:10, NASB).[42] Until then, we are engaged in an apprenticeship, learning to live out our vocation of ruling in the here and now. But what does this mean? Am I referring to the perverted *mélange* of church and state so common throughout Europe until modern times? Does this concept of ruling open the door to misconstrued political posturing in view of "taking back" America for Christ? Am I referring to the dominion theology or "reconstructionism" that urges Christians to occupy and control secular institutions until Christ returns? Is the New Humanity called to political activism in view of reforming society and forcefully establishing God's kingdom on earth?

When the biblical evidence is examined, I believe the renewal of the New Humanity's vocation of ruling is seen in three specific areas that together define our mission in this world. First, the mission of the New Humanity is to *rule over sin and satanic influence*. In God's words to Cain, "Sin is crouching at your door; it desires to have you, *but you must master it*" (Gen 4:7; emphasis mine). As the New Humanity, we

---

42. Cf. 1 Cor 6:2; Rev 5:10; 22:3–5.

"master" sin by putting off the old and putting on the new. We are called to put to death the "misdeeds of the body" (Rom 8:13) and whatever belongs to our earthly nature (Col 3:5) and to put on Christ (Rom 13:14) and the moral attributes of the New Humanity (Eph 4:24; Col 3:10). Furthermore, as we put on the armor of God, we are to exercise our spiritual authority over divisive, demonic powers (Eph 6:10–18). We do this knowing that the God of peace will soon crush Satan under our feet (Rom 16:20).

To what degree is the New Humanity to rule over sin and satanic influence in society? It is true that, as Martin Luther King often urged, the church is to be the "conscience" of society. He personally lived that out in appropriate ways to highlight the racial inequality of the day. The church today can and must do the same, using the appropriate avenues of expression and influence that are available to us. Furthermore, as the New Humanity we are to be wise in the way we live among "outsiders," making the most of opportunities for the gospel (Col 4:4). Members of the New Humanity recognize that one day *every* area of life will be fully restored and reconciled under the rule of God. With that hope in view, our role today is to be "salt" and "light" so that the world might see our good works and glorify our Father in heaven (Matt 5:13–16).

That being said, the New Testament writers seem relatively unconcerned about attempting to reconstruct the Old Humanity according to biblical values.[43] Aggressive attempts by certain professing believers to reform society according to biblical values are paradoxical if not hypocritical, given that the very sins often spoken against run rampant within the church. Moreover, when it concerns issues of reconciliation, what message does a fragmented church have for a fragmented world? When the Scriptures speak of ruling over sin and satanic influence, it is first of all in the context of "housecleaning" within the body of Christ. "It is time for judgment to begin with the family of God" (1 Pet 4:17). This is understandable, for we—as the New Humanity—best rule over sin and satanic influence in society as we resemble our Creator and relate harmoniously to one another as the body of Christ. This is because the three aspects of the representative role of the New Humanity—rule, resemblance, and relationship—are inseparable. In other words, collective resemblance to Christ and harmonious rela-

---

43. See especially 1 Cor 5:9–13; cf. Luke 12:30; John 14:17; 15:19; 17:14; 18:36; 1 John 2:17; 3:13.

tionships within the body of Christ are foundational to any initiative to rule over expressions of evil in society. In this way, the New Humanity truly becomes the conscious of society.

Second, the mission of the New Humanity is to *rule by making disciples of the nations* (Matt 28:19–20). This is the evangelistic mandate. We are not called to reform the nations, but we are called to make Christ-followers among the nations. In all the talk today of social justice, "working for the common good," and carrying out our original cultural mandate as the image of God, we can easily lose sight of our redemptive mission in this world—a mission that must remain our highest priority. Our mission as the New Humanity is not reformative, it is redemptive. As already observed, the stark contrast between the Old Humanity and the New Humanity is enough to remind us that any attempts to merely reform society will prove futile. On the other hand, one of the most effective strategies for making disciples among the nations is to be a church of the nations. In this sense, the local church *becomes* the mission rather than *doing* mission. A multiethnic and economically diverse church is well positioned to model community transformation precisely because it is a community in transformation.[44]

Finally, the mission of the New Humanity is to *rule by effectively stewarding creation and culture to the glory of God*. We have seen that the biblical hope of the New Humanity is not otherworldly. We are homesick for Eden, but not for a neo-Platonic sphere of celestial existence. While Christ's kingdom is not *of* this world, it will someday be *on* this world. Our original mandate to "subdue" and "rule" the earth (Gen 1:28) has not been abrogated. Even in the eternal state, the diverse cultural riches of the world will be brought into the New Jerusalem (Isa 60:16; Rev 21:26). As the New Humanity, we should set the pace in concern for both the stewardship of God's creation as well as the varied cultural expressions of beauty and art. If fallen humanity has misused and abused certain aspects of creation and culture, the New Humanity should be notorious for its wise stewardship of both.

CONCLUSION

Today, we experience only partially what one day we will realize fully. As we press toward our ultimate destiny, the church lives in the tension

---

44. See DeYmaz, *Ethnic Blends*, 93.

of the already/but not yet. Believers of all ethnicities are *already* one in Christ, having been co-enlivened, co-raised, and co-seated together in the heavenly realms. However, we have *not yet* experienced the fullness of this reality in our relationships this side of heaven. We live in the "in-between" times—in between Christ's reconciliatory cross work in the past and the experiential reconciliation of all things in the future. In these in-between times, our privileged vocation as the New Humanity is to *be* the answer to Jesus' prayer—"Your will be done on earth as it is in heaven." Each time we recognize and repent of ways in which we contribute to the present day dividing walls in Christ's church, each time we reaffirm our New Humanity identity, and each time we enlarge our boundaries to include the different "other," we are bringing the realities of heaven down to earth and the Trinity rejoices.

Conclusion

On October 31, 1517, Martin Luther posted his Ninety-Five Theses on the door of the Castle Church in Wittenberg, Germany. It was a summary of his main points of contention with the Catholic Church. As I conclude this book, I certainly don't have ninety-five theses as Luther proposed. Moreover, I have not written *against* something as much as *for* something. I do have, however, ten summary points or "theses" that bring together the essence of the first ten chapters of this book.

THESIS #1

We live in an increasingly multiethnic society. While the surrounding culture is becoming increasingly integrated, local churches remain largely segregated. The "building materials" used to construct the walls that divide us include the sociological dynamics of individualism, consumerism, choice, and competition, all of which contribute to a greater degree of ethnic homogeneity within local churches and consequent segregation among local churches.

THESIS #2

The biblical story begins with God who created mankind *as* his own image. Mankind does not *have* the image, nor was he created *in* the image, but he himself *is* the image. As such, humanity was mandated to rule over creation as God's authoritative vice-regent, to resemble his Creator, and to live in solidarity of relationship with God and with fellow humans. The community of the non-homogeneous Three-in-One is the template of the diversity in unity that God intends for all mankind.

THESIS #3

The intrusion of sin into the idyllic conditions of Eden brought about catastrophic consequences. The first man, Adam, gave birth to Old Humanity. Though remaining the *imago Dei*, humanity was deconstructed. Separation lies at the very heart of this deconstruction, having its impact upon the three expressions of man as the *imago Dei*: *rule*, *resemblance*, and *relationship*. The ecstasy of community that God intended was scandalously traded for hostile alienation. The epitome of this relational alienation is seen at the Tower of Babel. God's intervention by confusing humanity's language and dispersing the peoples was a severe mercy, designed to prevent mankind from self-destruction. God's purposes will not be thwarted. In the confusion and scattering of the nations, God chose a seed that would ultimately bring blessing to the peoples of the earth (Gen 11:27–15:11). Out of the Old Humanity scattered at Babel, a New Humanity would be gathered at Pentecost.

THESIS #4

The events on earth are a mere reflection of turmoil in the heavenlies. Because of this, we cannot understand the alienation of ethnicities on earth apart from what the Bible says about the divisive influence of Satan and his demonic minions. In Deuteronomy 32:8, we find a theological interpretation of the separation of the nations at the Tower of Babel. As an act of judgment on man's prideful arrogance, God "gave over" the ethnicities of the world to a form of intermediary, providential governance under spiritual powers. The glimpse into the celestial sphere described in Daniel 10 confirms the hypothesis of Deuteronomy 32:8—alienation, fear, mistrust, racism, hatred, and every form of evil that separates humanity from within himself and from his Creator is incited, to one degree or another, by fallen angelic powers that have attached themselves to the various peoples of this world.

THESIS #5

In stark contrast to the division and alienation of fallen Eden and Babel stands the New Humanity conceived at the cross and born at Pentecost. Here the dividing wall between Jew and Gentile—and by extension, between every ethnicity on earth—is deconstructed. In the New Humanity, mankind rediscovers his true vocation as the image of God along with its three corollaries: rule, resemblance, and relationship. As the New Humanity, we are both "body" and "bride"—one flesh with the Head and bride of the Head. Our identity as the New Humanity prohibits the segregation of the church along the lines of contrived boundary markers such as color, culture, and class. Such segregation is a return to Babel and a denial of our true identity.

THESIS #6

Pentecost was nothing less than a reversal of the experience of the Tower of Babel. If Babel depicts earth's divided nations, Pentecost describes God's "United Nations." The story of the church in Acts demonstrates the diversity in unity that should characterize the local church. Those who believed from "every nation under heaven" (Acts 2:5) were not siphoned off into ethnic specific churches. On the contrary, they associated with local churches marked by a distinct multiethnic flavor, whether in Jerusalem (Acts 2:42–47), in Antioch (Acts 11:19–20; 13:1), in Corinth (Acts 18:4; 1 Cor 12:13), or at Rome (Rom 2:17; 9:24; 11:13). The unity of New Humanity churches is not based on ethnicity, phenotype, language, culture, or socioeconomic class. Rather, it *transcends* all of these, bringing heaven to earth.

THESIS #7

From our study of the term *ekklēsia*, we discovered that an inseparable link exists between the universal church and the local church. The local church is intended to be in microcosm what the universal church is in macrocosm. This inseparable link between the universal and local church indicates that the diversity in unity that characterizes the former should be intentionally nurtured and ultimately reflected in the latter. We simply do not have biblical justification for the intentional establishment of homogeneous local churches. More positively, to the degree that such diversity in unity is nurtured and reflected in and among local churches, we fulfill Jesus' prayer that his followers may be brought to complete unity (John 17:23).

THESIS #8

The New Humanity created at the cross (Eph 2:15) and born at Pentecost (Acts 2) is now being renewed according to the image of his Creator

(Eph 4:22–24; Col 3:9–11). In this renewal, the three distinctive marks of humanity as the image of God are being restored—rule, resemblance, and relationship. As for the latter, in the New Humanity there is "no Greek or Jew, circumcised or uncircumcised, barbarian, Scythian, slave or free, but Christ is all, and is in all" (Col 3:11). By this affirmation, Paul is *not* arguing for a leveling of distinctions in the New Humanity. Christ calls us *past* our ethnicity, but not *out of* our ethnicity. Paul's declaration does affirm, however, that such distinctions should no longer have primary defining force. When such distinctions become the basis of defining our identity or determining our unity, they become boundary markers that fragment the body of Christ. For the New Humanity, such boundary markers have been replaced by Christ "who is all, and is in all."

THESIS #9

If Pentecost is the reversal of the debacle of Babel, Satan's intent is to *reverse the reversed*. Any fragmentation and segregation in the New Humanity can ultimately be attributed to the powers of darkness that strike at the "heel" of Christ (Gen 3:15). Our disunity as the body of Christ is not merely sociological, it is spiritual. We must remember the reality of the Babel-like powers that inspire such divisiveness and lay hold of the resources God places at our disposal to counteract their malicious attempts. We do this by taking our stand against the adversary and taking up the splendid armor that God has made available. Apart from this, our contrived efforts to nurture such diversity in unity in and among local churches will ultimately fail. Our encouragement is in the fact that the power that raised us together is more than sufficient to bring us together and to keep us together.

THESIS #10

We must allow God's design for history and our final destiny as the New Humanity to shape our life in the here and now. As we explore the destiny of the New Humanity recorded in the book of Revelation, we see the three aspects characteristic of humanity as the *imago Dei* fully restored: rule, resemblance, and relationship. The New Humanity reigns with Christ (Rev 22:5), resembles Christ (1 John 3:2), and is engaged in relationally harmonious worship of Christ (Rev 7:9–10). Indeed, the babble of Babel has become the beauty and purity of multiethnic, multigenerational praise before the Lamb of God. As his bride, the new Jerusalem is depicted as a mosaic of ethnic diversity and resurrected cultures. This is our future destiny that should determine our present practice.

A FINAL WORD

Yes, as Robert Frost says, "Something there is that doesn't love a wall, that wants it down." Jesus wanted the walls deconstructed. Within hours of praying that we might all be one, he offered himself up in answer to his own prayer. The cross and Pentecost are God's solution to the Fall and Babel. There is no other solution.

Jesus Christ has accomplished all that is necessary not only to make us one but also to keep us one. The theological vision of diversity in unity *is* an experiential possibility! For the possibility to become a reality, we must "want the walls down" as much as Christ does. After all, the church is *his* body, not ours. He is the head of the church, and we are to receive our directives from him alone. All the while appreciating earthly cultures, we must passionately pursue kingdom culture.

As this book was going to the publisher, I had the opportunity to once again visit the church building in southern France that I mentioned in chapter 1. Happily, that massive dividing wall is no longer there. Originally built in 1806, it was deconstructed in 2008 as a sign of unity between the Catholic and Protestant congregations occupying the building. Unfortunately, however, throughout America and around the world, dividing walls of color, culture, and class continue to fragment the body of Christ, compromising our witness to the world of the reality of the gospel. As believers of all ethnicities, let us reaffirm our New Humanity identity and be in this generation the living, tangible answer to the fervent intercession of Jesus Christ.

Bibliography

Abbot, T. K. *Epistles to the Ephesians and to the Colossians*. The International Critical Commentary. Edited by S. R. Driver et al. Edinburgh: T & T Clark, 1897.
Adamo, David T. "The African Wife of Moses: An Examination of Numbers 12:1–9." *African Theological Journal* 18 (1989) 230–37.
Alcorn, Randy. *Heaven*. Wheaton: Tyndale, 2004.
Aldrich, Joe. *Prayer Summits: Seeking God's Agenda for Your Community*. Portland: Multnomah, 1992.
Allan, John A. *The Epistle to the Ephesians*. London: SCM, 1959.
Aristotle. *Politica*. Translated by Philip W. Wicksteed and Francis M. Carnford. Loeb Classical Library. Cambridge: Harvard University Press, 1959.
Arnold, Clinton E. *Power and Magic: The Concept of Power in Ephesians in Light of Its Historical Setting*. Grand Rapids, Mich.: Baker, 1992.
———. *Powers of Darkness: Principalities & Powers in Paul's Letters*. Downers Grove, Ill.: InterVarsity, 1992.
———. *The Colossian Syncretism: The Interface Between Christianity and Folk Belief at Colossae*. Tübingen: J. C. B. Mohr, 1995.
Aune, David E. *Revelation 1–5*. Word Biblical Commentary. Edited by Ralph P. Martin. N.P.: Word, 1997.
Bacote, Vincent. "Fade to White: How White Is Evangelical Theology?" In *Building Unity in the Church of the New Millennium,* edited by Dwight Perry, 49–60. Chicago: Moody, 2002.
Banks, Robert. *Paul's Idea of Community: The Early House Churches in their Historical Setting*. Grand Rapids, Mich.: Eerdmans, 1980.
Barna, George. *Revolution*. George Barna, 2005.
Barna Group Update. "Spirituality May Be Hot in America, But 76 Million Adults Never Attend Church." March 20, 2006. No pages. Online: http://www.barna.org/barna-update/article/5-barna-update/158-spirituality-may-be-hot-in-america-but-76-million-adults-never-attend-church?q=unchurched.
Barndt, Joseph. *Dismantling Racism*. Minneapolis: Fortress, 1991.
Barnhouse, Donald Grey. *Romans: God's Remedy, Romans 3:21–4:25*. Vol 3 of Expository Messages on the Whole Bible Taking the Epistle to the Romans as a Point of Departure. 10 vols. Wheaton, Ill: Van Kampen, 1954.
Barr, James. "The Image of God in the Book of Genesis." *Bulletin of the John Rylands University Library of Manchester* 51 (1968) 11–26.
———. *The Semantics of Biblical Language*. London: Oxford University Press, 1961.
Barry, F. R. *Recovery of Man*. New York: Charles Scribner's Sons, 1949.

Bibliography

Barth, Markus. *Ephesians: Translation and Commentary.* 2 vols. The Anchor Bible. Garden City, New York: Doubleday & Company, 1974.

Beasley-Murray, G. R. *Baptism in the New Testament.* Grand Rapids, Mich.: Eerdmans, 1977.

Bellah, Robert N. et al. *Habits of the Heart: Individualism and Commitment in American Life.* New York: Harper & Row, 1985.

Berkhof, Hendrik. *Christ and the Powers.* Translated by John Howard Yoder. Scottdale, Penn.: Herald, 1962.

Berkhof, L. *Systematic Theology.* Grand Rapids, Mich.: Eerdmans, 1949.

Berkouwer, G. C. *Man: The Image of God.* Translated by Dick W. Jellerma. Studies in Dogmatics. Grand Rapids, Mich.: Eerdmans, 1962.

———. *Sin.* Translated by Philip C. Holtrop. Studies in Dogmatics. Grand Rapids, Mich.: Eerdmans, 1971.

Best, Ernest. *One Body in Christ.* London: SPCK, 1955.

Blaising, Craig A. and Darrell L. Bock. *Dispensationalism, Israel and the Church.* Grand Rapids, Mich.: Zondervan, 1992.

———. *Progressive Dispensationalism.* Grand Rapids, Mich.: Baker, 1993.

Blass, F. and A. Debrunner, *A Greek Grammar of the New Testament and Other Early Christian Literature.* Translated by Robert W. Funk. Chicago: The University of Chicago Press, 1961.

Block, Daniel Isaac. *The Gods of the Nations.* Studies in Ancient Near Eastern Theology. Mississippi: Evangelical Theological Society, 1988.

Bock, Darrell L. "'The New Man' as Community in Colossians and Ephesians." In *Integrity of Heart, Skillfulness of Hands.* Edited by Charles H. Dyer and Roy B. Zuck, 157–67. Grand Rapids, Mich.: Baker, 1994.

Bonilla-Silva, Eduardo and Amanda Lewis, "The 'New Racism': Toward an Analysis of the U.S. Racial Structure, 1960s–1990s." Center for Research on Social Organization at the University of Michigan, 536 (October 1996). Online: http://www.scribd.com/doc/20267888/Bonilla-Silva-and-Lewis-The-New-Racism-Toward-an-Analysis-of-the-U-S-Racial-Structure-1960s-1.

Boyd, Gregory A. *God at War: The Bible and Spiritual Conflict.* Downers Grove, Ill.: InterVarsity, 1997.

———. *The Myth of a Christian Nation.* Grand Rapids, Mich.: Zondervan, 2005.

Brown, Robert McAfee. *The Spirit of Protestantism.* New York: Oxford University Press, 1965.

Bruce, F. F. *The Acts of the Apostles: The Greek Text with Introduction and Commentary.* Grand Rapids, Mich.: Eerdmans, 1990

———. *The Epistle of Paul to the Romans.* London: Pickering & Inglis, 1961.

———. *The Epistle to the Hebrews.* Grand Rapids, Mich.: Eerdmans, 1964.

———. *New Testament History.* Garden City, N.Y.: Anchor, 1972.

Brunner, Emil. *The Misunderstanding of the Church.* Philadelphia: Westminster, 1953.

Bullinger, E. W. *Figures of Speech Used in the Bible.* 1898 Mssrs. Eyre and Spottiswoode, London. Reprint, Grand Rapids, Mich.: Baker, 1968.

Bultmann, Rudolph. *New Testament and Mythology.* Translated by Schubert M. Ogden. London: SCM Press, 1984.

Caird, C. B. *Principalities and Powers: A Study in Pauline Theology.* Oxford: Clarendon, 1956.

Calvin, John. *Institutes of the Christian Religion*. Edited by J. T. McNeill and F. L. Battles. 2 Vols. Philadelphia, Penn.: Westminster, 1960.

Campbell, William S. *Paul and the Creation of Christian Identity*. London: T & T Clark, 2008.

Cassuto, U. *Biblical and Oriental Studies*. Vol. 1. Jerusalem: Magnus, 1973.

———. *A Commentary of the Book of Genesis*. Translated by Israel Abrahams. 2 vols. Jerusalem: Magnes, 1972.

Chafer, Lewis Sperry. *He That is Spiritual*. Reprint, Grand Rapids, Mich.: Zondervan, 1961.

Chinn, Derek. "1+1=1: The Challenge of Creating a Multiracial Church from Single Race Congregations." DMin. diss., Western Seminary, 2009.

Clines, D. J. A. "Image of God in Man." *Tyndale Bulletin* 19 (1968) 53–103.

Colson, Charles and Ellen Vaughn. *Being the Body*. Nashville, Tenn.: W. Publishing, 2003.

Cooper, Rod. "People Just Like Me: Does the Bible Give Us Freedom to Build Deliberately Homogeneous Churches?" In *Building Unity in the Church of the New Millennium*, edited by Dwight Perry, 153–66. Chicago: Moody, 2002.

Coutts, J. "The Relationship of Ephesians and Colossians." *New Testament Studies* 4 (1957–58) 201–7.

Covey, Stephen R. *The Seven Habits of Highly Effective People*. New York: Simon and Schuster, 1989.

Craigie, P. C. *The Book of Deuteronomy*. New International Commentary on the Old Testament. Grand Rapids, Mich.: Eerdmans, 1976.

———. *Ugarit and the Old Testament*. Grand Rapids, Mich.: Eerdmans, 1983.

Cremer, Hermann. *Biblico Theological Lexicon of New Testament Greek*. Translated by William Urwick. Edinburgh: T & T Clark, 1962.

Cross, F. M. *Discoveries in the Judean Desert XIV Qumran Cave 4 IX*. Edited by Eugene Ulrich and Frank Moore Cross. Oxford: Clarendon Press, 1995.

Cullman, Oscar. *Christ and Time*. Translated by F. V. Wilson. Rev. ed. London: SCM, 1962.

———. *The State in the New Testament*. New York: Charles Scribner's Sons, 1956.

Custance, Arthur C. *Noah's Three Sons*. Grand Rapids, Mich.: Zondervan, 1975.

Dahl, N. A. "Christ, Creation and the Church." In *The Background of New Testament and its Eschatology*. Edited by W. E. Davies and D. Daube, 422–43. Cambridge: The University Press, 1956.

Dallaire, Roméo. *Shake Hands with the Devil: The Failure of Humanity in Rwanda*. New York: Carroll & Graff, 2004.

David, Pablo. "Daniel 11,1: A Late Gloss?" in *The Book of Daniel in the Light of New Findings*, edited by A. S. van der Woude, 505–14. Leuven: University Press, 1993.

Davies, W. E. *Paul and Rabbinic Judaism*. Philadelphia: Fortress, 1980.

Deissmann, Adolf. *Light from the Ancient East*. Translated by Lionel R. M. Strachan. 4th ed. Grand Rapids, Mich.: Baker, 1978.

Delcor, M. *Le Livre de Daniel*. SB. Paris: J. Gabalda et Cie Editeurs, 1971.

DeMoor, Johannes C. "El, the Creator." In *The Bible World: Essays in Honor of Cyrus H. Gordon*, 171–187. New York: KTAV, 1980.

DeYmaz, Mark. *Building a Healthy Multi-Ethnic Church*. San Francisco: Jossey-Bass, 2007.

———. *Homogeneous Unit Principle: Should Pastors Accept or Reject the Homogeneous Unit Principle?* Little Rock, Arkansas: Mosaix Global Network, 2011. No pages. Online: www.mosaix.info.

DeYmaz, Mark and Harry Li. *Ethnic Blends: Mixing Diversity into Your Local Church.* Grand Rapids, Mich.: Zondervan, 2010.

DeYoung, Curtiss Paul et al. *United by Faith: The Multiracial Congregation as the Answer to the Problem of Race.* Oxford: Oxford University Press, 2003.

Dibelius, Martin. *Die Geisterwelt in Glauben des Paulus.* Göttingen: Vandenhoeck und Ruprecht, 1909.

Driver, S. R. *The Book of Daniel.* Cambridge: University Press, 1922.

Dyer, Charles H. *The Rise of Babylon.* Wheaton: Tyndale, 1991.

Edersheim, Alfred. *The Life and Times of Jesus the Messiah.* Grand Rapids, Mich.: Eerdmans, 1971.

Eichrodt, Walter. *Theology of the Old Testament.* Translated by J. A. Baker. 2 vols. Philadelphia, Penn.: Westminster, 1967.

Emerson, Michael O. "Changing Demographics in a Context of Fear." *Outreach* (May/June 2011) 62–63.

Emerson, Michael O. and Christian Smith. "Color-Blinded." *Christianity Today* (October 2, 2000). Online: http://www.christianitytoday.com/ct/2000/october2/2.36.html

———. *Divided by Faith: Evangelical Religion and the Problem of Race in America.* Oxford: University Press, 2000.

Emerson, Michael O. with Rodney Woo. *People of the Dream.* Princeton: Princeton University Press, 2006.

Epictetus. *Discourses.* Translated by George Long. New York: D. Appleton, 1904.

Evans, Tony. *Oneness Embraced: A Fresh Look at Reconciliation, the Kingdom, and Justice.* Chicago: Moody, 2011.

Everling, O. *Die paulinische Angelologie and Dämonologie.* Göttingen: Vandenhoeck & Ruprecht, 1888.

Findley, Rowe. "Mountain with a Death Wish." *National Geographic.* January, 1981. No pages. Online: http://ngm.nationalgeographic.com/1981/01/mount-st-helens/findley-text/6.

Flood, Charles Bracelen. *Lee: The Last Years.* Boston: Houghton Mifflin, 1981.

Fokkelman, J. P. *Narrative Art in Genesis.* Sheffield: Sheffield Academic Press, 1991.

Fong, Bruce W. *Racial Equality in the Church: A Critique of the Homogeneous Unit Principle in Light of a Practical Theology Perspective.* Lanham, Maryland: University Press of America, 1996.

"The Foreign-Born Population: 2000." U.S. Census Bureau. No pages. Online: http://factfinder.census.gov/home/ saff/main.html?_lang=en.

Geller, Stephen A. "The Dynamics of Parallel Verse: A Poetic Analysis of Deut. 32.6–12," *Harvard Theological Review* 75:1 (1982) 35–56.

Goldingay, John E. *Daniel.* Vol. 30. Word Biblical Commentary. Eds. Hubbard et al., Dallas: Word Books, 1989.

Gould, Steven Jay. *Ontogeny and Phylogeny.* Cambridge: Belknap-Harvard Press, 1977.

Grenz, Stanley J. *The Social God and the Relational Self.* Louisville, Ky. Westminster John Knox Press, 2001.

Griffiths, Michael. *Cinderella with amnesia.* London: InterVarsity, 1975.

Gutherie, Donald. *New Testament Theology.* Downers Grove, Ill.: InterVarsity, 1976.

Habel, Norman C. "Appeal to Ancient Tradition as a Literary Form." *Zeitschrift für die alttestamentliche Wissenschaft* (88) 1976 253–72.

Hanson, Stig. *The Unity of the Church in the New Testament*. Uppsala: Almquist & Wiksells Biktryckeri AB, 1946.

Harris-Lacewell, Melissa. "Racial progress is far from finished." No pages. Online: http://www.cnn.com /2009/LIVING/07/07/lacewell.post.racial/.

Harrisville, R. A. *The Concept of Newness in the New Testament*. Minneapolis: Augsburg, 1960.

Hays, Daniel J. "The Cushites: A Black Nation in the Bible." *Bibliotheca Sacra* 153 (October–December 1996) 396–409.

―――. *From Every People and Nation: A biblical theology of race*. Edited by D. A. Carson. Downers Grove, Ill.: InterVarsity, 2003.

Heiser, Michael S. "Deuteronomy 32:8 and the Sons of God." *Bibliotheca Sacra* 158 (January–March 2001) 53–74.

Hendriksen, William. *Exposition of Ephesians*. New Testament Commentary. Grand Rapids, Mich.: Baker, 1967.

―――. *Exposition of Colossians and Philemon*. New Testament Commentary. Grand Rapids, Mich.: Baker, 1964.

Hens-Piazza, Gina. "A Theology of Ecology: God's Image and the Natural World." *Biblical Theology Bulletin* 13:4 (October 1983) 107–110.

Hiebert, D. Edmond. *An Introduction to the Pauline Epistles*. Chicago: Moody, 1954.

Hiebert, Paul G. "Western Images of Others and Otherness." In *This Side of Heaven: Race, Ethnicity, and Christian Faith*, edited by Robert J. Priest and Alvaro L. Nieves, 97–110. New York: Oxford University Press, 2007.

Hoch, Carl B. "The New Man of Ephesians 2." In *Dispensationalism, Israel and the Church*. Edited by Craig A. Blaising and Darrell L. Bock, 98–126. Grand Rapids, Mich.: Zondervan, 1992.

Hodges, Zane. "Notes on Acts." Unpublished class notes for Greek 219. Dallas Theological Seminary. Revised, 1973.

Hoehner, Harold W. *Chronological Aspects of the Life of Christ*. Grand Rapids, Mich.: Zondervan, 1977.

―――. *Ephesians: An Exegetical Commentary*. Grand Rapids, Mich.: Baker Academic, 2002.

Horst, P. W. van der. "Observations on a Pauline Expression." *New Testament Studies* 19 (1972–73) 181–82.

Humes, Karen R. et al. "Overview of Race and Hispanic Origin: 2010." 2010 Census Briefs. No pages. Online: www.census.gov/prod/cen2010/briefs/c2010br-02.pdf.

Jenkins, Philip. *The Next Christendom*. New York: Oxford University Press, 2002.

Jeppesen, Knud. "You are a Cherub, but no God!" *Scandinavian Journal of the Old Testament* 1 (1991) 83–94.

Jindra, Michael. "Culture Matters: Diversity in the United States and Its Implications." In *This Side of Heaven: Race, Ethnicity, and Christian Faith*, edited by Robert J. Priest and Alvaro L. Nieves, 63–80. New York: Oxford University Press, 2007.

Johnson, S. Lewis, Jr. "Christian Apparel." *Bibliotheca Sacra* 121 (January–March 1964) 23–33.

Josephus. Translated by H. St. J. Thackeray et al. 10 vols. Loeb Classical Library. Cambridge: Harvard University Press, 1926–1965.

Kautzsch, E. *Gesenius' Hebrew Grammar*. Translated by A. E. Cowley. 2nd ed. Oxford: Clarendon, 1910.

Keil, C. F. and F. Delitzsch. *The Pentateuch*. Vol 1 in Biblical Commentary on the Old Testament. Translated by James Martin et al., 27 vols. Reprint, Grand Rapids, Mich.: Eerdmans, 1971.

Kidner, Derek. *Genesis*. Downers Grove, Ill.: InterVarsity, 1967.

King, Martin Luther, Jr. "I Have A Dream." No pages. Online: http://www.americanrhetoric.com/ speeches/ mlkihaveadream.htm.

———. *A Knock at Midnight*. Edited by Clayborne Carson et al. New York: Warner Books, 1998.

———. *Why We Can't Wait*. New York: Penguin, 1964.

Kuhn, Thomas. *The Structure of Scientific Revolutions*. 3rd ed. Chicago: University of Chicago Press, 1996.

Lenski, R. C. H. *The Interpretation of St. Paul's Epistles to the Galatians and to the Ephesians and to the Philippians*. Minneapolis: Augsburg, 1937.

Lewis, C. S. *Christian Behaviour*. New York: Macmillan, 1948.

———. *The Last Battle*. New York: Harper Collins, 1956.

———. *Letters of C. S. Lewis*. Edited by W. H. Lewis. Revised edition edited by Walter Hooper. New York: Harcourt Brace, 1988.

———. *The Screwtape Letters*. New York: Macmillan, 1944.

Lightfoot, J. B. *Saint Paul's Epistles to the Colossians and to Philemon*. Reprint. Grand Rapids, Mich.: Zondervan, 1959.

Lincoln, A. T. "Liberation from the Powers: Supernatural Spirits or Societal Structures?" In *The Bible in Human Society*. Edited by M. Daniel Carroll et al., 335–54. Sheffield: Sheffield Academic, 1995.

Livingston, G. Herbert. *The Pentateuch in its Cultural Environment*. Grand Rapids, Mich.: Baker, 1974.

Lloyd-Jones, D. Martyn, *Life in the Spirit*. Grand Rapids, Mich.: Baker, 1975.

Lohse, Edward Lohse. *A Commentary on the Epistles to the Colossians and to Philemon*. Translated by William R. Poehlmann and Robert H. Karris. Hermenia—A Critical and Historical Commentary on the Bible. Edited by Helmut Koester. Philadelphia: Fortress, 1971.

MacGregor, G. H. C. "Principalities and Powers: the Cosmic Background of Paul's Thought," *New Testament Studies* 1 (1954–55) 17–28.

MacLeod, David J. "The Lion Who is a Lamb: An Exposition of Revelation 5:1–7." *Bibliotheca Sacra* 164 (July–September 2007) 323–40.

Maldame, Jean-Michel. "Les anges, les puissances, et la primauté du Christ." *Bulletin de Littérature Ecclésiastique* 1 (96/1995) 121–33.

Marty, Martin. "At the Crossroads." *Christianity Today* (February 2004): 38–40.

Mathews, Kenneth A. *Genesis 1—11:26*. New American Commentary. N.c.: Broadman & Holman, 1996.

McDannell, Colleen and Bernhard Lang. *Heaven: A History*. New York: Vintage, 1990.

McGavran, Donald A. *The Bridges of God: A Study in the Strategy of Missions*. London: World Dominion, 1955.

———. *Understanding Church Growth*. Grand Rapids, Mich.: Eerdmans, rev. ed. 1980.

McKay, J. *Religion in Judah under the Assyrians 732–609 BC*. Studies in Biblical Theology. Naperville: Alec R. Allenson, 1973.

McManners, John. *The Oxford History of Christianity*. Oxford: Oxford University Press, 1990.

Mead, Sidney E. *The Old Religion in the Brave New World: Reflections on the Relation Between Christendom and the Republic*. Los Angeles: University of California Press, 1977.

Meneses, Eloise Hiebert. "Science and the Myth of Bilogical Race." In *This Side of Heaven: Race, Ethnicity, and Christian Faith*. Edited by Robert J. Priest and Alvaro L. Nieves, 33–46. New York: Oxford University Press, 2007.

Merrill, Eugene H. "The Peoples of the Old Testament According to Genesis 10." *Bibliotheca Sacra* 154 (January–March 1997) 3–22.

Metzger, Paul Louis. *Consuming Jesus: Beyond Race and Class Divisions in a Consumer Church*. Grand Rapids, Mich.: Eerdmans, 2007.

Milne, Bruce. *Dynamic Diversity: Bridging Class, Age, Race and Gender in the Church*. Downers Grove, Ill.: InterVarsity, 2007.

Minear, Paul S. *Images of the Church in the New Testament*. Philadelphia: Westminster, 1960.

———. *The Obedience of the Faith: The Purpose of Paul in the Epistle to the Romans*. Studies in Biblical Theology, Second Series 19. Naperville, Ill.: SCM, 1971.

"Minorities expected to be majority in 2050." CNN-US. No pages. Online: http://articles.cnn.com/ 2008-08-13/us/census.minorities_1_hispanic-population-census-bureau-white-population?_s=PM:US.

The Mishnah. Translated by Herbert Danby. Oxford: Oxford University Press, 1933.

Morris, Henry M. *The Genesis Record: A Scientific and Devotional Commentary on the Book of Beginnings*. Grand Rapids, Mich.: Baker, 1976.

Mouw, Richard. *When the Kings Come Marching In*. Grand Rapids, Mich.: Eerdmans, 1983.

Mullen, E. Theodore. *The Assembly of the Gods: The Divine Council in Canaanite and Early Hebrew Literature*. Harvard Semitic Monographs. Vol. 24. California: Scholars Press, 1980.

Murray, John. *Principles of Conduct*. Grand Rapids, Mich.: Eerdmans, 1957.

Mussner, Franz. *Tractate on the Jews*. Translated by Leonard Swidler. Philadelphia: Fortress, 1984.

Nassar, Haya El. "U.S. Hispanic population to triple by 2050." USA Today (2/12/2008). Online: www.usatoday.com/news/nation/2008-02-11-population-study_N.htm#11.

"Nation's Foreign-Born Population Nears 37 Million." U.S. Census Bureau. Online: http://www.census.gov/newsroom/releases/archives/foreignborn_population/cb10-159.html.

Needham, David C. *Birthright*. Portland: Multnomah, 1979.

Newbigin, Leslie. *The Household of God*. New York: Friendship, 1954.

Newsom, C. "A Maker of Metaphors–Ezekiel's Oracles Against Tyre" *Interpretation* 38 (1984) 151–16.

Nida, Eugene A. *Customs and Cultures*. Pasadena: William Carey Library, 1954.

Nouwen, Henri. "Moving from Solitude to Community to Ministry." *Leadership: A Practical Journal for Church Leaders*. 16 no. 2 (Spring 1995) 81–85.

O'Brien, Peter T. *Colossians, Philemon*. Word Biblical Commentary. Vol. 44. Edited by David A. Hubbard et al. Waco: Word, 1982.

Olford, Stephen F. *Not I, But Christ*. Wheaton: Crossway Books, 1995.

Oppenheim, A. L. "Babylonian and Assyrian Historical Texts." *ANET*. Edited by J. B. Pritchard. 3rd edition. New Haven: CT: Princeton University Press, 1969.

Padilla, C. René. "The Unity of the Church and the Homogeneous Unit Principle." In *Exploring Church Growth*, edited by Wilbert R. Shenk, 285–305. Grand Rapids, Mich.: Eerdmans, 1983.

Page, Hugh Rowland. *The Myth of Cosmic Rebellion: A Study of its Reflexes in Ugaritic and Biblical Literature*. Leiden: E. J. Brill, 1996.

Paris, Jenell Williams. "Race: Critical Thinking and Transformative Possibilities." In *This Side of Heaven: Race, Ethnicity, and Christian Faith*, edited by Robert J. Priest and Alvaro L. Nieves, 19–32. New York: Oxford University Press, 2007.

Parker, Gary. *Creation Facts of Life*. Green Forest, Ark: Master Books, 1994.

Pearcey, Nancy R. *Total Truth: Liberating Christianity from Its Cultural Captivity*. Wheaton: Crossway, 2004.

Pentecost, Dwight J. *Pattern for Maturity*. Chicago: Moody Press, 1966.

"People of Color in U.S." *Catalyst* (October 2009). No pages. Online: http://www.catalyst.org/publication/356/people-of-color-in-the-us.

Perry, Dwight. *Building Unity in the Church*. Chicago: Moody, 2002.

Peters, G. W. "Demonology on the Mission Field." In *Demon Possession*. Edited by John Warwick Montgomery. Minneapolis: Bethany, 1976.

Priest, Robert J. and Alvaro L. Nieves, *This Side of Heaven: Race, Ethnicity, and Christian Faith*. New York: Oxford University Press, 2007.

"Race and Ethnicity." Polling Report. Article dated January 12–15, 2010. No pages. Online: www.pollingreport.com /race.htm.

Rad, Gerhard von, *Genesis*. Translated by John H. Marks. Philadelphia: Westminster, 1961.

Rader, William. *The Church and Racial Hostility: A History of the Interpretation of Ephesians 2:11–22*. Tübingen: J. C. B. Mohr, 1978.

Radmacher, Earl D. *The Nature of the Church*. Portland: Western Baptist, 1972.

Rah, Soong-Chan. *The Next Evangelicalism*. Downers Grove, Ill.: InterVarsity, 2009.

Rahlfs, Alfred. *Septuaginta* 2 vol. Stuttgart: Privilegierte Württembergische Bibelanstalt, 1935.

Rhoads, David. *The Challenge of Diversity: The Witness of Paul and the Gospels*. Minneapolis: Fortress, 1996.

Ricoeur, Paul. "Preface to Bultmann." In *Essays on Biblical Intepretation*, edited by Lewis S. Mudge, 49–72. Philadelphia: Fortress, 1980.

Ridderbos, Hermann. *Paul: An Outline of His Theology*. Translated by John Richard DeWitt. Grand Rapids, Mich.: Eerdmans, 1975.

———. *Paul and Jesus: Origin and General Character of Paul's Preaching of Christ*. Translated by David H. Freeman. Philadelphia: Presbyterian and Reformed, 1958.

Robertson, A. T. *The Acts of the Apostles*. Vol 3 of Word Pictures in the New Testament. Nashville, Tenn.: Broadman, 1930.

———. *A Grammar of the Greek New Testament in the Light of Historical Research*. Nashville, Tenn.: Broadman, 1934.

Robertson, O. Palmer. "Current Critical Questions Concerning the 'Curse of Ham' (Gen 9:20–27)," *Journal of the Evangelical Theological Society* 41:2 (June 1998) 177–88.

Robinson, H. Wheeler, *Corporate Personality in Ancient Israel*. Philadelphia: Fortress. 1964.

Robinson, J. Armitage. *Commentary on Ephesians*. Grand Rapids, Mich.: Kregel Publications, 1979.

Roon, A. Van. *The Authenticity of Ephesians*. Translated by S. Prescod-Jokel. Leiden: E. J. Brill, 1974.

Ross, Allen P. *Creation and Blessing: A Guide to the Study and Exposition of Genesis*. Grand Rapids, Mich.: Baker, 1988.

———. "The Table of Nations in Genesis 10—Its Structure." *Bibliotheca Sacra* 137 (October–December 1980) 340–353.

Rupp, Gordon. *Principalities and Powers: Studies in the Christian Conflict in History*. London: Epworth, 1952.

Russell, D. S. *The Method of Jewish Apocalyptic*. Philadelphia: Westminster Press, 1964.

Ryrie, Charles Caldwell. *Balancing the Christian Life*. Chicago: Moody, 1969.

Sailhamer, John H. *Genesis Unbound*. Sisters, Oreg.: Multnomah, 1996.

Saucy, Robert L. *The Church in God's Program*. Chicago: Moody Press, 1972.

Sauer, Eric. *The King of the Earth*. Grand Rapids: Eerdmans, 1962.

Schaeffer, Francis A. *Genesis in Space and Time*. Downers Grove, Ill.: InterVarsity, 1972.

Scroggs, Robin. *The Last Adam*. Philadelphia: Fortress, 1966.

Severson, Lucky. "Interview with Michael Emerson." *Religion & Ethics Newsweekly*. Article dated December 19, 2008. Online: http://www.pbs.org/wnet/religion and ethics/episodes/december-19-2008/interview-with-michael-emerson/1736/.

Shea, William H. "Wrestling with the Prince of Persia: A Study on Daniel 10." *Andrews University Seminary Studies* 21 (1983) 99–128.

Smalley, Stephen S. *The Revelation to John: A Commentary on the Greek Text of the Apocalypse*. Downers Grove, Ill.: InterVarsity, 2005.

Smith, Christian et al. *American Evangelicalism: Embattled and Thriving*. Chicago: University of Chicago Press, 1998.

Smith, Derwood. "The Two Made One: Some Observations on Ephesians 2:14–18." *Ohio Journal of Religious Studies* 1 (1973–75) 34–54.

Snodgrass, Klyne R. "Introduction to a Hermeneutics of Identity." *Bibliotheca Sacra* 168 (January–March 2011) 3–19.

———. "Jesus and Identity." *Bibliotheca Sacra* 168 (April–June 2011) 131–45.

———. Paul's Focus on Identity." *Bibliotheca Sacra* 168 (July–September 2011) 259–73.

———. "Pauline Perspectives on the Identity of a Pastor." *Bibliotheca Sacra* 168 (October–December 2011) 387–401.

Stark, Rodney. *The Rise of Christianity*. Princeton, N.J.: Princeton University Press, 1996.

Stevens, David E. "Daniel 10 and the Notion of Territorial Spirits." *Bibliotheca Sacra* (October—December 2000) 410–31.

———. "Does Deuteronomy 32:8 Refer to 'Sons of God' or 'Sons of Israel'"? *Bibliotheca Sacra* (April–June 1997) 131–41.

———. "La Notion Juive des 'Anges des Nations' à la Lumière du Texte Biblique." ThD. diss., La Faculté Libre de Théologie Evangélique, 1999.

Stott, John R. *God's New Society*. Downers Grove, Ill.: InterVarsity, 1979.

———. *The Spirit, the Church & the World*. Downers Grove, Ill.: InterVarsity, 1990.

Strauss, Stephen J. "The Significance of Acts 11:26 for the Church at Antioch and Today," *Bibliotheca Sacra* 168 (July–September 2011) 283–300.

Strickling, James E. "The Tower of Babel and the Confusion of Tongues." *Kronos* (Fall 1982) 53–62.

Tannehill, Robert C. *Dying and Rising with Christ*. Berlin: Verlag Alfred Topelmann, 1967.

Tellbe, Mikael. *Christ-Believers in Ephesus: A Textual Analysis of Early Christian Identity Formation in a Local Perspective*. Tübingen: Mohr-Siebeck, 2009.

Tov, Emanuel. *Textual Criticism of the Hebrew Bible*. Minneapolis, Minn.: Fortress Press, 1992.

Trench, R. C. *Synonyms of the New Testament*. Grand Rapids, Mich.: Eerdmans, 1948.

Twiss, Richard. *One Church, Many Tribes*. Ventura, Calif.: Regal, 2000.

Visser'T Hooft, W. A. *The Ecumenical Movement and the Racial Problem*. Paris: United Nations Educational, Scientific, and Cultural Organization, 1954. Online: http://unesdoc.unesco.org/images/0006/000643/064310eo.pdf.

Wagner, C. Peter, *Our Kind of People: The Ethical Dimensions of Church Growth in America*. Atlanta: John Knox, 1979.

Wallis, Jim. *The Call to Conversion*. San Francisco: Harper & Row, 1981.

Ware, Timothy Ware. *The Orthodox Church*. London: Penguin, 1997

Webster's Ninth New Collegiate Dictionary. Springfield, Mass.: Merriam-Webster, 1983.

Wenhem, Gordon J. *Genesis 1–15*. Word Biblical Commentary. Waco: Word, 1987.

Westcott, Brookes Foss. *Saint Paul's Epistle to the Ephesians*. Reprint. Minneapolis: Klock and Klock, 1978.

Wilcock, Michael. *I Saw Heaven Opened: The Message of Revelation* in The Bible Speaks Today. Edited John R. W. Stott. Downers Grove, Ill.: Inter-Varsity, 1975.

Wink, Walter. *Naming the Powers: The Language of Power in the New Testament*. Philadelphia: Fortress, 1984.

———. *Unmasking the Powers*. Philadelphia: Fortress, 1986.

———. *Engaging the Powers*. Minneapolis: Fortress, 1992.

Winslow, Ola Elizabeth. *Jonathan Edwards: Basic Writings*. New York: New American Library, 1966.

Woo, Rodney M. *The Color of Church*. Nashville, Tenn.: B & H Academic, 2009.

Wright, David F. "A Race Apart? Jews, Gentiles, Christians." *Bibliotheca Sacra* 160 (April–June 2003) 131–41.

Yamauchi, Edwin M. "Cultural Aspects of Marriage in the Ancient World," *Bibliotheca Sacra* 135 (July–September 1978) 241–52.

Yancey, George. *One Body, One Spirit*. Downers Grove, Ill.: InterVarsity. 2003.

Yee, Tet-Lim N. *Jews, Gentiles and Ethnic Reconciliation*. Society for New Testament Study Monograph Series. Cambridge: Cambridge University Press, 2005.

Yen, Hope. "Census estimates show big gains for U.S. minorities." *The Oregonian*. February 4, 2011.

Index of Ancient Documents

OLD TESTAMENT

Genesis

1:14–18	3
1:26–27	10, 36, 37, 41, 46, 48, 59, 69, 107, 113, 173, 205
1:28	173, 209, 251
2:4–4:26	60–63
3:7–10	61
3:11–13	61, 62
3:14–19	62
4:1–8	62, 111
4:16, 17	61, 62
5:1–6:8	63–64
5:3	59
5:22	59
6:9–9:29	64
6:6	41
6:7	50
7:23	50
8:21	41
9:1–3	69
9:6	38, 46, 50, 59
9:27	66
10:1–11:26	64, 65, 66, 67, 115
11:6	210
11:7	82
11:27–15:11	65, 254
12:1–3	65, 115, 145
12:2, 3	70
37:3, 23, 32	200
48:4–5	145
49:6	141

Exodus

3:1–12	41
4:22	80
6:3	42
9:25	50
19	123
19:6	225
20	50
20:13	46
22:27	41
33:18–23	41
31:18	123

Leviticus

15:16	50
23:15–21	122

Numbers

13	67, 68
17	50
18:26	42
22:4	141
33:53	40

Deuteronomy

1.13	42
4.12	41
5:4	123

Deuteronomy (continued)

14:1	80
25:5	50
29:25	78
32:1–4	82
32:8	8, 10, 77–94, 130, 182, 210, 211, 254, 263, 267,
32:6–12	262
32:39	49

Joshua

5:14–15	87
5:15	41
7	50

Judges

11:24	92
14:11	207

Ruth

1:3	49

1 Samuel

6:5	40
16:7	50
26:19–20	92

2 Samuel

7	115
21	50

1 Kings

22	80
22:19–22	80

2 Kings

3:27	92
11:18	40
17:16	182

1 Chronicles

17	115
21:1	89
29:1	50

2 Chronicles

6:41	166
7:14	230

Ezra

1–4	86
10:12	141

Job

1	80
1:6	79
4:18	80
15:15	80
20:4	50
26:7	49
32:8	47
38:7	79
39:14	166

Psalms

2:8	209
8	46, 60, 173
8:4, 37	50
8:4	44
8:5	45
8:6–8	45
10:14	41
14:1	70
19	83
29:1	80
33:6	49
39:6	40
72:8–11	208
73	225
73:20	40
78:51	66
78:55	42
82:1	80
89	115
89:6	80, 141
89:7	80
103:15	44
103:19, 20	80
104:1	166

104:29–30	49	Jeremiah	
106:22	66	3:1, 20	206
110	115	3:14	206
110:1	130	13:23	67
132	115	24:8	207
132:9	166	25:11	91
136:7–9	83	29:10	91
139	225	31:8	141
148:2	182	31:9	80
		31:33, 34	115
Proverbs		34:16	207
5:14	141	46:9	68
10:24	65		
20:27	47	Ezekiel	
		16:1–59	206
Ecclesiastes		16:11	40
12:7	41	17:14	225
		28:12–19	75
Isaiah		36:27	115
4:1	50	37:15–28	107
7:18	41	39:29	126
11:5	191, 192		
11:6–9	192	Daniel	
14:4–20	75	1:7–11, 18	87
14:13	80	3:4, 7	214
20:3–5	68	4:35	91
24:21	93, 245	5:19	214
31:3	41	6	89
40:18	41	6:25	214
43:6	80	7:13, 14	208, 209, 214
44:24	49	7:27	182
45:7	49	9:6, 8	87
45:15	68	9:25	86
49:18	206	10	8, 85, 87, 88, 89, 94, 182, 185, 187, 211, 254
51:4, 5	115		
51:9	166	10:1, 4	86
52:1	166	10:10–21	10, 84, 89, 93, 210
52:7	194	10:12	191
55:3–5	115	10:13	87, 182, 211
59:17	191, 194, 196	10:13, 20	187
60:16	251	11	91
61:10	207	11:1–45	89
62:5	206	11:5	87
66:18	214	12:1	87, 211

272 *Index of Ancient Documents*

Hosea
1:10	80
2:1	80
2:19–20	206
11:1	80

Joel
2:28, 29	126

Amos
5:26	40

Zephaniah
3:9, 10	68, 215

Zechariah
3:1–5	194
8:22	214
12:10	126

APOCRYPHA

Sirach
14:18	181
17:17	83
17:1–3	38

Wisdom of Solomon
2:23	38

PSEUDEPIGRAPHA

2 Baruch
48:24	107
85:14	107

1 Enoch
15:4	181
89:59–90:27	83
90:22–25	83

Testament of Naphtali
8:3–10:2	83

NEW TESTAMENT

Matthew
4:17	209
5:13	225
5:13–16	250
9:18, 23	186
9:34	186, 245
12:14	245
12:24	186
14:21	107
15:38	107
16:17	181
16:18	144, 152, 173, 211, 239
18:15–17	149
18:17	144, 147
18:20	148
19:3, 9	107
20:25	186
21:13	247
22:37–38	213
25	207
26:28	115
28:19–20	150, 251

Mark
1:19	243
3:22	186, 245
10:2	107
10:42	186
11:17	6
15:21	133

Luke
	9, 121, 122–28, 132–34, 143, 149, 190
2:1	121
4:6	209
5:8	108
8:41	186
11:15	186, 245
12:30	250
12:58	186
14:1	186
18:18	186

22:20	115	2	136
22:25	186	2:1–12	121
22:31	246	2:5–12	129
23:13, 35	186	2:5	124, 255
23:36	133	2:7	125
23:43	214	2:33–35	130
23:59	108	2:39	126
24:20	186	2:41	122
		2:41–47	128, 132, 147, 255
John		2:42	128, 136
	203, 205, 207, 208, 211,	2:44	128, 131
	213, 215, 217, 218, 219	3:17	186
1:46	125	4:32–37	132
3:1	186	4:32	131
3:8	123	4:36	133
7:26, 48	186	6	132, 235
7:52	125	6:1–6	147
8:32	192	6:1	132
10:16	122	6:5	132
12:31	182, 186, 245	6:7	132
12:42	186	6:9	99, 132
14:12–14	122, 201	7:13	225
14:17	250	7:38	142
14:30	182, 186, 245	7:42	84, 94
15:19	250	8	131–32
16:6	130	8:1–3	143
16:7	202	8:4	124
16:11	183, 186, 245	9:4	109
17	6	9:11	134
17:14	250	9:31	143
17:20–23	202	11:2–3	102
17:20	189	11:19–26	249
17:21–26	168	11:19–20	133, 255
17:21	24, 239	11:20	134
17:23	13, 138, 154, 155, 169, 170,	11:24	133
	255	11:26	134
18:10	197	13	133
18:36	250	13:1–3	249
		13:1	133, 255
Acts		14:16–17	83
	9, 247, 255	14:21–23	149
1	120, 122, 128, 255	15	135
1:4–5	123	15:2–4	149
1:15	123	17:26	53

Acts (continued)

18:4	127, 255
18:7	127
18:8	127
19	198
19:10	99
19:32–41	144
19:32, 39, 41	142
19:37	140
20:16	122
20:21	98
20:28	143
21:27	104
28:3	98
28:11–16	190
28:16	191
28:20	191

Romans

	162
1	62
1:4	130
1:7	225, 241
1:16	116
1:18–32	84
1:19, 21	83
1:24, 26, 28	94
2:17	134, 255
2:26	102
2:29	102
3:31	105
4:9	102
5	158
5:1	194
5:12–21	162
5:12–14	111
5:12, 21	109
5:15	161
5:19	108, 109, 111, 113
6	163, 225
6:1–23	162
6:1–15	109, 221
6:3	164
6:5	110
6:6	94, 116, 158, 160, 161, 169
7:2	107
7:22	161
8:3–9	160
8:11	163
8:13	250
8:22	62
9–11	113
9:24	116, 134, 255
11:1	113
11:13	134, 255
12:2	196
12:10, 16	148
12:18	195
13:1–7	186
13:3	186
13:8	148
13:12, 14	166
13:14	160, 250
14:13	148
15:5–6	135
15:7, 14	148
16	134
16:9	135
16:13	133
16:16	148
16:20	63, 173, 195, 250
16:21, 23	127
16:23	127

1 Corinthians

1:2	143, 225, 241
1:10–12	127
1:10	148
1:12, 13	197
1:13	24, 127
1:14	127
1:24	116
2:6–8	186
2:7	113
5:1–15	149
5:9–13	250
5:13	147
6:1–5	147

6:2	249	5:17	116, 159, 164
6:11	225	5:21	194
6:16	110	6:16	225
7:21–22	127, 175	7:10	229
8:1ff	127	7:11	231
9:20–23	155	10:3–4	7, 52
10:17	122, 227	10:3–5	196, 247
10:25ff	127	11:3	197
10:32	143	13:11	243
11:7	37, 115	13:12	148
11:16, 22	143		
11:17–18	228	Galatians	
11:18–34	150	1:2	241
11:20	140	1:13	143, 144
11:25	115	1:16	181
11:27–32	228	1:22–23	147
12	225	2:7–9	102
12:13	116, 127, 164, 165, 255	2:14–15	116
12:14–27	241	2:20	164
12:28	144	3:6–18	115
13:11	108	3:17	111
14:40	147	3:27	160, 164, 166, 194
15	158	3:28	109, 125, 161, 174
15:9	143, 144	4:3, 9	188
15:22	108, 111	5:6	102
15:24–58	93	5:13	148, 225
15:24	92, 93	5:17	160
15:31	169	5:24	164
15:45–49	160	6:1	243
15:45, 47	93, 109	6:15	102, 159
15:50	181		
16:20	148	Ephesians	
			97, 98
2 Corinthians		1:3–14	136, 168
1:1	143	1:3–6	205
2:11	189	1:3, 20	188
4:4	115, 172	1:3	198
4:10, 11, 14	163	1:4	173
4:10–11	169	1:7–8	205
4:16	161	1:10	209–10, 249
5:2–4	166	1:13	197
5:8	214	1:15–22	201
5:16, 1	172	1:15–18	198
5:16	225	1:20–23	200

Index of Ancient Documents

Ephesians (continued)
1:20–22	93
1:20	92, 93
1:22–23	145
1:22	144
2	96, 102, 106, 107, 120, 128, 136, 159, 160, 161, 163
2:1–3	99
2:2	186
2:3	160
2:4–6	99, 115, 169
2:2	186
2:5–6	169
2:6, 19	188
2:10	159
2:11–22	9, 129, 136
2:11–13	101, 111
2:13	126
2:14–15	195
2:14–16	105, 116
2:15b–18	106
2:15	5, 35, 40, 47, 60, 94, 96, 98, 106, 107, 116, 117, 157, 159, 160, 163, 170, 172, 176, 181, 255
2:18	136
2:19–22	136
2:21	225
3:2–6	112
3:6	112
3:7	119
3:10	144, 189, 200
3:16	161
3:13	119
3:14–21	201
3:14–19	201
3:17–19	167
3:19	223
4–6	118
4	159, 160, 161, 162, 163, 165, 171, 176
4:1–6	200
4:1	221
4:24	193
4:3–6	129
4:3	127, 136, 195
4:11–13	243
4:13	36
4:14	224
4:17–19	162
4:18	111
4:21	163, 193
4:22–24	10, 35, 40, 47, 60, 106, 109, 116, 136, 157, 169, 256
4:22	116, 161, 162, 166
4:23–24	115
4:23	161, 169, 171, 196
4:24	117, 160, 176, 193, 250
4:25–32	162
5:1–2	168
5:8	225
5:23–25	144
5:25, 26, 27	207
5:26	174, 197, 213
6	188, 197, 201
6:10–20	181, 247
6:10–18	191, 250
6:10–12	180–82
6:11–18	10
6:11	189
6:11, 13	191
6:12	92, 94
6:14	190
6:15	194
6:18–20	91, 201

Philippians
1:1	241
1:9–11	171
2:3	244
3:6	144
4:6–7	194
4:8	196

Colossians
	98, 145, 147
1:2	241
1:9	170
1:15	115, 172

1:18–19	147	Titus	
1:18, 24	144, 145	1:5	150
1:18	152		
1:20	209	Hebrews	
1:24	119, 169, 237, 240	2:5–9	93, 173
2:8, 20	188	2:5	44, 91, 92
2:11	102, 164	2:6–9	92
2:12	164	2:8–9	63
2:15	211	2:8	91, 199
3	159, 160, 161, 162, 163, 165, 166, 176	2:12	142
		2:14	93, 105, 181
3:1–3	165, 225	3:13	148
3:5–9	162	7:9–10	111
3:5	173, 250	8:10	123
3:8	170	10:16	123
3:9–11	5, 10, 35, 40, 47, 60, 106, 109, 116, 157, 158, 164, 169, 256	10:24	148
		11:16	219
3:9	116, 161	12:1	170
3:10–11	115	12:2	10
3:10	160, 169, 170, 171, 176, 250	12:22–23	205
		12:23	144
3:11	111, 117, 161, 174, 175, 176, 209, 237	13:14	219
3:12–25	162		
3:13, 16	148	James	
4:4	250	1:23–24	224
4:15–16	145		
4:15	147	1 Peter	
		1:1–2	241
1 Thessalonians		1:12	200
1:1	142, 148, 241	1:22	148
1:10	163	2:1	170
2:14	142, 143	2:6	152
5:8	168, 196	2:9	225
5:11	148	3:8	148
5:26–27	148	3:21–22	130
		4:9	148
2 Thessalonians		4:17	19, 50, 230
1:1	142	5:5, 14	148
1:4	142, 143	5:8–9	246
1 Timothy		2 Peter	
3:15	143	2:4–5	75

Index of Ancient Documents

1 John

1:7	148
2:17	250
3:2	256
3:8	211
3:11, 23	148
3:13	250
4:7, 11–12	148
5:19–20	245

2 John

5	148

Jude

6	75

Revelation

	204, 205, 240
1:5	186
1:10	140
2:26–27	210
5	209
5:9–10	214
5:9	214, 215
5:10	173, 210, 216, 249
7:9–14	213
7:9–10	215, 256
7:9	214
9:11	179
10:11	214
11:9	214
11:15	173, 209
12:7–9	211
13:2	212
13:4	211
13:7	214
14:6	214
16:13–14	212
17–18	219
17:11	212
17:15	214
19–21	10
19:6–9	205, 207
19:7–9	217
19:7–8	213
19:7	207
20	214, 217
20:6	173
20:10	212
21–22	217
21	209, 214
21:1–4	203, 205, 225
21:2, 9	205
21:2	213
21:3	217
21:12	217
21:13, 26	218
21:14	217
21:26	251
22:1–2	219
22:3–5	210, 249
22:5	173, 256

DEAD SEA SCROLLS

4 Qdt j/q	78

RABBINIC WRITINGS

'Abodah Zarah 2:1	103

GRECO-ROMAN WRITINGS

Politica

3.6.4	107

Discourses

3.1.25	225

EARLY CHRISTIAN WRITINGS

Against Apion 2.269	174

Jewish Antiquities

7:356–7	21
15:417	103

Index of Subjects and Names

A Knock at Midnight, 19, 264
Aaron, 68
Abbot, T. K., 106, 259
Abel, 62, 179
Aborigines/aboriginals, 52, 67, 124
Abraham, 42, 60, 65, 74, 111, 113, 115, 122, 145
Abrahamic covenant, 115
accountability, 27, 139, 149, 151
Achan, 50
Adam, 34, 41–42, 51, 59, 69, 73–74, 79, 82, 92– 96, 100, 211–13, 215, 219, 254
  as first man, 5, 36, 107, 111, 115, 254
  as head, 9, 36, 119
  sin of, 62–63, 108
  as prototype, 108
  contrasted to Christ 36, 96, 109, 111, 118, 160
  theology of, 158
Adamo, David T., 68, 259
Adversary. *See* Satan
affinity, 4, 7, 23–24, 26, 34, 97, 116–17, 125, 128, 155, 189, 234–35
Africa/Africans, 15, 52, 68, 124, 133–34, 178, 243, 249
Against Apion, 174
Akkadian, 70
Alcorn, Randy, 96, 205, 216–18, 220, 259
Aldrich, Joe, 239, 259
Alexander, 133

alienation
  at Babel 125
  of ethnicities, 8, 94
  of humanity, 9, 57–58, 60–61, 63–65, 72–74, 94–96, 100, 163, 180
  between Jew and Gentile, 87, 101–2, 104
Allan, John A., 158, 259
Americans, 17–18, 22, 24, 29, 52, 67, 124, 138, 146, 216, 232
Amos, 40
anakainoō, 170
analogia relationis, 39
ananeoō, 170
ananeousthai, 165
ancestry, 53–54, 111
aner, 107–8
ANET, 40, 86, 266
angelology, 83, 211
angels
  as rulers, 81, 87–88, 92, 94, 180, 182, 186–88, 200, 245
  guardian, 78, 85, 87, 94, 211
  malevolent, 88–90, 185
  messenger, 88–89, 94
  rebellion of, 60, 75, 210, 266
  tutelary, 85
animistic, 92
antediluvian, 70, 84
anthropology, 37
anthrōpos, 107–8, 158–60
Antioch, 132–34, 150, 249, 255, 267

Antipas, Herod, 134
Antiquities, 103, 214
apocalyptic literature, 90, 183, 187
APOT, 90
apothesthai, 165
Arabs, 66, 121, 125, 133
Aramaic, 125, 132-33
archai, 182, 187
archangel, 87, 89
archeology, 66, 72, 103
archōn, archontes, 182, 186-87
Aristotle, 107, 174, 259
Arnold, Clinton, 180, 182, 185-86, 188, 198, 259
Arnold, Eberhard, 137
Arrianus, 107
Artemis, 198
Aryans, 67
Asia/Asians, 21, 67, 121, 124, 134, 241, 249
assembly, 80, 141-44, 149, 151, 240, 265
assimilation, 233, 238
Assyrian/Assyrians 1125, 264, 266
astral deities, 84
astrological, 84, 187, 198
Athanasius, 38
Augustine, 38
Aune, David, 214, 259
authorities, 81, 87-89, 92, 94, 130, 180, 182, 186-88, 200, 211, 245
Awakenings, Great, 28-29
axios, 221

Babel, 8, 65, 67-75, 77, 79, 81-83, 85, 87, 89, 91, 93, 96-97, 113, 115-16, 120-21, 123-25, 127, 129-31, 133, 135-36, 179, 181, 200, 209-10, 215-16, 230, 254-57, 267
Bâbili, 70
Babylon/Babylonians 70-71, 84, 86, 125, 179, 219, 262
Bacote, Vincent, 27, 259

Baghdad, 70
balustrade, of temple, 103
baptism, 127-30, 150-51, 162, 164-65, 226-27, 260
Baptists, 1, 21, 30, 266
barbarian, 100, 158, 161, 174, 176, 256
Barna, George, 9, 29, 138-40, 146-48, 150, 152-53, 259
Barnabas, 133, 150
Barndt, Joseph, 54, 259
Barnhouse, Donald Grey, 111, 259
Barr, James, 37, 39, 186, 259
barriers. *See* dividing walls
Barry, F.R., 37, 259
Barth, Marcus, 38-39, 50, 97, 106, 156, 158-59, 192, 196, 260
BDB, 40, 47
Beasley-Murray, G.R., 165, 260
Bellah, Robert N., 27, 260
Berkhof, Hendrik, 184
Berkhof, L., 158
Berkouwer, G.C., 35, 47, 50, 62, 260
Biedermann, A.E., 38
Blaising, Craig A., 113, 260, 263
Bob Jones University, 20
Bock, Darrell L., 100, 113, 159, 260, 263
Bonhoeffer, Dietrich, 95, 169
Bonilla-Silva, Eduardo, 18, 260
boomers, 31, 232
boundaries, 25-26, 31, 33, 77, 79, 82-83, 101, 147, 174-76, 216, 220, 225-26, 231, 233, 235, 252
Boyd, Gregory A., 75, 80, 82, 89, 129, 186, 211, 245-46, 260
bride, 5, 10, 118, 197, 203, 205-08, 213, 217, 255, 257
breastplate of believer, 193-94, 196
bridegroom, 206-7
brokenness, 243
brotherhood, 16-17, 34
Bruce, F.F., 111, 132, 134-35, 260
Brunner, Emil, 2, 260

Bullinger, E.W., 158, 260
Bultmann, Rudolf, 76, 171, 183, 224, 260, 266

Cain, 61–62, 179, 249
Caird, C.B., 183, 260
Calvin, John, 2, 213, 240, 261
Cambyses, 86–87, 89–90, 185, 200
Campbell, William S., 222, 261
Canaanites, 67, 80, 82, 125, 265
Cappadocia, 121, 124, 241
Cassuto, U., 49, 80, 261
Caucasian, 67, 228, 230, 233
celestial, 80–81, 85, 87, 89–91, 94, 184, 212, 251, 254
census, 14, 23, 52, 262–63, 265, 268
Chafer, Lewis Sperry, 158, 261
Charles, R.H., 90
Chinn, Derek, 236, 261
Christology, 109, 159–60
Christos, 134
Christus Victor, 211
Church Dogmatics, 260
church
    betrothal of church, 205, 207, 213, 217, 219
    membership in, 127, 151–52, 231
churches
    autonomous nature of, 141–42, 145, 147, 149, 151
    competition among 7, 26, 30–31, 136, 218, 229, 253
circumcision, 100–102, 105, 135, 158, 161, 164, 174–76, 256
civilization, 67–68, 70, 72
clan, 66
classes, 9, 45, 181
Clines, D.J.A., 37–39, 42–43, 46, 49, 261
Clinton, Arnold, 185, 259
cocrucifixion, 169
colonization, 53–53, 65, 69, 210
Colson, Charles, 222, 261
commandments, 104, 123

communion. *See* Lord's supper.
communion sanctorum, 142, 145, 148
compassion, 167–68, 179, 206
Congo, 227
congregation, 21–23, 132, 138, 140–41, 144, 146, 152, 154, 168, 227–28, 231, 234, 236, 239, 241–42, 244, 262
congregational, 22, 24
consumerism, 3, 30–33, 131, 190, 230, 248, 265
Cooper, Rod, 15, 261
Coutts, J., 98, 105, 261
covenants, 101, 111, 113, 115
Covey, Stephen, 204, 222, 261
Craigie, P.C., 82, 84, 261
Creator, 10, 36, 38, 43–44, 47–49, 51–52, 56–61, 63, 70, 74, 79–81, 84, 91, 94, 97, 113, 115, 157, 160, 169, 171–74, 176–77, 212–13, 218, 229, 245, 249–50, 253–55, 261
Cremer, Hermann, 116, 261
Cretans, 67, 121, 125
crucified, 94, 164, 169
Cullman, Oscar, 130, 186, 261
culture (s)
    affinity of, 7, 128–29, 132
    and ethnic distinctions, 54
    and identity, 34, 97, 103, 110, 119–19, 235
    definition of, 54
    demonization of, 8
    differences of, 14, 31, 52, 55, 57, 80, 98–99, 116–17, 120, 135, 175, 216, 218, 233, 236,
    diversity of, 3, 6–7, 16, 69–70, 98, 131, 218
    Greek, 133, 174
    of slavery, 18
    segregation by, 135
    western, 27, 110
Cushites, 67–68, 215, 263
Custance, Arthur, 73, 261

customs, 52, 54, 72, 207, 265
Cyprus, 133
Cyrene, 121, 124, 133–34
Cyrus, 86–87, 89–90, 185, 261

Dahl, N.A., 109, 261
Dallaire, Roméo, 178–79, 261
Darius, 86, 89
Darwin, Charles, 44, 53, 57, 96
Darwinian, 53
David, Pablo, 90, 261
Davidic. *See* covenant.
Davies, W.E., 102, 261
DeBrunner, A., 161, 214, 260
deconstruction, of dividing walls, 9, 57–58, 61, 75–76, 79, 83–84, 96, 104, 117, 125, 197, 247, 254
deipnon, 140
Deissmann, Adolf, 103, 261
deities, 80, 84, 92, 187
Delcor, M., 85–86, 261
Delitzsch, F., 49, 72, 264
demographics, 3, 14–16, 236, 262
Demonology, 8, 75–77, 79, 81, 88, 179, 182, 185, 208, 240, 246, 266
DeMoor, Johannes C., 81, 261
demythologize, 77, 94, 183, 186, 188
denominations, 1–2, 7, 14, 20, 29–30, 125, 132, 136, 235
devil, 53, 75–76, 93, 178–80, 182, 189, 197, 209, 211, 245–46, 261
Deymaz, Mark, 6, 21, 32, 134, 238, 242, 251, 261–62
Deyoung, Curtiss Paul, 3, 6–7, 21, 133, 220, 223, 247, 262
diabolos, 182
dialects, 72, 123
Diana, 198
Dibelius, Martin, 183, 262
disciples 122–23, 126, 150, 154, 201–2, 220, 239, 246, 251
discipleship, 155, 240
disestablishment of the church, 31

Disraeli, Benjamin, 1
disunity, 70, 97, 104, 181, 190, 229–30, 256
dividing walls, 3–4, 7, 9–10, 13–14, 23–24, 26, 33–34, 37, 40, 55–56, 58, 75, 90, 96–98, 101, 103–5, 107, 116, 152, 159, 169, 173, 181, 195–96, 229–30, 247, 252–53, 257
divinities, 80
divinization, 46
divisions in the church, 3–4, 6–7, 13, 17, 20, 23–24, 34, 77, 90, 118–19, 125, 127, 190, 228, 265
doctrine, 19, 37, 39, 41, 45–46, 85, 97–98, 107, 177
dominion over the earth, 43, 46, 58, 63, 69, 91, 93, 158, 173, 199, 208–10, 249, 264
Driver, S.R., 85, 259, 262
Dyer, Charles H., 71, 260, 262
dynameis, 182

ecclesiology, 29, 31, 159, 162
ecology, 43, 263
ecumenical, 2, 20, 71–72, 238, 268
Eden, 60, 65, 70, 96, 200, 204, 213, 218–19, 251, 254
Edersheim, Alfred, 83, 262
Edwards, Jonathan, 204, 268
église, 140
eglwys, 140
Egypt, 66–67, 80, 83–84, 121, 124–25, 128, 216, 228
Eichrodt, Walter, 42, 262
Einstein, Albert, 248
ekklēsia, 9, 24, 137, 139–55, 255
elders, 81, 149–50, 243
election, 101
emergent churches, 31
Emerson, Michael O., 3–4, 7, 14–15, 18, 20, 22, 25–26, 28–31, 33, 179, 233, 235, 262, 267
empire, 88, 91, 100, 194

Index of Subjects and Names   283

enculturation, 237
endysasthai, 165
enemy. *See also* Devil, 179–82, 187, 189–91, 193, 196, 199, 246
Enlightenment, 27–28
Enoch, 59, 63, 83, 181
Ephesus, 99, 198, 268
Epictetus, *Discourses*, 225, 262
epinosis, 171
equality, racial, 6, 17, 55, 113, 262
Erastus, 127
eschatology, 93, 108–9, 118, 158–59, 171, 217, 261
establishment, 31–32, 60, 70, 99, 119, 133, 155, 214, 255
eternity, eternal state, 57, 167, 208, 213, 217, 219, 251
Ethiopian, 67, 133, 238
ethnē, 100–101, 104
ethnic
  distinctions, 45, 54–55, 66, 73, 108–9, 116–17, 135–36, 161, 174–76, 231–33, 237, 256
  hostility, 18, 68, 96, 103–6, 113, 195, 200, 216, 266
  mosaic of, 3, 6, 9, 125, 217, 257
ethnicity, 2–3, 7, 9–10, 14, 17, 22–24, 26, 33–34, 36, 40, 45–46, 52, 54–55, 66–68, 75, 85, 89–90, 98–100, 103–4, 107, 115–18, 125, 127, 129–30, 135–36, 145, 152, 154–55, 175–77, 179, 189, 194, 198, 215–18, 221, 227–29, 231, 234, 236, 240, 244, 246, 254–56, 263, 265–66
ethnocentrism, 23, 54, 85, 87, 94, 101–2, 113, 131, 190, 226
ethnos, 107, 214
eugenics, 95–96
Europeans, 52, 68, 100
evangelicals, 17–18, 20, 22, 24, 27, 29–30, 173, 224
evangelism, 32, 239
Evans, Tony, 20, 229–30, 262

Eve, 50–51, 60–62, 113, 118, 172, 208–9, 213, 218–19
Everling, Otto, 183, 262
evolution, 45, 53, 139
exclusivism, 165
exousia, 182, 187

fellowship
  definition of, 128
  of local church, 153
  within Godhead, 49
Filipinos, 216, 228
Findley, Rowe, 199, 262
Firstfruits, 122
Fokkelman, J.P., 69, 262
Fong, Bruce W., 6, 262
foreigners, 100–103
foreskin, 102
forgiveness, 21, 115, 129, 168, 190
freedom, 30–31, 98, 261
Frost, Robert, 13, 100, 257

Gabriel, 51, 85, 88–91, 94
Galatia, 241
Galileans, 121, 125, 131
Galilee, 125, 134, 143–44
Gallup Poll, 2
Galton, Frances, 95
Geller, Stephen, 79, 262
gender, 14, 127, 155, 265
genealogy, 65
Generation X, 31
generational preferences, 3, 7, 14, 23–24, 34, 97, 136, 176, 189–90, 222, 231, 237
generations, 31, 59, 81, 95, 111–12, 174, 234, 257
Gentiles, 97–106, 112–13, 117, 127, 134–35, 168, 268
Gnosticism, 166
gods, 40, 42, 45, 70, 80–81, 83–84, 92, 174, 183, 212, 260, 265
Goldingay, John E., 184, 262
Goodwin, Thomas, 111

Gould, Steven Jay, 53, 262
government, 20, 46, 69, 95, 184, 186, 210, 216
gôy, 66, 79, 82, 92, 211
Graham, Billy, 18
Greeks, 100, 127, 132–33, 165, 174–75, 209
Grenz, Stanley, 51, 262
Griffiths, Michael, 30, 140, 262
Gutherie, Donald, 159, 262

Habel, Norman, 81–82, 263
Hades, 152, 211
halakic, 105
Ham, 59, 64–67, 125, 266
hamartias, 160
Hamites, 67, 73
Hanson, Stig, 106, 263
Harris-Lacewell, Melissa, 17, 263
Harrisville, R.A., 116, 263
Hays, Daniel, 6, 66–68, 133, 263
heavenlies, 8, 74, 89, 91, 254
Hebraic Jews, 99, 132, 235
Hegel, F., 38
Heiser, Michael S., 78, 263
Hellenists, 99, 131–32, 166
helmet of salvation, 196
Hendriksen, William, 101, 165, 263
Herbert, G., 264–65
hermeneutics, 222, 224, 267
Herod, 103, 133–34
heterogeneity, 24
Hiebert, D. Edmond, 263
Hiebert, Paul G., 55, 100, 263
Hinduism, 218
Hispanic, 3–4, 15, 21, 24, 195, 263, 265
HIV, 179, 243
Hobbes, Thomas, 28
Hoch, Carl B., 163, 263
Hodges, Zane, 240, 263
Hoehner, Harold, 97, 104, 121, 221, 263
holiness, 38, 48, 58, 61, 157, 160, 193

holos, 145
homogeneity
  and identity, 32, 175
  of churches, 3–4, 7, 24, 103, 118, 234, 253
  of ethnicity, 22, 153, 177
  of New Humanity, 127
  societal, 26
Horst, P.W. van der, 166, 263
humanity
  dignity of, 27, 38, 44–45, 49, 59
  dispersion of, 65–66, 68–69, 73, 79, 91, 124, 210
humankind, 5, 8, 35–36, 41, 44–46, 48, 50, 55, 73, 96, 157, 160, 210
Humbert, P., 39
Humes, Karen R., 14–15, 263
Hutu, 54, 100, 179
Huxley, Thomas, 44
Hystaspes, Darius, 86, 89

Iconium, 150
identity
  collective nature of, 4, 7, 9–11, 32, 36, 60, 97, 100, 108–10, 117–18, 159–63, 171–72, 190, 193, 197, 217, 222–23, 225–27, 232, 243
  formation of, 30, 120, 135, 151, 190–91, 196–98, 221–22, 225–26, 237–38, 242, 244, 268
ideology, 52, 188
idolatry, 40, 83–84, 184, 189
Ignatius, 145
imago Dei, 8–9, 35, 37–39, 41, 43, 45, 47, 49, 51, 53, 55, 57, 59, 61, 63, 65, 67–69, 71–73, 75–76, 83–84, 91, 93–94, 96, 113, 128, 208, 212, 225, 245–46, 249, 254, 256
immigrants, 15, 21, 237
immigration, 3, 21, 243
inclusio, 89

Index of Subjects and Names   285

inclusiveness, relational, 55, 98, 105, 113, 115, 126, 175, 208, 215, 217, 233, 238
inclusivism, 165, 214, 229, 232
indigenous peoples, 23, 52, 100, 125, 179
individualism, 26–27, 29–30, 33, 49, 103, 110, 118, 128, 136, 139, 189–90, 229, 232, 240, 253, 260
indwelling of Spirit, 125, 129
inheritance, 77, 79, 83, 98, 196, 208–9
injustice, 184
integration, 19, 22, 233–34, 238, 242, 253
interbreeding, 73
intercession, 91, 248, 257
interchurch relations, 147, 236
interethnic, 22
internationals, 238, 248
intertestamental period, 38
Islander, 52
isolationism, generational and cultural, 23, 72
Israel, 15, 46, 50, 62, 66–68, 77–81, 83, 85–92, 94, 97, 100–103, 105, 112–13, 122–23, 142, 200, 206–7, 211, 214, 217, 239, 260–61, 263, 266–67

Jamestown, 53
Japheth, 59, 64–67, 125
Javan, 67
Jenkins, Philip, 16, 263
Jeppesen, Knud, 75, 263
Jerusalem, 67, 87, 120, 122–28, 131–33, 135, 141, 143, 147, 203–5, 217–19, 251, 255, 257, 261
Jesus Christ
  lordship of, 130
  as Peacemaker, 99, 101, 104
Jews, 15, 87, 98–102, 104–6, 112–13, 117, 120–22, 124, 126–27, 131–35, 141, 148, 165, 168, 175, 235, 265, 268
Jindra, Michael, 54, 263
Johnson, S. Lewis, 165–66, 263
Joktan, 67
Josephus, 103, 124, 174, 214, 263
Judah, 84, 126, 264
Judaism, 83, 99–100, 102, 121, 124–25, 183, 187, 261
Jungian analysis, 184
justice, 38, 40, 48, 58, 76, 164, 174, 184, 206, 231, 251, 262
justification, 155, 236, 255

kainos, 108, 116, 159, 170
kaleo, 141
kata, 78, 145, 172
katarge, 105
katartizō, 243
Kautzsch, E., 41–43, 264
Keil, C.F., 49, 72, 264
Kidner, Derek, 36, 264
King, Martin Luther Jr., 16, 247, 250, 264
Kipling, Rudyard, 53
Kirche, 140
Kittim (Crete), 67
koinōnia, 128, 136
Koreans, 24, 67, 117, 216
kosmokratores, 182, 187
ktisis, 107, 160
Kurdish, 117
kûshî, 67
kyriakos, 140
kyriotētes, 182

Lamb of God, 205, 207, 209–10, 213–15, 217–18, 257, 264
Laodicea, 147
laos, 107, 215, 217
Latinos, 21, 54
leaders as equippers, 242, 244
leadership, 2, 71, 132–33, 138, 150–51, 242, 244, 249, 265

lectio difficilior, 78
Lee, Robert E., 188, 231, 262
legalism, 172
Lenski, R.C.H., 106, 264
Lewis, C.H., 76, 117, 156–57, 203–4, 264
Lightfoot, J.B., 116, 161, 264
Lincoln, A.T., 90, 183, 264
linguistic, 32–33, 54, 66, 139, 183, 216
Livingston, G. Herbert, 73, 264
Lloyd-Jones, D. Martyn, 208, 264
Locke, John, 28
Loeb Classical Library, 259, 263
logos, 38
Lohse, Edward, 98, 166, 264
Lord's Supper, 140, 150–51, 205, 207, 217, 226–29, 231, 244
Luther, Martin, 2, 140, 197, 253
LXX, 39, 78, 141

Macedonians, 125
MacGregor, G.H.C., 183–84, 264
MacLeod, David, 208–9, 264
magic, 76–77, 180, 182, 186, 198, 259
mandate, cultural, 55, 58, 60, 63, 70, 74, 173, 187, 210, 218, 242, 244, 251
mankind, repartition of, 78, 81–82, 84
manuscripts, 78
Marcel, Gabriel, 51
marginalized, 101, 244
marketplace, church as, 29–31, 139, 148, 151, 232
Marty, Martin, 224, 264
Masoretic text, 77
materialism, 33, 189
Mathews, Kenneth A., 49, 67, 264
maxaira, 197
McAfee, Robert, 260
McDannell, Colleen, 213, 264
McGavran, Donald, 32, 264
McKay, J., 84, 264

McManners, John, 19, 265
Mead, Sidney E., 28, 265
Medes, 121, 124
Mediterranean, 124, 131, 134, 226, 249
mega-mall environment, 31, 128
Melchizedek, 111
membership. *See* church. Meneses, Eloise Hiebert, 53, 95, 265
mergers, 20
Merrill, Eugene H., 65–68, 70, 73, 265
Mesopotamia, 70, 73, 80, 121, 124
Messiah, 87, 99, 102, 134, 191–92, 194, 196, 218, 262
methodeia, 189
Metzger, Paul Louis, 32, 190, 241, 265
Michael, the archangel, 4, 7, 14, 30, 85, 87–89, 94, 179, 211, 233, 235, 262–63, 267–68
millennials, 232
millennium, 84, 259, 261
Milligan, G., 108
Milne, Bruce, 209, 265
Minear, Paul, 135, 225, 265
minorities, 14–15, 265, 268
Mishnah, 38, 102, 265
mission. *See* New Humanity.
Moffatt, James, 78
mongoloid, 52
Morris, Henry M., 69, 73, 82, 84, 265
Mosaic law, 105
Mosaix, 262
Moulton, J.H., 108
Mouw, Richard, 51, 265
Mullen, Theodore, 80, 265
multicultural, 125, 131, 200, 233, 244
multiethnicity, 6–9, 137, 146, 154, 168, 236–37, 243–44
multigenerational, 257
multilingual, 121, 131
multinational, 121

multiracial, 6, 22, 131, 233, 236, 261–62
Multnomah, 259, 265, 267
Murray, John, 158, 265
Muslum, 248
Mussner, Franz, 113, 265
mystery
   of New Humanity, 112–13, 118–20, 174
   of unity in diversity, 174
   religions, 133, 166, 187
myth, 49, 53, 95, 185, 260, 265–66

nationalism, 71, 210
nationality, 9, 21, 55, 100, 126, 128, 215
nations, 6, 10, 27, 34, 62, 65–67, 70, 72, 74, 77–85, 88, 90, 92–94, 100, 103–5, 113, 115, 122, 124, 131, 133–34, 145, 179, 182, 187, 207–12, 214, 218–19, 237–38, 246–49, 251, 254–55, 260, 267–68
Nebuchadnezzar, 71
Needham, David, 106, 158, 265
Negroes, 20, 52
neos, 108, 116, 170
Nero, 190
New Humanity
   as organism, 9, 118–19, 121, 136
   interdependence in, 195
   lifestyle of, 19, 157–58, 162–63, 165–66, 170–71, 176, 193, 221, 229–30
   mission of, 60, 238, 245, 248–49, 251, 266
   renewal of, 10, 40, 56, 161, 169–72, 174–75, 232, 237, 249, 256
   transformation of, 158, 219, 221, 223, 237, 251
Newbigen, Leslie, 152
Newsom, C., 75, 265
niche affinities, 31, 153, 228, 237
Nida, Eugene A., 54, 265

Niebuhr, Reinhold, 71
Nieves, Alvaro L., 3, 15, 22, 263, 265–66
Nimrod, 70–71, 125
Ninevah, 70
Noah, 46, 59, 64–66, 68, 73, 79, 261
nonnative, 73
Nouwen, Henri, 234, 265

obedience, 109, 135, 180, 265
occultism, 189
odyrmos, 229
Ohio, 267
oikoumenē, 92, 211
Olford, Stephen, 242, 265
oneness, 8, 20, 35, 48, 113, 121, 132, 135, 145, 169, 230, 262
ordo salutis, 158
organic community, 5, 29, 113
Oriental, 67, 261
Origen, 85
Oromo speakers, 226, 236, 238
Orthodox, 174, 268

Pablo, David, 261
Padilla, René, 33, 118, 120, 132, 135, 239, 266
Paine, Thomas, 64
palaion, 159
Palestine, 67, 125, 134
Palestinian, 131
Palmer, O., 266
Pamphylia, 121, 124
panoplia, 191
papyri, 183
paradigm, 222, 224
paradise, 44, 179, 204–5, 213, 246
Parker, Gary, 73, 266
partnership, 128, 146
Passover, 122, 124
pastor(s), 19, 22, 151, 168, 179, 227, 240, 242, 247, 267
Pearcey, Nancy, 28–29, 49, 59, 64, 173, 239, 266

Index of Subjects and Names

Peleg, 67
Pentateuch, 49, 72–73, 264
Pentecost
  and the powers, 129–31
  as birth of New Humanity, 9, 74, 115, 120–21, 127, 255
  as remedy to Babel, 115, 119–20, 255–56
  definition of, 122–26
Perry, Dwight, 7, 259, 261, 266
Persia, 85–91, 94, 100, 125, 133, 185, 187, 211, 267
personhood, 41–42
phenotype, 54, 136, 255
Philo, 38
philosophy, 28, 95
Phoenicia, 80
Phrygia, 121, 124
phylē, 214
Phylogeny, 53, 262
physis, 160
pigmentation, 68
Platonic, 42, 154, 251
plausibility structure, 238–41
plurality in the Godhead, 49, 113
pneumatika, 182
PollingReport, 17, 266
polytheism, 82
ponērias, 182
Portland, Oregon, 3, 23, 227, 241, 248, 259, 265–66
postmodern, 27, 52
powers, cosmic, 75, 85, 88, 91, 130, 184–85, 198, 208, 246, 264, 266
Praetorian guard, 191
pragmatism, 32, 224
prayer, 13, 91, 132, 201, 235, 248
preaching, 124, 200, 209, 266
prejudice, 18, 24, 31–32, 54, 68, 71, 190, 233
presuppositions, 39, 185
pride, 70–71, 94, 125

priest, 3, 6, 15, 22, 27, 29, 86, 103, 132, 169, 197, 210, 214, 263, 265–66
Prince of Persia, 85–91, 182, 185, 187, 267
principalities, 183, 185–86, 246, 259–60, 264, 267
Pritchard, James B., 266
privatization, 27–28
prophets, 67, 87–88, 90–91, 93, 126, 133, 192, 203, 205–6, 208, 245
proselytes, 124, 126
Protestant, 13, 18–20, 27, 257, 260
protoevangelium, 59, 63, 115, 179, 240
pseudepigraphal, 108
psychology, 246

Qumran, 78, 183, 261

rabbinic, 102, 108, 261
rabbis, 38, 83
race/racial, 3–4, 6–7, 14, 16–18, 20–23, 31–33, 52, 54–55, 68, 71–72, 95, 104, 129, 183, 190, 238, 242, 250, 260, 262–63, 266, 268
racial inequality, 18, 46, 250
racialization, 8, 14, 17–19, 179
racism, 17–18, 23–24, 30, 45, 53–55, 85, 94, 129, 131, 189, 218, 242, 246, 254, 259–60
Rad, Gerhard von, 71, 266
Rader, William, 104, 266
Radmacher, Earl D., 141–42, 266
Rah, Soong-Chan, 16, 55, 244, 266
Rahlfs, Alfred, 266
reconciliation, 4–6, 9–11, 17–18, 21, 34, 94, 96–97, 101–2, 104–6, 110, 115–17, 125, 136, 160, 164, 170, 181, 190, 200, 205, 246, 250, 252, 262, 268
redemption, 37, 98, 122, 150
redemptive historical, 161, 163

Index of Subjects and Names   289

reductionism, 185
Reformation, 13, 27–28
Reformers, 27, 38, 48
refugees, 227, 243
relational oneness, 8, 48, 50–52, 58, 62, 91, 97, 104, 110–11, 113, 116, 149, 153, 161–63, 165–68, 172, 194, 223, 246, 249, 254, 262
religions, 46, 86–87, 131, 133, 166, 187–88
repentance, 19, 98, 209, 229–30, 252
resemblance of Creator, 8, 40, 47, 55–58, 60–61, 74, 91, 115, 157, 208, 212, 219, 249–50, 254–56
resurrection of/with Christ, 109–10, 115, 122, 130, 163–64, 199, 209, 226
revival, 29, 223, 242
revivalists, 28
revolutionaries, 138–39, 146, 152, 155
Rhoads, David, 131, 266
rhēma, 197
rîb, 81
Ricoeur, Paul, 224, 266
Ridderbos, Hermann, 108, 159, 208, 266
righteousness, 41, 56, 58, 61, 101, 111, 113, 116, 157, 160, 164, 166, 191–94, 196, 206, 212–13
rituals, 150, 244
Robertson, A.T., 141, 144, 161
Robertson, O. Palmer, 67, 266
Robinson, H. Wheeler, 50, 110–11, 266
Robinson, J. Armitage, 98, 267
Roon, A. Van, 158, 267
Ross, Allen P., 42, 46–48, 64, 66, 69–71, 73–74, 267
Rousseau, Jacques, 27–28
Rupp, Gordon, 183, 267
Russell, D.S., 83, 267
Ruth, 49

Rwanda, 17, 100, 178–79, 216, 228, 233, 261
Ryrie, Charles Caldwell, 110, 158, 267

Sailhamer, John H., 60, 267
salvation, 113, 135, 164, 166, 196–97, 201, 213, 215, 229–30
Samaria, 143–44
sameness, 125, 136
sandals of peace, 194
sarx, 160, 164
Satan
    as adversary, 180, 189–90, 192, 199, 201, 256
    as serpent, 60, 63, 75–76, 211
    schemes of, 88, 180, 188–90, 217, 245
satyr, 100
Saucy, Robert L., 151, 267
Sauer, Eric, 43–44, 267
Saul, 50, 133–34, 143
Schaeffer, Francis, 58, 136, 267
scientists, 46, 53, 95
Screwtape Letters, 76, 264
Scroggs, Robin, 108–9, 267
Scythian, 158, 161, 174, 176, 256
sectarianism, 7
segregation, of the church, 4, 6–7, 17–20, 22–24, 33, 36, 90, 96–97, 116, 135, 152, 170, 181, 189, 197, 222, 229, 232, 237, 248, 253, 255–56
selem, 40–41, 47
semantics, 186, 259
seminaries, 20, 22
Semitic, 41, 69, 265
separation, 57, 63, 70, 72, 74, 81–83, 93, 105, 129, 141, 254
separatism, 29
Septuagint, 78, 91, 141, 182, 187, 200
Serb, 54
Seth, 41
Shea, William H., 86–87, 267

Shem, 59, 64–66, 125
Shemites, 66
shield of faith, 195–96
Shinar, 65, 70
Silas, 148
Simeon, 133
Simon, 261
sinfulness, 55, 111
Sitaki, Emmanuel, 179
skotous, 182, 187
slavery, 19, 21, 52
Smalley, Stephen S., 216, 267
Smith, Christian, 4, 14, 18, 20, 22, 25–26, 28–31, 33, 110, 179, 235, 262
Smith, Derwood, 267
Smyrnaeans, 145
Snodgrass, Klyne R., 169, 222, 224, 226, 267
society, 18, 27, 30, 76, 94–95, 166, 182, 184–86, 245–46, 264
socioeconomic factors, 3, 7, 9, 14, 23–24, 26, 36, 116, 118, 127, 129, 132, 136, 181, 190, 221–22, 246, 255
sociological currents, 24, 190, 220, 247
sociologists, 7, 32, 238
sociopolitical, 82, 92, 187, 245–46
soldiers, Roman, 190–92, 194, 196
solidarity, of Old/New Humanity, 8, 25–26, 33, 50–51, 56, 101, 108, 110–11, 116, 125, 145, 159–61, 175, 253
Solomon, 38, 65, 208
sons of God, 8, 74–78, 87–89, 91–94, 211, 263, 267
sorcery, 198
Sosipater, 127
soul, 38, 41–42, 48, 118, 123, 128, 131, 142, 188, 213, 228
species, 45, 53
spirituality, 38, 184, 259
Spurgeon, Charles H., 75

Stachys, 135
Stephanas, 127
Stephen, 53, 142–43, 204, 222, 242, 261–62, 265, 267
sterilization, 96
Stevens, David E., 78, 86, 88, 182, 187, 267
Stewart, J.S., 110
stoicheia, 182, 188
Stott, John R., 119, 125, 185, 267–68
stratopedarchēs, 191
Strauss, Stephen J., 134, 267
Strickling, James E., 72, 267
strongholds, demonic, 7, 196, 247
structural evil, 189
subjection, 60, 91, 173
Sumerians, 67
Susa, 86
sword of the Spirit, 192, 197
syn, 99
synagogue, 127, 132, 148
syncretism, 188, 259
Syrians, 67, 125, 132–33

T
tabernacle, 60
Talmud, 70, 102
Tannehill, Robert C., 158, 268
Targum, 38
Tarshish, 67
Tarsus, 134
TDNT, 92, 116, 171, 187, 214–15, 221
Tellbe, Mikael, 99, 222, 268
temple, 60, 70–71, 84, 86–87, 90–91, 103–5, 218, 225, 230, 248
temptation, 71, 209
Terah, 59, 65, 74
territorial, spirits, 78, 86, 88, 182, 187, 267
territories, geographical, 82, 92
tertium genus, 117
theocracy, 102
theologians, 50, 137, 183

theology, 8, 35–36, 40, 42–43, 49, 72, 80–81, 96, 108, 158–59, 185, 249, 259–60, 262–66
theophanies, 41
theou, 78
thronoi, 182
Tigris, 70
Timothy, 148, 268
togetherness, 97, 99, 104, 109, 112–13, 118, 128, 180–81, 235
tôlᵉdôt, 58–65
Tolkien, J.R.R., 245
Tov, Emanuel, 78, 268
Tozer, A.W., 121
Tractate on the Jews, 113, 265
translations, 99, 140, 158, 160, 224
tribes, 10, 23, 27, 66, 73, 111, 178–79, 213–17, 268
Trinity, 49, 51, 117, 119, 124, 139, 168, 174, 214, 252
truth, 7, 28–29, 45–46, 49, 59, 64, 72, 81, 100, 111–13, 119, 123, 125, 129, 136, 163, 167–68, 173, 188, 191–97, 201, 210, 222, 226–29, 239, 266
Turkey, 124
Tutsi, 54, 100, 179
Twiss, Richard, 23, 268
TWOT, 89
Tyndale, William, 140–41

U
Ugarit, 81–82, 261, 266
unchurched, 259
uncircumcised, 101–2, 158, 161, 174–76, 256
undressing, the Old Humanity, 162, 164
universe, 60, 75, 80, 199, 205–6, 208
unleavened bread, 122
Urbanus, 135

V
Vaughn, Ellen, 222, 261
Venema, Cornelius, 218

vice-regent, humanity as, 40, 43, 45–46, 52, 55, 58, 74, 91, 113, 157, 173, 218, 253
virtues, 167–68
Visser'T Hooft, W.A., 2, 20, 71–72, 238, 268

W
Wagner, C. Peter, 32, 131, 154, 268
Walls, 15, 17, 19, 21, 23, 25, 27, 29, 31, 33
Walls, Andrew, 3
Ware, Timothy, 174, 268
warfare
  angelic, 60, 75–78, 83–85, 87, 89–91, 185, 210–12, 217, 254
  spiritual, 180–82, 185–89, 191–93, 197, 199–201, 211, 245–47
wealth, 17, 132
Weltanschauung, 28, 30
weltbild, 76, 185
Wenhem, Gordon J., 69–70, 74, 268
Wesley, John, 2
whites, 18, 22, 31, 231–32
widows, 132, 179
Wittenberg, 253
women, 103, 126, 139, 143, 168, 238
workplace, 28, 234
worldview, 23, 28, 53, 100, 124, 139, 183, 185, 198, 223

Y
Yahweh, 66, 70, 80–83, 101, 111, 206
Yamauchi, Edwin M., 207, 268
Yancey, George, 7, 18, 268
Yee, Tet-Lin N., 101–2, 104–5, 117, 268
Yen, Hope, 14, 268

Z
ziggurat, 71, 84
Zion, 206
ziqqurratu, 84
zodiac, 84, 198